# *Rick Steves'*

# ITALY

# 2001

AVALON
TRAVEL
publishing

**Other ATP travel guidebooks by Rick Steves**
*Rick Steves' Europe Through the Back Door*
*Rick Steves' Europe 101: History and Art for the Traveler*
  (with Gene Openshaw)
*Rick Steves' Mona Winks: Self-Guided Tours of Europe's Top Museums*
  (with Gene Openshaw)
*Rick Steves' Postcards from Europe*
*Rick Steves' Best of Europe*
*Rick Steves' France, Belgium & the Netherlands* (with Steve Smith)
*Rick Steves' Germany, Austria & Switzerland*
*Rick Steves' Great Britain & Ireland*
*Rick Steves' Scandinavia*
*Rick Steves' Spain & Portugal*
*Rick Steves' London* (with Gene Openshaw)
*Rick Steves' Paris* (with Steve Smith and Gene Openshaw)
*Rick Steves' Rome* (with Gene Openshaw)
Rick Steves' Phrase Books: German, Italian, French,
  Spanish/Portuguese, and French/Italian/German

Avalon Travel Publishing, 5855 Beaudry Street, Emeryville, CA 94608

Printed in the United States of America
First printing December 2000.

For the latest on Rick Steves' lectures, guidebooks, tours, and public
television series, contact Europe Through the Back Door, Box 2009,
Edmonds, WA 98020, tel. 425/771-8303, fax 425/771-0833,
www.ricksteves.com, or e-mail: rick@ricksteves.com.

ISSN 1084-4422
ISBN 1-56691-229-6

**Europe Through the Back Door Editor** Risa Laib
**Avalon Travel Publishing Editor** Kate Willis
**Copy Editor** Donna Leverenz
**Research Assistance** Risa Laib, Lisa Friend
**Production & Typesetting** Kathleen Sparkes, White Hart Design,
  Albuquerque, NM
**Design** Linda Braun
**Cover Design** Janine Lehmann
**Maps** David C. Hoerlein
**Printer** Publishers Press
**Cover Photo** Santa Croce, Florence; copyright © John Elk III

Distributed to the book trade by
Publishers Group West, Berkeley, California

*Although the author and publisher have made every effort to provide accurate,*
*up-to-date information, they accept no responsibility for loss, injury, bad pasta,*
*or inconvenience sustained by any person using this book.*

# CONTENTS

# Italy's Best Destinations

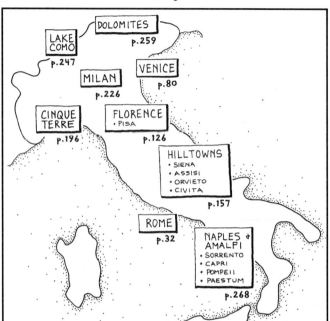

# INTRODUCTION

This book breaks Italy into its top big-city, small-town, and rural destinations. It then gives you all the information and opinions necessary to wring the maximum value out of your limited time and money in each of these destinations.

If you plan a month or less in Italy and have a normal appetite for information, this lean and mean little book is all you need. If you're a travel info fiend (like me), this book sorts through all the superlatives and provides a handy rack upon which to hang your supplemental information.

Italy is my favorite country. Experiencing its culture, people, and natural wonders economically and hassle-free has been my goal for over 25 years of traveling, researching, and tour guiding. With this book, I pass on to you the lessons I've learned, updated (in mid-2000) for 2001.

*Rick Steves' Italy* is a tour guide in your pocket, offering a comfortable mix of big cities and cozy towns, from brutal but *bello* Rome to *tranquillo*, traffic-free Riviera villages. It covers the predictable biggies and adds a healthy dose of "Back Door" intimacy. Along with marveling at Michelangelo's masterpieces, you'll enjoy a *bruschetta* snack as a village boy rubs fresh garlic on your toast. I've been selective, including only the top sights. For example, after visiting dozens of hill towns, I recommend just the best five.

The best is, of course, only my opinion. But after more than two busy decades of travel writing, lecturing, and tour guiding, I've developed a sixth sense for what tickles the traveler's fancy.

## This Information Is Accurate and Up-to-Date

This book is updated every year. Most publishers of guidebooks that cover a country from top to bottom can afford an update only every two or three years (and even then, it's often by letter). Since this book is selective, I'm able to get it personally updated each summer. Even with an annual update, things change. But if you're traveling with the current edition of this book, I guarantee you're using the most up-to-date information available (for the latest, check www.ricksteves.com/update). This book will help you have an inexpensive, hassle-free trip. Use this year's edition. I tell you, you're crazy to save a few bucks by traveling on old information. If you're packing an old book, you'll learn the seriousness of your mistake . . . in Italy. Your trip costs about $10 per waking hour. Your time is valuable. This guidebook saves lots of time.

## Planning Your Trip

This book is organized by destinations. Each destination is a mini-vacation on its own, filled with exciting sights and comfortable, good-value places to stay. In each chapter you'll find:

**Planning Your Time,** a suggested schedule with thoughts on how to best use your limited time.

**Orientation,** including tourist information, city transportation, and an easy-to-read map designed to make the text clear and your arrival smooth.

**Sights with ratings: ▲▲▲**—Don't miss; **▲▲**—Try hard to see; **▲**—Worthwhile if you can make it; no rating—Worth knowing about.

**Sleeping** and **Eating,** with addresses and phone numbers of my favorite hotels and restaurants.

**Transportation Connections** to nearby destinations by train and route tips for drivers.

The **appendix** is a traveler's tool kit, with telephone tips, a climate chart, events calendar, and survival phrases.

Browse through this book, choose your favorite destinations, and link them up. Then have a great trip! You'll travel like a temporary local, getting the absolute most out of every mile, minute, and dollar. You won't waste time on mediocre sights because, unlike other guidebook authors, I cover only the best. Since your major financial pitfalls are lousy, expensive hotels, I've worked hard to assemble the best accommodations values for each stop. And as you travel the route I know and love, I'm happy you'll be meeting some of my favorite Italian people.

## Trip Costs

Six components make up your trip cost: airfare, surface transportation, room and board, sightseeing/entertainment, shopping/miscellany, and gelato.

**Airfare:** Don't try to sort through the mess. Find and use a good travel agent. A basic round-trip U.S.A.-to-Milan (or Rome) flight should cost $700 to $1,000, depending on where you fly from and when. Always consider saving time and money in Europe by flying "open jaw" (flying into one city and out of another).

**Surface Transportation:** For a three-week whirlwind trip of all my recommended destinations, allow $300 per person for public transportation (train and buses) or $500 per person (based on 2 people sharing a car) for a three-week car rental, tolls, gas, and insurance. Car rental is cheapest if arranged from the United States. Some train passes are available only outside of Europe. You might save money by getting an Italian railpass or buying tickets as you go (see "Transportation," below).

**Room and Board:** You can thrive in Italy on $70 a day for room and board (allow $80/day for Rome). This $70/day budget allows $10 for lunch, $20 for dinner, and $40 for lodging (based on 2 people splitting the cost of an $80 double room that includes breakfast). If you've got more money, I've listed great ways to spend it. And students and tightwads can enjoy Italy for as little as $40 a day ($20 for a bed, $20 for meals and snacks). But budget sleeping and eating require the skills covered later in this chapter (and in more depth in my book *Rick Steves' Europe Through the Back Door*).

**Sightseeing and Entertainment:** In big cities, figure about $5 to $7 per major sight (museums, Colosseum), $2 for minor ones (climbing church towers), and $25 to $30 for splurge experiences (tours or gondola ride—per person). An overall average of $15 a day works for most. Don't skimp here. After all, this category directly powers most of the experiences all the other expenses are designed to make possible.

**Shopping and Miscellany:** Figure $1 per postcard, coffee, and soft drink and $2 per gelato. Shopping can vary in cost from nearly nothing to a small fortune. Good budget travelers find that this category has little to do with assembling a trip full of lifelong and wonderful memories.

## Exchange Rate
I've priced things in lire (L) throughout the book.

L2,000 = about $1.

To figure lire quickly and easily, cover the last three digits and cut what's left by half (e.g., a L27,000 dinner costs about $13.50).

**Euro:** The euro, adopted as a currency by 11 European countries (including Italy), won't materialize into actual bills and coins until 2002. For travelers in 2001, it's not an issue.

## Prices, Times, and Discounts
The prices in this book, as well as the hours and telephone numbers, are accurate as of mid-2000—but once you pin Italy down, it wiggles. At each major destination, ask the local tourist information office for a current list of the city's sights, hours, and prices. Any guidebook on Italy starts to yellow even before it's printed.

In Italy—and in this book—you'll use the 24-hour clock. It's the same through 12:00 noon, then keep going—13:00, 14:00.... For anything over 12, subtract 12 and add p.m. (14:00 is 2:00 p.m.).

Peak season is roughly May through October. Off-season, November through April, expect shorter hours, more lunchtime breaks, and fewer activities.

While discounts for sights and transportation are not listed in this book, seniors (60 and over), students (with International Student Identity Cards), and youths (under 18) may snare a deal—although these days many discounts are limited to European residents.

## When to Go

Italy's best travel months are May, June, September, and October. November through April usually has pleasant weather with generally none of the sweat and stress of the tourist season. Peak season offers the longest hours and the most exciting slate of activities—but terrible crowds and, at times, suffocating heat. During peak times many resort-area hotels maximize business by requiring that guests buy dinner in their restaurants. August, the local holiday month, isn't as bad as many make it out to be, but big cities tend to be quiet (with discounted hotel prices), and beach and mountain resorts are jammed (with higher hotel prices). If you anticipate crowds, arrive early in the day or call hotels in advance (call from one hotel to the next; your fluent-in-Italian receptionist can help you).

Summer temperatures range from the 70s in Milan to the high 80s and 90s in Rome. In the winter it often drops to the 40s in Milan and the 50s in Rome. Spring and fall can be cold, and many hotels do not turn on their heat. Air-conditioning, when available, usually doesn't kick in until June 1. Most mid-range hotels come with air-conditioning—a worthwhile splurge in the summer. (See climate chart in the Appendix.)

## Sightseeing Priorities

Depending on the length of your trip, here are my recommended priorities:

|  |  |
|---|---|
| 3 days: | Florence, Venice |
| 5 days, add: | Rome |
| 7 days, add: | Cinque Terre |
| 10 days, add: | Civita di Bagnoregio and Siena |
| 14 days, add: | Sorrento, Naples, Pompeii, Amalfi, Paestum |
| 18 days, add: | Milan, Lake Como, Varenna, Assisi |
| 21 days, add: | Dolomites, Verona, Ravenna |

(This includes everything on the "Whirlwind Three-Week Tour" map on page 7.)

Considering how you're likely to go both broke and crazy driving in Italian cities and how handy and affordable Italy's trains and buses are, I'd do most of Italy by public transportation. If you want to drive, consider doing the big intense stuff (Rome, Naples area, Milan, Florence, and Venice) by train or bus and renting a car for the hill towns of Tuscany and Umbria and for the Dolomites. A car is a worthless headache on the Riviera and in the Lake Como area.

## Red Tape, Business Hours, and Banking

You need a passport but no visa or shots to travel in Italy.

**Business Hours:** Traditionally, Italy uses the siesta plan. People work from 8:00 or 9:00 to 13:00 and from 15:30 to 19:00, Monday through Saturday. Many businesses have adopted the government's new recommended 8:00 to 14:00 workday. In tourist areas, shops are open longer. If you're buying more than $200 worth of souvenirs, ask in the shops about getting the 10 to 19 percent tax back at the airport upon departure.

**Banking:** You'll want to spend local hard cash. The fastest way to get it is by using plastic: your ATM, credit, or debit card at a cash machine (Bancomat).

Bring some traveler's checks only as a backup. Regular banks have the best rates for cashing traveler's checks. For a large exchange, it pays to compare rates and fees. Bank of Sicily consistently has good rates. Banking hours are generally 8:30 to 13:30 and 15:30 to 16:30 Monday through Friday but can vary wildly. Banks are slow; simple transactions can take 15 to 30 minutes. Post offices and train stations usually change money if you can't get to a bank.

To get a cash advance from a bank machine, you'll need a four-digit PIN (numbers only, no letters, seven-digit PIN won't work) with your bank card. Before you go, verify with your bank that your card will work.

Visa and MasterCard are more commonly accepted than American Express. Bring two cards in case one is demagnetized, eaten by a machine, or rejected by a temperamental cash machine. Just like at home, credit or debit cards work easily at larger hotels, restaurants, and shops, but smaller businesses prefer payment in hard lire. Note that few businesses want to take large (L100,000) bills, especially for small purchases. Either use large bills for larger purchases or break them down for free at a bank.

Use a money belt. Thieves target tourists. A money belt (call 425/771-8303 for our free newsletter/catalog) provides peace of mind and allows you to carry lots of cash safely.

Don't be petty about changing money. The greatest avoidable money-changing expense is having to waste time every few days returning to a bank. Change a week's worth of money, get big bills, stuff them in your money belt, and travel!

## Language Barrier

Many Italians in larger towns and the tourist trade speak at least some English. Still, you'll get more smiles and results by using at least the Italian pleasantries. In smaller nontouristy towns, Italian is the norm. See the "Survival Phrases" near the end of this book (excerpted from *Rick Steves' Italian Phrase Book*). Note that Italian is pronounced much like English with a few exceptions, such as: *c* followed by *e* or *i* is pronounced *ch* (to ask "*Per centro?*"—"To the center?"—you say pehr CHEN-troh). In Italian, *ch* is pronounced like the hard *c* in Pinocchio (*chiesa*—church—is pronounced kee-AY-zah). Give it your best shot. Italians appreciate your efforts.

## Italy's Best Three-Week Trip

| Day | Plan | Sleep in |
|---|---|---|
| 1 | Arrive in Milan | Milan |
| 2 | Milan to Lake Como | Varenna |
| 3 | Lake Como | Varenna |
| 4 | To Dolomites via Verona (pick up car at Lake Como) | Castelrotto |
| 5 | Dolomites | Castelrotto |
| 6 | To Venice | Venice |
| 7 | Venice | Venice |
| 8 | To Florence | Florence |
| 9 | Florence | Florence |
| 10 | To Cinque Terre | Vernazza |
| 11 | Cinque Terre | Vernazza |
| 12 | To Siena | Siena |
| 13 | Siena | Siena |
| 14 | To Orvieto | Orvieto |
| 15 | Orvieto | Orvieto |
| 16 | To Sorrento via Pompeii | Sorrento |
| 17 | Sorrento | Sorrento |
| 18 | To Paestum | Sorrento |
| 19 | To Rome, drop car | Rome |
| 20 | Rome | Rome |
| 21 | Rome | Rome |
| 22 | Rome, fly home | |

This trip is designed to be done by car but works fine by rail with a few modifications. An Italy Rail Card (8 days in 1 month) works well—pay out of pocket for short runs such as Milan to Varenna or the small hops between villages in the Cinque Terre. While you can fly into Milan or Rome, I'd choose Milan and work my way south, flying out of Rome. Upon landing in Milan, go directly to Lake Como to relax and get over jet lag. Then see Milan for a half day but sleep in cozier Verona. Consider basing in Bolzano in the Dolomites. From Venice go straight to the Cinque Terre (2 direct trains/day), then do Florence and Siena. A car makes things more efficient in the hill towns of Tuscany and Umbria but is a headache elsewhere. Sorrento is a good home base for the Naples Bay sights. Skip Paestum unless you love Greek ruins. If you'd like to save Venice for near the end of your trip, you could start in Milan, seeing everything but Venice on the way south, then sleeping through everything you've already seen by catching the night train from Naples to Venice. This saves you a day and gives you an early arrival in Venice.

## Whirlwind Three-Week Tour of Italy

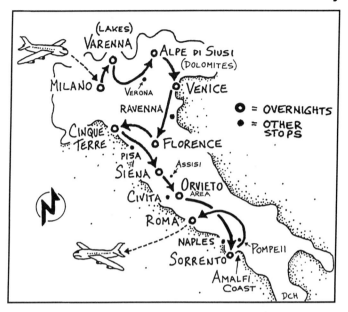

## Travel Smart

Many people travel through Italy thinking it's a chaotic mess.
They feel any attempt at efficient travel is futile. This is dead
wrong—and expensive. Italy, which seems as orderly as spilled
spaghetti, actually functions quite well. Only those who understand this and travel smart can enjoy Italy on a budget.

Upon arrival in a new town, lay the groundwork for a smooth
departure. Write down the schedule for the train or bus you'll take
when you depart. Reread this book as you travel and visit local
tourist information offices. Buy a phone card and use it for reservations, reconfirmations, and double-checking hours. Enjoy the
friendliness of the local people. Ask questions. Most locals are
eager to point you in their idea of the right direction. Learn the
currency and develop a simple formula to estimate prices in dollars
quickly. Keep a notepad in your pocket for organizing your
thoughts. Those who expect to travel smart, do.

Sundays have the same pros and cons as they do for travelers
in the United States. Sightseeing attractions are generally open
but have shorter hours, shops and banks are closed, and minor
transportation connections are more frustrating (e.g., no bus service
to or from Civita). City traffic is light. Rowdy evenings are rare on
Sundays. Saturdays are virtually weekdays with earlier closing

## Tips on Sightseeing in Italy

• Churches offer some amazing art (usually free), a cool respite from heat, and a welcome seat. A modest dress code (no bare shoulders or shorts for men or women) is enforced at larger churches such as Venice's St. Mark's and the Vatican's St. Peter's. A coin box near a piece of art often illuminates the art for a coin (and a better photo). Whenever possible, let there be light.

• Advance reservations are advisible for some of the more famous museums (Florence: Uffizi) and mandatory at others (Milan: Da Vinci's *Last Supper*, Padua: Scrovigni Chapel, Rome: Borghese Gallery and Nero's Golden House).

• Some sights are open throughout the evening, allowing easy viewing without crowds. Ask the local TI for a current listing of museum hours.

• Art historians and Italians refer to the great Florentine centuries by dropping a thousand years. The *Trecento* (300s), *Quattrocento* (400s), and *Cinquecento* (500s) were the 1300s, 1400s, and 1500s.

• In Italian museums, art is dated with A.C. (for Avanti Cristo, or B.C.) and D.C. (for Dopo Cristo, or A.D.). O.K.?

• Audioguides are becoming increasingly common at museums. These small portable devices give you information in English on what you're seeing. After you dial a number that appears next to a particular piece of art, you listen to the spiel (cutting it short if you want). Though the information can be dry, it's usually worthwhile (about L7,000, extra for 2 earphones—not always available).

• In museums, rooms can begin closing about 30 to 60 minutes before actual closing time. If your heart is set on one piece of art, don't save it for the finale.

• WCs at museums are usually free and clean.

• About half the visitors at Italian museums are English (not Italian) speakers. If a museum lacks audioguides and the only English you encounter explains how to pay, politely ask if there are plans to include English descriptions of the art. Think of it as a service to those who follow.

hours. Hotels in tourist areas are often booked up at Easter, in August, and on Fridays and Saturdays. Religious holidays and train strikes can catch you by surprise anywhere in Italy.

Plan ahead for banking, laundry, post-office chores, and picnics. Mix intense and relaxed periods. Every trip (and every traveler) needs at least a few slack days. Pace yourself. Assume you will return. Drink your water *con gas*.

## Tourist Information

During your trip, your first stop in each town should be the tourist office (abbreviated "TI" in this book and "i," "*turismo*, "'and "APT" in Italy). While Italian TIs are about half as helpful as those in other countries, their information is twice as important. Prepare. Have a list of questions and a proposed plan to double-check. If you're arriving late, telephone ahead (and try to get a map for your next destination from a TI in the town you're departing from).

Be wary of the travel agencies or special information services that masquerade as TIs but serve fancy hotels and tour companies. They are crooks and liars selling things you don't need.

While the TI is eager to book you a room, use their room-finding service only as a last resort. Across Europe, room-finding services are charging commissions from hotels, taking fees from travelers, and blacklisting establishments that buck their material-istic rules. They are unable to give hard opinions on the relative value of one place over another. The accommodations stakes are too high to go potluck through the TI. You'll do better going direct with the listings in this book.

## Italian Tourist Offices in the United States

Before your trip, contact the nearest Italian TI, briefly describe your trip, and request information. You'll get the general packet and, if you ask for specifics (individual city maps, a calendar of festivals, good hikes around Lake Como, info on wine tasting in Umbria, and so on), an impressive amount of help. If you have a specific problem, they're a good source of sympathy.

Write, call, or fax the office nearest you...

In New York: 630 Fifth Ave., #1565, New York, NY 10111, brochure hotline tel. 212/245-4822, tel. 212/245-5618, fax 212/586-9249.

In Illinois: 500 N. Michigan Ave., #2240, Chicago, IL 60611, brochure hotline tel. 312/666-0990, tel. 312/644-0996, fax 312/644-3019, e-mail: enitch@italiantourism.com.

In California: 12400 Wilshire Blvd., #550, Los Angeles, CA 90025, brochure hotline tel. 310/820-0098, tel. 310/820-1898, fax 310/820-6357, e-mail: enitla@earthlink.net.

Web sites: www.italiantourism.com (Italian Tourist Board in the United States) and www.vatican.va (Vatican).

## Recommended Guidebooks

Especially if you'll be traveling beyond my recommended destina-tions, you may want some supplemental information. When you consider the improvements they'll make in your $3,000 vacation, $30 for extra maps and books is money well spent. Especially for several people traveling by car, the weight and expense are neg-ligible. One budget tip can save the price of an extra guidebook.

Lonely Planet's *Italy* is thorough, well researched, and packed with good maps and hotel recommendations for low- to moderate-budget travelers, but it's not updated annually. Use it only with a one- or two-year-old copyright. The hip *Rough Guide to Italy* (British researchers, more insightful) and the highly opinionated *Let's Go: Italy* (by Harvard students, better hotel listings) are great for students and vagabonds. If you're a low-budget train traveler interested in the youth and night scene (which I have basically ignored), get *Let's Go: Italy*. The Italy section in the bigger *Let's Go: Europe* is sparse.

**Cultural and Sightseeing Guides:** The colorful Eyewitness series is popular with travelers (editions covering Italy, Tuscany, Rome, Florence, Venice). They are fun for their great, easy-to-grasp graphics and photos and just right for people who want only factoids. But the Eyewitness written content is relatively skimpy, and the books weigh a ton. I buy them in Italy (no more expensive than in the United States) or simply borrow them for a minute from other travelers at certain sights to make sure I'm aware of that place's highlights. The tall green Michelin guides to Italy and Rome have nothing on room and board but do have great maps for drivers and lots of solid encyclopedic coverage of sights, customs, and culture (sold in English in Italy). The Cadogan guides to various parts of Italy offer an insightful look at the rich and confusing local culture. Those heading for Florence or Rome should read Irving Stone's *The Agony and the Ecstasy* for a great— if romanticized—rundown on Michelangelo, the Medici family, and the turbulent times of the Renaissance.

## Rick Steves' Books and Videos

*Rick Steves' Europe Through the Back Door 2001* gives you budget travel skills for minimizing jet lag, packing light, planning your itinerary, traveling by car or train, finding budget beds without reservations, changing money, avoiding rip-offs, outsmarting thieves, hurdling the language barrier, staying healthy, taking great photographs, using your bidet, and much more. The book also includes chapters on 35 of my favorite "Back Doors," six of which are in Italy.

Rick Steves' **Country Guides**, a series of seven guidebooks including this book, cover the Best of Europe; Great Britain/Ireland; France/Belgium/Netherlands; Spain/Portugal; Germany/Austria/Switzerland; and Scandinavia. All are updated annually and come out each December.

Rick Steves' **City Guides** cover Rome, Paris, and London. Updated annually (and available in January), these practical guides offer in-depth coverage of Europe's three greatest cities, complete with extensive self-guided tours through the greatest museums. To make your visit to Italy's secular and religious capital more meaningful, consider getting the Rome city guide.

*Europe 101: History and Art for the Traveler* (with Gene Open-shaw, 2000), which gives you the story of Europe's people, history, and art, is heavy on Italy's ancient, Renaissance, and modern history. Written for smart people who were sleeping in their history and art classes before they knew they were going to Europe, *101* helps resurrect the rubble.

*Rick Steves' Mona Winks: Self-Guided Tours of Europe's Top Museums* (with Gene Openshaw, 1998) gives you one- to three-hour self-guided tours through Europe's 20 most exhausting and important museums. Nearly half of the book is devoted to Italy, with tours of Venice (St. Mark's, Doge's Palace, and Accademia Gallery), Florence (Uffizi Gallery, Bargello, Michelangelo's *David*, and a Renaissance walk through the town center), and Rome (Colosseum, Forum, Pantheon, Vatican Museum, and St. Peter's Basilica). If you want to enjoy the great sights and museums of Italy, *Mona* will be a valued friend.

In Italy, a phrase book is as fun as it is necessary. My *Rick Steves' Italian Phrase Book* will help you meet the people and stretch your budget. It's written by a monoglot who, for more than 25 years, has fumbled through Italy struggling with all the other phrase books. Use this fun and practical communication aid to make accurate hotel reservations over the telephone, ask for a free taste of cantaloupe-flavored gelato at the *gelatería*, have the man in the deli make you a sandwich, and tell your cabbie that if he doesn't slow down you'll throw up.

My public television series—*Rick Steves' Europe*—airs 16 brand-new shows in 2001, including two shows on Rome (Classical and Baroque) and one on the Best of Sicily. All 52 of the earlier shows, which include six half-hour shows on Italy, still air throughout the United States on public television stations and the Travel Channel. Each episode is also available in information-packed home videos, as is my two-hour slide-show lecture on Italy (call us at 425/771-8303 for our free newsletter/catalog or check www.ricksteves.com).

*Rick Steves' Postcards from Europe*, my autobiographical book, packs more than 25 years of travel anecdotes and insights into the ultimate 3,000-mile European adventure. Through my guidebooks, I share my favorite European discoveries with you. *Postcards* introduces you to my favorite European friends. Half of *Postcards* is set in Italy: Venice, Florence, Rome, and the Cinque Terre.

All of my books are published by Avalon Travel Publishing (www.travelmatters.com).

## Maps

The maps in this book, drawn by Dave Hoerlein, are concise and simple. Dave, who is well traveled in Italy, designed the maps to help you locate recommended places and the tourist

offices, where you can pick up more in-depth maps of the city
or region (cheap or free).

For an overall map of Europe, consider my new Rick Steves'
Europe Planning Map—geared to travelers' needs—with sightseeing destinations listed prominently (for our free newsletter/
catalog, contact us at 425/771-8303 or www.ricksteves.com).

Train travelers can do fine with a simple rail map (such as
the one that comes with your railpass) and city maps from the
TI as they travel. But drivers shouldn't skimp on maps. Excellent
maps are available throughout Italy at bookstores, newsstands,
and gas stations. Get a good 1:200,000 map to get the most out
of your miles and study the key to get the most sightseeing value
out of your map.

## Tours of Italy

Travel agents will tell you about normal tours of Italy, but they
won't tell you about ours. At Europe Through the Back Door,
we offer 20-day tours of Italy featuring most of the highlights in
this book (departures April–Oct, 26 people on a big roomy bus
with 2 great guides) and one-week, off-season getaways to Rome
(departures Oct–March, 20 people). For information, call 425/
771-8303 or see www.ricksteves.com.

## Transportation

### By Car or Train?

Each mode of transportation has pros and cons. Public transportation is one of the few bargains in Italy. Trains and buses are
inexpensive and good. City-to-city travel is faster, easier, and
cheaper by train than by car. Trains give you the convenience
and economy of doing long stretches overnight. By train I arrive
relaxed and well rested—not so by car.

Parking, gas (about $4 per gallon), and tolls are expensive in
Italy. But drivers enjoy more control, especially in the countryside.
Cars carry your luggage for you, generally from door to door—
especially important for heavy packers (such as chronic shoppers
and families traveling with children). And groups know that the
more people you pack into a car or minibus, the cheaper it gets
per person.

### Trains

To travel by train cheaply in Italy, simply buy tickets as you go.
But Italy's train ticket system confounds even the locals, and, for
convenience alone, I'd go with the Italian State Railway's Italy Rail
Card (see chart on the next page). If you're traveling with a group,
consider Italy's Kilometric Ticket. Unlike the Rail Card, the Kilometric Ticket—while a headache because it doesn't cover fast-train

# Cost of Public Transportation

My free *Rick Steves' Guide to European Railpasses* has the latest on 2001 prices. To get the railpass guide, call us at 425/771-8303 or visit www.ricksteves.com/rail (you can order most passes online). All Italy passes are also sold in Italy at travel agencies and major train stations.

## ITALY RAIL CARD (2000)

|                              | 1st class | 2nd class |
| ---------------------------- | --------- | --------- |
| 10 consec. days              | $299      | $199      |
| 17 consec. days              | 373       | 249       |
| 24 consec. days              | 433       | 289       |
| 33 consec. days              | 522       | 348       |
| Any 5 days in 1 month flexi  | 239       | 159       |
| Any 10 days in 1 month flexi | 334       | 223       |
| Any 14 days in 1 month flexi | 429       | 286       |

Passes cover supplements EXCEPT for the fast-n-classy T.A.V.; passes do not cover any reservations. Children 4-11 pay half the adult fare; under 4 free.

**Italy:**
This schematic map indicates the cost in dollars for a one-way 2nd class trip (first #) and the number of kilometers (second #) between the cities shown.

## ITALIAN KILOMETRIC TICKET

Also known as the "Biglietto Chilometrico," this ticket features coupons for up to 20 trips totaling up to 3,000 kilometers that can be used for up to five people. Sold quick and easy at any major Italian travel agency or train station, the pass costs about $180 for first class or $120 for second class. For example, a group of five could go the 570 km from Venice to Rome on a Kilometric Ticket for $24 each vs. the normal $45 regular ticket price. The Kilometric Ticket does not cover supplements charged for the faster intercity trains.

supplements—can be an economical deal for groups. (One to five people can travel up to 3,000 kilometers on it for around $120 second class, $180 first class—buy it at major Italian stations; it's also available in the United States but costs much more.) For travel exclusively in Italy, a 17-country Eurailpass is a bad value, though a cheaper five-country Europass is worth considering. New for 2001, the Eurail Selectpass ($476 for 10 days in 2 months) allows you to tailor a pass to your trip, provided you're traveling in three adjacent countries, directly connected by rail or ferry. For instance, you could choose France-Italy-Greece or Germany-Austria-Italy.

You'll encounter several types of trains in Italy. Along with the various milk-run trains, there are the slow IR (Interregional) and *directo* trains, the medium *expresso*, the fast IC (Intercity), and the bullet-train T.A.V. (Treno Alta Velocita). The T.A.V., which requires about a L30,000 supplement even if you have a railpass, provides two-thirds of the train service from Rome to Milan, Florence, Venice, or Naples. Even with supplements, fast trains

## Italy's Public Transportation

KEY: — RAIL  — — BUS  •••• SHIP

*NOT TO SCALE*  ● GOOD OVERNIGHT STOPS

## Deciphering Italian Train Schedules

At the station, look for the big yellow posters labeled *Partenze*—Departures (ignore the white posters, which show arrivals). Schedules are listed chronologically, hour by hour, showing the trains leaving the station throughout the day. The first column (*Ora*) lists the time of departure. The next column (*Treno*) shows the type of train. The third column (*Classi Servizi*) lists the services available (first- and second-class cars, dining car, couchettes, etc.) and, more important, whether you need reservations (usually denoted by an *R* in a box). The next column lists the destination of the train (*Principali Fermate Destinazioni*), often showing intermediate stops, followed by the final destination, with arrival times listed throughout in parentheses. Note that *your* final destination may be listed in fine print as an intermediate destination. If you're going from Milan to Florence, scan the schedule and you'll notice that virtually all trains that terminate in Rome stop in Florence en route. Travelers who read the fine print end up with a greater choice of trains. The next column (*Servizi Diretti e Annotazioni*) has pertinent notes about the train, such as "also stops in. . ." (*ferma anche a. . .*), "doesn't stop in. . ." (*non ferma a. . .*) , "stops in every station" (*ferma in tutte le stazioni*), and so on. The last column lists the track (*Binario*) the train departs from. Confirm the *binario* with an additional source: a ticket seller, the electronic board listing immediate departures, TV monitors on the platform, or the railway officials who are usually standing by the train unless you really need them. For any odd symbols on the poster, look at the key at the end. Some of the phrasing can be deciphered easily: such as *servizio periodico* (periodical service—doesn't always run). For the tricker ones, ask a local or railway official or simply take a different train.

are affordable (e.g., a second-class Rome-to-Venice ticket costs about $50 with express supplement). Buying supplements on the train comes with a nasty penalty, and buying them at the station can waste time. Try to buy them at travel agencies (CIT or American Express) in towns. The cost is the same, the lines and language barrier are smaller, and you'll save time.

First-class tickets cost 50 percent more than second-class. While second-class cars go as fast as their first-class neighbors, Italy is one country where I would consider the splurge of first class. The easiest way to upgrade a second-class ticket once onboard a crowded train is to nurse a drink in the snack car.

If you anticipate a crowd, you can get a firm seat reservation in advance for about L7,000. Newsstands sell up-to-date regional and all-Italy timetables (L8,000, ask for the *orario ferroviaro*). There is an all-Italy telephone number for train information—1478-88088 (daily 7:00–21:00, English generally spoken). On the Web, check http://bahn.hafas.de/english.html or www.fs-on-line.com.

Italian trains are famous for their thieves. Never leave a bag unattended. There have been cases of bandits gassing an entire car before looting the snoozing gang. I've noticed that police now ride the trains, and things seem more controlled. Still, for an overnight trip, I'd feel safe only in a *cuccetta* (a berth in a special sleeping car with an attendant who keeps track of who comes and goes while you sleep—approximately L25,000 in a 6-bed compartment, L35,000 in a less-cramped 4-bed compartment). Avoid big-city train station lines whenever you can. For either the same cost or a minimal charge (about L4,000), you can buy tickets and reserve a *cuccetta* at a travel agency.

Most stations have a *deposito* (or *bagagli*) where you can safely leave your bag for L5,000 per 12-hour period (payable when you pick up the bag). Larger stations also have lockers which are a bit complicated to figure out (the smiley slot takes bills).

Strikes are common. Strikes generally last a day, and train employees will simply say, "*Sciopero*" (strike). But, in actuality, sporadic trains, following no particular schedule, lumber down the tracks during most strikes.

## Car Rental
Research car rental before you go. It's cheaper to arrange for car rentals through your travel agent while still in the United States. Rent by the week with unlimited mileage. If you need a car for three or more weeks, it's cheaper to lease (you'll save money on insurance and taxes). Explore your drop-off options (south of Rome can be a problem).

For peace of mind, I spring for the Collision Damage Waiver (CDW) insurance (about $10–15 per day), which gives a zero deductible rather than the standard value-of-the-car "deductible." A few "gold" credit cards cover CDW insurance; quiz your credit-card company on the worst-case scenario. Travel Guard sells CDW insurance for $6 a day (U.S. tel. 800/826-1300).

Theft insurance (separate from CDW insurance) is mandatory when you're renting a car for use in Italy. The insurance usually costs about $10 to $15 a day, payable when you pick up the car.

A rail-and-drive pass (such as a EurailDrive, EuropassDrive, or Italy Rail and Drive) can be put to thoughtful use. Certain areas are great by car, such as the Dolomites and the hill towns of Tuscany and Umbria, while most of Italy is best by train.

## Standard European Road Signs

STOP — DUH | No Entry For Cars | All Vehicles Prohibited | No Entry | Speed Limit (in km) | Yield | No Passing | Danger | Parking

### *Driving*

Driving in Italy is frightening—a video game for keeps, and you only get one quarter. All you need is a U.S. driver's license and a car. According to everybody but the Italian police, international driver's licenses are not necessary. The police fine you if they can't read your license.

**Autostradas:** Italy's freeway system is as good as our interstate system, but you'll pay about a dollar for every 10 minutes of use. (I paid L40,000 for the four-hour drive from Bolzano to Pisa.) While I favor the autostradas because I feel they're safer, cheaper (saving time and gas), and less nerve-racking than smaller roads, savvy local drivers know which toll-free "*superstradas*" are actually faster and more direct than the autostrada (e.g., Florence to Pisa). For more information, visit www.autostrade.it.

**Gas:** Most cars take unleaded (green pumps, available everywhere). Autostrada rest stops are self-service stations open daily without a siesta break. Small-town stations are usually cheaper and offer full service but shorter hours. Many 24-hour-a-day stations are entirely automated, with machines that trade gas for paper money.

**Metric:** A liter is about a quart, four to a gallon; a kilometer is about .6 of a mile. Figure kilometers to miles by cutting them in half and adding back 10 percent of the original (120 km: 60 + 12 = 72 miles, 300 km: 150 + 30 = 180 miles).

**Parking:** White lines generally mean parking is free. Blue lines mean you'll have to pay—usually L1,500 to L2,000 per hour. If there's no meter, there is probably a roving attendant who will take your money. Study the signs. Many free zones are cleared out (by car owners or tow trucks) one day a week for street cleaning. Often the free zones have a 30- or 60-minute time limit. *Zona disco* has nothing to do with dancing. Italian cars have a time disc, which you set at your arrival time and lay on the dashboard so the attendant knows how long you've been parked. This is a fine system that all drivers should take advantage of. (If your rental car doesn't come with a *zona disco*, pick one up at a tobacco shop or just write your arrival time on a piece of paper and place it on the dashboard.) Garages are safe, save time, and help you avoid the stress of parking tickets. Take the parking voucher with you to pay the cashier before you leave.

**Theft:** Cars are routinely vandalized and stolen. Try to make your car look locally owned: Hide the "tourist-owned" rental company decals and put a local newspaper in your back window.

## Telephones, Mail, and E-mail

Smart travelers use the telephone every day—especially in Italy—to make hotel reservations, call tourist information offices, and phone home. Dialing long distance is easy with an Italian phone card.

Italy's phone cards are cards you insert in the phone instead of coins. They're sold in L5,000, L10,000, and L15,000 denominations at tobacco shops, post offices, and machines near phone booths (many phone booths indicate where the nearest phone-card sales outlet is located). Rip off the perforated corner to "activate" the card before you insert it into the phone.

The orange SIP public telephones are everywhere and take cards or coins. About a quarter of the phones are broken (which could explain why so many Italians carry cell phones). The rest of the phones work reluctantly. Dial slowly and deliberately, as if the phone doesn't understand numbers very well. Often a recorded message will break in, brusquely informing you that your number does not exist. Dial again with confidence to convince the phone of your number's existence. If you fail, try a different phone. Repeat as needed.

Italian phone numbers vary in length; a hotel can have, say, a 10-digit phone number and 11-digit fax number. When spelling out your name on the phone, you'll find *i* (pronounced "ee" in Italian) and *e* (pronounced "ay") are confusing. Say "*i*, Italia" and "*e*, Empoli" to clear up that problem. If you plan to access your voice mail from Italy, be advised that you probably can't dial extensions or secret codes once you connect (you're on vacation—relax). European time is six/nine hours ahead of the east/west coast of the United States.

**Dialing Direct:** Italy has dispensed with area codes. To call anywhere within Italy, just dial the number. For example, the number of one of my recommended Venice hotels is 041-522-7131. To call it from the Venice train station, dial 041-522-7131. If you call it from Rome, it's the same: 041-522-7131.

When dialing internationally, dial the international access code (of the country you're calling from), the country code (of the country you're calling), and the local number. To call the Venice hotel from the United States, dial 011 (the U.S. international access code), 39 (Italy's country code), and then 041-522-7131. (Isn't there always an exception? If you're making an international call to an Italian cell phone number, follow the instructions above, but drop the initial zero of the cellular number. Cellular numbers listed in this book are preceded by the word "cellular.") To call my office from Italy, I dial 00 (Italy's international access code), 1 (the U.S. country code),

425 (Edmonds' area code), and 771-8303. For international access codes and country codes, see the appendix.

Hotel-room phones are reasonable for calls within Italy (the faint beeps stand for L200 phone units) but a terrible rip-off for calls to the United States (unless you use a PIN card—see below—or your hotel allows toll-free access to your USA Direct service—see below). If you have phone-card phobia, look for the easy-to-use "talk now, pay later" metered phones in some bars or in the central post office or train station in big cities.

Italy has toll-free numbers that start with 800 (like the U.S.A.'s 800 numbers, though in Italy you don't dial a "1" first). In Italy, you can dial these 800 numbers—called *freephone* or *numero verde* (green number)—free from any phone without using a card or coins.

**Calling Home:** Calling the United States from Italy is now cheapest with the new PIN cards (sold for L5,000, L10,000, and L20,000 at newsstands and hole-in-the-wall long-distance phone shops; because there are so many brand names, just ask for an international telephone card). Buy a card, scratch off and reveal your Personal Identification Number, dial the toll-free number, punch in your PIN, and talk. You'll get about three minutes per dollar. Because you don't insert these cards into a phone, you can use them at most phones, including your hotel room (unless it's an older touch-tone phone). If the PIN doesn't work on one phone, try another phone. Get a lower denomination (L10,000 instead of L20,000) in case the card is a dud. On my last trip, I had difficulty using PIN cards to make local calls, so I used Italian phone cards, coins, or hotel room phones for local calls, and saved the PIN card for international calls.

USA Direct services, such as AT&T, MCI, and Sprint, while still convenient, are no longer a good value. It's much cheaper to call the United States using a PIN card or Italian phone card, but some people prefer to use their easier, pricier calling cards. Each card company has a toll-free number in each European country (for Italy: AT&T—tel. 172-1011, MCI—tel. 172-1022, Sprint—tel. 172-1877) which puts you in touch with an English-speaking operator who takes your card number and the number you want to call, puts you through, and bills your home phone number for the call. Oddly, you need to use a 200-lire coin or Italian phone card to dial the toll-free number. You'll be billed $2 per minute plus a $4 service charge. Hanging up when you hear an answering machine is expensive ($6). First use a coin or an Italian phone card to call home for five seconds—long enough to say "call me" or to make sure an answering machine is off so you can call back using your USA Direct number to connect with a person. It's a rip-off to use USA Direct for calls between European countries; it's much cheaper to call direct using an Italian phone card.

**Mail:** Mail service is miserable in Italy. Postcards get last priority. If you must have mail stops, consider a few prereserved hotels along your route or use American Express offices. Most American Express offices in Italy will hold mail for one month. This service is free to anyone using an Amex card or traveler's checks (and available for a small fee to others). Allow 14 days for U.S.-to-Italy mail delivery, but don't count on it. Federal Express makes pricey two-day deliveries. Phoning is so easy that I've completely dispensed with mail stops. If possible, mail nothing precious from Italy.

**E-mail:** E-mail use among Italian hoteliers is increasing. I've listed e-mail addresses when possible. Little, hole-in-the-wall cybercafés are popular in the bigger cities, giving you inexpensive and easy Internet access.

## Sleeping

For hassle-free efficiency, I favor hotels and restaurants handy to your sightseeing activities. Rather than list hotels scattered throughout a city, I describe two or three favorite neighborhoods and recommend the best accommodations values in each, from $20 bunks to plush $200 doubles with all the comforts.

Sleeping in Italy is expensive. Cheap big-city hotels can be depressing. Tourist information services cannot give opinions on quality. A major feature of this book is its extensive listing of good-value rooms. I like places that are clean, small, central, quiet at night, traditional, inexpensive, friendly, with firm beds—and those not listed in other guidebooks. (In Italy, for me, 6 out of 9 is a keeper.)

### Hotels

Double rooms listed in this book will range from about $50 (very simple, toilet and shower down the hall) to $200 (maximum plumbing and more), with most clustering around $90 (with private bathrooms). Prices are higher in big cities and heavily touristed cities and lower off the beaten path. Three or four people economize by requesting larger rooms. Solo travelers find that the cost of a *camera singola* is often only 25 percent less than a *camera doppia*. Most listed hotels have rooms for anywhere from one to five people. If there's room for an extra cot, they'll cram it in for you.

The Italian word for "hotel" is *albergo*. A few places have kept the old titles, *locanda* or *pension*, indicating that they offer budget beds.

You normally get close to what you pay for. Prices are fairly standard. Shopping around earns you a better location and more character but rarely a cheaper price.

However, prices at nearly any hotel can get soft if you do any of the following: arrive direct (without using a pricey middleman

## Sleep Code

To pack maximum information into minimum space, I use this code to describe accommodations in this book. When there is a range of prices in one category, the price will fluctuate with the season, size of room, or length of stay. Prices listed are per room, not per person.

**S** = Single room or price for one person using a double.

**D** = Double or twin room. "Double beds" are often two twins sheeted together and are usually big enough for nonromantic couples.

**T** = Three-person room (often a double with a single bed moved in).

**Q** = Four-adult room (an extra child's bed is usually cheaper).

**b** = Private bathroom with a toilet and shower or tub.

**t** = Private toilet only. (The shower is down the hall.)

**s** = Private shower or tub only. (The toilet is down the hall.)

**CC** = Accepts credit cards (**V** = Visa, **M** = MasterCard, **A** = American Express). Many places also accept Diners' (which I don't note). If CC isn't mentioned, assume you'll need to pay cash.

**SE** = Speaks English. This code is used only when it seems predictable that you'll encounter English-speaking staff.

**NSE** = Does not speak English. Used only when it's unlikely you'll encounter English-speaking staff.

According to this code, a couple staying at a "Db-L160,000, CC:V, SE" hotel would pay a total of L160,000 (about $80) for a double room with a private bathroom. The hotel accepts Visa or Italian cash. The staff speaks English.

like the TI), offer to pay cash, stay at least three nights, or visit off-season. Breakfasts are legally optional (though some hotels insist they're not). Initial prices quoted often include breakfast and a private bathroom. Offer to skip breakfast for a better price.

You'll save $10 to $20 if you ask for a room without a shower and just use the shower down the hall. Generally rooms with a bath or shower also have a toilet and a bidet (which Italians use for quick sponge baths). Tubs usually come with a frustrating "telephone shower" (handheld nozzle). If a shower has no curtain, the entire bathroom showers with you. The cord that dangles over the tub or shower is not a clothesline. You pull it when you've fallen and can't get up.

Double beds are called *matrimoniale*, even though hotels aren't interested in your marital status. Twins are *due letti singoli*.

Many hotel rooms have a TV and phone. Rooms in fancier hotels usually come with air-conditioning (sometimes you pay an extra per-day charge for this), a tiny safe, and a small stocked fridge called a *frigo* bar (FREE-goh bar).

When you check in, the receptionist will ask for your passport and keep it for a couple of hours. Hotels are required to register each guest with the police. Relax. Americans are notorious for making this chore more difficult than it needs to be.

The hotel breakfast, while convenient, is often a bad value— $8 for a roll, jelly, and usually unlimited *caffè latte*. You can sometimes request cheese or salami (about L5,000 extra). I enjoy taking breakfast at the corner café. It's OK to supplement what you order with a few picnic goodies.

Rooms are safe. Still, zip cameras and keep money out of sight. More pillows and blankets are usually in the closet or available on request. In Italy towels and linen aren't always replaced every day. Hang your towel up to dry.

While bed-and-breakfasts (*affitta camere*) and youth hostels (*ostello della gioventù*) are not as common in Italy as elsewhere in Europe, I've listed many in this book. Big-city hostels are normally overrun with the *Let's Go* crowd, but small-town hostels can be an enjoyable way to save money and make friends.

Regardless of where you stay, you'll avoid the time-wasting crowd at the reception desk in the morning if you pay the evening before you leave.

## Making Reservations

It's possible to travel at any time of year without reservations, but, given the high stakes and the quality of the gems I've found for this book, I'd recommend making reservations. You can call long in advance from home or grab rooms a few days to a week in advance as you travel. (If you have difficulty, ask the fluent receptionist at your current hotel to call for you.) If you like more spontaneity (or if you're traveling off-season), you might make a habit of calling between 9:00 and 10:00 on the day you plan to arrive, when the hotel clerk knows who'll be checking out and just which rooms will be available. I've taken great pains to list telephone numbers with long distance instructions (see "Telephones," above; also see the Appendix). Use the telephone and the convenient telephone cards. Most hotels listed are accustomed to English-only speakers. A hotel receptionist will trust you and hold a room until 16:00 without a deposit, though some will ask for a credit-card number. Honor (or cancel by phone) your reservations. Long distance is cheap and easy from public phone booths. Don't let these people down—I promised you'd call and cancel if for some reason you won't show up. Don't needlessly confirm rooms through the tourist office; they'll take a commission.

If you know where you want to stay each day (and you don't need or want flexibility), reserve your rooms a month or two in advance from home. To reserve from home, telephone first to confirm availability and then fax or e-mail your formal request. Phone and fax costs are reasonable, e-mail is a steal, and simple English is usually fine. To fax, use the handy form in the appendix (online at ricksteves.com/reservation). If you don't get an answer to your fax request, consider that a "no." (Many little places get 20 faxes a day after they're full and can't afford to respond.)

A two-night stay in August would be "two nights, 16/8/01 to 18/8/01" (Europeans write the date in this order—day/month/year—and hotel jargon uses your day of departure). You'll often receive a response back requesting one night's deposit. A credit card will usually be accepted. If you use your credit card for the deposit, you can pay with your card or cash when you arrive; if you don't show up, you'll be billed for one night. Always reconfirm your reservations a day in advance by phone.

### Agriturismo

*Agriturismo* (or agricultural tourism) began in the 1960s to encourage farmers to remain on their land, produce food, and offer accommodation to tourists. These rural Italian B&Bs are ideal for couples or families traveling by car.

Some properties are simple and rustic, while others are downright luxurious, offering amenities such as swimming pools. The quality of the rooms varies, but they are usually simple, clean, and comfortable. Most serve tasty home-grown food. And most require a minimum-night stay, usually a week. July and August are especially busy. Off-season shorter stays are possible.

Be aware that agricultural tourism is organized *"alla Italiana,"* which means, among other things, a lack of a single governing body. In this book you'll find some *agriturismo* farms you can contact directly. Otherwise, consider one of several agencies that handle bookings, such as Farm Holidays in Tuscany. They book rooms and apartments at 300 farms in Tuscany, Umbria, and elsewhere in Italy (Mon–Fri 9:00–13:00, 15:00–18:00, plus May–Sept Sat 16:00–18:00, closed Sun, Via Manin 20, 58100 Grosseto, tel. 0564-417-418, www.it-farmholidays.it, English spoken). Book several months in advance for high season (May–Sept). Generally, a 25 or 30 percent deposit is required (lost if you cancel), and the balance is due one month before arrival.

For more information on *agriturismo*, visit www.initaly.com, www.italyfarmholidays.com, and www.agriturismo.com.

## Eating Italian

The Italians are masters of the art of fine living. That means eating...long and well. Lengthy, multicourse lunches and dinners and endless hours sitting in outdoor cafés are the norm. Americans eat on their way to an evening event and complain if the check is slow in coming. For Italians, the meal is an end in itself, and only rude waiters rush you. When you want the bill, mime-scribble on your raised palm or ask for it: "*Il conto?*"

Even those of us who liked dorm food will find that the local cafés, cuisine, and wines become a highlight of our Italian adventure. Trust me, this is sightseeing for your palate, and even if the rest of you is sleeping in cheap hotels, your taste buds will relish an occasional first-class splurge. You can eat well without going broke. But be careful; you're just as likely to blow a small fortune on a disappointing meal as you are to dine wonderfully for $20.

## Restaurants

When restaurant hunting, choose places filled with locals, not the place with the big neon signs boasting, "We speak English and accept credit cards." Restaurants parked on famous squares generally serve bad food at high prices to tourists. Locals eat better at lower-rent locales. Family-run places operate without hired help and can offer cheaper meals. The word *osteria* (normally a simple, local-style restaurant) makes me salivate.

For unexciting but basic values, look for a *menu turistico* (also called *menu del giorno*—menu of the day), a three- or four-course, set-price meal (price includes service charge, no need to tip). Galloping gourmets order à la carte with the help of a menu translator. (The *Marling Italian Menu Master* is excellent. *Rick Steves' Italian Phrase Book* has enough phrases for intermediate eaters.) Some restaurants have self-serve antipasti buffets, offering a variety of cooked appetizers spread out like a salad bar (pay per plate, not weight; usually costs around L11,000-16,000); a plate of antipasti combined with a pasta dish makes a healthy, affordable, interesting meal.

A full meal consists of an appetizer (antipasto, L5,000–10,000), a first course (*primo piatto*, pasta or soup, L8,000–14,000), and a second course (*secondo piatto*, expensive meat and fish dishes, L10,000–20,000). Seafood and steak is sometimes sold by weight (if you see "100 g" by the price, you'll pay that price *per* 100 grams—about a quarter pound). Some special dishes come in large quantities meant for two people; the shorthand way of showing this on a menu is "X2" (meaning "times two"). Vegetables (*contorni, verdure*) may come with the *secondo* course or cost extra (L6,000) as a side dish. Restaurants normally pad the bill with a cover charge (*pane e coperto*, around L2,000) and a service charge (*servizio*, 15 percent); these charges are listed on the menu. Italian waiters are paid well, and tipping is not expected if the *servizio* charge is included in the bill. At restaurants that don't tack on a service charge, tip 10 to 15 percent.

As you will see, the lire add up in a hurry. Light and budget eaters get by with a *primo piatto* each and sharing an antipasto. Italians admit that *secondi* are the least interesting aspect of the local cuisine.

## Delis, Cafeterias, Pizza Shops, and Tavola Calda (Hot Table) Bars

Italy offers many cheap alternatives to restaurants. Stop by a *rosticcería* (for great cooked deli food, ready for take out), a self-service cafeteria (which feeds you without the add-ons), a *tavola calda* bar (for an assortment of veggies), or a Pizza Rustica shop (for stand-up or take-out pizza).

Pizza is cheap and everywhere. Key pizza vocabulary: *capricciosa* (generally ham, mushrooms, and artichokes), *funghi* (mushrooms), *margherita* (tomato sauce and mozzarella), *marinara* (tomato sauce, oregano, garlic, no cheese), *quattro formaggi* (4 different cheeses), and *quattro stagioni* (different toppings on each of the four quarters for those who can't choose just one menu item). If you ask for *peperoni* on your pizza, you'll get green or red peppers, not sausage. Kids like *margherita* and *diavola* (closest thing in Italy to American "pepperoni"). At Pizza Rustica take-out shops, slices are sold by weight (100 grams, or *un etto*, is a hot cheap snack; 200 grams, or *due etti*, makes a light meal).

For a fast, cheap, and healthy lunch, find a *tavola calda* bar with a buffet spread of meat and vegetables and ask for a mixed plate of vegetables with a hunk of mozzarella (*piatto misto di verdure con mozzarella*). Don't be limited by what you can see. If you'd like a salad with a slice of cantaloupe and a hunk of cheese, they'll whip that up for you in a snap. Belly up to the bar and, with a pointing finger and key words in the chart on the next page, you can get a fine mixed plate of vegetables. If something's a mystery, ask for *un assaggio* (a little taste).

## Italian Bars/Cafés

Italian "bars" are not taverns but cafés. These local hangouts serve coffee, mini-pizzas, sandwiches, and cartons of milk from the cooler. Many dish up plates of fried cheese and vegetables from under the glass counter, ready to reheat. This is my budget choice, the Italian equivalent of English pub grub.

For quick meals, bars usually have trays of cheap ready-made sandwiches (*panini* or *tramezzini*)—some kinds are delightful grilled. To save time for sightseeing and room for dinner, my favorite lunch is a ham and cheese *panini* at a bar (called *tost*, grilled twice to get really hot). To get food "to go," say, "*Da portar via*" (for the road).

Bars serve great drinks—hot, cold, sweet, or alcoholic. Chilled bottled water (*natural* or *frizzante*) is sold cheap to go.

## Ordering Food at *Tavola Caldas*

| plate of mixed veggies | *piatto misto di verdure* | pee-AH-toh MEES-toh dee vehr-DOO-ray |
|---|---|---|
| "Heated, please." | *Scaldare, per favore.*" | skahl-DAH-ray, pehr fah-VOH-ray |
| "A taste, please." | *"Un assaggio, per favore"* | oon ah-SAH-joh, pehr fah-VOH-ray |
| artichoke | *carciofo* | kar-CHOH-foh |
| asparagus | *asparagi* | ah-spah-RAH-jee |
| beans | *fagioli* | fah-JOH-lee |
| green beans | *fagiolini* | fah-joh-LEE-nee |
| broccoli | *broccoli* | BROK-oh-lee |
| canteloupe | *melone* | may-LOH-nay |
| carrots | *carote* | kah-ROT-ay |
| ham | *prosciutto* | proh-SHOO-toh |
| mushrooms | *funghi* | FOONG-ghee |
| potatoes | *patate* | pah-TAH-tay |
| rice | *riso* | REE-zoh |
| spinach | *spinaci* | speen-AH-chee |
| tomatoes | *pomodori* | poh-moh-DOH-ree |
| zucchini | *zucchine* | zoo-KEE-nay |
| breadsticks | *grissini* | gree-SEE-nee |

*Excerpted from *Rick Steves' Italian Phrase Book*

If you ask for "*un caffè*," you'll get espresso. Cappuccino is served to locals before noon and tourists any time of day. (To an Italian, cappuccino is a breakfast drink and a travesty after anything with tomatoes.) Italians like it only warm. To get it hot, request "*Molto caldo*" (very hot) or "*Più caldo, per favore*" (hotter, please; pron. pew KAHL-doh, pehr fah-VOH-ray).

Experiment with a few of the options...

- *caffè freddo*: sweet and iced espresso
- *cappuccino freddo*: iced cappuccino
- *caffè hag*: espresso decaf (decaf is easily available in Italian bars)
- *macchiato*: with only a little milk
- *caffè latte*: coffee with lots of hot milk, no foam
- *caffè Americano*: espresso diluted with water
- *caffè corretto*: espresso with a shot of liqueur

Beer on tap is "*alla spina*." Get it *piccola* (33 cl), *media* (50 cl), or *grande* (a liter). To order a glass (*bicchiere*; pron. bee-kee-AY-ree) of red (*rosso*) or white (*bianco*) wine say, "*Un bicchiere di vino rosso/bianco.*" House wine often comes in a quarter-liter carafe (*un quarto*).

All bars have a WC (*toilette, bagno*) in the back, and the public is entitled to use it.

**Prices:** You'll notice a two-tiered price system. Drinking a cup of coffee while standing at the bar is cheaper than drinking it at a table. If you're on a budget, don't sit without first checking out the financial consequences.

If the bar isn't busy, you'll often just order and pay when you leave. Otherwise: 1) decide what you want; 2) find out the price by checking the price list on the wall, the prices posted near the food, or by asking the barman; 3) pay the cashier; and 4) give the receipt to the barman (whose clean fingers handle no dirty lire) and tell him what you want.

## Picnics

In Italy picnicking saves lots of lire and is a great way to sample local specialties. In the process of assembling your meal you get to deal with the Italians in the market scene. On days you choose to picnic, gather supplies early. You'll probably visit several small stores or market stalls to put together a complete meal, and many close around noon. While it's fun to visit the small specialty shops, a local *alimentari* is your one-stop corner grocery store (most will slice and stuff your sandwich for you if you buy the ingredients there). A *supermercato* gives you more efficiency with less color for less cost.

Juice lovers can get a liter of O.J. for the price of a Coke or coffee. Look for "100% *succo*" (juice) on the label. Hang onto the half-liter mineral-water bottles (sold everywhere for about L1,000). Buy juice in cheap liter boxes, drink some and store the extra in your water bottle. (I drink tap water—*acqua del rubinetto.*)

Picnics can be an adventure in high cuisine. Be daring. Try the fresh mozzarella, *presto* pesto, shriveled olives, and any UFOs the locals are excited about. Shopkeepers are happy to sell small quantities of produce. But in a busy market, a merchant may not want to weigh and sell small, three-carrot-type quantities. In this case, estimate generously what you think it should cost, and hold out the lire in one hand and the produce in the other. Wear a smile that says, "If you take the money, I'll go." He'll grab the money. A typical picnic for two might be fresh rolls, 100 grams of cheese, 100 grams of meat (100 grams = about a quarter pound, called *un etto* in Italy), two tomatoes, three carrots, two apples, yogurt, and a liter box of juice. Total cost—about $10.

## Culture Shock—Accepting Italy as a Package Deal

We travel all the way to Italy to enjoy differences—to become temporary locals. You'll experience frustrations. Certain truths that we find "God-given" or "self-evident," like cold beer, ice in drinks, bottomless cups of coffee, hot showers, body odor smelling bad, and bigger being better, are suddenly not so true. One of the benefits of travel is the eye-opening realization that there are logical, civil, and even better alternatives. A willingness to go local ensures that you'll enjoy a full dose of Italian hospitality.

If there is a negative aspect to the image Italians have of Americans, it is that we are big, loud, aggressive, impolite, rich, and a bit naive. While Italians look bemusedly at some of our Yankee excesses—and worriedly at others—they nearly always afford us individual travelers all the warmth we deserve.

## Send Me a Postcard, Drop Me a Line

If you enjoy a successful trip with the help of this book and would like to share your discoveries, please fill out and send the survey at the end of this book to me at Europe Through the Back Door, Box 2009, Edmonds, WA 98020. I personally read and value all feedback. Thanks in advance—it helps a lot.

For our latest travel information on Italy, tap into our Web site at www.ricksteves.com. To check on any updates for this book, visit www.ricksteves.com/update. My e-mail address is rick@ricksteves.com. Anyone is welcome to a free issue of our 64-page *Back Door* quarterly newsletter.

Judging from all the positive feedback and happy postcards I receive from travelers who have used this book, it's safe to assume you'll enjoy a great, affordable vacation—with the finesse of an independent, experienced traveler. Thanks and *buon viaggio!*

# BACK DOOR TRAVEL PHILOSOPHY
## As Taught in *Rick Steves' Europe Through the Back Door*

*Travel is intensified living—maximum thrills per minute and one of the last great sources of legal adventure. Travel is freedom. It's recess, and we need it.*

*Experiencing the real Europe requires catching it by surprise, going casual...* "Through the Back Door."

*Affording travel is a matter of priorities. (Make do with the old car.) You can travel—simply, safely, and comfortably—anywhere in Europe for $70 a day plus transportation costs. In many ways, spending more money only builds a thicker wall between you and what you came to see. Europe is a cultural carnival, and, time after time, you'll find that its best acts are free and the best seats are the cheap ones.*

*A tight budget forces you to travel close to the ground, meeting and communicating with the people, not relying on service with a purchased smile. Never sacrifice sleep, nutrition, safety, or cleanliness in the name of budget. Simply enjoy the local-style alternatives to expensive hotels and restaurants.*

*Extroverts have more fun. If your trip is low on magic moments, kick yourself and make things happen. If you don't enjoy a place, maybe you don't know enough about it. Seek the truth. Recognize tourist traps. Give a culture the benefit of your open mind. See things as different but not better or worse. Any culture has much to share.*

*Of course, travel, like the world, is a series of hills and valleys. Be fanatically positive and militantly optimistic. If something's not to your liking, change your liking. Travel is addicting. It can make you a happier American as well as a citizen of the world. Our Earth is home to 6 billion equally important people. It's humbling to travel and find that people don't envy Americans. They like us, but, with all due respect, they wouldn't trade passports.*

*Globe-trotting destroys ethnocentricity. It helps you understand and appreciate different cultures. Travel changes people. It broadens perspectives and teaches new ways to measure quality of life. Many travelers toss aside their hometown blinders. Their prized souvenirs are the strands of different cultures they decide to knit into their own character. The world is a cultural yarn shop. And Back Door Travelers are weaving the ultimate tapestry. Come on, join in!*

# ITALY

- 120,000 square miles (a little larger than Arizona)
- 60 million people (500 people per square mile)
- 800 miles long, 100 miles wide
- 2,000 lire = about U.S. $1. And 1,000 lire = about 50 cents.

*Bella Italia!* It has Europe's richest, craziest culture. If you take it on its own terms, Italy is a cultural keelhauling that actually feels good.

Some people, often with considerable effort, manage to hate it. Italy bubbles with emotion, corruption, stray hairs, inflation, traffic jams, body odor, strikes, rallies, holidays, crowded squalor, and irate ranters shaking their fists at each other one minute and walking arm in arm the next. Have a talk with yourself before you cross the border. Promise yourself to relax and soak in it; it's a glorious mud puddle.

There are two Italies: The north is industrial, aggressive, and "time-is-money" in its outlook. The south is crowded, poor, relaxed, farm oriented, and traditional. Families here are very strong and usually live in the same house for many generations. Loyalties are to the family, city, region, soccer team, and country—in that order.

Economically, Italy has had its problems, but somehow things have always worked out. Today Italy is the Western world's seventh largest industrial power. Its people earn more per capita than the British. Italy is the world's leading wine producer. It is sixth in cheese and wool output. Tourism is big business. Cronyism, which complicates my work, is an integral part of the economy.

Italy, home of the Vatican, is Catholic, but the dominant religion is life—motor scooters, soccer, fashion, girl watching, boy watching, good coffee, good wine, and *la dolce far niente* ("the sweetness of doing nothing"). The Italian character shows itself on the streets in the skilled maniac drivers and the classy dressers who star in the ritual evening stroll, or *passeggiata*.

The language is fun. Be melodramatic and talk with your hands. Hear the melody; get into the flow. Italians are outgoing. They want to communicate, and they try harder than any other Europeans. Play with them.

Italy, a land of extremes, is also the most thief-ridden country you'll visit. Tourists suffer virtually no violent crime—but plenty of petty purse snatchings, pickpocketings, and shortchangings. Wear your money belt! The scruffy-looking women and children loitering around the major museums aren't there for the art.

Take advantage of the cheap, colorful, and dry-but-informative city guidebooks sold on the streets. Use the information telephones you'll find in most historic buildings. Just set the dial on English, pop in your coins, and listen. The narration is often accompanied by a brief slide show.

Some important Italian churches require modest dress: no shorts or bare shoulders on men, women, and sometimes even children. With a little imagination (except at the ultrastrict Vatican's St. Peter's), those caught by surprise can improvise something—a jacket for your knees and maps for your shoulders. I wear a superlightweight pair of long pants for my hot and muggy big-city Italian sightseeing.

While no longer a cheap country, Italy is still a hit with shoppers. Glassware (Venice), gold, silver, leather, prints (Florence), and high fashion (Rome and Milan) are good souvenirs, but do some price research at home so you'll recognize the good values.

Many tourists are mind-boggled by the huge prices: L30,000 for dinner! L120,000 for the room! L136,000 for the taxi ride! Since there are roughly L2,000 in a dollar, figure Italian prices by covering the last three zeros with your finger and cutting the remaining figure in half. That L30,000 dinner costs about $15 in U.S. money; the L120,000 room, about $60; and the taxi ride. . .uh-oh!

Don't sweat the small stuff—the coins. The biggest-value coin (the rarely-used L1,000) is worth only 50 cents. The rest of the coins can be baffling (the old and new versions of the same-value coin come in different sizes), but remember, they're all worth very little.

Beware of the "slow count." After a transaction, you may get your change back in batches of bills. The salesperson (or bank teller) hopes you're so confused by all the zeros that you'll gather up your money and say *"grazie"* before he or she finishes the count.

Never part with a 100,000 lire note (say "CHEN-toh MEE-lah"—one hundred thousand) without making clear you know it's not a 10,000. There are legitimate extras (café prices as much as double when you sit down instead of stand at the bar, taxis get L5,000 extra after 22:00, and so on) at which paranoid tourists wrongly take offense. But the waiter who charges you L70,000 for a pizza and beer assumes you're too polite to involve the police. If you have any problem with a restaurant, hotel, or taxi, get a cop to arbitrate.

*La dolce far niente* is a big part of Italy. Zero in on the fine points. Don't dwell on the problems. Accept Italy as Italy. Savor your cappuccino, dangle your feet over a canal (if it smells, breathe through your mouth), and imagine what it was like centuries ago. Ramble through the rabble and rubble of Rome and mentally resurrect those ancient stones. Look into the famous sculpted eyes of Michelangelo's *David* and understand Renaissance man's assertion of himself. Sit silently on a hilltop rooftop. Get chummy with the winds of the past. Write a poem over a glass of local wine in a sun-splashed, wave-dashed Riviera village. If you fall off your moral horse, call it a cultural experience. Italy is for romantics.

# ROME
# (ROMA)

Rome is magnificent and brutal at the same time. Your ears will ring, if you're careless you'll be run down or pickpocketed, you'll be frustrated by the kind of chaos that only an Italian can understand. You may even come to believe Mussolini was a necessary evil. But Rome is required, and in the wake of improvements made for Jubilee Year 2000, it's more exciting and easier than ever.

If your hotel provides a comfortable refuge, if you pace yourself and accept and even partake in the siesta plan, if you're well organized for sightseeing, and if you protect yourself and your valuables with extra caution and discretion, you'll do fine. You'll see the sights and leave satisfied.

Rome at its peak meant civilization itself. Everything was either civilized (part of the Roman Empire, Latin- or Greek-speaking) or barbarian. Today Rome is Italy's political capital, the capital of Catholicism, and a splendid ... "junk pile" is not quite the right term ... of Western civilization. As you peel through its fascinating and jumbled layers, you'll find its buildings, cats, laundry, traffic, and 2.6 million people endlessly entertaining. And then, of course, there are its magnificent sights.

Tour St. Peter's, the greatest church on earth, and scale Michelangelo's 100-meter-tall dome, the world's largest. Learn something about eternity by touring the huge Vatican Museum. You'll find the story of creation—bright as the day it was painted—in the newly restored Sistine Chapel. Do the "Caesar Shuffle" through ancient Rome's Forum and Colosseum. Savor Europe's most sumptuous building—the Borghese Gallery—and take an early evening "*Dolce Vita* Stroll" down the Via del Corso with Rome's beautiful people. Enjoy an after-dark walk from Trastevere to the Spanish Steps, lacing together Rome's Baroque and bubbly night spots.

## Rome Area

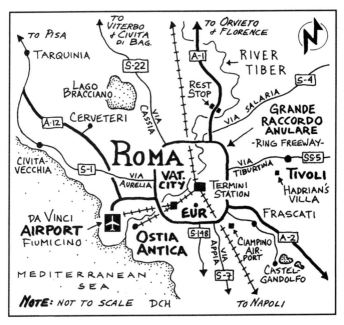

# Planning Your Time

For most travelers, Rome is best done quickly. It's a great city, but it's exhausting. Time is normally short, and Italy is more charming elsewhere. To "do" Rome in a day, consider it as a side trip from Orvieto or Florence and maybe before the night train to Venice. Crazy as that sounds, if all you have is a day, it's a great one.

**Rome in a day:** Vatican (2 hours in the museum and Sistine Chapel and 1 hour in St. Peter's), taxi over the river to the Pantheon (munch a bar-snack picnic on its steps), then hike over Capitol Hill, through the Forum, and to the Colosseum. Have dinner on Campo de' Fiori and dessert on Piazza Navona.

**Rome in two days:** Do the "Caesar Shuffle" from the Colosseum and Forum over Capitol Hill to the Pantheon. After a siesta, join the locals strolling from Piazza del Popolo to the Spanish Steps. Have dinner near your hotel. On the second day, see Vatican City (St. Peter's, climb the dome, tour the Vatican Museum). Spend the evening walking from Trastevere to Campo de' Fiori (atmospheric place for dinner) to the Trevi Fountain. With a third day, add the Borghese Gallery (reservations required) and the National Museum of Rome.

## Orientation

The modern sprawl of Rome is of no interest to us. Our Rome
actually feels small when you know it. It's the old core—within
the triangle formed by the train station, Colosseum, and Vatican.
Get a handle on Rome by considering it in these layers:

**The ancient city** had a million people. Tear it down to size
by walking through just the core. The best of the classical sights
stand in a line from the Colosseum to the Pantheon.

**Medieval Rome** was little more than a hobo camp of
50,000—thieves, mean dogs, and the pope, whose legitimacy
required a Roman address. The medieval city, a colorful tangle
of lanes, lies between the Pantheon and the river.

**Window-shoppers' Rome** twinkles with nightlife and ritzy
shopping near medieval Rome, on or near Rome's main drag—
Via del Corso—and around the ritzy Spanish Steps.

**Vatican City** is a compact world of its own with two great,
huge sights: St. Peter's Basilica and the Vatican Museum.

**Trastevere**, the seedy, colorful, wrong-side-of-the-river
neighborhood/village, is Rome at its crustiest—and perhaps
most "Roman."

**Baroque Rome** is an overleaf that embellishes great squares
throughout the town with fountains and church facades.

Since no one is allowed to build taller than St. Peter's dome,
the city has no modern skyline. And the Tiber River is ignored.
It's not navigable, and after the last floods (1870), the banks were
built up very high and Rome turned its back on its naughty river.

## Tourist Information

While Rome has three main tourist information offices (abbreviated in this book as TI), the dozen or so handy TI kiosks scattered
around the town at major tourist centers are handy and just as
helpful. If all you need is a map, forget the TI and pick one up
at your hotel.

You'll find TIs at the airport (daily 8:15–19:00, tel. 06-6595-
6074) and the train station (daily 8:00–21:00, off-season 9:00–
20:00, near track #3, accessible from platforms or lobby, marked
"Informazioni Turistiche/Tourist Info," crowded, combined with
travel agency, tel. 06-4890-6300).

The central TI office, near Piazza della Repubblica's huge
fountain, covers the city and the region. It's a five-minute walk
out the front of the train station (Mon–Fri 8:15–19:15, Sat 8:15–
13:30, next to Saab dealership, Via Parigi 5, tel. 06-4889-9253).
It's air-conditioned, less crowded, and more helpful than the
station TI, and it has a table to plan on—or sit under to overcome
your frustration.

At any TI, ask for a city map, a listing of sights and hours (in
the free *Tesori di Roma* booklet), and *L'Evento*, the free bimonthly

# Rome

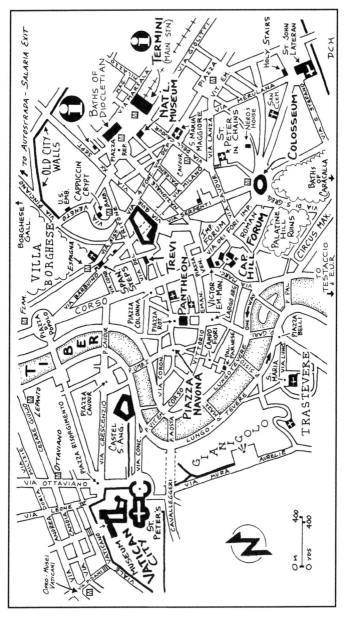

periodical entertainment guide for evening events and fun. All hotels list an inflated rate to cover the hefty commission any TI room-finding service charges. Save money by booking direct.

Smaller TIs (daily 9:00–18:00) include kiosks near the entrance to the Forum (on Piazza del Tempio della Pace), at Via del Corso (on Largo Goldoni), in Trastevere (on Piazza Sonnino), on Via Nazionale (at Palazzo delle Esposizioni), at Castel Sant' Angelo, and at San Giovanni in Laterano. For more information, call 06-3600-4399 (daily 9:00–19:00, www.comune.roma.it, www.informaroma.it).

*Roma c'è* is a cheap little weekly entertainment guide with a helpful English section (at the back) on musical events and the pope's schedule for the week (new edition every Thu, sold at newsstands for L2,000, www.romace.it, Web site in Italian). Fancy hotels carry a free English monthly, *Un Ospite a Roma* (A Guest in Rome).

## Arrival in Rome

**By Train:** Rome's main train station, Termini, is a minefield of tourist services: a TI (daily 8:00–21:00, off-season 9:00–20:00), train info office (daily 7:00–21:45), ATMs, late-hours banks, public showers (downstairs), luggage lockers (near track 24), 24-hour thievery, a pharmacy (daily 7:30–22:00, downstairs, at west end of station), the main city-bus hub (in front of train station), a subway stop, a grocery (oddly named "Drug Store," daily 7:00–24:00, downstairs), and the handy, cheery Chef Express Self-Service Ristorante (daily 11:00–22:30, easy WC at entrance, near east end of station; although there are several Chef Express bars scattered throughout station, the most comfortable is this sit-down Ristorante). The closest Internet point is downstairs near Dunkin Donuts (Thenetgate, daily 6:00–23:30, cheapest to buy a L10,000 60-minute card, can return or use at branches at Trevi Fountain or Vatican). The station has some sleazy sharks with official-looking cards. In general, avoid anybody selling anything at the station if you can.

Most of my hotel listings are easily accessible by foot (those near the train station) or by Metro (those in the Colosseum and Vatican neighborhoods). The train station has its own Metro stop (Termini).

**By Plane:** If you arrive at the airport, catch a train (hrly, 30 min, L16,000) to Rome's train station or take (or share) a taxi to your hotel. For details, see "Transportation Connections," below.

## Helpful Hints

**Plan Ahead:** The marvelous Borghese Gallery and Nero's Golden House both require reservations. For the Borghese Gallery, it's safest to make reservations well in advance before your trip. You can wait until you're in Rome to call for a reservation time at

Nero's Golden House, though it's wise to book farther ahead.
For specifics on these museums, look in "Sights," below.

**Museums:** Outdoor sights like the Colosseum, the Forum,
and Ostia Antica are open roughly 9:00 to 18:00. The Vatican
Museum is closed on Sunday (except for last Sun of month when
it's free and crowded), some sights close early on Sunday (such as
the Pantheon and E.U.R.'s Museum of Roman Civilization), and
some close all day Monday (National Museum of Rome, Borghese
Gallery, Capitol Hill Museum, Castel Sant' Angelo, Ostia Antica,
and more). Some museums stay open later in summer (usually on
Sat). The helpful TI booklet, *Tesori di Roma*, has a current listing
of museum hours, or check the last pages of the daily *Messaggero*
newspaper. On holidays, expect shorter hours or closures. Hours
listed anywhere can vary. Confirm sightseeing plans each morning
with a quick L200 telephone call asking, "Are you open today?"
("*Aperto oggi?*"; ah-PER-toh OH-jee) and "What time do you
close?" ("*A che ora chiuso?*"; ah kay OH-rah kee-OO-zoh). I've
included telephone numbers for this purpose.

A combo ticket—covering the National Museum of Rome,
Colosseum, Palatine Hill, and Baths of Caracalla—which was
offered in 2000 may be offered again in 2001 (around L30,000,
basically allows you to see 4 sights for price of 3, purchase at
participating sites, valid for 5 days).

**Churches:** Churches generally open early (around 7:00),
close for lunch (roughly 12:00–15:00), and close late (around
19:00). Kamikaze tourists maximize their sightseeing hours by
visiting churches before 9:00 and seeing the major sights that
stay open during the siesta (St. Peter's, Colosseum, Forum, Capitol Hill Museum, National Museum of Rome) while Romans
are taking it cool and easy. Many churches have "modest dress"
requirements, which means no bare shoulders, miniskirts, or
shorts—for men or women. This dress code is strictly enforced
at St. Peter's (elsewhere you'll see many tourists in shorts touring
many churches).

**Shops:** Shops are usually open 9:00 to 13:00 and 16:00
to 19:00. Grocery stores are often closed on Sunday. While
the summer break is not what it used to be, during the holiday
month of August many shops and restaurants still close up for
vacation, and "*Chiuso per ferie*" signs decorate locked doors all
over town.

**Travel Agencies:** Your hotel can direct you to the nearest
travel agency. Buy train tickets and get railpass-related reservations and supplements at travel agencies rather than dealing with
the congested train station. The cost is usually the same as at the
station (otherwise a minimal charge worth paying).

**Books:** The American Bookstore sells all the major guidebooks (Via Torino 136, Metro: Repubblica, tel. 06-474-6877).

## Dealing with (and Avoiding) Problems

**Theft Alert:** With sweet-talking con artists meeting you at the station, well-dressed pickpockets on buses, and thieving gangs of children at the ancient sites, Rome is a gauntlet of rip-offs. There's no great physical risk, but green tourists will be ripped off. Thieves strike when you're distracted. Don't trust kind strangers. Keep nothing important in your pockets. Assume you're being stalked. (Then relax and have fun.) Be most on guard while boarding and leaving buses and subways. Thieves crowd the door, then stop and turn while others crowd and push from behind. The sneakiest thieves are well-dressed business men (generally with something in their hands); lately many are posing as tourists with Tevas, fanny packs, and cameras. Scams abound: Don't give your wallet to self-proclaimed "police" who stop you on the street, warn you about counterfeit (or drug) money, and ask to see your wallet.

If you know what to look out for, the gangs of children picking the pockets and handbags of naive tourists are no threat but an interesting, albeit sad, spectacle. Gangs of city-stained children (sometimes as young as 8–10 years old), too young to prosecute but old enough to rip you off, troll through the tourist crowds around the Colosseum, Forum, Piazza Repubblica, and train and Metro stations. Watch them target tourists who are overloaded with bags or distracted with a video camera. The kids look like beggars and hold up newspapers or cardboard signs to confuse their victims. They scram like stray cats if you're onto them. A fast-fingered mother with a baby is often nearby. The terrace above the bus stop near the Colosseum Metro stop is a fine place to watch the action and maybe even pick up a few moves of your own.

**Reporting Losses:** To report lost or stolen passports and documents or to file an insurance claim, you must file a police report (with Polizia at track 1 or with Carabinieri at track 20, also at Piazza Venezia). To replace a passport, file the police report, then go to your embassy (see below). To report lost traveler's checks, call your bank (Visa tel. 800-874-155, Thomas Cook/Mastercard tel. 800-872-050, American Express tel. 800-872-000; these toll-free 800 numbers are Italian, not American), then file a police report. To report stolen or lost credit cards, call the company (Visa tel. 800-877-232, Mastercard tel. 800-870-866, American Express tel. 800-874-333), then file a police report.

**Embassies:** United States (Mon–Fri 8:30–13:00, 14:00–17:30, Via Veneto 119, tel. 06-46741) and Canada (Via Zara 30, tel. 06-445-981).

**Emergency Numbers:** Police tel. 113. Ambulance tel. 118.

**Hit and Run:** Walk with extreme caution. Scooters don't need to stop at red lights, and even cars exercise what drivers call the "logical option" of not stopping if they see no oncoming traffic. As Vespa scooters become electric, they'll get quieter (hooray) but more dangerous for pedestrians. Follow locals like a shadow when you cross a street (or spend a good part of your visit stranded on curbs).

**Staying/Getting Healthy:** The siesta is a key to survival in summertime Rome. Lie down and contemplate the extraordinary power of gravity in the eternal city. I drink lots of cold, refreshing water from Rome's many drinking fountains (the Forum has three). There's a pharmacy (marked by a green cross) in every neighborhood, including a handy one in the train station (daily 7:30–22:00, located downstairs, at west end). A 24-hour pharmacy is on Piazza dei Cinquecento 51 (next to train station on Via Cavour, tel. 06-488-0019). Embassies can recommend English-speaking doctors. Consider MEDline, a 24-hour home medical service (tel. 06-808-0995, doctors speak English). Anyone is entitled to free emergency treatment at public hospitals. The hospital closest to the train station is Policlinico Umberto 1 (entrance for emergency treatment on Via Lancisi, translators available, Metro: Policlinico).

## Getting around Rome

Sightsee on foot, by city bus, or by taxi. I've grouped your sightseeing into walkable neighborhoods.

Public transportation is efficient, cheap, and part of your Roman experience. It starts running around 5:30 and stops around 23:30, sometimes earlier. After midnight there are a few very crowded night buses, and taxis become more expensive and hard to get. Don't try to hail one—go to a taxi stand.

Buses and subways use the same ticket. You can buy tickets at newsstands, tobacco shops, or at major Metro stations or bus stops, but not on board (L1,500, good for 75 minutes—one Metro ride and unlimited buses); all-day bus/Metro passes cost L6,000 (for more info, visit www.atac.roma.it).

Buses (especially the touristic #64) and the subway are havens for thieves and pickpockets. Assume any commotion is a thief-created distraction.

**By Subway:** The Roman subway system (Metropolitana) is simple, with two clean, cheap, fast lines. While much of Rome is not served by its skimpy subway, these stops are helpful: Termini (train station, National Museum of Rome at Palazzo Massimo, recommended hotels), Repubblica (Baths of Diocletian/Octagonal Hall, main TI, recommended hotels), Barberini (Cappuccin Crypt, Trevi Fountain), Spagna (Spanish Steps, Villa Borghese, classy shopping area), Flaminio (Piazza del Popolo, start of recommended Via del Corso Dolce Vita stroll), Ottaviano (St. Peter's and Vatican City), Cipro-Musei Vaticani (Vatican Museum, recommended hotels), Colosseo (Colosseum, Roman Forum, recommended hotels), and E.U.R. (Mussolini's futuristic suburb).

## Metropolitana: Rome's Subway

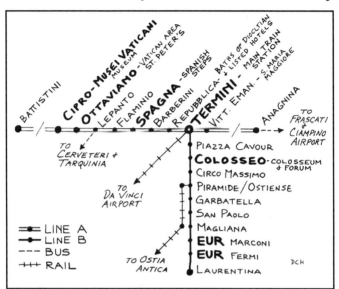

**By Bus:** Bus routes are clearly listed at the stops. Punch your ticket in the orange stamping machine as you board—or you are cheating. Riding without a stamped ticket on the bus, while relatively safe, is stressful. Inspectors fine even innocent-looking tourists L100,000. If you hop a bus without a ticket, locals who use tickets rather than a monthly pass can sell you a ticket from their wallet bundle. Ideally buy a bunch of tickets so you can hop a bus without first having to search for an open tobacco shop.

Learn which buses serve your neighborhood. Here are a few worth knowing about:

#64: Termini (train station), Piazza della Repubblica, Via Nazionale (recommended hotels), Piazza Venezia (near Forum), Largo Argentina (near Pantheon), St. Peter's Basilica. Ride it for a city overview and to watch pickpockets in action (can get horribly crowded).

#8: This tram connects Largo Argentina with Trastevere (get off at Piazza Mastai).

Electrico #116: Through the medieval core of Rome from Campo de' Fiori to Piazza Barberini via the Pantheon (runs daily except Sun).

**By Taxi:** Taxis start at about L5,000 (surcharges of L2,000 on Sun, L5,000 for night hours of 22:00–7:00, L2,000 surcharge for luggage, L14,000 extra for airport, tip about 10 percent by rounding up to the nearest thousand lire). Sample fares: Train station to Vatican-L16,000; train station to Colosseum-L10,000; Colosseum to Trastevere-L12,000. Three or four companions with more money than time should taxi almost everywhere. It's tough to wave down a taxi in Rome. Find the nearest taxi stand. (Ask a local or in a shop *"Dov'è* [DOH-vay] *una fermata dei tassi?"* Some are listed on my maps.) Unmarked, unmetered taxis at train stations and the airport are usually a rip-off. Taxis listing their telephone number on the door have fair meters—use them. To save time and energy, have your hotel call a taxi; the meter starts when the call is received. (Some Rome cab telephone numbers: 06-4994, 06-88177, and 06-3570.)

## Tours of Rome

**Scala Reale**—Tom Rankin (an American architect in love with Rome and his Roman wife) runs Scala Reale, a company committed to sorting out the rich layers of Rome for small groups with a longer-than-average attention span. Their excellent walking tours vary in length from two to four hours and start at L30,000 per person. Try to book in advance since their groups are limited to six and fill up fast. Their fascinating "Rome Orientation" walks lace together lesser-known sights from antiquity to the present, helping you get a sense of how Rome works (U.S. tel. 888/467-1986, Italy tel. 06-445-1477, www.scalareale.org, e-mail: info@scalareale.org.

**Through Eternity**—This company offers four tours, all led by native English speakers with relevant university degrees and an emphasis on storytelling: St. Peter's and Vatican Museum (L50,000, museum entry not included, 5.5 hrs, daily except Sun, meet at 10:00 at Piazza Pio XII); Colosseum and Roman Forum (L30,000, 2.5 hrs, starts daily at 13:00 at Arch of Constantine); Rome at Twilight (L30,000, starts nightly at 19:00 at fountain at base of Spanish Steps); and a Wine Sampling Tour (L30,000, nightly at 19:00 at central fountain in Piazza Navona). Confirm details and book in advance (max of 25 people, tel. 06-700-9336, cellular 0347-336-5298, private tours possible, www.througheternity.com).

**Walks of Rome**—Students working for "Walks of Rome" give free 45-minute tours of the Colosseum in order to promote their other guided walks. The tours bring the Colosseum to life and they hope you'll join—and pay for—their other walks: Ancient City (L30,000, 2 hrs), Vatican City (L50,000/full day of St. Peter's/Vatican Museum; L30,000 for just Vatican Museum Tour), Roman Sunset (L30,000, great Renaissance and Baroque squares, nightly at 19:00), and Catacombs (L50,000, 3 hrs, by bus with some of the city included). Admissions cost extra. Their pub crawl tours meet at 20:00 at the Spanish Steps (March–Sept) and at the Colosseum Metro stop (year-round) and finish at a disco six pubs later around midnight. I've never seen 50 young, drunk people having so much fun (tel. 06-484-853 or cellular 0347-795-5175, private tours possible, www.walksofeurope.com, e-mail: walkingtours@yahoo.com).

**Hop-on Hop-off Bus Tour**—The ATAC city bus tour offers your best budget orientation tour of Rome. In 1.75 hours you'll have 80 sights pointed out to you (by a live guide in English and maybe one other language) and have a chance to get out at nine different stops and catch a later bus. The stops are: Piazza Barberini, Via Veneto, Villa Borghese, Piazza Cavour, St. Peter's Square, Corso Vittorio Emanuele (for Piazza Navona), Piazza Venezia, Colosseum, and Via Nazionale (L15,000, bus #110 departs every 30 minutes—at top and bottom of hour, runs 9:00–20:00 March–Sept, 10:00–18:00 Oct–Feb, departs from front of station, near platform C, buy tickets at info kiosk there—marked "i metro," tel. 06-4695-2252). Avoid their unprofessional competitor, Stop 'n' Go, which runs only at whim.

## Sights—From the Colosseum Area to Capitol Hill

▲**St. Peter-in-Chains Church (San Pietro in Vincoli)**—Built in the fifth century to house the chains of St. Peter, this church is most famous for its Michelangelo statue. Check out the much-venerated chains under the high altar and then focus on *Moses* (free, but pop in L500 to light the statue, Mon–Sat 7:00–12:30, 15:30–19:00, Sun 7:30–12:30, a short 5- to 10-minute walk uphill from Colosseum; modest dress required).

Pope Julius II commissioned Michelangelo to build a massive tomb with 48 huge statues crowned by a grand statue of this ego-maniac pope. When Julius died, the work had barely started, and no one had the money or concern for Julius to finish the project. Michelangelo finished one statue, *Moses*, and left a few unfinished statues: *Leah* and *Rachel* flanking *Moses* in this church, the *Prisoners* now in Florence's Accademia, and the *Slaves* now in Paris' Louvre. Study the powerful statue; it's mature Michelangelo. He worked on it in fits and starts for thirty years. Moses has received the Ten Commandments. As he holds the stone tablets, his eyes show a man determined to stop his tribe from worshiping the golden calf and idols...determined to win salvation for the people of Israel. Why the horns? Centuries ago, the Hebrew word for "rays" was mistranslated as "horns."

▲▲**Nero's Golden House (Domus Aurea)**—The remains of Emperor Nero's "Golden House" were recently opened to the public. Nero's huge house used to sprawl across the valley where the Colosseum now stands. Nero was your quintessential bad emperor: killed his mother and crucified St. Peter. The story goes that he fiddled while Rome burned in A.D. 64; Romans suspected he started the fires to clear land for an even bigger house. While only hints of the splendid colored frescoes survive, the towering vaults and basic immensity of the place is impressive. As you wander, look up at the holes in the ceiling and imagine how much of Rome hides underground...and why the subway is limited to two lines.

Visits are allowed only with an escort (25 people every 15 minutes) and a reservation (L12,000, Wed–Mon 9:00–19:45, last entry at 18:45, closed Tue, tour lasts 45 min, escort speaks Italian, audioguides-L3,000, 200 meters northeast of Colosseum, through a park gate, up a hill and on the left). To reserve a place, call 06-3996-7700. If you just show up (particularly on a late afternoon on a weekday), you could luck out and get on a tour; if tours aren't booked up, the remaining seats are sold to drop-ins.

▲▲**Colosseum**—This 2,000-year-old building is the great example of Roman engineering. Using concrete, brick, and their trademark round arches, Romans constructed much larger buildings than the Greeks. But in deference to the higher Greek culture, notice how they finished their no-nonsense megastructure by pasting all three orders of Greek columns (Doric, Ionic, and Corinthian) as exterior decorations. The Flavian Amphitheater's popular name, "Colosseum," comes from the colossal statue of Nero that once stood in front of it.

Romans were into "big." By putting two theaters together, they created a circular amphitheater. They could fill and empty its 50,000 numbered seats as quickly and efficiently as we do our superstadiums. Teams of sailors hoisted canvas awnings over the stadium to give fans shade. This was where ancient Romans, whose taste for violence was the equal of modern America's, enjoyed their Dirty Harry and *Terminator*. Gladiators, criminals, and wild animals fought to the death in every conceivable scenario. The floor of the Colosseum is missing, exposing underground passages. Animals in cages were kept here and then lifted up in elevators; they'd pop out from behind blinds into the arena. The gladiator didn't know where, when, or by what he'd be attacked.

**Cost, Hours, Tours**: L10,000, daily 9:00–19:00, off-season 9:00–15:00 (public WC is behind Colosseum, face ticket entrance and go right—WC under stairway; Metro: Colosseo, tel. 06-3974-9907). As you stand in the ticket line, students may offer you a free tour. The tours are good (and free because they'll try to get you to pay for their other tours—see "Tours of Rome," above). The stairs to the upper level are near the exit (west end). Beware of young pickpockets—ragged children carrying cardboard or newspapers—between the Colosseum and its Metro stop (see "Theft Alert," above).

▲**Arch of Constantine**—The well-preserved arch that stands between the Colosseum and the Forum commemorates a military coup and, more important, the acceptance of Christianity in the

## The Forum Area

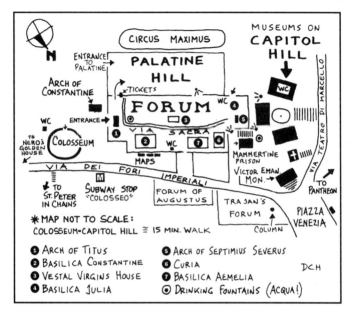

❶ Arch of Titus
❷ Basilica Constantine
❸ Vestal Virgins House
❹ Basilica Julia

❺ Arch of Septimius Severus
❻ Curia
❼ Basilica Aemelia
⊙ Drinking Fountains (Acqua!)

DCH

Roman Empire. In A.D. 312, Emperor Constantine (who had a vision he could win under the sign of the cross) defeated his rival Maxentius. Constantine promptly legalized Christianity.

▲▲▲**Roman Forum (Foro Romano)**—Ancient Rome's birthplace and civic center, the Forum was the common ground between Rome's famous seven hills (free admission to Forum, L12,000 for Palatine Hill, both keep the same hours: daily 9:00–19:30 or an hour before dark, off-season 9:00–15:00, Metro: Colosseo, tel. 06-3974-9907).

To help resurrect this confusing pile of rubble, study the before-and-after pictures in the cheap city guidebooks sold on the streets. (Check out the small red *Rome, Past and Present* books with plastic overlays to un-ruin the ruins. They're priced at L20,000—pay no more than L15,000.) With the help of the map in this section, follow this basic walk (assuming you enter from the Colosseum side near the Arch of Constantine):

**1.** Start by the small **Arch of Titus** (drinking fountain opposite) overlooking the remains of what was the political, social, and commercial center of the Roman Empire. The Via Sacra—the main street of ancient Rome—cuts through the Forum from here to Capitol Hill and the Arch of Septimius Severus on the opposite side. On the left a ticket booth welcomes you to the Palatine Hill (described below)—once filled with the palaces of Roman emperors. Study the Arch of Titus—carved with propaganda celebrating the A.D. 70 defeat of the Jews, which began the Diaspora that ended with the creation of Israel in 1947. Notice the gaggle of soldiers carrying the menorah.

**2.** Ahead of you on the right are the massive ruins of the **Basilica of Constantine.** Follow the path leading there from the Via Sacra. Only the giant barrel vaults remain, looming crumbly and weed eaten. As you stand in the shadow of the Basilica of Constantine, reconstruct it in your mind. The huge barrel vaults were just side niches. Extend the broken nub of an arch out over the vacant lot and finish your imaginary Roman basilica with rich marble and fountains. People it with plenty of toga-clad Romans. Yeow.

**3.** Next hike past the semicircular Temple of Vesta to the **House of the Vestal Virgins.** Here, the VVs kept the eternal flame lit. A set of ponds and a marble chorus line of Vestal Virgins mark the courtyard of the house.

**4.** The grand **Basilica Julia,** a first-century law court, fills the corner opposite the Curia. Notice how the Romans passed their time; ancient backgammon-type game boards are cut into the pavement.

**5.** The **Arch of Septimius Severus,** from about A.D. 200, celebrates that emperor's military victories. In front of it a stone called Lapis Niger covers the legendary tomb of Romulus. To the left of the arch, the stone bulkhead is the Rostra, or speaker's platform. It's named for the ship's prows that used to decorate it as big shots hollered, "Friends, Romans, countrymen...."

**6.** The plain, intact brick building near the Arch of Septimius Severus was the **Curia,** where the Roman senate sat. (Peek inside.) Roman buildings were basically brick and concrete, usually with a marble veneer, which in this case is long lost.

**7.** The **Basilica Aemilia** (second century B.C.) shows the floor plan of an ancient palace. This pre-Christian "basilica" design was later adopted by medieval churches. From here a ramp leads up and out (past a WC and a fun headless statue to pose with). The entire area between here and Trajan's Column may eventually become an archeological park.

**Palatine Hill**—The hill above the Forum contains scanty remains of the Imperial palaces and the Roman Quadrata (Iron Age huts and the legendary house of Romulus—under corrugated tin roof in far corner). We get our word *palace* from this hill, where the emperors chose to live. The Palatine was once so filled with palaces that later emperors had to build out. (Looking up at it from the Forum you see the substructure that supported these long-gone palaces.)

The newly opened Palatine museum has sculptures and fresco fragments but is nothing special. From the pleasant garden, you'll get an overview of the Forum. On the far side, look down into an emperor's private stadium and then beyond at the dusty Circus Maximus, once a chariot course. Imagine the cheers, jeers, and furious betting. But considering how ruined the ruins are, the heat, the hill to climb, the L12,000 entry fee, and the relative difficulty in understanding what you're looking at, the Palatine Hill is a disappointment (same hours as Forum, above).

▲**Mammertine Prison**—The 2,500-year-old cisternlike prison that once imprisoned saints Peter and Paul is worth a look. Stepping into the room you hit a modern floor. Erase that in your mind and look up at the hole in the ceiling through which prisoners were lowered. Then take the stairs down to the actual prison floor level. Imagine humans, amid rotting corpses, awaiting slow deaths. Then consider the legend of the saints baptizing the prisoners from a miraculous spring. On the walls near the entry are lists of notable prisoners (Christian and non-Christian) and how they were executed: *strangolati, decapitato, morto di fame* . . . (donation requested, daily 9:00–12:00, 14:30–18:00).

Leaving the prison, turn right and climb the stairs leading to Capitol Hill. Halfway up, you'll find a refreshing water fountain. Block the spout with your fingers; it spurts up for drinking. Romans, who call this *il nasone* (the nose), joke that cheap Roman boys take their dates out for a drink at *il nasone*.

▲▲**Capitol Hill (Campidoglio)**—This hill was the religious and political center of ancient Rome. It's still the home of the city's government. Michelangelo's Renaissance square is bounded by two buildings of the Capitol Hill Museum and the mayoral palace. Its centerpiece is a copy of the famous equestrian statue of Marcus Aurelius (the original is behind glass in the adjacent museum). To approach the great square the way Michelangelo wanted you to, walk halfway down the grand stairway toward Piazza Venezia, spin around, and walk back up. This was the new Renaissance face of Rome, with its back to the Forum and facing the new city. Notice how Michelangelo gave the buildings the "giant order," with huge pilasters making the existing two-story buildings feel one story and a more harmonious part of the new square. Notice also how the statues atop these buildings first welcome you and then draw you in. There's a fine view of the Forum from the terrace just past the mayor's palace (downhill on the right).

▲▲**Capitol Hill Museum**—This museum encompasses two buildings (Palazzo dei Conservatori and Palazzo Nuovo), connected by an underground passage that leads to the Tabularium and a panoramic overlook of the Forum (L12,000, free on last Sun of month, Tue–Sun 9:00–21:00, shorter hours off-season, last entry 60 min before closing, closed Mon, tel. 06-3996-7800 or 06-6710-2071). For an orientation to the museum's two buildings, face the equestrian statue on Capitol Hill Square (with your back to the grand stairway). The Palazzo Nuovo is on your left and the

Palazzo dei Conservatori is on your right (closer to the river). Ahead is the mayor's palace (Palazzo Senatorio); below it and out of sight is the Tabularium and underground passage.

You can buy your ticket at either building (but if you want to rent an L7,000 audioguide, go to Palazzo dei Conservatori).

The **Palazzo dei Conservatori** is one of the world's oldest museums, at 500 years old. Outside the entrance, notice the marriage announcements and, very likely, wedding-party photo ops. Inside the courtyard, have a look at giant chunks of a statue of Emperor Constantine; when intact, this imposing statue held court in the Basilica of Constantine in the Forum. The museum is worthwhile, with lavish rooms and several great statues. Tops is the original (500 B.C.) Etruscan *Capitoline Wolf* (the little statues of Romulus and Remus were added in the Renaissance). Don't miss the *Boy Extracting a Thorn* or the enchanting *Commodus as Hercules*. The second-floor painting gallery—except for two Caravaggios—is forgettable. The café upstairs has a splendid patio with city views (lovely at sunset).

Connect the two museums with the underground passage that leads to the **Tabularium**. Built in the first century A.D., this once held the archives of ancient Rome. The word *Tabularium* comes from tablet, on which the Romans wrote their laws. You won't see any tablets, but you will see a superb head-on view of the Forum from the windows.

The **Palazzo Nuovo** houses mostly portrait busts of forgotten emperors. But it has three must-see statues: the *Dying Gaul*, the *Capitoline Venus* (both on the first floor up), and the original gilded bronze equestrian statue of Marcus Aurelius (behind glass in museum courtyard). This greatest surviving equestrian statue of antiquity was the original centerpiece of the square. While most such pagan statues were destroyed by Dark Age Christians, Marcus was mistaken as Constantine (the first Christian emperor) and therefore spared.

**From Capitol Hill to Piazza Venezia**—Leaving Capitol Hill, descend the stairs leading to Piazza Venezia. At the bottom of the stairs, look left several blocks down the street to see a condominium actually built around surviving ancient pillars and arches of Teatro Marcello—perhaps the oldest inhabited building in Europe.

Still at the bottom of the stairs, look up the long stairway to your right (which pilgrims climb on their knees) for a good example of the earliest style of Christian church. While pilgrims find it worth the climb, sightseers can skip it. As you walk toward Piazza Venezia, look down into the ditch on your right and see how everywhere modern Rome is built on the forgotten frescoes and mangled mosaics of ancient Rome.

**Piazza Venezia**—This vast square is the focal point of modern Rome. The Via del Corso, starting here, is the city's axis, surrounded by Rome's classiest shopping district. From the Palazzo Venezia's balcony above the square (to your left with back to Victor Emmanuel Monument), Mussolini whipped up the nationalistic fervor of Italy. Fascist masses filled the square screaming, "Four more years!" or something like that. (Fifteen years later, they hung him from a meat hook in Milan.)

**Victor Emmanuel Monument**—This oversized monument to an Italian king was part of Italy's rush to overcome the new country's strong regionalism and to create a national identity after unification in 1870. Romans think of it not as an altar of the fatherland but as "the wedding cake," "the typewriter," or "the dentures." It wouldn't be so bad if it weren't sitting on a priceless acre of ancient Rome and if they chose better marble (this is too in-your-face white and picks up the pollution horribly). Soldiers guard Italy's Tomb of the Unknown Soldier as the eternal flame flickers. Stand directly in front of it and see how Via del Corso bisects Rome.

▲**Trajan's Column, Market, and Forum**—This offers the grandest column and best example of "continuous narration" from antiquity. Over 2,500 figures scroll around the 40-meter-high column telling of Trajan's victorious Dacian campaign (circa A.D. 103, in present-day Romania), from the assembling of the army at the bottom to the victory sacrifice at the top. The ashes of Trajan and his wife were held in the mausoleum at the base while the sun once glinted off a polished bronze statue of Trajan at the top. Today St. Peter is on top. Study the propaganda that winds up the column like a scroll, trumpeting Trajan's wonderful military exploits. You can view this close-up for free (it's just off Piazza Venezia, across the street from the Victor Emmanuel Monument). Viewing balconies once stood on either side, but it seems likely Trajan fans only came away with a feeling that the greatness of their emperor and empire was beyond comprehension (for a rolled-out version of the Column's story, visit the Museum of Roman Civilization at E.U.R., below). This column marked **Trajan's Forum**, built to handle the shopping needs of a wealthy city of over a million. Commercial, political, religious, and social activities all mixed in the Forum.

For a fee, you can go inside **Trajan's Market** and part of Trajan's Forum; the entrance is uphill from the column on Via IV Novembre. The market was once filled with shops selling goods from all over the Roman Empire (L12,000, summer Tue–Sat 9:00–18:30, winter 9:00–16:30, closed Mon).

Rome is in the slow process of excavating Trajan's Forum, closing down the busy street Via dei Fori Imperiali (controversial for the traffic problems this would create), and turning the entire area into a vast archaeological park.

## Sights—Heart of Rome

▲▲▲**Pantheon**—For the greatest look at the splendor of Rome,
antiquity's best-preserved interior is a must (free, Mon–Sat 9:00–
18:30, Sun and holidays 9:00–13:00, tel. 06-6830-0230). Because
it became a church dedicated to the martyrs just after the fall of
Rome, the barbarians left it alone, and the locals didn't use it as
a quarry. The portico is called Rome's umbrella—a fun local
gathering in a rainstorm. Walk past its one-piece granite columns
(biggest in Italy, shipped from Egypt) and through the original
bronze doors. Sit inside under the glorious skylight and enjoy
classical architecture at its best.

The dome, 47 meters (142 feet) high and wide, was
Europe's biggest until the Renaissance. Michelangelo's dome
at St. Peter's, while much higher, is one meter smaller. The
brilliance of its construction astounded architects through the
ages. During the Renaissance, Brunelleschi was given permission
to cut into the dome (see the little square hole above and to
the right of the entrance) to analyze the material. The concrete
dome gets thinner and lighter with height—the highest part
is volcanic pumice.

This wonderfully harmonious architecture greatly inspired
Raphael and other artists of the Renaissance. Raphael, along with
Italy's first two kings, chose to be buried here.

As you walk around the outside of the Pantheon, notice the
"rise of Rome"—about 5 meters (15 feet) since it was built.

▲▲**Curiosities near the Pantheon**—The only Gothic church
you'll see in Rome is **Santa Maria sopra Minerva**. On a little
square behind the Pantheon to the east, past the Bernini statue of
an elephant carrying an Egyptian obelisk, this Dominican church
was built *sopra* (over) a pre-Christian temple of Minerva. Before
stepping in, notice the high-water marks on the wall (right of door).
Inside you'll see that the lower parts of the frescoes were lost to
floods. (After the last great flood, in 1870, Rome built the present
embankments, finally breaking the spirit of the Tiber River.)

Rome was at its low ebb, almost a ghost town, through
much of the Gothic period. Little was built during this time (and
much of what was built was redone Baroque). This church is a
refreshing exception.

St. Catherine's body lies under the altar (her head is in
Siena). In the 1300s, she convinced the pope to return from
France to Rome, thus saving Italy from untold chaos.

Left of the altar stands a little-known Michelangelo statue,
*Christ Bearing the Cross*. Michelangelo gave Jesus an athlete's or
warrior's body (a striking contrast to the more docile Christ of
medieval art) but left the face to one of his pupils. Fra Angelico's
simple tomb is farther to the left, on the way to the back door.
Before leaving, head over to the right (south transept), pop in a

# Heart of Rome

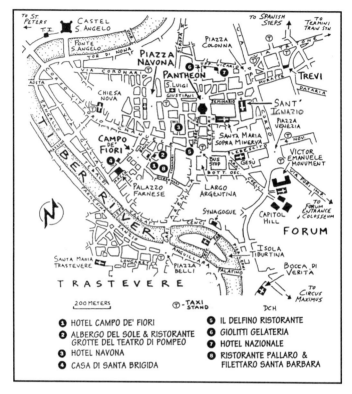

**① HOTEL CAMPO DE' FIORI**

**② ALBERGO DEL SOLE & RISTORANTE GROTTE DEL TEATRO DI POMPEO**

**③ HOTEL NAVONA**

**④ CASA DI SANTA BRIGIDA**

**⑤ IL DELFINO RISTORANTE**

**⑥ GIOLITTI GELATERIA**

**⑦ HOTEL NAZIONALE**

**⑧ RISTORANTE PALLARO & FILETTARO SANTA BARBARA**

L500 coin for light, and enjoy a fine Filippo Lippi fresco showing scenes from the life of St. Thomas Aquinas.

Exit the church via its rear door (behind the Michelangelo statue), walk down Fra Angelico lane (spy any artisans at work), turn left, and walk to the next square. On your right you'll find the **Chiesa di St. Ignazio** church, a riot of Baroque illusions. Study the fresco over the door and the ceiling in the back of the nave. Then stand on the yellow disk on the floor between the two stars. Look at the central (black) dome. Keeping your eyes on the dome, walk under and past it. Church building project runs out of money? Hire a painter to paint a fake, flat dome. (Both churches open early, take a siesta—Santa Maria sopra Minerva closes at 12:00, St. Ignazio at 12:30—reopen around 15:30, and close at 19:00. Modest dress is recommended.)

A few blocks away, back across Corso Vittorio Emanuele, is the rich and Baroque **Gesu Church**, headquarters of the

Jesuits in Rome. The Jesuits powered the Church's Counter-Reformation. While Protestants were teaching that all roads to heaven didn't pass through Rome, the Baroque churches of the late 1500s were painted with spiritual road maps that said they did.

Walk out the Gesu Church and two blocks down Corso V. Emanuele to the **Sacred Area** (Largo Argentina), an excavated square facing the boulevard, about four blocks south of the Pantheon. Walk around this square looking into the excavated pit at some of the oldest ruins in Rome. It was here that Caesar was assassinated. Today this is a refuge for cats. Some 250 cats are cared for by volunteers. You'll see them—and their refuge—at the far (west) side of the square.

## Sights—Near the Train Station

These sights are within a three- to 10-minute walk northwest of the train station. By Metro, use the Piazza Repubblica stop for all of these sights except the National Museum of Rome and the Museum of the Bath (Metro: Termini).

▲▲▲**National Museum of Rome in Palazzo Massimo**—Rome's National Museum houses the greatest collection of ancient Roman art I've seen anywhere. The ground floor is a historic yearbook of marble statues from the second century B.C. to the second century A.D., with rare Greek originals.

The first floor is peopled by statues from the first through fourth centuries A.D. The second floor (which requires an appointment) contains frescoes and mosaics that once decorated the walls and floors of Roman villas. Finally, descend into the basement to see the mummified eight-year-old girl, fine gold jewelry, dice, an abacus, and vault doors leading into the best coin collection in Europe, with fancy magnifying glasses maneuvering you through cases of coins from ancient Rome to modern times.

**Cost and Hours**: L12,000, Tue–Sun 9:00–18:45, closed Mon, last entry 60 min before closing (L7,000 audioguide available at bookshop after you buy ticket). The second floor can be visited only with a guide (get time for 45-minute tour—in Italian—upon arrival, not possible to reserve in advance). The museum is about 100 meters from the Termini train station. As you leave the station, it's the sandstone-brick building on your left. Enter at the far end, at Largo di Villa Peretti (Metro: Termini, tel. 06-481-5576).

**Baths of Diocletian**—Around A.D. 300, Emperor Diocletian built the largest baths in Rome. This sprawling meeting place, with baths and schmoozing spaces to accommodate 3,000 bathers at a time, was a big deal in ancient Rome. While much of it is still closed, three sections are open: the Octagonal Hall, the Church of St. Mary of the Angels and Martyrs (both face Piazza della Repubblica), and the Museum of the Bath (across from the train station).

▲▲**Octagonal Hall**—The Aula Ottagona or Rotunda of Diocletian was a private gymnasium in the Baths of Diocletian. Built
around A.D. 300, these functioned until 537, when the barbarians
cut Rome's aqueducts. The floor would have been seven meters
lower (look down the window in the center of the room). The
graceful iron grid supported the canopy of a 1928 planetarium.
Today, the hall's a gallery, showing off fine bronze and marble
statues—the kind that would have decorated the baths of imperial
Rome. Most are Roman copies of Greek originals...gods,
athletes, portrait busts. Two merit a close look: the *Defeated
Boxer* (first century B.C., Greek and textbook Hellenistic) and
the *Roman Aristocrat*. The aristocrat's face is older than the body.
This cat-bronze statue is typical of the day: take a body modeled
on Alexander the Great and pop on a portrait bust. (Free, Tue–
Sat 9:00–14:00, Sun 9:00–13:00, closed Mon.)

▲**Church of St. Mary of the Angels and Martyrs (Santa Maria
degli Angeli e dei Martiri)**—From Piazza della Repubblica, step
through the Roman wall into what was the great central hall of the
baths and is now a church (since the 16th century) designed by
Michelangelo. When the church entrance was moved to Piazza
Repubblica, the church was reoriented 90 degrees, turning the
nave into long transepts and the transepts into a short nave.
The 12 red granite columns still stand in their ancient positions.
The classical floor was 15 feet lower. Project the walls down and
imagine the soaring shape of the Roman vaults.

**Museum of the Bath (Museo Nazionale Romano—Terme di
Diocleziano)**—This newly opened museum, located on the grounds
of the ancient Baths of Diocletian, has a misleading name. Rather
than featuring the Baths, it displays ancient Roman inscriptions on
tons of tombs, steles, and tablets. Although well displayed and
described in English, the museum is difficult to appreciate quickly,
and most travelers will find more history presented on a grander
scale in the National Museum of Rome a block away (L8,000,
Tue–Sun 9:00–19:45, closed Mon, audioguide-L7,000—confirm it's
in English, Viale E. De Nicola 79, entrance faces Termini station,
tel. 06-488-0530).

▲**Santa Maria Della Vittoria**—This church houses Bernini's
statue of a swooning *St. Theresa in Ecstasy* (free, daily 6:30–11:30,
16:30–19:00, Largo Susanna, about 5 blocks northwest of the
train station, Metro: Repubblica).

## Sights—North Rome

▲**Villa Borghese**—Rome's unkempt "Central Park" is great
for people watching (plenty of modern-day Romeos and Juliets).
Take a row on the lake or visit its fine museums.

▲▲▲**Borghese Gallery** (Galleria Borghese)—This private
museum, filling a cardinal's mansion in the park, offers one of

Europe's most sumptuous art experiences. Because of the gallery's slick mandatory reservation system, you'll enjoy its collection of world-class Baroque sculpture, including Bernini's *David* and his exciting statue of Apollo chasing Daphne, as well as paintings by Caravaggio, Raphael, Titian, and Rubens, with manageable crowds.

The essence of the collection is the connection of the Renaissance with the classical world. Notice the second-century Roman reliefs with Michelangelo-designed panels above either end of the portico as you enter. The villa was built in the early 17th century by the great art collector Cardinal Borghese, who wanted to prove that the glories of ancient Rome were matched by the Renaissance.

In the main entry hall, opposite the door, notice the thrilling relief of the horse falling (first century A.D., Greek). Pietro Bernini, father of the famous Bernini, completed the scene by adding the rider.

Each room seems to feature a Baroque masterpiece. The best of all is in Room 3: Bernini's Apollo chasing Daphne. It's the perfect Baroque subject—capturing a thrilling, action-filled moment. In the mythological story, Apollo races after Daphne. Just as he's about to reach her, she turns into a tree. As her toes turn to roots and branches spring from her fingers, Apollo is in for one rude surprise. Walk slowly around. It's more air than stone.

**Cost, Hours, Reservations:** L14,000, Tue–Sun 9:00–21:00, maybe until 23:00 on Sat June–Sept, closed Mon. No photos are allowed.

Reservations are mandatory and easy to get in English over the Internet (www.ticketeria.it) or by phone: call 06-32810 (if you get an Italian recording, press 2 for English; office hours: Mon–Fri 9:00–19:00, Sat 9:00–13:00, office closed Sat in Aug). Every two hours, 360 people are allowed to enter the museum. Entry times are 9:00, 11:00, 13:00, 15:00, 17:00, and 19:00 (plus 21:00 on Sat). Reserve a minimum of several days in advance for a weekday visit, at least a week ahead for weekends. When you reserve, request a day and time (which you'll be given if available), and you'll get a claim number. While you'll be advised to come 30 minutes before your appointed time, you can arrive a few minutes beforehand, but don't be late as no-show tickets are given to standbys.

Visits are strictly limited to two hours. Concentrate on the first floor but leave yourself 30 minutes for the paintings of the Pinacoteca upstairs; highlights are marked by the audioguide icons. The fine bookshop and cafeteria are best visited outside your two-hour entry window.

If you don't have a reservation, just show up (or call first and ask if there are openings; a late afternoon on a weekday is usually your best bet). Reservations are tightest at 11:00 and on weekends. No-shows are released a few minutes after the top of the hour.

Generally out of 360 reservations a few will fail to show (but more than a few may be waiting to grab those spots).

**Tours:** Guided English tours are offered at 9:10 and 11:10 for L8,000; reserve with entry reservation (or consider the excellent audioguide tour-L8,000).

**Location**: The museum is in the Villa Borghese park. A taxi (tell the cabbie your destination: gah-leh-REE-ah bor-GAY-zay) can get you within 100 meters of the museum. Otherwise, Metro to Spagna and take a 15-minute walk through the park.

▲**Cappuccin Crypt**—If you want bones, this is it. It's below the church Santa Maria della Immaculata Concezione on Via Veneto, just off Piazza Barberini. The bones of over 4,000 monks who died between 1528 and 1870 are in the basement, all artistically arranged for the delight—or disgust—of the always-wide-eyed visitor. The soil in the crypt was brought from Jerusalem 400 years ago, and the monastic message on the wall explains that this is more than just a macabre exercise. Pick up a few of Rome's most interesting postcards (donation, Fri–Wed 9:00–12:00, 15:00–18:00, closed Thu, Metro: Barberini). A painting of St. Francis by Caravaggio is upstairs. Just up the street you'll find the American embassy, Federal Express, and fancy Via Veneto cafés filled with the poor and envious looking for the rich and famous.

**Castel Sant' Angelo**—Built as a tomb for Emperor Hadrian; used through the Middle Ages as a castle, prison, and place of last refuge for popes under attack; and hosting a museum today, this giant pile of ancient bricks is packed with history (L10,000, Tue–Sun 9:00–20:00, closed Mon, Metro: Lepanto or bus #64, near Vatican City, tel. 06-681-9111).

## Sights—Vatican City

This tiny independent country of just over 100 acres, contained entirely within Rome, has its own postal system, armed guards, helipad, mini–train station, and radio station (KPOP). Politically powerful, the Vatican is the religious capital of 800 million Roman Catholics. If you're not one, become a Catholic for your visit.

Small as it is, Vatican City has two huge sights: St. Peter's Basilica and the Vatican Museum (with the Sistine Chapel). A helpful TI is just to the left of St. Peter's Basilica (Mon–Sat 8:30–18:30, closed Sun, tel. 06-6988-1662, Vatican switchboard tel. 06-6982, www.vatican.va; facing the church, WCs are to the right and left—near TI, and also on roof). Nearest Metro stops are still a 10-minute walk away from either sight: for St. Peter's, the closest stop is Ottaviano; for the Vatican Museum, it's Cipro-Musei Vaticani.

**Post Office**: The Vatican post, with an office in the Vatican Museum and one on St. Peter's Square, is more reliable than the Italian mail service (comfortable writing rooms,

## Vatican City Overview

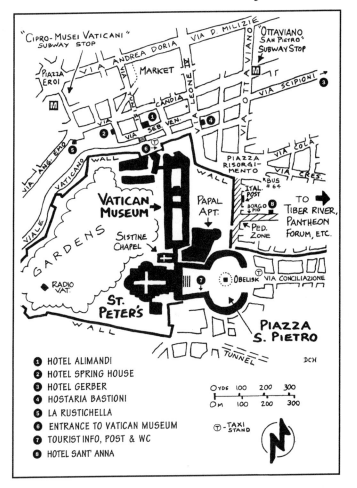

1. HOTEL ALIMANDI
2. HOTEL SPRING HOUSE
3. HOTEL GERBER
4. HOSTARIA BASTIONI
5. LA RUSTICHELLA
6. ENTRANCE TO VATICAN MUSEUM
7. TOURIST INFO, POST & WC
8. HOTEL SANT' ANNA

Mon–Fri 8:30–19:00, Sat 8:30–18:00). The stamps are a collectible bonus (Vatican stamps are good throughout Rome; Italian stamps are not good at the Vatican).

**Tours**: The Vatican TI conducts free 90-minute tours of St. Peter's (depart from TI at 15:00 on Mon, Wed, and Fri, no need to book ahead but do confirm schedule with TI, tel. 06-6988-1662). Tours of the Vatican Gardens offer the only way to see the gardens; book tours at least one day in advance by calling 06-6988-4466 (L17,000, Mon–Sat 10:00–12:00). For a tour of the necropolis of St. Peter's and the saint's tomb, fax the Excavations Office at 06-6988-5518 (L15,000, 2 hrs, office open Mon–Fri 9:00–17:00, tel. 06-6988-5318).

**Seeing the Pope:** Your best chances for a sighting are on Sundays and Wednesdays. Because he's a travelin' man, the following schedule can vary. The pope gives a blessing at noon on Sunday from his apartment on St. Peter's Square (except Aug–Sept when he speaks at his summer residence at Castel Gandolfo, 40 km from Rome; train leaves Rome's Termini station at 8:35, returns after his talk). On Wednesday at 10:00, the pope blesses the crowds at St. Peter's from a balcony or canopied platform on the square (except in winter, when he speaks at 11:00 in 7,000-seat Aula Paola VI Auditorium, next to St. Peter's Basilica). To find out the pope's schedule or to book a free spot for the Wednesday blessing (either for a seat on the square or in the auditorium), call 06-6988-3114. Smaller ceremonies celebrated by the pope require reservations. The weekly entertainment guide *Roma c'è* always has a "Seeing the Pope" section. If you don't want to see the pope, minimize crowd problems by avoiding these times.

▲▲▲**St. Peter's Basilica**—There is no doubt: This is the richest and most impressive church on earth. To call it vast is like calling God smart. Marks on the floor show where the next-largest churches would fit if they were put inside. The ornamental cherubs would dwarf a large man. Birds roost inside, and thousands of people wander about, heads craned heavenward, hardly noticing each other. Don't miss Michelangelo's *Pietà* (behind bullet-proof glass) to the right of the entrance. Bernini's altar work and seven-story-tall bronze canopy (*baldacchino*) are brilliant.

For a quick self-guided walk through the basilica, follow these points (see map on page 56):

**1.** The atrium is larger than most churches. Notice the historic doors (the Holy Door, on the right, won't be opened until the next Jubilee Year, in 2025—see point 13 below).

**2.** The purple circular porphyry stone marks the site of Charlemagne's coronation in A.D. 800 (in the first St. Peter's church that stood on this site). From here get a sense of the immensity of the church, which can accommodate 95,000 worshippers standing on its six acres.

**3.** Michelangelo planned a Greek-cross floor plan rather than the Latin-cross standard in medieval churches. A Greek cross, symbolizing the perfection of God, and by association the goodness of man, was important to the humanist Michelangelo. But accommodating large crowds was important to the Church in the fancy Baroque age, which followed Michelangelo, so the original nave length was doubled. Stand halfway up the nave and imagine the stubbier design Michelangelo had in mind.

**4.** View the magnificent dome from the statue of St. Andrew.

# St. Peter's Basilica

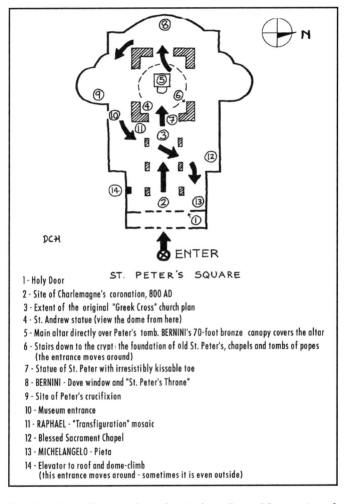

N

DCH

ENTER

ST. PETER'S SQUARE

1 - Holy Door
2 - Site of Charlemagne's coronation, 800 AD
3 - Extent of the original "Greek Cross" church plan
4 - St. Andrew statue (view the dome from here)
5 - Main altar directly over Peter's tomb. BERNINI's 70-foot bronze canopy covers the altar
6 - Stairs down to the crypt: the foundation of old St. Peter's, chapels and tombs of popes
   (the entrance moves around)
7 - Statue of St. Peter with irresistibly kissable toe
8 - BERNINI - Dove window and "St. Peter's Throne"
9 - Site of Peter's crucifixion
10 - Museum entrance
11 - RAPHAEL - "Transfiguration" mosaic
12 - Blessed Sacrament Chapel
13 - MICHELANGELO - Pieta
14 - Elevator to roof and dome-climb
   (this entrance moves around - sometimes it is even outside)

See the vision of heaven above the windows: Jesus, Mary, a ring of saints, rings of angels, and, on the very top, God the Father.

**5.** The main altar sits directly over St. Peter's tomb and under Bernini's 70-foot-tall bronze canopy.

**6.** The stairs lead down to the crypt to the foundation, chapels, and tombs of popes. (Do this last since it leads you out of the church.)

**7.** The statue of St. Peter, with an irresistibly kissable toe, is one of the few pieces of art that predate this church. It adorned the first St. Peter's church.

**8.** St. Peter's throne and Bernini's star-burst dove window is the site of a daily mass (Mon–Sat at 17:00, Sun at 17:45).

**9.** St. Peter was crucified here when this location was simply "the Vatican Hill." The obelisk now standing in the center of St. Peter's square marked the center of a Roman racecourse long before a church stood here.

**10.** For most, the treasury (in the sacristy) is not worth the admission.

**11.** The church is filled with mosaics, not paintings. Notice the mosaic version of Raphael's *Transfiguration*.

**12.** Blessed Sacrament Chapel.

**13.** Michelangelo sculpted his *Pietà* when he was 24 years old. A pietà is a work showing Mary with the dead body of Christ taken down from the cross. Michelangelo's mastery of the body is obvious in this powerfully beautiful masterpiece. Jesus is believably dead, and Mary, the eternally youthful "handmaiden" of the Lord, still accepts God's will...even if it means giving up her son.

The Holy Door (just to the right of the *Pietà*) was bricked shut at the end of the Jubilee Year 2000 and won't be opened until 2025. Every 25 years the Church celebrates an especially festive year derived from the Old Testament idea of the Jubilee Year (originally every 50 years), which encourages new beginnings and the forgiveness of sins and debts. In the Jubilee Year 2000, the pope tirelessly promoted debt relief for the Third World.

**14.** An elevator leads to the roof and the stairway up the dome. The dome, Michelangelo's last work, is (you guessed it) the biggest anywhere. Taller than a football field is long, it's well worth the sweaty climb for a great view of Rome, the Vatican grounds, and the inside of the basilica—particularly heavenly while there is singing. Look around—Rome has no modern skyline. No building is allowed to exceed the height of St. Peter's. The elevator takes you to the rooftop of the nave. From there a few steps take you to a balcony at the base of the dome looking down into the church interior. After that the one-way, 300-step climb (for some people claustrophobic) to the cupola begins.

The rooftop level (below the dome) has a gift shop, WC, drinking fountain, and a commanding view (L8,000 elevator, allow an hour to go up and down, May–Sept daily 8:30–18:00, Oct–April daily 8:30–17:00).

The church strictly enforces its dress code: no shorts or bare shoulders (men and women); no miniskirts. You might be required to check any bags at a free cloakroom near the entry.

**Hours:** St. Peter's is open daily May through September from 7:00 to 19:00, until 18:00 October through April (ticket booth to treasury closes 1 hour earlier). All are welcome to join in the hour-long Mass at the front altar (Mon–Sat at 17:00, Sun at 17:45).

The church is particularly moving at 7:00, while tourism is still sleeping. Volunteers who want you to understand and appreciate St. Peter's give free 90-minute tours (3/week, see "Tours," above); these are generally excellent but non-Christians can find them preachy. Seeing the *Pietà* is neat; understanding it is divine.

▲▲▲**Vatican Museum**—Too often the immense Vatican Museum is treated as an obstacle course, with four nagging miles of displays separating the tourist from the Sistine Chapel. Even without the Sistine, this is one of Europe's top three or four houses of art. It can be exhausting, so plan your visit carefully, focusing on a few themes. Allow two hours for a quick visit, three or four for time to enjoy it. The museum has a nearly impossible-not-to-follow, one-way system (although, for the rushed visitor, the museum does clearly mark out 4 color-coded visits of different lengths—A is shortest, D longest).

Start, as civilization did, in Egypt and Mesopotamia. Next, the Pio Clementino collection features **Greek and Roman statues**. Decorating its courtyard are some of the best Greek and Roman statues in captivity, including the *Laocoön* group (1st century B.C., Hellenistic) and the *Apollo Belvedere* (a 2nd-century Roman copy of a Greek original). The centerpiece of the next hall is the *Belvedere Torso* (just a 2,000-year-old torso, but one that had a great impact on the art of Michelangelo). Finishing off the classical statuary are two fine fourth-century porphyry sarcophagi; these royal purple tombs hold the remains of Constantine's mother and daughter. Crafted in Egypt at a time when a declining Rome was unable to do such fine work, the details are fun to study.

After long halls of tapestries, old maps, broken penises, and fig leaves, you'll come to what most people are looking for: the Raphael Rooms (or *stanza*), and Michelangelo's Sistine Chapel.

These outstanding works are frescoes. A fresco (meaning "fresh" in Italian) is technically not a painting. The color is mixed into wet plaster, and, when the plaster dries, the painting is actually part of the wall. This is a durable but difficult medium, requiring speed and accuracy as the work is built slowly, one patch at a time.

After fancy rooms illustrating the "Immaculate Conception of Mary" (a hard-to-sell, 19th-century Vatican doctrine) and the triumph of Constantine (with divine guidance, which led to his conversion to Christianity), you enter the first room completely done by **Raphael** and find the newly restored *School of Athens*. This is remarkable for its blatant pre-Christian classical orientation wallpapering the apartments of Pope Julius II. Raphael honors the great pre-Christian thinkers—Aristotle, Plato, and company—who are portrayed as the leading artists of Raphael's day. The bearded figure of Plato is Leonardo da Vinci. Diogenes, history's first hippie, sprawls alone in bright blue on the stairs, while Michelangelo broods in the foreground—supposedly added late. Apparently Raphael snuck a peek at the Sistine Chapel and decided that his arch competitor was so good he had to put their personal differences aside and include him in this tribute to the artists of his generation. Today's St. Peter's was under construction as Raphael was working. In the *School of Athens*, he gives us a sneak preview of the unfinished church.

Next (unless you detour through the refreshingly modern Catholic art section) is the brilliantly restored **Sistine Chapel**. The Sistine Chapel, the pope's personal chapel, is where, upon the death of the ruling pope, a new pope is elected. The College of Cardinals meets here and votes four times a day until a two-thirds-plus-one majority is reached and a new pope is elected.

The Sistine is famous for Michelangelo's pictorial culmination of the Renaissance, showing the story of Creation, with a powerful God weaving in and out of each scene through that busy first week. This is an optimistic and positive expression of the High Renaissance and a stirring example of the artistic and theological maturity of the 33-year-old Michelangelo, who spent four years on this work.

Later, after the Reformation wars had begun and after the Catholic army of Spain had sacked the Vatican, the reeling Church began to fight back. As part of its Counter-Reformation, a much older Michelangelo was commissioned to paint the *Last Judgment* (behind the altar). Brilliantly restored, the message is as clear as the day Michelangelo finished it: Christ is returning, some will go to hell and some to heaven, and some will be saved by the power of the rosary.

In the recent and controversial restoration project, no paint was added. Centuries of dust, soot (from candles used for lighting and Mass), and glue (added to make the art shine) were removed, revealing the bright original colors of Michelangelo. Photos are allowed (without a flash) elsewhere in the museum, but as part of the deal with the company who did the restoration, no photos are allowed in the Sistine Chapel.

For a shortcut, a small door at the rear of the Sistine Chapel allows tour groups and speedy individuals (without an audioguide) to escape directly to St. Peter's Basilica (ignore sign saying "Tour Groups Only"). If you squirt out here, you're done with the museum. The Pinacoteca is the only important part left. Consider doing it at the start. Otherwise it's a 10-minute, heel-to-toe slalom through tourists from the Sistine Chapel to the entry/exit.

After this long march to the entry/exit, you'll find the **Pinacoteca** (the Vatican's small but fine collection of paintings, with Raphael's *Transfiguration*, Leonardo's unfinished *St. Jerome*, and Caravaggio's *Deposition*), a cafeteria (long lines, mediocre food), and the underrated early-Christian-art section, before you exit via the souvenir shop.

**Cost:** L18,000, free on last Sunday of each month.

**Hours:** March–Oct Mon–Fri 8:45–16:45, Sat 8:45–13:45, Nov–Feb Mon–Sat 8:45–13:45, closed Sun except last Sun of the month (when it's free and open 8:45–13:45). The last entry is 75 minutes before closing time. The Sistine Chapel closes 30 minutes early. The museum is closed on many holidays, including: Jan 1 and 6, Feb 11, March 19, Easter and Easter Monday, May 1, Ascension Day, Corpus Christi, June 29, Aug 15 plus 14 or 16, Nov 1, Dec 8, 25, and 26.

It's generally hot and crowded. Saturday, the last Sunday of the month, and Monday are the worst; late afternoons are best. Modest dress (no short shorts or bare shoulders) is appropriate and often required.

**Information:** An information window is in the entry hall (look for "i" symbol; it's probably in the bank of windows to your left, under "Special Permits"; some English spoken). Also in the entry you'll find a book kiosk plus a bookshop just up the stairs (with other shops scattered throughout the museum). You can rent an audioguide (L10,000) after you buy your ticket. Tel. 06-6988-4947 or 06-6988-3333.

## Sights—South Rome

**Baths of Caracalla (Terme di Caracalla)**—Today it's just a shell—a huge shell—with all of its sculptures and most of its mosaics moved to museums. Inaugurated by Emperor Caracalla in A.D. 216, this massive complex could accommodate 1,600 visitors at a time. Today you'll see a huge two-story, roofless brick building surrounded by a garden, bordered by ruined walls. The two huge rooms at either end of the building were used for exercise. In between the exercise rooms was a pool flanked by two small mosaic-floored dressing rooms. Niches in the walls once held statues. In its day, this was a remarkable place to hang out. For ancient Romans, the baths were a social experience.

The Baths of Caracalla functioned until Goths severed the aqueducts in the sixth century. In modern times, operas were held here from 1938 to 1993. For the same reason concerts no longer occur in the Forum—to keep the ruins from getting more ruined— operas were discontinued here (L8,000, Mon 9:00–14:00, Tue– Sun 9:00–19:15, ask if audioguides are available, fine L15,000 guidebook—can read in shaded garden while sitting on a chunk of column, Metro: Circus Maximus, and a 5-minute walk south along Via delle Terme di Caracalla). Look for Caracalla's statues in Rome's Octagonal Hall and Naples' Archaeological Museum.

**E.U.R.**—In the late 1930s, Italy's dictator, Mussolini, planned an international exhibition to show off the wonders of his fascist

society. But the "wonders of fascism" brought us World War II
first, and Il Duce's celebration never happened. Italy made the
best of the unfinished mega-project, finishing it in the 1950s to
house government offices and big obscure museums. If Hitler
and Mussolini had won the war, our world might look like E.U.R.
(pronounced "ai-oor"). From the Magliana subway stop, stairs
lead uphill to E.U.R.'s skyscraper, the blocky **Palace of the
Civilization of Labor** (Palazzo del Civilta del Lavoro). With
its giant, no-questions-asked, patriotic statues and its black-and-
white simplicity, this is the essence of fascist architecture. It's
understandably nicknamed the "Square Colosseum."

The **Museum of Roman Civilization** (Museo della Civilta
Romana) fills 59 rooms with plaster casts and models illustrating
the greatness of classical Rome. It also has a scrolled-out version
of Trajan's Column, but the highlight is the 1:250 scale model of
Constantine's Rome—c. A.D. 300 (L8,000, Tue–Sat 9:00–18:45,
Sun 9:00–13:30, closed Mon, Piazza G. Agnelli, Metro: E.U.R.
Fermi, tel. 06-592-6041).

## Sights—Near Rome
▲▲**Ostia Antica**—Rome's ancient seaport, less than an hour from
downtown, is the next best thing to Pompeii. Ostia had 80,000
people at the time of Christ, later became a ghost town, and is now
excavated. Start at the 2,000-year-old theater, buy a map, explore the
town, and finish with its fine little museum (note that museum closes
at 14:00). To get there take the subway's B Line to the Piramide
stop and then catch the Lido train to Ostia Antica (2/hrly), walk over
the overpass, go straight to the end of that road, and follow the signs
to (or ask for) "*scavi* Ostia Antica" (L8,000, Tue–Sun 9:00–18:00 in
summer, 9:00–16:00 in winter, closed Mon, museum closes at 14:00,
tel. 06-5635-8099). Just beyond is Rome's filthy beach (*lido*).

## Self-Guided Walks of Rome
▲▲▲**Floodlit Rome Hike: Trastevere to the Spanish Steps**—
Rome can be grueling. But a fine way to enjoy this historian's rite
of passage is an evening walk lacing together Rome's floodlit night
spots. Enjoying fine urban spaces, observing real-life theater
vignettes, sitting so close to a Bernini fountain that traffic noises
evaporate, watching water flicker its mirror on the marble, jostling
with local teenagers to see all the gelato flavors, enjoying lovers
straddling more than the bench, jaywalking past flak-proof vested
*polizia*, marveling at the ramshackle elegance that softens this brutal city for those who were born here and can imagine living
nowhere else—these are the flavors of Rome best tasted after dark.
This walk is about three kilometers (2 miles) long; for a shortcut,
start at Campo de' Fiori.

Taxi or ride the bus (from Vatican area, take #23; from Via

Nazionale hotels, take #64, #70, #115, or #640 to Largo Argentina and then transfer to #8) to Trastevere, the colorful neighborhood across (*tras*) the Tiber (*tevere*) River.

**Trastevere** offers the best look at medieval-village Rome. The action all marches to the chime of the church bells. Go to Trastevere and wander. Wonder. Be a poet on Rome's Left Bank. This proud neighborhood was long an independent working-class area. Now becoming trendy, high rents are driving out the source of so much color. Still, it's a great people scene, especially at night. Start your exploratory stroll at Piazza di Santa Maria in Trastevere. While today's fountain is 17th century, there's been a fountain here since Roman times.

**Santa Maria in Trastevere**, one of Rome's oldest churches, was made a basilica in the fourth century, when Christianity was legalized (free, daily 7:30–13:00, 15:00–19:00). It was the first church dedicated to the Virgin Mary. The portico (covered area just outside the door) is decorated with fascinating ancient fragments filled with early Christian symbolism. Most of what you see today dates from around the 12th century, but the granite columns come from an ancient Roman temple, and the ancient basilica floor plan (and ambience) survives. The 12th-century mosaics behind the altar are striking and notable for their portrayal of Mary—the first showing her at the throne with Jesus in heaven. Look below the scenes from the life of Mary to see ahead-of-their-time paintings (by Cavallini, from 1300) that predate the Renaissance by 100 years.

Before leaving Trastevere, wander the back streets (if you're hungry, see "Eating," below). Then, from the church square (Piazza di Santa Maria), take Via del Moro to the river and cross on Ponte Sisto, a pedestrian bridge with a good view of St. Peter's dome. Continue straight ahead for one block. Take the first left, which leads down Via di Capo di Ferro through the scary and narrow darkness to Piazza Farnese, with its imposing Palazzo Farnese. Michelangelo contributed to the facade of this palace, now the French embassy. The fountains on the square feature huge one-piece granite hot tubs from the ancient Roman Baths of Caracalla.

One block from there (opposite the palace) is **Campo de' Fiori** (Field of Flowers), which is my favorite outdoor dining room after dark (see "Eating," below). The statue of Giordano Bruno, a heretic who was burned in 1600 for believing the world was round and not the center of the universe, marks the center of this great and colorful square. Bruno overlooks a busy produce market in the morning and strollers after dark. This neighborhood is still known for its free spirit. When the statue of Bruno was erected in 1889, local riots overcame Vatican protests against honoring a heretic. Bruno faces his executioner, the Vatican Chancellory (the big white building in the corner a bit to his right), while his pedestal reads: "And the flames rose up." The square is lined and surrounded by fun eateries. Bruno also faces La Carbonara, which gave birth to pasta carbonara. The Forno, next door, is a popular place for hot and tasty take-out *pizza bianco* (plain but spicy pizza bread).

If Bruno did a hop, step, and jump forward and turned right and marched 200 meters, he'd cross the busy Corso Vittorio Emanuele and find **Piazza Navona**. Rome's most interesting night scene features street music, artists, fire eaters, local Casanovas, ice cream, outdoor cafés (splurge worthy if you've got time to sit and enjoy the human river of Italy), and fountains by Bernini, the father of Baroque art. The Tartufo "death by chocolate" ice cream (L5,500 to go, L12,000 at a table) made the Tre Scalini café (left of obelisk) world famous among connoisseurs of ice cream and chocolate alike. This oblong piazza is molded around the long-gone stadium of Domitian, an ancient chariot racetrack.

Leave Piazza Navona directly across from Tre Scalini café, go (east) past rose peddlers and palm readers, jog left around the guarded building, and follow the brown sign to the **Pantheon** straight down Via del Salvatore (cheap pizza place on left just before the Pantheon, easy WC at McDonald's). Sit for a while under the Pantheon's floodlit, moonlit portico.

With your back to the Pantheon, head right, passing Bar Pantheon on your right. The Tazza d'Oro Casa del Caffè, one of Rome's top coffee shops, dates back to the days when this area was licensed to roast coffee beans. Look back at the fine view of the Pantheon from here.

With the coffee shop on your right, walk down Via degli Orfani to Piazza Capranica, with the big plain Florentine Renaissance–style Palazzo Capranica. Big shots, like the Capranica family, built stubby towers on their palaces—not for any military use . . . just to show off. Leave the piazza to the right of the palace, between the palace and the church. Via in Aquiro leads to a sixth-century B.C. Egyptian **obelisk** (taken as a trophy by Augustus after his victory in Egypt over Mark Antony and Cleopatra). Walk into the guarded square past the obelisk and face the huge parliament building. A short detour to the left (past Albergo National) brings you to some of Rome's best gelato. Gelateria Caffè Pasticceria Giolitti is cheap to go or elegant, pricey, and worthwhile for a sit among classy locals (open daily until very late, your choice: cone or *bicchierini*—cup, Via Uffici del Vicario 40). Or head directly from the parliament into the next, even grander, square.

**Piazza Colonna** features a huge second-century column honoring Marcus Aurelius, the philosopher-emperor. The big, important-looking palace is the prime minister's residence. Cross Via del Corso, Rome's noisy main drag, and jog right (around the Y-shaped shopping gallery from 1928) and head down Via dei Sabini to the roar of the water, light, and people of the Trevi Fountain.

The **Trevi Fountain** is an example of how Rome took full advantage of the abundance of water brought into the city by its great aqueducts. This watery Baroque avalanche was built in 1762 by a pope celebrating his reopening of the ancient aqueduct that powers it. Romantics toss two coins over their shoulder thinking it will give them a wish and assure their return to Rome. That may sound silly, but every year I go through this touristic ritual . . . and it actually seems to work.

Take some time to people watch (whisper a few breathy *bello*s or *bella*s) before leaving. Facing the fountain, go past it on the right down Via delle Stamperia to Via del Triton. Cross the busy street and continue to the Spanish Steps (ask, *"Dov'è Piazza di Spagna?"*; doh-vay pee-aht-zah dee spahn-yah) a few blocks and thousands of dollars of shopping opportunities away.

The **Piazza di Spagna** (rhymes with "lasagna"), with the very popular Spanish Steps, got its name 300 years ago, when this was the site of the Spanish Embassy. It's been the hangout of many Romantics over the years (Keats, Wagner, Openshaw, Goethe, and others). The Boat Fountain at the foot of the steps, which was done by Bernini's father, Pietro Bernini, is powered by an aqueduct. (All of Rome's fountains are aqueduct powered; their spurt is determined by the water pressure provided by the various aqueducts. This one, for instance, is much weaker than Trevi's gush.) The piazza is a thriving night scene. Facing the steps, walk to your right about a block to tour one of the world's biggest and most lavish McDonald's. About a block on the other side of the steps is the Spagna Metro stop, which (usually until 23:30) will zip you home.

▲**The Dolce Vita Stroll down Via del Corso**—This is the city's chic and hip "cruise" from Piazza del Popolo (Metro: Flaminio) down a wonderfully traffic-free section of Via del Corso and up Via Condotti to the Spanish Steps each evening around 18:00 (Sat and Sun are best). Strollers, shoppers, and flirts on the prowl fill this neighborhood of Rome's most fashionable stores (open after siesta 16:30–19:30). Throughout Italy, early evening is time to stroll.

Start on **Piazza Popolo**. Historians: This area was once just inside medieval Rome's main entry. The delightfully car-free square is marked by an obelisk that was brought to Rome by Augustus after he conquered Egypt. (It once stood in the Circus Maximus.) The Baroque Church of **Santa Maria del Popolo**— with Raphael's Chigi Chapel (pron. kee-gee, third chapel on left) and two Caravaggio paintings (side paintings in chapel left of altar)—is next to the gate in the old wall, on the far side of Piazza del Popolo, to the right as you face the gate (church open Mon–Sat 7:00–12:00, 16:00–19:00, Sun 8:00–13:30, 16:30–19:30).

From Piazza del Popolo, shop your way down **Via del Corso**. To rest your feet, join the locals sitting on the steps of various churches along the street.

At Via Pontefici, historians turn right and walk a block to
see the massive, rotting, round brick **Mausoleum of Augustus**,
topped with overgrown cypress trees. Beyond it, next to the
river, is Augustus' Ara Pacis, or Altar of Peace (due to reopen in
2001...maybe).

From the mausoleum, return to Via del Corso and the 21st
century, continuing straight until **Via Condotti**. Shoppers, take
a left to join the parade to the **Spanish Steps**. The streets that
parallel Via Condotti to the south (Borgogno and Frattini) are just
as popular. You can catch a taxi home at the taxi stand a block
south of the Spanish Steps (at Piazza Mignonelli, near American
Express and McDonald's).

Historians: Ignore Via Condotti. Continue a kilometer
down Via del Corso—straight since Roman times—to the Victor
Emmanuel Monument. Climb Michelangelo's stairway to his
glorious (especially when floodlit) square atop Capitol Hill and
catch the lovely views of the Forum (from either side of the
mayor's palace) as the horizon reddens and cats prowl the
unclaimed rubble of ancient Rome.

## Sleeping in Rome
### (L2,000 = about $1, country code: 39)
Sleep Code: **S** = Single, **D** = Double/Twin, **T** = Triple, **Q** = Quad,
**b** = bathroom, **t** = toilet only, **s** = shower only, **CC** = Credit Card
(**V**isa, **M**asterCard, **A**mex), **SE** = Speaks English, **NSE** = No
English. Breakfast is normally included in the expensive places.

The absolute cheapest doubles in Rome are L70,000, without
shower or breakfast. You'll pay L30,000 in a backpacker-filled
dorm or hostel. A nicer hotel (L240,000 with a bathroom and
air-conditioning) provides an oasis and refuge, making it easier
to enjoy this intense and grinding city. If you're going door to
door, prices are soft—so bargain. Built into a hotel's official price
list is a kickback for a room-finding service or agency; if you're
coming direct, they pay no kickback and may lower the price for
you. Many hotels have high-season (mid-March–June, Sept–Oct)
and low-season prices. Room rates are lowest in sweltering August.
Easter and September are most crowded and expensive. On Easter,
April 25, and May 1, the entire city gets booked up.

Some of my recommended hotels are small, with huge, murky
entrances that make you feel like a Q-Tip in a gas station. English
works in all but the cheapest places. Traffic in Rome roars, so my
challenge has been to find friendly places on quiet streets. With
the recent arrival of double-paned windows and air-conditioning,
night noise is not the problem it was. Even so, light sleepers
should always ask for a *tranquillo* room. Many prices here are
promised only to people who show this book and come direct
without using a room-finding service.

Scala Reale, the company that runs tours (see "Tours of Rome," above), can help you find short-term accommodations if you contact them in advance (U.S. tel. 888/467-1986, Italy tel. 06-445-1477, www.scalareale.org, e-mail: info@scalareale.org).

Your hotel can point you to the nearest **Laundromat** (usually open daily 8:00–22:00, about L12,000 to wash and dry a 15-pound load). The Bolle Blu chain comes with Internet access (L8,000/hr, near train station at Via Milazzo 20, Via Palestro 59, and Via Principe 116, tel. 06-446-5804).

### *Sleeping on Via Firenze (zip code: 00184)*

I generally stay on Via Firenze because it's tranquil, safe, handy, and central. It's a 10-minute walk from the central train station and airport shuttle, and two blocks beyond the Piazza della Repubblica and TI. The defense ministry is nearby, and you've got heavily armed guards all night. Virtually all the orange buses that rumble down Via Nazionale (#64, #70, #115, #640) take you to Piazza Venezia (Forum) and Largo Argentina (Pantheon). From Largo Argentina, #8 goes to Trastevere (first stop after crossing the river) and #64 (jammed with people and thieves) continues to St. Peter's.

**Hotel Oceania** is a peaceful slice of air-conditioned heaven. This nine-room manor house–type hotel is spacious and quiet, with newly renovated and spotless rooms, run by a pleasant father-and-son team (Sb-L190,000, Db-L240,000, Tb-L300,000, Qb-L355,000, these prices through 2001 with this book only, additional 20 percent off in Aug and winter, includes breakfast, phones, English newspaper, CC:VMA, Via Firenze 38, tel. 06-482-4696, fax 06-488-5586, www.hoteloceania.it, e-mail: hoceania@tin.it, son Stefano SE, dad Armando serves world-famous coffee).

**Hotel Aberdeen** is classier and more professional for about the same price. It has mini-bars, phones, and showers in its 36 modern, air-conditioned, and smoke-free rooms; includes a fine breakfast buffet; and is warmly run by Annamaria, with support from her cousins Sabrina and Cinzia, and trusty Reda riding shotgun after dark (Sb-L180,000, Db-L250,000, Tb-L300,000, Qb-L350,000, prices through 2001 with this book only, L60,000 less per room in Aug and winter, CC:VMA, garage-L40,000, Via Firenze 48, tel. 06-482-3920, fax 06-482-1092, check for deals on Web, www.travel.it/roma/aberdeen, e-mail: hotel .aberdeen@travel.it, SE).

**Residence Adler**, with its wide halls, garden patio, and eight quiet, elegant, and air-conditioned rooms in a great locale, is another good deal. It's run the old-fashioned way by a charming family (Db-L200,000, Tb-L280,000, Qb-L340,000, includes breakfast, prices through 2001 with this book only, CC:VMA, additional 5 percent off if you pay cash, elevator, Via Modena 5, tel. 06-484-466, fax 06-488-0940, NSE).

# Rome's Train Station Neighborhood

| | |
|---|---|
| ❶ HOTEL OCEANIA & NARDIZZI | ⓭ ALBERGO SILEO |
| ❷ HOTEL ABERDEEN | ⓮ HOTEL DUCA D'ALBA |
| ❸ RESIDENCE ADLER | ⓯ HOTEL GRIFO |
| ❹ HOTEL REX | ⓰ SUORE DI SANT ANNA |
| ❺ HOTEL BRITTANIA | ⓱ SNACK BAR GASTRONOMIA |
| ❻ HOTEL SONYA | ⓲ PASTICCERIA DAGNINO |
| ❼ HOTEL PENSIONE ITALIA | ⓳ HOSTARIA ROMANA |
| ❽ HOTEL CORTINA & CAFFETTERIA NAZIONALE | ⓴ RISTORANTE GIOVANNI |
| ❾ YWCA CASA STUDENTESSE | ㉑ PHARMACY |
| ❿ SUORE SANTA ELISABETTA | ㉒ RIST. CINESE INT'L. |
| ⓫ HOTEL MONTREAL | ㉓ BEEHIVE HOSTEL |
| ⓬ HOTEL FENICIA & MAGIC | ㉔ CASA OLMATA HOSTEL |

**Hotel Nardizzi Americana**, with 18 simple, pleasant, air-conditioned rooms and a rooftop terrace, is loosely run (Sb-L150,000, Db-L200,000, Tb-L240,000, Qb-L260,000, prices through 2001 with this book only, includes breakfast, discounts for off-season and long stays, CC:VMA, additional 10 percent off with cash, elevator, drinks available evenings, Via Firenze 38, tel. 06-488-0368, fax 06-488-0035, SE).

**Hotel Seiler** is a quiet, serviceable place with 30 decent rooms (Sb-L160,000, Db-L230,000, Tb-L280,000, these discounted prices good only with this book, includes continental breakfast, CC:VMA, fans, elevator, Via Firenze 48, tel. 06-485-550, fax 06-488-0688, e-mail: acropoli@rdn.it, Silvio and Alessia SE).

**Hotel Texas Seven Hills**, a stark institutional throwback to the 1960s, rents 18 quiet but depressing rooms (D-L160,000, Db-L200,000, often soft prices, CC:VMA, air-con planned for 2001, Via Firenze 47, elevator, tel. 06-481-4082, fax 06-481-4079, e-mail: what's that?, NSE).

## Sleeping between Via Nazionale and Basilica Santa Maria Maggiore

**Hotel Pensione Italia**, in a busy, interesting, handy locale, is placed safely on a quiet street next to the Ministry of the Interior. Thoughtfully run by English-speaking Andrea, Lena, and Alberico, it's comfortable, airy, clean, and bright (31 rooms, Sb-L130,000, Db-L180,000, Tb-L240,000, Qb-L280,000, includes breakfast, prices through 2001 with this book and cash only, all rooms 20 percent off in mid-July–Aug and winter, elevator, air-con for L15,000 extra, Via Venezia 18, just off Via Nazionale, 00184 Roma, tel. 06-482-8355, fax 06-474-5550, www.hotelitaliaroma.com, e-mail: hitalia@pronet.it). Their singles are all on the quiet courtyard and the nine annex rooms across the street are a cut above the rest.

**Hotel Sonya** is a small, family-run but impersonal place with 20 comfortable, well-equipped rooms, a great location, and low prices; reserve well in advance (Db-L220,000, Tb-L250,000, Qb-L290,000, CC:VMA, air-con, elevator, facing the Opera at Via Viminale 58, tel. 06-481-9911, fax 06-488-5678, Francesca SE).

**Hotel Cortina** rents 14 modern, air-conditioned rooms for a decent price on a busy street. Ask for a quieter room on the courtyard or side street (Db-L250,000, includes breakfast, CC:VMA, 10 percent discount with this book and cash only, Via Nazionale 18, 00184 Roma, tel. 06-481-9794, fax 06-481-9220, www.travel.it/roma/hotelcortina, John Carlo and Angelo SE).

**YWCA Casa Per Studentesse** accepts men and women. It's an institutional place, filled with white-uniformed maids, more-colorful Third World travelers, and 75 single beds. It's closed from midnight to 7:00; in case of an emergency, a live-in

manager can let people out, but not in (L50,000 per person in 3-
and 4-bed rooms, S-L70,000, Sb-L90,000, D-L120,000, Db-
L140,000, includes breakfast except on Sun, elevator, Via C. Balbo
4, 00184 Roma, tel. 06-488-0460, fax 06-487-1028). The YWCA
faces a great little street market.

**Suore di Santa Elisabetta** is a heavenly Polish-run convent
booked long in advance, but it's an incredible value (Sb-L63,000,
Db-L115,000, Tb-L148,000, Qb-L180,000, includes breakfast,
CC:VM, elevator, fine view roof terrace, a block southwest of
Basilica Santa Maria Maggiore at Via dell' Omata 9, tel. 06-488-
8271, fax 06-488 1066).

**Hotel Montreal**, run with care, is a bright, solid, business-
class place on a big street a block southeast of Santa Maria
Maggiore (Db-L220,000 most of year, L170,000 in July–Aug,
L150,000 in winter, CC:VMA, 21 of its 27 rooms have air-con,
elevator, good security, 1 block from Metro: Vittorio, 3 blocks
west of train station, Via Carlo Alberto 4, 00185 Roma, tel.
06-445-7797, fax 06-446-5522, www.hotelmontrealroma.com).

**Splurges: Hotel Britannia** stands like a marble fruitcake,
offering all the comforts in tight quarters on a quiet and safe-
feeling street. Lushly renovated with over-the-top classical motifs,
its 32 air-conditioned rooms are small but comfortable with bright,
modern bathrooms (Db-L430,000 in May–June and Sept–Oct,
Db-L275,00 in Aug, Db-L380,000 the rest of the year, extra
bed-L90,000, children up to 10 stow away for free, babysitting
service, CC:VMA, phones, TV, safes, mini-bar, free parking,
Via Napoli 64, 00184 Roma, tel. 06-488-3153, fax 06-488-2343,
e-mail: britannia@venere.it).

**Hotel Rex** is a business-class Art Deco fortress—a quiet,
plain, and stately four-star place with all the comforts  (50 rooms,
Sb-L370,000, Db-L470,000, Tb-L550,000, CC:VMA, elevator,
air-con, some smoke-free rooms, 2 phones per room—next to bed
and toilet, 2 blocks south of Via Nazionale at Via Torino 149, tel.
06-482-4828, fax 06-488-2743, e-mail: hotel.rex@alfanet.it, SE).

## Sleeping Cheap, Northeast of the Train Station

The cheapest hotels in town are northeast of the station.
Some travelers feel this area is weird and spooky after dark.
With your back to the train tracks, turn right and walk two
blocks out of the station.

**Hotel Fenicia** rents 11 comfortable, well-equipped rooms
at a fine price. Their bigger rooms are on fourth floor—quiet
but there's no elevator (Sb-L85,000, Db-L135,000, Tb-L185,000,
prices through 2001 with this book only, air-con-L20,000/day,
breakfast-L10,000, CC:VMA, TVs, safes, 2 blocks from station at
Via Milazzo 20, tel. & fax 06-490-342, www.fenicia.web-page.net,
e-mail: hotel.fenicia@tiscalinet.it, Georgio and Anna SE).

**Hotel Magic**, a clean, marbled place run by a mother-daughter team, is high enough off the road to escape the traffic noise (10 rooms, Sb-L90,000, one D-L100,000, Db-L130,000, Tb-L180,000, Qb-L200,000, air-con-L20,000/day, breakfast-L7,000, prices through 2001 with this book only, cheaper in Aug and winter, CC:VM, thin walls, phones, safes, TV, midnight curfew, Via Milazzo 20, 3rd floor, 00185 Roma, tel. & fax 06-495-9880, little English spoken).

**Albergo Sileo** is a shiny-chandeliered, 10-room place with an elegant touch that has a contract to house train conductors who work the night shift. With maids doing double time, they offer simple, pleasant rooms from 19:00 to 9:00 only. If you can handle this, it's a great value. During the day they store your luggage, and though you won't have access to a room, you're welcome to hang out in their lobby or bar (D-L75,000, Db-L90,000, Tb-L115,000, elevator, Via Magenta 39, tel. & fax 06-445-0246, Alessandro and Maria Savioli NSE).

## Sleeping near the Colosseum *(zip code: 00184)*
These places are buried in a very Roman world of exhaust-stained medieval ambience. For the first three, take the subway one stop from the train station to Metro: Cavour). The handy electrico bus line #117 connects you with the sights.

**Hotel Duca d'Alba** is a tight and modern pastel-marble-hardwood place just half a block from the Metro station (Sb-L260,000, Db-L390,000, much cheaper July–Aug and winter, extra bed-L40,000, breakfast buffet, CC:VMA, air-con, safes, phones, TV, elevator, Via Leonina 14, tel. 06-484-471, fax 06-488-4840, check Web site for deals, www.hotelducadalba.com, SE).

**Hotel Grifo** has a homey, tangled floor plan with 20 modern rooms and a roof terrace. The double-paned windows almost keep out the Vespa noise (Db-L230,000, L210,000 in July, CC:VMA, elevator, air-con, some rooms have terraces, 2 blocks off Via Cavour at Via del Boschetto 144, tel. 06-487-1395, fax 06-474 2323, e-mail: alez@dds.nl, son Alessandro SE).

**Suore di Sant Anna** was built for Ukrainian pilgrims. The sisters are sweet. It's difficult (little English plus 23:00 curfew), but once you're in, you've got a comfortable home in a classic Roman-village locale. Reserve well in advance (Sb-L65,000, Db-L120,000, Tb-L180,000, includes breakfast, consider dinner for L29,000, off the corner of Via dei Serpenti and Via Baccina at Piazza Madonna dei Monti 3, Metro: Cavour, tel. 06-485-778, fax 06-487-1064, e-mail: santasofia@tiscalinet.it).

**Pensione Per Pelligrini** is another nun-run place with simple, clean rooms and lots of twin beds. The language barrier is a challenge, but the price is right (39 rooms, S-L60,000, Sb-L80,000, D-L128,000, Db-L148,000, Tb-L172,000, breakfast-L8,000, closed

Aug, just off Piazza Vittorio Emmanuele II with morning market scene, Istituto Buon Salvatore, Via Leopardi 17, from station take bus # 714, #649, or #360, tel. 06-446-7147 or 06-446-7225, fax 06-4461382, Sister Anna Maria SE).

**Near the Palatine:** The **Hotel Casa Kolbe**, located in a former monastery, rents out monkish, spartan rooms with no fans or air-conditioning. But the location is magical, across from the Palatine ruins on a quiet side street about a block from a little-used entrance to the Forum. This place isn't for everybody but perfect for some—you know who you are. Ask for a room with a view of Palatine Hill (63 rooms, Sb-L120,000, Db-L150,000, Qb-L210,000, breakfast-L8,000, CC:VM, elevator, garden, courtyard, Via S. Teodoro 44, tel. 06-679-4974 or 06-679-8866, fax 06-6994-1550, Maurizio SE).

## *Sleeping near Campo de' Fiori and Piazza Navona (zip code: 00186)*

**Hotel Campo de' Fiori** is ideal for wealthy bohemians who value centrality over peace and comfort. Just off Campo de' Fiori, it has an unreal rooftop terrace, 27 smallish rooms, and rickety windows and furniture (D-L180,000–190,000, Db-L280,000, includes breakfast, CC:VM, narrow hallways, fans, lots of stairs and no elevator, Via del Biscione 6, tel. 06-6874886, fax 06-687-6003, Andreas and others SE). They also have apartments very close by that can house five or six people (Db-L280,000, extra person-L50,000); these are a better (roomier) deal than staying at the hotel.

**Albergo del Sole**, with 60 simply decorated rooms, is impersonal and filled with German groups but well located (D-L150,000, small Db-L180,000, Db-L220,000, no breakfast, fans, elevator, multitiered terrace, Via del Biscione 76, tel. 06-6880-6873, fax 06-689-3787, www.venere.it/roma/sole, e-mail: sole@italyhotel.com).

**Casa di Santa Brigida**, also near the characteristic Campo de' Fiori, overlooks the elegant Piazza Farnese. With soft-spoken sisters gliding down polished hallways, and pearly gates instead of doors, this lavish convent makes the exhaust-stained Roman tourist feel like he's died and gone to heaven. If you're unsure of your destiny (and don't need a double bed), this is worth the splurge (23 rooms, Sb-L125,000, Db-L250,000, 4 percent extra with CC, great-value dinners, roof garden, plush library, air-con, walk-in address: Monserrato 54, mailing address: Piazza Farnese 96, reserve months in advance, tel. 06-6889-2596, fax 06-6889-1573, www.brigidine.org, e-mail: brigida@mclink.it, many of the sisters are from India and speak English).

**Piazza Navona:** **Hotel Navona** is a fine value, offering 35 basic rooms in an ancient building in a perfect locale a block off Piazza Navona. The rooms on the top floor come with more character (wood beams) and more stairs (D-L160,000, Db-L190,000, Db with air-con-L230,000, family rooms, Via dei Sediari 8, tel. 06-686-4203, fax 06-6880-3802, www.hotelnavona.com, run by a friendly Australian named Corry). **Residenza Zanardelli**, also owned by Corry, has six airy, pleasant rooms two blocks north of Piazza Navona (Db-L260,000, CC:VM but prefer cash, TV, phone, air-con, on busy street but double-paned windows minimize noise, Via G. Zanardelli 7, look for tiny name next to buzzer at door, tel. 06-6821-1392 or 06-6880-9760, fax 06-6880-3802).

**Hotel Nazionale**, a four-star landmark, is a 16th-century palace sharing a well-policed square with the national parliament. Its 90 rooms are served by lush public spaces, fancy bars, and a uniformed staff. It's a big hotel and even has a revolving front door, but if you want security, comfort, and the heart of old Rome at your doorstep (the Pantheon is 3 blocks away and Rome's top gelateria is just around the corner), this is a worthy splurge (Sb-L360,000, Db-L560,000, extra person-L120,000, suites-L850,000—gasp, less in Aug and winter, CC:VMA, air-con, elevator, Piazza Montecitorio 131, tel. 06-695-001, fax 06-678-6677, www.nazionaleamontecitorio.it, e-mail: nazionale@montecitorio.it, SE).

### Sleeping "Three Stars" near the Vatican Museum (zip code: 00192)

To locate hotels, see map on page 55.

**Hotel Alimandi** is a good value, run by the friendly and entrepreneurial Alimandi brothers: Paolo, Enrico, Luigi, and Germano. Their 35 rooms are air-conditioned, modern, and marbled in white (Sb-L160,000 or L170,000 with breakfast; Db-L240,000 or L260,000 with breakfast; Tb-L280,000 or L315,000 with breakfast; 5 percent discount with this book and cash, CC:VMA, grand breakfast-L15,000 unless included in room price—see above, elevator, great roof garden, self-service washing machines, Internet access-L5,000, pool table, free parking, down the stairs directly in front of Vatican Museum, Via Tunisi 8, near Metro: Cipro-Musei Vaticani, reserve by phone, no reply to fax means they are full, tel. 06-3972-6300, toll free in Italy tel. 800-122-121, fax 06-3972-3943, www.alimandi.org, e-mail: alimandi@tin.it, SE). They offer their guests free airport pickup and drop off (saving you L80,000 if you were planning on taking a taxi), though you must reserve when you book your room and conform to their set schedule (which can mean waiting). Maria Alimandi rents out three rooms in her apartment, a 20-minute bus ride from the Vatican (Db-L140,000, see Web site above).

**Hotel Spring House**, with a hotelesque feel, offers 51 attractive rooms—some with balconies which don't cost extra (ask for a balcony). Mention this book to get a special price (Db-L250,000 instead of normal L280,000 rate, includes breakfast, 5 percent discount for cash payment, 15 percent discount July–Aug and winter, Internet access-L10,000/30 min, CC:VMA, phones, TV, air-con, fridges in room, elevator, parking-L25,000/day, Metro: Cipro-Musei Vaticani, Via Mocenigo 7, 2 blocks from Vatican Museum, tel. 06-3972-0948, fax 06-3972-1047, www.hotelspringhouse.com, Stefano Gabbani).

**Hotel Gerber** is sleek, modern, air-conditioned, business-like, and set in a quiet residential area (27 rooms, S-L120,000, Sb-L180,000, Db-L250,000, Tb-L290,000, Qb-L330,000, 10 percent discount with this book, includes breakfast buffet, air-con, CC:VMA, 1 block from Lepanto subway stop, Via degli Scipioni 241, at intersection with Ezio, tel. 06-321-6485, fax 06-321-7048, www.hotelgerber.it, Peter SE).

**Hotel Sant' Anna** is much pricier than the rest but closer to the city center and located on a charming-for-Rome pedestrian street that fills with restaurant tables at dinnertime. Its 20 rooms are overly decorated with classical themes, but the furnishings are comfy (Db-L350,000, Db-L280,000 in July–Aug and winter, CC:VM, air-con, elevator, courtyard, Borgo Pio 133, near inter-section with Mascherino, a couple blocks from entrance of St. Peter's, tel. 06-6880-1602, fax 06-6830-8717, www.travel.it/roma/santanna, SE).

## Sleeping in Hostels and Dorms

Rome's one real youth hostel is big, institutional, and not central or worth the trouble. For cheap dorm beds, consider the following places:

**Near Basilica Santa Maria Maggiore: Casa Olmata** is a laid-back backpackers' place midway between the Termini train station and Colosseum (beds in shared quads-L30,000, S-L60,000, bunkbed D-L70,000, one queen-size D-L100,000, lots of stairs, laundry service, free Internet access, video rentals, games, roof-top terrace, communal kitchen, dinners twice weekly, English dominant language, a block southwest of Basilica Santa Maria Maggiore, Via dell' Omata 36, 3rd floor, tel. 06-483-019, fax 06-474-2854, www.casaolmata.com, e-mail: casaolmata30@hotmail.com, Mirella and Marco). **The Beehive** is especially good for older travelers. This tidy little place, with three six-bed dorms and a guests' kitchen on one floor, is thoughtfully run by a friendly young American couple, Steve and Linda (L30,000 beds, CC:VM, closed 13:00–16:00, 2 blocks south of Basilica Santa Maria Maggiore at Via Giovanni Lanza 99, tel. 06-474-0719, fax 06-4788-1190, www.the-beehive.com). The Beehive has some doubles in a building a 15-minute walk away (S-L50,000, D-L100,000, T-L150,000, reserve and check in at Beehive) and can also refer you to B&Bs, private rooms, and apartments elsewhere in Rome (www.cross-pollinate.com).

**Near the Vatican: Pensione Ottaviano** offers a fun, easy-going clubhouse feel and a good location near the Vatican (25 beds in 2- to 7-bed rooms, L30,000 per bed with sheets, D-L90,000, 6 blocks south of Ottaviano Metro stop, Via Ottaviano 6, near Piazza Risorgimento, reservations only after 21:00 the night before, tel. 06-3973-7253, www.pensioneottaviano.com).

# Eating in Rome
Romans spend their evenings eating rather than drinking and the preferred activity is to simply enjoy a fine, slow meal buried deep in the old city. Rome's a fun and cheap place to eat, with countless little eateries serving fine $20 meals. Tourists wander the streets just before midnight wondering, "Why did I eat so much?"

Although I've listed a number of restaurants, I recommend that you just head for a scenic area and explore. Piazza Navona, the Pantheon area, Campo de' Fiori, and Trastevere are neighborhoods full of places ranging from expensive sit-down to cheap take-out.

## Eating in Trastevere
Guidebooks list Trastevere's famous places, but I'd wander the fascinating maze of streets near Piazza Santa Maria in Trastevere and find a mom-and-pop place with barely a menu. Check out the tiny streets north of the church. You might consider these places before making a choice:

For outdoor seating on romantic Piazza della Scala, check out **Taverna della Scala**, the local choice for pizza (Wed–Mon 12:30–15:00, 19:00–24:00, closed Tue, tel. 06-581-4100) and **La Scala**, chic and popular with Generation X Romans (daily 12:00–15:00, 19:00–24:00, tel. 06-580-3763). Don't miss the fine little *gelatería* with oh-wow pistachio (across from church on Piazza della Scala).

At **Taverna del Moro da Tony**, Tony scrambles—with a great antipasti table—to keep his happy eaters well fed and returning (but too much mayo on bruschetta, Tue–Sun 14:00–02:00, closed Mon, off Via del Moro at Vicolo del Cinque 36, tel. 06-580-9165). For a basic meal with lots of tourists, you can eat cheap at **Mario's** (Mon–Sat 12:00–14:00 19:00–24:00, closed Sun, 3 courses with wine and service for L20,000, Via del Moro 53, tel. 06-580-3809).

**Ristorante Alle Fratte di Trastevere** is lively and inexpensive (closed Tue, Via dell Fratte di Trastevere, tel. 06-583-5775).

**Da Otello**, on Piazza San Edigio, has good antipasti and pizzas, and cooks up meat dishes on a wood-burning stove in the dining room (Thu–Tue 12:30–14:30, 19:30–24:00, closed Wed, Via della Pelliccia 47, tel. 06-589-6848).

### Eating on and near Campo de' Fiori

For the ultimate romantic square setting, eat at whichever place looks best on Campo de' Fiori. Circle the square, considering each place. **La Carbonara** claims to be the birthplace of pasta carbonara (closed Tue). Meals on small nearby streets are a better value but lack that Campo de' Fiori magic. Bars and pizzerias seem to be overwhelming the popular square. The **Taverna** and **Vineria** at numbers 16 and 15 offer good perches from which to people watch and nurse a glass of wine.

Nearby, on the more elegant and peaceful Piazza Farnese, **Ostaria Da Giovanni Ar Galletto** has a dressier local crowd, great outdoor seating, moderate prices, and fine food (closed Sun, tucked in corner of Piazza Farnese at #102, tel. 06-686-1714).

**Filetti de Baccala** is a tradition for many Romans. Basically a fish bar with paper tablecloths and cheap prices, its grease-stained, hurried waiters serve old-time favorites—fried cod fillets, a strange bitter *puntarelle* salad, and delightful anchovies with butter—to nostalgic locals (Mon–Sat 17:30–23:10, closed Sun, a block east of Campo de' Fiori tumbling onto a tiny and atmospheric square, Largo dei Librari 88, tel. 06-686-4018).

**Trattoria der Pallaro** has no menu but plenty of return eaters. Paola Fazi, with a towel wrapped around her head turban-style, and her family serve up a five-course festival of typically Roman food for L33,000, including wine, coffee, and a wonderful mandarin liqueur. Their slogan: "Here, you'll eat what we want to feed you." Look like Oliver asking for more soup and get seconds on the mandarin liqueur (Tue–Sun 12:00–15:30, 19:30–24:00, closed Mon, indoor/outdoor seating on quiet square, a block south of Corso Vittorio Emanuele down Largo del Chiavari to Largo del Pallaro 15, tel. 06-6880-1488).

**Ristorante Grotte del Teatro di Pompeo**, sitting atop an ancient theater, serves good food at fair prices with a smile (closed Mon, Via del Biscione 73, tel. 06-6880-3686).

For interesting bar munchies, try **Cul de Sac** on Piazza Pasquino (daily 12:00–18:00, 19:00–24:00, a block southwest of Piazza Navona). **L'Insalata Ricca**, a popular chain that specializes in hearty and healthy salads, is next door (daily 12:00–15:45, 18:45–22:00, Piazza Pasquino 72, tel. 06-6830-7881). Another branch is nearby with more spacious outdoor seating (just off Corso Vittorio Emanuele on Largo del Chiavari).

**Brek**, on Largo Argentina just south of the Pantheon, is an appealing, new self-service restaurant—which it calls "free flow" (daily 12:00–15:30, 18:30–23:00, sandwiches and pizza slices downstairs, "free flow" upstairs, northwest corner of square, Largo Argentina 1, tel. 06-6821-0353).

**Il Delfino**, also on Largo Argentina and near Brek, is a tired but handy self-service cafeteria that serves throughout the day (daily 7:00–21:00, not cheap but fast). Across the side street, **Frullati di Frutta** sells refreshing fruity frappés. The *alimentari* (grocery store) on the Pantheon square will make you a sandwich for a temple-porch picnic.

## Eating near Via Firenze and Via Nazionale Hotels

**Snack Bar Gastronomia** is a great local hole-in-the-wall for lunch or dinner (daily 7:00–21:00, really cheap hot meals dished up from under glass counter, tap water with a smile, Via Firenze 34). There's an *alimentari* across the street.

**Pasticceria Dagnino**, popular for its top-quality Sicilian specialties—especially pastries and ice cream—is where those who work at my recommended hotels eat (daily 7:00–22:00, in Galleria Esedra off Via Torino, a block from hotels, tel. 06-481-8660). Their *arancino*—a rice, cheese, and ham ball—is a greasy Sicilian favorite. Direct the construction of your meal at the bar, pay for your trayful at the cashier, and climb upstairs, where you'll find the dancing Sicilian girls (free).

**Hostaria Romana** is a great place for traditional Roman cuisine. For an air-conditioned, classy local favorite run by a jolly group of men who enjoy their work, eat here (closed Sun, midway between Trevi fountain and Piazza Barberini, Via del Boccaccio 1, at intersection with Via Rasella, no reservations needed before 20:00, tel. 06-474-5284). Go ahead and visit the antipasto bar in person to assemble your plate. They're happy to serve an *antipasti misto della casa* and pasta dinner. Take a hard look at their *Specialita Romane* list.

**Ristorante da Giovanni** is a serviceable, hardworking place that has been feeding locals and travelers for 50 years (L23,000 menu, Mon–Sat 12:00–15:00, 19:00–22:30, closed Sun, CC:VM, just off Via XX Septembre at Via Antonio Salandra 1, tel. 06-485-950).

**Cafetteria Nazionale**, with woody elegance, offers light lunches—including salads—at reasonable prices (set menu or buffet, Mon–Sat 7:00–20:00, closed Sun, CC:VM, Via Nazionale 26–27, at intersection with Via Agostino de Pretis, tel. 06-4899-1716).

**Ristorante Cinese Internazionale** is your best neighborhood bet for Chinese (daily 12:00–15:00, 18:00–23:00, inexpensive, no pasta, just off Via Nazionale behind Hotel Luxor at Via Agostino de Pretis 98, tel. 06-474-4064).

The **McDonald** restaurants on Piazza della Repubblica (free piazza seating outside), Piazza Barberini, and Via Firenze offer air-conditioned interiors and salad bars.

**Flann O'Brien Irish Pub** is a great place for a quick light meal (pasta or something *other* than pasta), fine Irish beer, and the most Italian crowd of all (daily 7:30–01:00, Via Nazionale 17, at intersection with Via Napoli, tel. 06-488-0418).

## Eating near the Vatican Museum

**Antonio's Hostaria dei Bastioni** is tasty and friendly. It's conveniently located midway between your walk from St. Peters' to the Vatican Museum, with noisy streetside seating and a quiet interior (hot when hot—no air-con, Mon–Sat 12:00–15:00, 19:00–23:30, closed Sun, L10,000–12,000 pastas, L15,000 *secondi*, no cover charge, at corner of Vatican wall, Via Leone IV 29, tel. 06-3972-3034).

**La Rustichella** has a great and fresh antipasti buffet (L15,000, enough for a meal) and fine pasta dishes. Arrive when they open at 19:30 to avoid a line and have the pristine buffet to yourself (Tue–Sun 12:30–15:00, 19:30–23:00, closed Mon, near Metro: Cipro-Musei Vaticani stop, opposite church at end of Via Candia, Via Angelo Emo 1, tel. 06-3972-0649). Consider the fun and fruity **Gelatería Millennium** next door.

Avoid the restaurant pushers handing out fliers near the Vatican: bad food, expensive menu tricks. Viale Giulio Cesare is lined with cheap **Pizza Rustica** shops and fun eateries, such as **Cipriani Self-Service Rosticcería** (closed Mon, pleasant outdoor seating, near Ottaviano subway stop, Viale Guilio Cesare 195).

Turn your nose loose in the wonderful **Via Andrea Doria** open-air market three blocks north of the Vatican Museum (Mon–Sat roughly 7:00–13:30, until 16:30 on Tue and Fri except summer, between Via Tunisi and Via Andrea Doria). If the market is closed, try the nearby **IN's supermarket** (Mon–Sat 8:30–13:30, 16:00–20:00 but closed Thu eve, a half block straight out from Via Tunisi entrance of open-air market, Via Francesco 18).

## Transportation Connections—Rome

Termini is the central station. Long-distance buses (e.g., from Siena and Assisi) arrive at Rome's small Tiburtina station, which is on Metro line B, with easy connections to the main train station (a straight shot 4 stops away) and the entire Metro system.

**By train from Rome to: Venice** (6/day, 5–8 hrs), **Florence** (12/day, 2 hrs, stop at Orvieto en route), **Pisa** (8/day, 3–4 hrs), **Genova** (7/day, 6 hrs, overnight possible), **Milan** (12/day, 5 hrs, overnight possible), **Naples** (6/day, 2 hrs), **Brindisi** (2/day, 9 hrs), **Amsterdam** (2/day, 20 hrs), **Bern** (5/day, 10 hrs), **Frankfurt** (4/day, 14 hrs), **Munich** (5/day, 12 hrs), **Nice** (2/day, 10 hrs), **Paris** (5/day, 16 hrs), **Vienna** (3/day, 13–15 hrs).

## Rome's Airports

Rome's two airports—Fiumicino (a.k.a. Leonardo da Vinci) and the small Ciampino—share the same Web site (www.adr.it).

**Fiumicino Airport**: Rome's major airport has a TI (daily 8:15–19:00, tel. 06-6595-4471), ATMs, banks, luggage storage, shops, and bars.

A slick, direct train connects the airport and Rome's central

Termini train station in 30 minutes. Trains run twice hourly in both directions from roughly 7:30 to 21:30. From the airport, trains depart at :07 and :37 past the hour (from airport's arrival gate, follow signs to "Stazione/Railway Station"; buy ticket from a machine or the Biglietteria office; L16,000, CC:VM, or free with first-class railpass). From Termini, trains depart at :21 and :51 past the hour from Track 25 (L16,000, buy ticket from any *Tabacchi* shop in station or at Alitalia desk near entrance to Track 25; to reach Track 25, walk along Track 24 midway through the station, then follow signs that take you inside—to Alitalia desk—and down the escalator). Read the ticket. If validation is required, stamp it in a yellow machine on the platform.

Your hotel can arrange a taxi to the airport at any hour for about L80,000. To get from the airport into town cheaply by taxi, try teaming up with any tourist also just arriving (most are heading for hotels near yours in the center). Splitting a taxi and hopping out once downtown at a taxi stand to take another to your hotel will save you L30,000. Avoid unmarked, unmetered taxis.

Airport information (tel. 06-65951 or 06-6595-3640) can connect you directly to your airline. (British Air tel. 147-812-266, Alitalia tel. 06-65643, Delta tel. 800-864-114, KLM tel. 06-652-9286, SAS tel. 06-6501-0771, TWA tel. 800-841-843, United tel. 0266-7481, Lufthansa tel. 06-6568-4004, Swiss Air tel. 06-847-0555.)

**Ciampino Airport**: Rome's smaller airport (tel. 06-794-941) handles budget and charter flights. To get to downtown Rome from the airport, take the LILA/Cotral bus (2/hrly) to the Anagnina Metro stop, where you can connect by Metro to the stop nearest your hotel.

## Driving in Rome

Greater Rome is circled by the Grande Raccordo Anulare. This ring road has spokes that lead you into the center. Entering from the north, leave the autostrada at the Settebagni exit. Following the ancient Via Salaria (and the black-and-white "Centro" signs), work your way doggedly into the Roman thick of things. This will take you along the Villa Borghese park and dump you right on Via Veneto (where there's an Avis office). Avoid rush hour and drive defensively: Roman cars stay in their lanes like rocks in an avalanche. Parking in Rome is dangerous. Park near a police station or get advice at your hotel. The Villa Borghese underground garage is handy (L35,000/day, Metro: Spagna).

Consider this: Your car is a worthless headache in Rome. Avoid a pile of stress and save money by parking at the huge, easy, and relatively safe lot behind the Orvieto station (follow "P" signs from autostrada) and catch the train to Rome (every 2 hrs, 75 min).

# VENICE (VENEZIA)

Soak all day in this puddle of elegant decay. Venice is Europe's best-preserved big city. This car-free urban wonderland of 100 islands—laced together by 400 bridges and 2,000 alleys—survives on the artificial respirator of tourism.

Born in a lagoon 1,500 years ago as a refuge from barbarians, Venice is overloaded with tourists and is slowly sinking (unrelated facts). In the Middle Ages, the Venetians, becoming Europe's clever middlemen for east-west trade, created a great trading empire. By smuggling in the bones of St. Mark (San Marco, in about A.D. 830), Venice gained religious importance as well. With the discovery of America and new trading routes to the Orient, Venetian power ebbed. But as Venice fell, her appetite for decadence grew. Through the 17th and 18th centuries, Venice partied on the wealth accumulated through earlier centuries as a trading power.

Today Venice is home to about 70,000 people in its old city, down from a peak population of around 200,000. While there are about 500,000 in greater Venice (counting the mainland, not counting tourists), the old town has a small-town feel. Locals seem to know everyone. To see small-town Venice through the touristic flak, get away from the Rialto-San Marco tourist zone and savor the town early and late without the hordes of vacationers day-tripping in from nearby beach resorts. A 10-minute walk from the madness puts you in an idyllic Venice few tourists see.

## Planning Your Time

Venice is worth at least a day on even the speediest tour. Hyper-efficient train travelers take the night train in and/or out. Sleep in the old center to experience Venice at its best: early and late. For a one-day visit, cruise the Grand Canal, do the major sights on

# Venice

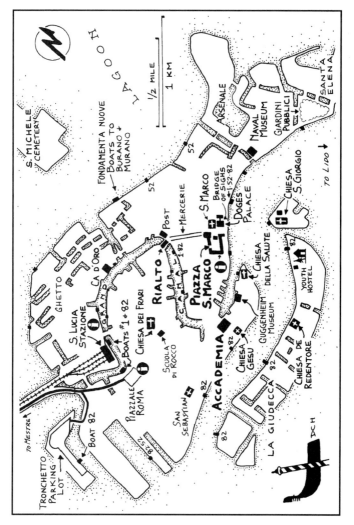

St. Mark's Square (the square itself, Doge's Palace, St. Mark's Basilica), see the Church of the Frari (Chiesa dei Frari) for art, and wander the back streets on a pub crawl (see "Eating," below). Venice's greatest sight is the city itself. Make time to simply wander. While doable in a day, Venice is worth two. It's a medieval cookie jar, and nobody's looking.

## Orientation

The island city of Venice is shaped like a fish. Its major thorough-fares are canals. The Grand Canal winds through the middle of the fish, starting at the mouth where all the people and food enter, passing under the Rialto Bridge, and ending at St. Mark's Square (San Marco). Park your 21st-century perspective at the mouth and let Venice swallow you whole.

Venice is a carless kaleidoscope of people, bridges, and odor-less canals. The city has no real streets, and addresses are hope-lessly confusing. There are six districts: San Marco (most touristy), Castello (behind San Marco), Cannaregio (from the station to the Rialto), San Polo (other side of the Rialto), Santa Croce, and Dor-soduro. Each district has about 6,000 address numbers. Luckily it's easy to find your way, since many street corners have a sign point-ing you to the nearest major landmark, such as San Marco, Accad-emia, Rialto, and Ferrovia (the train station). To find your way, navigate by landmarks, not streets. Obedient visitors stick to the main thoroughfares as directed by these signs and miss the charm of backstreet Venice.

## Tourist Information

There are TIs at the train station (daily 8:10–18:50, crowded and surly), at the far end of St. Mark's Square (Mon–Sat 9:00–17:00, friendly), and near St. Mark's Square on the lagoon (daily 10:00–18:00, sells *vaporetto* tickets, rents audioguides for self-guided walking tours). For a quick question, save time by phoning (tel. 041-529-8711, www.turismovenezia.it). At any TI, pick up a free city map and the free *Leo* bimonthly magazine, which comes with an insert, *Leo Bussola*, that lists museum hours, exhibitions, and musical events (in Italian and English). Confirm your sight-seeing plans. Ask for the fine brochures outlining three offbeat Venice walks. The free periodical entertainment guide *Un Ospite de Venezia* (a monthly listing of events, nightlife, museum hours, train and *vaporetto*—motorized bus-boat—schedules, emergency telephone numbers, and so on) is available at the TI or fancy hotel reception desks. The cheap Venice map on sale at postcard racks has much more detail than the TI map. Also consider the little guidebook (sold alongside the postcards), which comes with a city map and explanations of the major sights.

**Walking Tours:** The TI offers audioguides for self-guided walking tours of Venice's neighborhoods (5 to choose from: San Marco, Rialto, Santa Croce, Cannaregio, and Castello; prices range from L4,000 for 1 tour to L30,000 for all; available at TI at lagoon near St. Mark's Square—maybe also at other TIs in 2001).

Local guide Alessandro Schezzini gets beyond the clichés and into offbeat Venice (L175,000, 2.5 hrs, tel. & fax 041-534-5367, cellular 033-5530-9024) e-mail: venische@tiscalinet.it.

## Arrival in Venice

A three-kilometer-long causeway (with highway and train lines) connects Venice to the mainland. Mestre, Venice's sprawling mainland industrial base, has fewer crowds, cheaper hotels, plenty of parking lots, but no charm. Don't stop here (unless you're parking your car in a lot). Trains regularly connect Mestre with Venice's Santa Lucia station (6/hrly, 5 min).

**By Train:** Venice's Santa Lucia train station plops you right into the old town on the Grand Canal, an easy *vaporetto* ride or fascinating 40-minute walk from St. Mark's Square. Upon arrival, skip the station's crowded TI (the two TIs at St. Mark's Square are better); it's not worth a long wait for a miminal map (if you want a map now, buy one at a newsstand). Confirm your departure plan (stop by train info desk or just study the *partenze*—departure—posters on walls). Consider storing unnecessary heavy bags, although it's not worth it if the lines for baggage check are long, sweaty, and dreary (baggage check at platform 14, L5,000/12 hrs, L10,000/24 hrs, daily 03:45–00:30; or lockers at platform 1—L3,000–5,000, often either in use or broken). Then walk straight out of the station to the canal. The dock for *vaporetti* #1 and #82 is on your left (for downtown Venice, most recommended hotels, and Grand Canal Tour); the dock for #51 and #52 is on your right (for two recommended hotels). Buy a L6,000 ticket at the ticket window and hop on a boat for downtown (direction: Rialto or San Marco).

**By Car:** The freeway ends at Venice. Follow the green lights directing you to a parking lot with space, probably Tronchetto (across the causeway and on the right), which has a huge, multi-storied garage (L30,000/day, half price with discount coupon from your hotel). From there you'll find travel agencies masquerading as TIs and *vaporetto* docks for the boat connection (#82) to the town center. Don't let taxi boatmen con you out of the cheap (L6,000) *vaporetto* ride. Parking in Mestre is easy and cheap (open-air lots L8,000/day, L10,000/day garage across from Mestre train station).

**By Plane:** Romantics can jet to St. Mark's Square by Alila-guna speedboat (L17,000, hrly, 70 min, 6:15–24:00 from airport, 4:50–22:50 from St. Mark's Square). Or, catch a bus from the airport to the Tronchetto *vaporetto* stop: either the handy blue ATVO shuttle bus (L5,000, 2/hrly, 20 min, 5:30–20:40 to airport, 8:30–24:00 from airport, www.atvo.it) or the cheaper orange ACTV bus #5 (L1,500, 1–3/hrly, 20–40 min, 4:40–01:00). Airport info: tel. 041-260-611, flight info: tel. 041-260-9260.

## Helpful Hints

The Venice fly trap lures us in and takes our money any way it can. Count your change carefully—I catch someone shortchanging me about once a day. Accept the fact that Venice was a tourist town 400 years ago. It was, is, and always will be crowded. While 80 percent of Venice is actually an untouristy place, 80 percent of the tourists never notice. Hit the back streets.

**Get Lost:** Venice is the ideal town to explore on foot. Walk and walk to the far reaches of the town. Don't worry about getting lost. Get as lost as possible. Keep reminding yourself, "I'm on an island, and I can't get off." When it comes time to find your way, just follow the directional arrows on building corners or simply ask a local, *"Dov'è San Marco?"* ("Where is St. Mark's?"). People in the tourist business (that's most Venetians) speak some English. If they don't, listen politely, watching where their hands point, say *"Grazie,"* and head off in that direction. If you're lost, pop into a hotel and ask for their business card—it comes with a map and a prominent "you are here."

**Rip-Offs, Theft, and Help:** While pickpockets work the crowded main streets, docks, and *vaporetti*, the dark, late-night streets of Venice are safe. A service called Venezia No Problem tries to help tourists who've been mistreated by any Venetian business (toll-free tel. 800-355-920, for complaints only, not for information).

**Water:** Venetians pride themselves on having pure, safe, and tasty tap water piped in from the foothills of the Alps (which you can actually see from Venice bell towers on crisp, clear winter days).

**Money:** ATMs are plentiful and the easiest way to go. Bank rates vary. I like the Banca di Sicilia, a block toward St. Mark's Square from Campo San Bartolomeo. The American Express change desk is just off St. Mark's Square (Mon–Sat 8:30–20:00). Thomas Cook's two offices waive their commission on Thomas Cook checks but charge 4.5 percent for others (Mon–Sat 9:00–19:45, Sun 9:30–17:00, at St. Mark's Square, nearly under the tower with digital clock; or Mon–Sat 9:00–19:45, Sun 9:30–17:00, at Rialto *vaporetto* dock). Nonbank exchange bureaus like Exacto will cost you $10 more than a bank for a $200 exchange. A 24-hour cash machine near the Rialto *vaporetto* stop exchanges U.S. dollars and other currencies for lire at fair rates.

**Travel Agencies:** If you need to get train tickets, pay supplements, or make reservations, try Kele & Teo Viaggi e Turismo (cash only, Mon–Fri 8:30–12:30, 15:00–18:00, Sat 9:00–12:00, at Ponte dei Bareteri on the Mercerie midway between Rialto and St. Mark's Square, tel. 041-520-8722) or American Express (Mon–Fri 9:00–17:30, Sat 9:00–12:30, CC:A for rail tickets, CC:VMA for supplements and reservations; also offer tours of Venice April–Oct; just off St. Mark's Square at 1471, en route to the Accademia, tel. 041-520-0844). Either agency saves travelers time-consuming trips to the train station (sold at the same price as at the station).

**Post Office:** A large post office is off the far end of St. Mark's Square (on the side of square opposite the St. Mark's church, Mon–Sat 8:10–18:00, shorter hours off-season), and a branch is near the Rialto (on St. Mark's side, Mon–Fri 8:10–13:30, Sat 8:10–12:30).

**Church Services:** The San Zulian Church offers a Mass in English at 9:30 on Sunday (May–Sept, 2 blocks toward Rialto off St. Mark's Square). Gregorians would enjoy the sung Gregorian Mass at 11:00 on Sunday at San Giorgio Maggiore church (on island of San Giorgio Maggiore, visible from Doge's Palace, catch *vaporetto* #10 or #20 from San Zaccaria dock). Confirm times of Mass at TI.

**The "Rolling Venice" Youth Discount Pass:** This worthwhile L5,000 pass gives those under 30 discounts on sights and transportation plus information on cheap eating and sleeping. In summer, they have a kiosk in front of the train station (July–Sept daily 8:00–20:00). Their main office, near St. Mark's Square, is open year-round (Mon–Fri 9:30–13:00, from American Express head toward St. Mark's Square, first left, first left again through "Contarina" tunnel, follow white sign to Commune di Venezia and see the sign, Corte Contarina 1529, third floor, tel. 041-274-7651).

**Pigeon Poop:** If bombed by a pigeon, resist the initial response to wipe it off immediately—it'll just smear into your hair. Wait until it dries and flake it off cleanly.

**Laundry:** Near St. Mark's Square and many of my hotel listings is the full-service Lavanderia Gabriella (Mon–Fri 8:00–19:00, 985 Rio Terra Colonne, near St. Mark's Square, from San Zulian Church go over Ponta dei Ferali, take first right down Calle dei Armeni, tel. 041-522-1758). Near the Rialto is Lavanderia S.S. Apostoli (Mon–Sat 8:30–12:00, 15:00–19:00, closed Sun, just off Campo S.S. Apostoli on Salizada del Pistor, tel. 041-522-6650). At either place you can get nine pounds of laundry washed and dried for L30,000—confirm price carefully. Drop it by in the morning; pick it up that afternoon. (Call to be sure they're open.) Don't expect to get your clothes back ironed, folded, or even entirely dry. The modern and much cheaper Bea Vita self-serve *lavanderia* is across the canal from the station (daily 8:00–22:00, go over bridge, take first right, first left, first right).

**Etiquette:** Walk on the right and don't loiter on bridges. Picnicking is technically forbidden (keep a low profile). Dress modestly. Men should keep their shirts on. When visiting St. Mark's or other major churches, men, women, and even children should cover their knees and shoulders (or risk being turned away).

**Haircuts:** I've been getting my hair cut at Coiffeur Benito for 15 years. Benito has been keeping local men and women trim for 25 years. He's an artist—actually a "hair sculptor"— and a cut is a fun diversion from the tourist grind (L35,000, Tue–Sat 8:30–13:30, 15:30–19:30, behind San Zulian Church near St. Mark's Square, Calle S. Zulian Gia del Strazzanol 592A, tel. 041-528-6221).

## Downtown Venice

**LODGING:**

| | | |
|---|---|---|
| ❶ GUERATTO | ⓫ BEL SITO | ㉑ GIORGIONE |
| ❷ STURION | ⓬ MARIN | ㉒ AMERICAN |
| ❸ CANADA | ⓭ LEVI | ㉓ BELLE ARTI |
| ❹ ASTORIA | ⓮ GAMBERO | ㉔ LA CALCINA |
| ❺ CANEVA | ⓯ CAMPIELLO | ㉕ CHIESA VALDESE |
| ❻ RIVA | ⓰ PAGANELLI | |
| ❼ PIAVE | ⓱ ACCADEMIA | |
| ❽ FONTANA | ⓲ GALLERIA | |
| ❾ DONI | ⓳ ALBORETTI | ● 1·82 VAPORETTI STOPS |
| ❿ CORONA | ⓴ ALLA SCALA |       W/ LINE #'S |
| | | ●····● TRAGHETTO ROUTES |

## Getting around Venice

The public transit system is a fleet of motorized bus-boats called
*vaporetti*. They work like city buses except that they never get a
flat, the stops are docks, and if you get off between stops, you may
drown. For most, only two lines matter: #1 is the slow boat, taking
45 minutes to make every stop along the entire length of the
Grand Canal, and #82 is the fast boat that zips down the Grand

Canal in 25 minutes, stopping mainly at Tronchetto (car park), Piazzale Roma (bus station), Ferrovia (train station), Rialto Bridge, and San Marco. Buy a L6,000 ticket ideally before boarding or from a conductor on board. (Families of 3 or more pay L5,000 per person.) A round-trip (*andata e ritorno*) costs L10,000 (good for 2 trips within a day on any line).

You can buy a pass for a 24-hour period (L18,000, families of 3 or more pay L15,000 apiece), 72 hours (L35,000), and one week (L60,000)—it's fun to be able to hop on and off spontaneously. Technically, luggage costs the same as dogs—L6,000—but I've never been charged. Riding free? There's a one-in-six chance a conductor will fine you L32,000.

Only three bridges cross the Grand Canal, but *traghetti* (little L700 ferry gondolas, marked on better maps) shuttle locals and in-the-know tourists across the Grand Canal at several handy locations (see Downtown Venice map). Take advantage of these time savers. They can also save money. For instance, while most tourists take the L6,000 *vaporetto* to connect St. Mark's with Salute Church, a L700 *traghetto* also does the job.

## Grand Canal Tour of Venice

For a ▲▲▲ joyride, introduce yourself to Venice by boat. You can ride boat #82 (too fast, 25 minutes, be certain you're on a "San Marco via Rialto" boat) or #1 (slow, 45 minutes). Either way, cruise the entire Canale Grande from Tronchetto (car park) or Ferrovia (train station) to San Marco. If you can't snag a front seat, lurk nearby and take one when it becomes available or find an outside seat in the stern. This ride has the best light and least crowds early in the morning. Twilight is also good. While Venice is a barrage on the senses that hardly needs a narration, these notes give the cruise a little meaning and help orient you to this great city. Some city maps (on sale at postcard racks) have a handy Grand Canal map on the back.

Venice, built in a lagoon, sits on pilings—pine trees driven 15 feet into the clay. About 25 miles of **canals** drain the city, dumping like streams into the Grand Canal. Technically, there are three canals (Grand, Giudecca, and Cannaregio), and the other 45 "canals" are rivers.

Venice is a city of **palaces**. The most lavish were built fronting this canal. This cruise is the only way to really appreciate the front doors of this unique and historic chorus line of mansions from the days when Venice was the world's richest city. Strict laws prohibit any changes in these buildings, so while landowners gnash their teeth, we can enjoy Europe's best-preserved medieval city—slowly rotting. Many of the grand buildings are now vacant. Others harbor chandeliered elegance above mossy, empty ground floors.

Start at **Tronchetto** (the bus and car park) or the **train**

**station**. The station, one of the few modern buildings in town, was built in 1954. It's been the gateway into Venice since 1860, when the first station was built. "F.S." stands for "Ferrovie dello Stato," the Italian state railway system. The bridge at the station is the first of only three that cross the Canale Grande.

The **ghetto** is shortly after the train tation, on the left. Look down Cannaregio Canal (opposite the Riva di Biasio stop). The twin pink six-story buildings (known as the "skyscrapers") are a reminder of how densely populated the world's original ghetto was. Set aside as the local Jewish quartei in 1516, the area became extremely crowded. This urban island (behind the San Marcuola stop) developed into one of the most closely knit business and cultural quarters of all Jewish communities in Italy.

As you cruise, notice the traffic signs. Venice's main thorough-fare is busy with traffic. You'll see all kinds of **boats**: taxis, police boats, garbage boats, and even brown-and-white UPS boats. Venice's sleek, black, graceful **gondolas** are a symbol of the city. While used gondolas cost around $10,000, new ones run up to $30,000 apiece. They're built with a slight curve so that one oar propels them in a straight line. Today, with over 500 gondoliers joyriding around the churning *vaporetti*, there's a lot of conges-tion on the Grand Canal. Watch your *vaporetto* driver curse the gondoliers.

Opposite the San Stae stop look for the faded frescoes. Imagine the facades of the Grand Canal in its day: frescoed by masters like Tintoretto and glittering with mosiacs.

At the Ca d'Oro stop notice the lacy Gothic palace. Named the **"House of Gold"**—the frilly edge of the roof was once gilded—it's considered the most elegant Venetian Gothic palace on the canal. Unfortunately there's little to see inside (L6,000, daily 8:15–16:00, free peek through hole in door of courtyard).

On the right, the outdoor **fish and produce market** bustles with people in the morning but is quiet the rest of the day. (This is a great scene to wander through—even though new European hygiene standards required a less-colorful remodeling job last year.) Can you see the *traghetto* gondola ferrying shoppers—standing like Washingtons crossing the Delaware—back and forth? Ahead, above the post office, the golden angel of the Campanile faces the wind and marks St. Mark's Square (where this tour ends). The huge **post office**, with *servizio postale* boats moored at its blue posts, is on the left just before the Rialto Bridge.

A major landmark of Venice, the **Rialto Bridge** is lined with shops and tourists. The third bridge on this spot, it was built in 1592. Earlier Rialto Bridges could open to let in big ships. After 1592, the Grand Canal was closed to shipping and became a canal of palaces. With a span of 42 meters and founda-tions stretching 200 meters on either side, the Rialto was an impressive engineering feat in its day. Locals call the summit of this bridge the "icebox of Venice" for its cool breeze. Tourists call it a great place to kiss. *Rialto* means "high river." The restaurants beyond the bridge feature high prices and low quality.

**The Rialto**, a separate town in the early days of Venice, has always been the commercial district, while San Marco was the religious and governmental center. Today a street called the Mercerie connects the two, providing travelers with human traffic jams and a gauntlet of shopping temptations.

Beyond the Rialto on the left, notice the long stretch of **merchants' palaces**, each with proud and different facades. Many feature the Roman palace design of twin towers flanking a huge set of central windows. These were showrooms designed to let in maximum sunlight.

Take a deep whiff of Venice. What's all this nonsense about stinky canals? All I smell is my shirt. By the way, how's your captain? Smooth dockings? To get to know him, stand up in the bow and block his view.

The rising water level takes its toll. Many canal-level floors are abandoned. Notice how many buildings have a foundation of waterproof white stone (*pietra d'Istria*) upon which the bricks sit high and dry. The posts—historically painted gaily with the equivalent of family coats of arms—don't rot under water. But the wood at the water line does rot. Notice how the rich marble facades are just a veneer covering no-nonsense brick buildings. Look up at the characteristic chimneys.

After the San Silvestro stop you'll see (on the right) a **13th-century admiral's palace**. Venetian admirals marked their palaces with twin obelisks.

After the San Tomá stop look down the side canal (on the right) before the bridge to see the traffic light, the **fire station**, and the fireboats ready to go.

These days, when buildings are being renovated, huge murals with images of the building mask the ugly scaffolding. Corporations hide the scaffolding out of goodwill (and get their name— e.g., Frette—on the mural).

The wooden Accademia Bridge crosses the Grand Canal and leads to the **Accademia Gallery** (neoclassical facade just after the British consulate on the right), filled with the best Venetian paintings. The bridge was put up in 1932 as a temporary fix for the original iron one. Locals liked it, so it stayed.

Cruising under the bridge, you'll get a classic view of the **Salute Church** (ahead), built as a thanks to God when the devastating plague of 1630 passed. It's claimed that more than a million trees were piled together to build a foundation upon the solid clay 35 meters below sea level. Much of the surrounding countryside was deforested by Venice. Trees were needed both to fuel the furnaces of its booming glass industry and to prop up this city in the mud.

The low white building on the right (between the bridge and the church) is the **Peggy Guggenheim Gallery**. She willed the city a fine collection of modern art. The Salviati building (with the fine mosaic) is a glass factory.

Just before the Salute stop (on the right), the house with the big view windows and the red and wild Andy Warhol painting on the living-room wall (often behind white drapes) was lived in by Mick Jagger. In the 1970s this was famous as Venice's rock-and-roll-star party house.

The building on the right with the golden ball is the **Dogana da Mar**, a 16th-century customs house. Its two bronze Atlases hold a statue of Fortune riding the ball. While there are no hotels on this side, all the buildings on the left are fancy Grand Canal hotels.

As you prepare to deboat at San Marco, look from left to right out over the lagoon. A wide harborfront walk leads past the town's most elegant hotels to the green area in the distance. This is the public garden, the only sizable park in town. Farther out is the **lido**, Venice's beach. It's tempting, with its sand and casinos, but its car traffic breaks into the medieval charm of Venice.

The dreamy church that seems to float is the architect Palladio's **San Giorgio Maggiore**. It's just a *vaporetto* ride away (#10 or #20 from San Zaccaria dock). Find the Tintoretto paintings in the church (such as the *Last Supper*) and take the elevator up the tower for a terrific view (L3,000, daily 9:30–13:00, 14:30–18:30, Gregorian Mass at 11:00 on Sun, tel. 041-522-7827). Across the lagoon (to your right) is a residential island called Giudecca.

Get out at the San Marco stop. Directly ahead is Harry's Bar. Hemingway drank here when it was a characteristic no-name *osteria* and the gondoliers' hangout. Today, of course, it's the overpriced hangout of well-dressed Americans who don't mind paying triple for their Bellinis (peach juice with Prosecco wine) to make the scene. St. Mark's Square is just around the corner.

For more *vaporetto* fun, ride a boat around the city and out into the lagoon and back (ask for the *circulare;* pron. cheer-koo-LAH-ray). Plenty of boats leave from San Marco for the beach (*lido*), and speedboats offer tours of nearby islands: Burano is a quiet, picturesque fishing and lace town, Murano specializes in glassblowing, and Torcello has the oldest churches and mosaics but is otherwise dull and desolate. Boat #12 takes you to these remote points slower and cheaper.

## Sights—Venice, on St. Mark's Square

▲▲▲**St. Mark's Square (Piazza San Marco)**—Surrounded by splashy and historic buildings, Piazza San Marco is filled with music, lovers, pigeons, and tourists by day and is your private rendezvous with the Middle Ages late at night. Europe's greatest dance floor is the romantic place to be. In a hard rain, St. Mark's Square is the first place in Venice to flood (you might see stacked wooden benches; when the square floods, these are put end to end to make elevated sidewalks).

Venice's best TIs (and WCs) are here; one TI is on the square, the other on the lagoon. To find the TI on the square, stand with your back to the church, and go to the far corner on your left; the office is tucked away in the arcade (daily 9:00–17:00, near this TI is a L1,000 WC open daily 8:00–21:00—it's a few steps beyond St. Mark's Square en route to American Express office and Accademia; see Albergo Diorno—marked on pavement). The other TI is on the lagoon (daily 10:00–18:00, walk out to water by Doge's Palace, go right; nearby WCs open daily 9:00–19:00).

With your back to the church, survey one of Europe's great urban spaces and the only square in Venice to merit the title "Piazza." Nearly two football fields long, it's surrounded by the offices of the republic. On the right are the "old offices" (16th-century Renaissance). On the left are the "new offices" (17th-century Baroque). Napoleon, after enclosing the square with the more simple and austere neoclassical wing across the far end, called this "the most beautiful drawing room in Europe."

The clock tower, a Renaissance tower built in 1496, marks the entry to the Mercerie, the main shopping drag, which connects St. Mark's Square with the Rialto. From the piazza you can see the bronze men (Moors) swing their huge clappers at the top of each hour. In the 17th century one of them knocked an unsuspecting worker off the top and to his death—probably the first-ever killing by a robot. Notice the world's first "digital" clock on the tower facing the square (with dramatic flips every 5 minutes).

For a slow and pricey evening thrill, invest L12,000 (plus L7,000 if the orchestra plays) in a beer or coffee in one of the elegant cafés with the dueling orchestras. If you're going to sit awhile and savor the scene, it's worth the splurge. For the most thrills L2,000 can get you in Venice, buy a bag of pigeon seed and become popular in a flurry. To get everything airborne, toss your sweater in the air.

▲▲**St. Mark's Basilica**—Since about A.D. 830 this basilica has housed the saint's bones. The mosaic above the door at the far left of the church shows two guys carrying Mark's coffin into the church. Mark looks pretty grumpy after the long voyage from Egypt.

To enter the church, modest dress is required even of kids (no shorts or bare shoulders); T-shirt sales at kiosks outside the entrance are brisk. In peak season, there can be long lines of people waiting to get into the church. People who ignore the dress code hold up the line while they plead fruitlessly with—or put on extra clothes under the watchful eyes of—the dress code police.

## Floods and a Dying City

Venice floods about 60 times a year—normally in winter.
Venetian floods start in St. Mark's Square. The entry of the
church is the lowest spot in town. The meters at the base of
the outside of the bell tower, or campanile (near the exit,
facing the grand square), show the current sea level (*livello
marea*). Find the mark showing the high-water level from the
terrible floods of 1966 (waist level on right). When wind and
tide combine to raise the water level to one meter, a warning
siren sounds. It repeats if a serious flood is imminent.

In 1965 Venice's population was over 150,000. Since
the flood of 1966 the population has been shrinking. Today
the population is about 70,000 ... and geriatric. Sad, yes,
but imagine raising a family here: the fragile nature of things
means piles of regulations (no biking, and so on), and costs
are high—even though the government is now subsidizing
rents to keep people from moving out. You can easily get
glass and tourist trinkets, but it's hard to find groceries.
And floods and the humidity make house maintenance an
expensive pain.

The church has 4,000 square meters of Byzantine mosaics,
the best and oldest of which are in the atrium (turn right as you
enter and stop under the last dome—this may be roped off, but
dome is still partially visible). Facing the church, gape up (it's
OK, no pigeons), and read clockwise the story of Adam and Eve
that rings the bottom of the dome. Now, facing the piazza, look
domeward for the story of Noah, the ark, and the flood (two by
two, the wicked being drowned, Noah sending out the dove, a
happy rainbow, and a sacrifice of thanks).

Step inside the church (stairs on right lead to bronze horses)
and notice the rolling mosaic marble floor. As you shuffle under the
central dome, look up for the Ascension (free, no photos, Mon–Sat
9:45–17:30, Sun 14:00–17:00, tel. 041-522-5205). See the schedule
board in the atrium listing two free English guided tours (July–Aug
Mon–Fri up to 4 tours/day, Sat 1/day, off-season 2/weekly, 30–90
minutes depending on guide and group). The church is particularly
beautiful when lit (unpredictable schedule, maybe middays 11:00–
12:00, Sat–Sun 14:00–17:00 plus 18:45 Mass on Sat).

In the **museum** upstairs (L3,000, daily 9:45–16:00, sometimes
until 17:00, enter from atrium either before or after you tour
church), you can see an up-close mosaic exhibition, a fine view of
the church interior, a view of the square from the horse balcony,
and (inside, in their own room) the newly restored original bronze

horses. These well-traveled horses, made during the days of
Alexander the Great (4th century B.C.), were taken to Rome by
Nero, to Constantinople/Istanbul by Constantine, to Venice by
crusaders, to Paris by Napoleon, back "home" to Venice when
Napoleon fell, and finally indoors and out of the acidic air.

The **treasury** and **altarpiece** of the church (L3,000 each,
daily 9:45–17:10, 16:10 in winter) give you the best chance outside
of Istanbul or Ravenna to see the glories of Byzantium. Venetian
crusaders looted the Christian city of Constantinople and brought
home piles of lavish loot (until the advent of TV evangelism,
perhaps the lowest point in Christian history). Much of this
plunder is stored in the treasury (*tesoro*) of San Marco. As you
view these treasures, remember most were made in A.D. 500,
while Western Europe was still rutting in the mud. Beneath
the high altar lies the body of St. Mark ("Marxus") and the Pala
d'Oro, a golden altar piece made with 80 Byzantine enamels
(A.D. 1000–1300). Each shows a religious scene set in gold and
precious stones. Both of these sights are interesting and historic,
but neither is as much fun as two bags of pigeon seed.

▲▲▲**Doge's Palace (Palazzo Ducale)**—The seat of the Venetian
government and home of its ruling duke, or doge, this was the most
powerful half acre in Europe for 400 years (April–Oct daily 9:00–
19:00, Nov–March daily 9:00–17:00, last entry 90 minutes before
closing, tel. 041-522-4951). The L18,000 combo ticket includes
admission to a number of lesser museums: Museo Correr (see
below), Palazzo Mocenigo (textiles and costumes, closed Mon),
Museo del Vetro di Murano (glass museum on Murano, closed
Wed), and Museo del Merletto di Burano (lace museum on Burano,
closed Tue). The ticket is valid for three months.

While each room in the Doge's Palace has a short English
description, the fast-moving, 90-minute, tape-recorded guided
tour wand is wonderfully done and worth the L7,000 if you don't
have *Rick Steves' Mona Winks* and you're planning to really understand the Palace. Vagabond lovers, sightseeing cheek to cheek,
can crank up the volume and split one wand. Audioguides are
rentable up to two hours before closing (until 17:00 April–Oct,
until 15:00 Nov–March).

The new "Secret Itineraries Tour," which follows the Doge's
tracks into rooms not included in the general admission price,
must be booked in advance (L24,000, at 10:00 and 11:30 in English,
1.25 hrs, call 041-522-4951 to confirm times and to reserve).

The palace was built to show off the power and wealth of the
republic and remind all visitors that Venice was number one.
In typical Venetian Gothic style, the bottom has pointy arches,
and the top has an Eastern or Islamic flavor. Its columns sat on
pedestals, but in the thousand years since they were erected, the
palace has settled into the mud, and the bases have vanished.

Enjoy the newly restored facades from the courtyard. Notice a grand staircase (with nearly naked Moses and Paul Newman at the top). Even the most powerful visitors climbed this to meet the doge. This was the beginning of an architectural power trip. The doge, the elected-for-life king of this "dictatorial republic," lived with his family on the first floor near the halls of power. From his lavish quarters you'll follow the one-way tour through the public rooms of the top floor, finishing with the Bridge of Sighs and the prison. The place is wallpapered with masterpieces by Veronese and Tintoretto. Don't worry much about the great art. Enjoy the building.

In room 12, the Senate Room, the 200 senators met, debated, and passed laws. From the center of the ceiling, Tintoretto's *Triumph of Venice* shows the city in all her glory. Lady Venice, in heaven with the Greek gods, stands high above the lesser nations who swirl respectfully at her feet with gifts.

The Armory shows remnants of the military might the empire employed to keep the east-west trade lines open (and the local economy booming). Squint out the window at the far end for a fine view of Palladio's San Giorgio Maggiore Church and the lido (cars, casinos, crowded beaches) in the distance.

After the huge brown globes, you'll enter the giant Hall of the Grand Council (180 feet long, capacity 2,000), where the entire nobility met to elect the senate and doge. Ringing the room are portraits of 76 doges (in chronological order). One, a doge who opposed the will of the Grand Council, is blacked out. Behind the doge's throne, you can't miss Tintoretto's monsterpiece, *Paradise*. At 1,700 square feet, this is the world's largest oil painting. Christ and Mary are surrounded by a heavenly host of 500 saints.

Walking over the Bridge of Sighs, you'll enter the prisons. The doges could sentence, torture, and jail their opponents secretly and in the privacy of their own homes. As you walk back over the bridge, squeeze your arm through the marble lattice window and wave to the gang of tourists gawking at you.

▲▲**Museo Civico Correr**—The city history museum is now included (whether you like it or not) with the Doge's Palace admission. In the Napoleon Wing you'll see fine neoclassical works by Canova. Then peruse armor, banners, and paintings recreating festive days of the Venetian Republic. The top floor lays out a fine overview of Venetian art. And just before the cafeteria a room is filled with traditional games. There are fine English descriptions and great Piazza San Marco views throughout (L18,000 combo ticket with Doge's Palace and other museums, enter in arcade directly opposite church, April–Oct daily 9:00–19:00, Nov–March daily 9:00–17:00, tel. 041-522-4951).

▲**Campanile di San Marco**—Ride the elevator 300 feet to the top of the bell tower for the best view in Venice. This tower crumbled into a pile of bricks in 1902, a thousand years after it was built. For an ear-shattering experience, be on top when the bells ring (L10,000, daily 9:00–21:00 in summer, until 19:00 otherwise). The golden angel at its top always faces into the wind. Beat the crowds and enjoy crisp air at 9:00.

## More Sights—Venice

▲▲**Galleria dell' Accademia**—Venice's top art museum, packed with highlights of the Venetian Renaissance, features paintings by Bellini, Veronese, Tiepolo, Giorgione, Testosterone, and Canaletto. It's just over the wooden Accademia Bridge. Expect long lines in the late morning because they allow only 300 visitors in at a time; visit early or late to miss crowds (L12,000, Mon 8:15–14:00, Tue–Sun 8:15–19:15, shorter hours off-season, audioguide-L7,000 or L10,000 with 2 earphones, English info sheets in some rooms, guidebook-L15,000, no photos, tel. 041-522-2247). Hour-long guided tours run Monday through Friday at 10:00, 11:00, and 12:00 for L10,000 (you can skip to the front of the line if buying a tour).

There's a decent pizzeria at the bridge (Pizzeria Accademia Foscarini; see "Eating," below), a public WC under it, and usually a classic shell game going on on top of it (study the system as partners in the crowd win big money).

▲**Peggy Guggenheim Collection**—This popular collection of far-out art offers one of Europe's best reviews of the art styles of the 20th century. Stroll through Cubism (Picasso, Braque), surrealism (Dalí, Ernst), futurism (Boccione, Carra), American abstract expressionism (Pollock), and a sprinkling of Klee, Calder, and Chagall (L12,000, Wed–Mon 10:00–18:00, Sat until 22:00 April–Oct, closed Tue, audioguide-L8,000, guidebook-L8,000, free baggage check, photos allowed only in garden and terrace— overlooking Grand Canal, near Accademia, tel. 041-240-5411).

▲▲**Chiesa dei Frari**—This great Gothic Franciscan church, an artistic highlight of Venice featuring three great masters, offers more art per lira than any other Venetian sight. Freeload on English-language tours to get the most out of the Titian *Assumption* above the high altar. Then move one chapel to the right to see Donatello's wood carving of St. John the Baptist almost live. And, for the climax, continue right through an arch into the sacristy to sit before Bellini's *Madonna and the Saints*. The genius of Bellini, perhaps the greatest Venetian painter, is obvious in the pristine clarity, believable depth, and reassuring calm of this three-paneled altar piece. Notice the rich colors of Mary's clothing and how good it is to see a painting in its intended setting. For many, these three pieces of art make a visit to the Accademia Gallery unnecessary (or they may whet your appetite for more). Before leaving, check out the neoclassical, pyramid-shaped tomb of Canova and (opposite that) the grandiose tomb of Titian the Venetian. Compare the carved marble Assumption behind his tombstone portrait with the painted original above the high altar (L4,000, Mon–Sat 9:00–18:00, Sun 13:00–18:00).

▲**Scuola di San Rocco**—Next to the Frari Church, another lavish building bursts with art, including some 50 Tintorettos. The best paintings are upstairs, especially the *Crucifixion* in the smaller room. View the neck-breaking splendor with one of the mirrors (*specchio*) available at the entrance (L9,000, daily 9:00–17:30). For *molto* Tiepolo (14 stations of the cross), drop by the nearby Church of San Polo.

**Ca' Rezzonico**—This 18th-century Grand Canal *palazzo* is the Museo del '700 Veneziano, offering a good look at the life of Venice's rich and famous in the 1700s (at a *vaporetto* stop of the same name, tel. 041-522-4543). It will probably be closed for restoration through Spring of 2001.

**Santa Elena**—For a pleasant peek into a completely untouristy residential side of Venice, catch the boat from St. Mark's Square to the neighborhood of Santa Elena (at the fish's tail). This 100-year-old suburb lives as if there were no tourism. You'll find a kid-friendly park, a few lazy restaurants, and beautiful sunsets over San Marco.

## Gondola Rides

A rip-off for some, this is a traditional must for romantics. Gondoliers charge about L120,000 for a 40-minute ride during the day; from 20:00 on, figure on L150,000 to L200,000 (for *musica*—singer and accordionist, it's an additional L170,000 during day, L190,000 after 20:00). You can divide the cost—and the romance—among up to six people (only 2 people get to sit side by side). Glide through nighttime Venice with your head on someone else's shoulder. Follow the moon as it sails past otherwise unseen buildings. Silhouettes gaze down from bridges while window glitter spills onto the black water. You're anonymous in the city of masks as the rhythmic thrust of your striped-shirted gondolier turns old crows into songbirds. This is extremely relaxing (and I think worth the extra to experience at night). Since you might get a narration plus conversation with your gondolier, talk with several and choose one you like who speaks English well.

For a glimpse at the only gondola workshop in Venice, visit the Accademia neighborhood. Walk down the Accademia side of the canal Fondamente Nani. As you approach Giudecca Canal you'll see the beached gondolas on your right across the Nani Canal.

For cheap gondola thrills, stick to the L700 one-minute ferry ride on a Grand Canal *traghetto* or hang out on a bridge along the gondola route and wave at (or drop leftover pigeon seed on) romantics.

## Festivals

Venice's most famous is **Carnevale** (Feb. 17–27 in 2001). Carnevale, which means "farewell to meat," originated centuries ago as a wild two-month-long party leading up to the austerity of Lent. In Carnevale's heyday—the 1600s and 1700s—you could do pretty much anything with anybody from any social class if you were wearing a mask. These days it's a tamer 10-day celebration, culminating in a huge dance lit with fireworks on St. Mark's Square. Sporting masks and costumes, Venetians from kids to businessmen join in the fun. Drawing the biggest crowds of the year, Carnevale has nearly been a victim of its success, driving away many Venetians (who skip out on the craziness to go ski in the Dolomites).

The **Feast of the Redeemer** features a parade and fireworks (July 21 in 2001). The colorful **Historical Regatta** fills the Grand Canal with old-time boats and pageantry (Sept 2 in 2001).

## Shopping

Shoppers like Carnevale masks, lace (a specialty of Burano, see below, but sold in Venice as well), empty books with handmade covers, and paintings—especially of Venice. If you're buying a substantial amount from nearly any shop, bargain. It's accepted and almost expected. Offer less and offer to pay cash; merchants are very conscious of the bite taken by credit-card companies.

Popular Venetian glass is available in many forms: vases, tea sets, decanters, glasses, jewelry, lamps, sculptures (such as solid-glass aquariums), and on and on. Shops will ship it home for you (snap a photo of it before it's packed up). If you're serious about glass, visit the small shops on Murano Island. Murano's glass-blowing demonstrations are fun; you'll usually see a vase and a "leetle 'orse" made from molten glass. In Venice, demos are given by various companies around St. Mark's Square, but they're only for groups; to see a demo, you'd have to sneak in with a group waiting outside. In Venice, glass-bead necklaces—simple, packable souvenirs—are cheap at vendors' stalls, expensive at shops.

Salizada San Samuele is a nontouristy street with several artsy shops. Livio de Marchi's wood sculpture shop is delightful even when it's closed. Check out the window displays for his latest creations: socks, folded shirts, teddy bears, "paper" sacks, all carved from wood (Mon–Fri 9:30–12:30, 13:30–18:30, nearest major landmark is Accademia Bridge—on St. Mark's side, Salizada San Samuele 3157, *vaporetto* stop: San Samuele, or if approaching by foot, follow signs to Palazzo Grassi, tel. 041-528-5694, www.liviodemarchi.com).

## Sights—Venice Lagoon

Several interesting islands hide out in the Venice Lagoon. **Burano**, famous for its lace, is a sleepy island with a sleepy

## Venice Lagoon

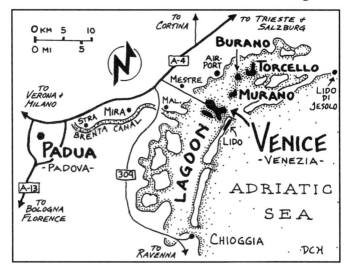

community—village Venice without the glitz. Lace fans enjoy Scuola di Merletti (L8,000, Wed–Mon 10:00–17:00, closed Tue, tel. 041-730-034).

**Torcello**, another lagoon island, is dead except for its church, which claims to be the oldest in Venice (L5,000, daily 10:30–17:30, tel. 041-730-084). It's impressive for its mosaics but not worth a look on a short visit unless you really have your heart set on Ravenna but can't make it there.

The island of **Murano**, famous for its glass factories, has the Museo Vetrario, which displays the very best of 700 years of Venetian glassmaking (L8,000, Thu–Tue 10:00–17:00, closed Wed, tel. 041-739-586).

The islands are reached easily, cheaply, and slowly by *vaporetto* (depart from San Zaccaria dock nearest the Bridge of Sighs/Doge's Palace, line #12 connects all 3 islands, can also take #41 to Murano, then #12 to the other islands). Four-hour speed-boat tours of these three lagoon destinations leave twice a day (usually 9:30 and 14:30; 1/day winter at 14:30, L30,000, tel. 041-523-8835) from the dock near the Doge's Palace; the tours are indeed speedy, stopping for roughly 35 minutes at each island.

## Nightlife in Venice

Venice is quiet at night, as tour groups are back in the cheaper hotels of Mestre, and the masses of day-trippers return to their beach resorts. Gondolas cost nearly double but are doubly romantic and relaxing under the moon. *Vaporettos* are nearly empty, and it's a great time to cruise the Grand Canal on the slow boat #1.

Take your pick of traditional Vivaldi concerts in churches throughout town. Vivaldi is as trendy here as Strauss in Vienna and Mozart in Salzburg. In fact, you'll find frilly young Vivaldis all over town hawking concert tickets. The TI has a list of this week's concerts (tickets from L35,000). If you see a concert at Scuola di San Rocco, you can enjoy the art (which you're likely to pay L9,000 for during the day) for free during the intermission.

On St. Mark's Square, the dueling café orchestras entertain. Every night, enthusiastic musicians play the same songs, creating the same irresistible magic. Hang out for free behind the tables (which allows you to easily move on to the next orchestra when the musicians take a break) or spring for a seat and enjoy a fun and gorgeously set concert. If you sit awhile it can be L20,000 well spent (drink L12,000 plus a one-time L7,000 fee for entertainment).

You're not a tourist, you're a living part of a soft Venetian night...an alley cat with money. Streetlamp halos, live music, floodlit history, and a ceiling of stars make St. Mark's magic at midnight. In the misty light, the moon has a golden hue. Shine with the old lanterns on the gondola piers where the sloppy Grand Canal splashes at the Doge's Palace...reminiscing. Comfort the small statues of the four frightened tetrarchs (ancient Byzantine emperors) where the Doge's Palace hits the basilica. Cuddle history.

## Sleeping in Venice
### (L2,000 = about $1, country code: 39)
Sleep Code: **S** = Single, **D** = Double/Twin, **T** = Triple, **Q** = Quad, **b** = bathroom, **t** = toilet only, **s** = shower only, **CC** = Credit Card (**V**isa, **M**asterCard, **A**mex), **SE** = Speaks English, **NSE** = No English. Breakfast is included unless otherwise noted. Air-conditioning, when available, is usually only turned on in summer. See map on page 86 for hotel locations. Virtually all of these hotels are central.

Reserve a room as soon as you know when you'll be in town. Book direct—not through any tourist agency. Call first to see what's available. Follow up with a fax or phone call to reconfirm. Most places will take a credit card for a deposit. If everything's full, don't despair. Call a day or two in advance and fill in a cancellation. If you arrive on an overnight train, your room may not be ready. Drop your bag at the hotel and dive right into Venice.

I've listed prices for peak season: April, May, June, September, and October. Prices can get soft in July, August, and winter. Hotels sometimes give discounts if you stay at least three nights and/or pay cash. If on a budget, ask for a cheaper room or a discount. Always ask. I've listed rooms in two neighborhoods: in the Rialto-San Marco action and in a quiet Dorsoduro area behind the Accademia Gallery. If a hotel has a Web site, check it.

Hotel Web sites are particularly valuable for Venice, because they often come with a map that at least gives you the illusion you can easily find the place.

### Sleeping between St. Mark's Square and Campo Santa Maria di Formosa (zip code: 30122)

**Hotel Riva,** with gleaming marble hallways and bright modern rooms, is romantically situated on a canal along the gondola serenade route. You could actually dunk your breakfast rolls in the canal (but don't). Sandro may hold a corner (*angolo*) room if you ask. Confirm prices and reconfirm reservations, as readers have had trouble with both (2 D with adjacent showers-L170,000, Db-L200,000, Tb-L280,000, Ponte dell' Angelo, #5310 Castello, 30122 Venezia, tel. 041-522-7034, fax 041-528-5551, unenthusiastic receptionists don't speak English). Face St. Mark's cathedral, walk behind it on the left along Calle de la Canonica, take the first left (at blue "Pauly & C" mosaic in street), continue straight, go over the bridge, and angle right to the hotel.

   **Locanda Piave,** with 15 fine rooms above a bright and classy lobby, is fresh, modern, and comfortable (Db-L260,000, Tb-L340,000, family suites-L370,000 for 3, L410,000 for 4, L420,000 for 5 people, prices with this book, CC:VMA but 10 percent discount with cash, air-con; *vaporetto* #1 to San Zaccaria, to the left of Hotel Danieli is Calle de le Rasse, take it, turn left at end, turn right nearly immediately at square—S.S. Filippo e Giacomo—on Calle Rimpeto La Sacrestie, go over bridge, take second left, hotel is two short blocks ahead on Ruga Giuffa #4838/40, Castello, 30122 Venezia, tel. 041-528-5174, fax 041-523-8512, www.elmoro.com/alpiave, e-mail: hotel .alpiave@iol.it, Mirella, Paolo, and Ilaria SE, faithful Molly NSE). They have a couple of apartments for L350,000 to L440,000 (for 3–5 people, cash only, includes kitchenette, 2-night minimum during high season: mid-March–mid-July, Sept–mid-Nov, cheaper in Aug for 2-night stays).

### Sleeping on or near the Waterfront, east of St. Mark's Square

These places, about one canal down from the Bridge of Sighs on or just off the Riva degli Schiavoni waterfront promenade, rub drainpipes with Venice's most palatial five-star hotels. The first three—while pricey for the location and not particularly friendly—are professional and comfortable. Ride *vaporetto* #1 to San Zaccaria.

   **Hotel Campiello,** a lacy and bright little 16-room, air-conditioned place, was once part of a 19th-century convent. It's ideally located 50 meters off the waterfront (Sb-L200,000, Db-L230,000–300,000, includes buffet breakfast, CC:VMA,

5 percent discount with cash, 30 percent discount mid-Nov–Feb excluding Christmas and Carnevale; behind Hotel Savoia, up Calle del Vin off the waterfront street—Riva Schiavoni, San Zaccaria #4647, tel. 041-520-5764, fax 041-520-5798, www.hcampiello.it, e-mail: campiello@hcampiello.it, family run for 4 generations, sisters Monica and Nicoletta).

**Albergo Paganelli** is right on the waterfront—on Riva degli Schiavoni—and has a few incredible view rooms (S-L160,000, Sb-L220,000, D-L220,000, Db-L260,000–350,000, Db with view-L350,000, request *"con vista"* for view, CC:VMA, air-con, prices often soft, at San Zaccaria *vaporetto* stop, Riva degli Schiavoni #4182, Castello, 30122 Venezia, tel. 041-522-4324, fax 041-523-9267, www.gpnet.it/paganelli, e-mail: hotelpag@tin.it). With spacious rooms, carved and gilded headboards, chandeliers, and hair dryers, this hotelesque place is a good value. Seven of their 22 rooms are in a less interesting but equally comfortable *dependencia* a block off the canal.

**Albergo Doni** is a dark, hardwood, clean, and quiet place with 12 dim-but-classy rooms run by a likable smart aleck named Gina (D-L130,000, Db-L170,000, T-L180,000, Tb-L230,000, ceiling fans, air-con for L20,000 extra per night, use credit card to secure telephone reservations but must pay in cash, Riva Schiavoni, San Zaccaria N. #4656 Calle del Vin, tel. & fax 041-522-4267, Niccolo and Gina SE). Leave Riva Degli Schiavoni on Calle del Vin and go 100 meters with a left jog.

**Hotel Fontana** is a cozy, two-star, family-run place with 14 rooms and lots of stairs on a touristy square two bridges behind St. Mark's Square (Sb-L100,000–180,000, Db-L150,000–270,000, family rooms, fans, 10 percent discount with cash, CC:VMA; *vaporetto* #1 to San Zaccaria, find Calle de le Rasse—to left of Hotel Danieli—take it, turn right at end, continue to first square, Campo San Provolo, Castello 4701, tel. 041-522-0579, fax 041-523-1040, www.hotelfontana.it).

**Albergo Corona** is a clean, confusing, Old World place with eight basic rooms (D-L105,000, lots of stairs; *vaporetto* #1 to San Zaccaria dock, take Calle de le Rasse—to left of Hotel Daneli, turn left at end, take right at square—Campo S.S. Filippo e Giacomo—on Calle Rimpeto La Sacrestie, take first right, then next left on Calle Corona to #4464, tel. 041-522-9174, SE).

## Sleeping North of St. Mark's Square
**Hotel Astoria** is a clean, simple place with 28 comfortable rooms tucked away a few blocks off St. Mark's Square (D-L180,000, Db-L240,000, July–Aug Db-L180,000, closed mid-Nov–mid-March, CC:VMA, 2 blocks from San Zulian Church at Calle Fiubera #951; from Rialto *vaporetto* #1 dock go straight inland on Calle le Bembo, which becomes Calle dei Fabbri, turn left

on Calle Fiubera, tel. 041-522-5381, fax 041-520-0771, e-mail: hotelastoria@inwind.it).

**Locanda Gambero**, with 27 rooms, is the biggest one-star hotel in the San Marco area (S-L110,000, old D-L170,000, new Db-L250,000, T-L220,000, Tb-L320,000, CC:VM, rooms with bath also have TV and air-con; from Rialto *vaporetto* #1 dock go straight inland on Calle le Bembo, which becomes Calle dei Fabbri; or from St. Mark's Square go through Sotoportego dei Dai then down Calle dei Fabbri to #4687, at intersection with Calle del Gambero, tel. 041-522-4384, fax 041-520-0431, e-mail: hotgamb@tin.it). Gambero runs the pleasant Art Deco–style La Bistrot on the corner, which serves old-time Venetian cuisine.

### Sleeping West/Northwest of St. Mark's Square
**Hotel Bel Sito**, friendly for a three-star hotel, has Old World character and a picturesque location—facing a church on a small square between St. Mark's Square and the Accademia. With solid wood furniture, its rooms feel elegant, even the few with peely paint (Sb-L204,000–238,000, Db-L227,000–362,000, includes breakfast, CC:VM, air-con, some rooms with canal or church views, *vaporetto* #1 to Santa Maria del Giglio stop, take narrow alley to square, hotel at far end to your right, San Marco 2517, Santa Maria del Giglio, tel. 041-522-3365, fax 041-520-4083, e-mail: belsito@iol.it).

**Alloggi Alla Scala**, a comfy and tidy five-room place run by Senora Andreina della Fiorentina, is homey, central, and tucked away on a quiet square that features a famous spiral stairway called Scala Contarini del Bovolo (small Db-L130,000, big Db-L150,000, extra bed-L40,000, breakfast-L12,000, CC:VM, Campo Manin #4306, San Marco, tel. 041-521-0629, fax 041-522-6451, daughter SE). From Campo Manin follow signs to (on statue's left) "Scala Contarini del Bovolo" (L4,000, daily 10:00–17:30, views from top).

### Sleeping near the Rialto Bridge
**(zip code: 30125)**
The first three hotels are located on the west side of the Rialto Bridge (away from St. Mark's Square).

**Locanda Sturion**, with air-conditioning and all the modern comforts, is pricey because it overlooks the Grand Canal (Db-L230,000–340,000, Tb-L350,000–450,000, family deals, canal-view rooms cost about L60,000 extra, includes breakfast, CC:VMA, miles of stairs, 100 meters from Rialto Bridge opposite *vaporetto* dock, San Polo, Rialto, Calle Sturion #679, 30125 Venezia, tel. 041-523-6243, fax 041-522-8378, www.locandasturion.com, e-mail: sturion@tin.it, SE). They require a personal check or traveler's check for a deposit.

**Hotel Locanda Ovidius**, with an elegant view terrace, wood-beamed-ceilinged breakfast room, and nine bright, comfortable rooms, is also on the Grand Canal. It has far fewer stairs than the Locanda Sturion next door (Sb-L150,000–300,000, Db-L200,000–390,000, Db with view-L300,000–450,000, off-season deal: get 1 night free for 4-night stay during Sun–Thu, CC:VMA, air-con, Calle del Sturion #677a, tel. 041-523-7970, fax 041-520-4101, www.hotelovidius.com, e-mail: info@hotelovidius.com).

**Albergo Guerrato**, overlooking a handy and colorful produce market, one minute from the Rialto action, is run by friendly, creative, and hardworking Roberto and Piero. Giorgio takes the night shift. Their 800-year-old building is Old World simple, airy, and wonderfully characteristic (D-L140,000, Db-L185,000, T-L180,000, Tb-L240,000, Q-L190,000, Qb-L280,000, including a L4,000 city map, prices promised through 2001 with this book, cash only; walk over the Rialto away from St. Mark's Square, go straight about 3 blocks, turn right on Calle drio la Scimia—not Scimia, the block before—and you'll see the hotel sign, Calle drio la Scimia #240a, 30125 San Polo, tel. & fax 041-522-7131 or 528-5927, e-mail: hguerrat@tin.it, SE). My tour groups book this place for 50 nights each year. Sorry. If you fax without calling first, no reply within three days means they are booked up. (It's best to call first.)

The next three hotels are located on the east side of the Rialto Bridge (St. Mark's side).

**Hotel Canada** has 25 small, pleasant rooms (S-L150,000, Sb-L210,000, 2 D with adjacent bath-L220,000, Db-L270,000, Tb-L330,000, Qb-L420,000, CC:VM, air-con L15,000 extra per night, rooms on canal come with view, noise, and aroma, rooms facing church are quiet and fresh, Castello San Lio #5659, 30122 Venezia, tel. 041-522-9912, fax 041-523-5852, SE). Canada is ideally located on a small, lively square, just off Campo San Lio between the Rialto and St. Mark's Square.

**Hotel Caneva** is an institutional, vinyl feeling, canalside place with plain, big, bright rooms and a tired management (S-L70,000, Sb-L110,000, Db-L155,000, Tb-L205,000, prices good with this book and cash, CC:VMA but prices increase with a credit card; midway between Rialto and St. Mark's Square near Chiesa la Fava; coming from San Bartolomeo square—at east end of Rialto Bridge—take a left at Stagneri/Disney store, go straight over bridge, then right—around church, Ramo Dietro La Fava #5515, 30122 Venezia, tel. 041-522-8118, fax 041-520-8676).

**Hotel Giorgione**, a four-star hotel in a 15th-century palace on a quiet lane, is superprofessional, with plush public spaces, pool tables, Internet access, a garden terrace, and 70 spacious over-the-top rooms with all the comforts (Sb-L170,000–280,000, Db-L250,00–430,000, pricier superior rooms and

suites available, extra bed-L100,000, 20 percent off in July and
August, check Web for discounts, CC:VMA, elevator, air-con,
Piazza S.S. Apostoli #4587, tel. 041-522-5810, fax 041-523-9092,
www.hotelgiorgione.com).

### Sleeping near S.S. Giovanni e Paoli

**Locanda la Corte**, with three stars, has 16 attractive, high-ceilinged,
wood-beamed rooms—done in pastels—bordering a small, quiet
courtyard (Sb-L180,000, standard Db-L320,000, superior Db-
350,000, suites available, CC:VM, air-con; *vaporetto* #52 from train
station to Fondamente Nove, exit boat to your left, follow waterfront, turn right after second bridge to get to S.S. Giovanni e Paolo
square; facing Rosa Salva bar, take street to left—Calle Bressana,
hotel is a short block away at bridge; Castello 6317, tel. 041-241-
1300, fax 041-241-5982, www.locanda.lacorte.it).

### Sleeping near the Accademia

When you step over the Accademia Bridge, the commotion of
touristy Venice is replaced by a sleepy village laced with canals.
This quiet area, next to the best painting gallery in town, is a
10-minute walk from St. Mark's Square and the Rialto. All are
within 12 minutes from the station or car park and three minutes
from St. Mark's Square on the fast boat #82. The hotels are
located near the south end of the Accademia Bridge except for
the last listing (Fondazione Levi), which is at the north end of
the bridge (St. Mark's side).

    **Pensione Accademia** fills the 17th-century Villa Maravege.
While its 27 comfortable and air-conditioned rooms are nothing
extraordinary, you'll feel aristocratic gliding through its grand
public spaces and lounging in its breezy garden (Sb-L150,000–
220,000, standard Db-L240,000–350,000, superior Db-L290,000–
420,000, family deals, CC:VMA; facing Accademia Gallery,
take first right, cross first bridge, go right, Dorsoduro #1058,
30123 Venezia, tel. 041-523-7846, fax 041-523-9152, www
.pensioneaccademia.it, e-mail: pensione.accademia@flashnet.it).

    **Hotel Galleria** is a compact and velvety little 10-room
place (S-L100,000, D-L150,000–160,000, Db-L180,000, big Db-
L220,000, CC:VMA, fans, includes breakfast in room, views
overlooking Grand Canal, near Accademia Gallery and next to
recommended Foscarini restaurant, Dorsoduro #878a, 30123
Venezia, tel. 041-523-2489, tel. & fax 041-520-4172, www
.galleria.it, e-mail: galleria@tin.it, SE).

    **Hotel Agli Alboretti** is a cozy, family-run, 25-room place
in a quiet neighborhood a block behind the Accademia Gallery.
With red carpeting and wood-beamed ceilings, it feels elegant
(Sb-L175,000, 2 small Db-L215,000, Db-L270,000, Tb-L320,000,
Qb-L370,000, includes breakfast, CC:VMA, air-con; 100 meters

from the Accademia *vaporetto* stop on Rio Terra a Foscarini at #884 Accademia; facing Accademia Gallery, go left, then forced right, tel. 041-523-0058, fax 041-521-0158, www.cash.it/alboretti, e-mail: alborett@gpnet.it, SE).

**Hotel American** is a small, cushy, three-star place on a lazy canal next to the delightful Campo San Vio (a tiny overlooked square facing the Grand Canal). At this Old World hotel with 18 rooms, you'll get better rates Sundays through Thursdays (Sb-L150,000–280,000, Db-L230,000–400,000, Db with view-L260,000–450,000, rates vary by day and season, extra bed-L50,000–100,000, includes big buffet breakfast, CC:VMA, air-con, 30 meters off Campo San Vio and 200 meters from Accademia Gallery; facing Accademia Gallery, go left, forced right, take second left—following yellow sign to Guggenheim Museum, cross bridge, take immediate right, 628 Accademia, 30123 Venezia, tel. 041-520-4733, fax 041-520-4048, check www.hotelamerican.com for deals).

**Hotel Belle Arti** is the place if you want to be in the old center without the commotion and intensity of Venice. With a grand entry and all the American hotel comforts, it's a big 67-room, modern, three-star place sitting on a former schoolyard (Sb-L200,000–240,000, Db-L280,000–360,000, Tb-L360,000–440,000, the cheaper rates apply to July–Aug and winter, CC:VMA, includes buffet breakfast, plush public areas, air-con, quiet, elevator, 100 meters behind Accademia Gallery; facing Gallery, take left, then forced right, Via Dorsoduro 912, tel. 041-522-6230, fax 041-528-0043, www.hotelbellearti.com, info@hotelbellearti.com).

**Domus Cavanis**, nearly across the street from—and owned by—Belle Arti, is a two-star hotel that recently opened and still feels new. Its 27 simple rooms are quiet and affordable (Db-L200,000, includes breakfast at Hotel Belle Arti, elevator, TV, phones, Dorsoduro 896, tel. 041-528-7374, fax 041-522-8505).

**Pensione La Calcina**, the home of English writer John Ruskin in 1876, comes with all the three-star comforts in a professional yet intimate package. Its 29 rooms are squeaky clean, with good wood furniture, hardwood floors, and a peaceful canalside setting facing Giudecca (S-L110,000–130,000, Sb-L150,000, Sb with view-L170,000, Db-L200,000–230,000, Db with view-L260,000–300,000, depending on size and season, CC:VMA, air-con, can reserve rooftop terrace for 60-minute visit, canalside buffet breakfast terrace, Dorsoduro #780, at the south end of Rio di San Vio, tel. 041-520-6466, fax 041-522-7045, e-mail: la.calcina@libero.it). From the car park or station catch *vaporetto* #51 to Zattere (at *vaporetto* stop, exit right, and walk along canal to hotel).

**Locanda San Trovaso** is sparkling new, with seven classy, spacious rooms—three with canal views—and a peaceful location on a small canal (Sb-L150,000, Db-L200,000, CC:VM, small roof terrace, Dorsoduro 1351, take *vaporetto* #82 from Tronchetto or #51 from Piazzale Roma or train station, get off at Zattere, exit left, cross bridge, continue along canal, turn right at tiny Calle Trevisan, cross bridge, cross adjacent bridge, take immediate right, first left, tel. 041-277-1146, fax 041-277-7190, www.locandasantrovaso.com, e-mail: s.trovaso@tin.it).

**Fondazione Levi**, a guest house run by a foundation that promotes research on Venetian music, offers 18 quiet, comfortable rooms (Sb-L110,000, Db-L180,000, Tb-L210,000, Qb-L240,000, only twin beds, elevator; 80 meters from base of Accademia Bridge on St. Mark's side; from Accademia *vaporetto* stop, cross Accademia Bridge, take immediate left—crossing the bridge Ponte Giustinian and going down Calle Giustinian directly to the Fondazione, buzz the "Foresteria" door to the right, San Vidal #2893, 30124 Venezia, tel. 041-786-711, fax 041-786-766, SE).

## Sleeping near the Train Station
**Hotel Marin** is three minutes from the train station but completely out of the touristic bustle of the Lista di Spagna. Just renovated, cozy, and cheery, it seems like a 19-bedroom home the moment you cross the threshold and is one of the best values in town (S-L100,000, D-L125,000, Db-L155,000, T-L170,000, Tb-L200,000, Q-L205,000, Qb-L225,000, prices good with this book and if you pay cash, pricier with CC:VMA, San Croce #670b, tel. 041-718-022, fax 041-721-485, www.hotelmarin.it). It's family run by helpful, friendly, English-speaking Bruno, Nadia, and son Samuel (they have city maps). It's immediately across the canal from the train station, behind the green dome (over bridge, right, first left, first right, first right). There's an Internet café and handy Laundromat nearby.

## Dormitory Accommodations
**Foresteria della Chiesa Valdese**, warmly run by a Protestant church, offers cheap dorm beds and doubles in a handy location (halfway between St. Mark's Square and Rialto). This run-down but charming old palace has elegant paintings on the ceilings (dorm bed-L35,000, D-L90,000, Db-L120,000, includes breakfast, more expensive for 1-night stays, some larger apartments for families with up to 5 people-L190,000, office open Mon–Sun 9:00–13:00, 18:00–20:00, from Campo Santa Maria di Formosa, walk past Bar all' Orologio to the end of Calle Lunga and cross the bridge, Castello #5170, reserve 3 months in advance, tel. & fax 041-528-6797, fax 041-241-6328).

The **Venice youth hostel**, on Giudecca Island, is crowded, cheap, and newly remodeled (L30,000 beds with sheets and breakfast in 10- to 16-bed rooms, membership required, office open daily 7:00–9:30, 13:30–23:00, catch *vaporetto* #82 from station to

Zittele, tel. 041-523-8211). Their budget cafeteria welcomes nonhostelers (nightly 17:00–23:30).

# Eating in Venice

While touristy restaurants are the scourge of Venice, there are plenty of good alternatives. The first trick: Walk away from triple-language menus.

## *Eating between Campo Santi Apostoli and Campo S.S. Giovanni e Paolo*

**Trattoria da Bepi** caters to a local crowd and specializes in fresh seafood and Venetian cuisine. Bepi's son, Loris, who speaks English, makes a smooth *panna cotta* (pudding) and a mean licorice grappa (Fri–Wed 12:00–14:30, 19:00–22:00, closed Thu, CC:VM, allow L65,000 per person, on Salizada del Pistor next to Santi Apostoli Church, tel. 041-528-5031).

**Antiche Cantine Ardenghi de Lucia e Michael** is a leap of local faith and an excellent splurge. Michael—an effervescent former Murano glass salesman—and his wife, Lucia, cook for a handful of people each night by reservation only. You must call first. You pay L80,000 per person and trust them to wine, dine, and serenade you with Venetian class. The evening can be quiet or raucous depending on who and how many are eating. When you call, ask for a festival of fruit and vegetables or you'll get nothing but crustaceans. There's no sign, and the door's locked. Find #6369 and knock. The password: La Repubblica Serenissima. From Campo S.S. Giovanni e Paolo, pass the churchlike hospital (notice the illusions painted on its facade), go over the bridge to the left, and take the first right—the street is Calle della Testa—to #6369 (Tue–Sat 20:00–24:00, closed Sun–Mon, tel. 041-523-7691).

Two colorful *osterias* are good for *cicchetti*, (munchies) wine tasting, or a simple, rustic, sit-down meal surrounded by a boisterous local ambience: **Osteria da Alberto** (Mon–Sat 12:00–15:00, 18:00–21:30, closed Sun, CC:VM, midway between Campo Santi Apostoli and Campo S.S. Giovanni e Paolo, next to Ponte de la Panada on Calle Larga Giacinto Gallina, tel. 041-523-8153) and **Osteria Candela** on Calle de l'Oca. You'll find local pubs in the side streets opposite Campo St. Sofia across Strada Nuova.

For great local cuisine far beyond the crowds in a rustic Venetian setting, hike to **Osteria Al Bacco** in Cannaregio (closed Mon, Fondamenta Capuzine, Cannaregio #3054, reservations wise, tel. 041-717-493).

## *Eating near the Accademia*

**Restaurant/Pizzeria Accademia Foscarini**, next to the Accademia Bridge and Galleria, offers decent L9,000 to L13,000 pizzas in a great canalside setting (Wed–Mon 7:00–23:00, closed Tue).

**Trattoria Al Cugnai** is an unpretentious place run by three sisters serving good food at a good price with friendly service (Tue–Sun 12:00–15:00, 19:00–22:00, closed Mon, midway between the Accademia Gallery and the forgotten and peaceful Campo San Vio, tel. 041-528-9238). They are happy to let you sip your sweet *fragolino bianco* (L2,000) on Campo San Vio (benches with Grand Canal view) and return the glass.

**Taverna San Trovaso** is a restaurant/pizzeria with nice gnocchi and a good L30,000 menu (Tue–Sun 12:00–14:50, 19:00–21:50, closed Mon, CC:VM, air-con, 100 meters from Accademia Gallery on San Trovaso canal; facing Accademia take a right, then a forced left at canal).

Just west of St. Mark's Square, consider **Osteria Da Carla** (a.k.a. Pietro Panizzolo), a fun and very local hole-in-the-wall where the food is good, the price is right, and Carla mothers you (Mon–Sat 7:00–23:00, closed Sun; from American Express head toward St. Mark's Square, first left, first left again through "Contarina" tunnel, at Sotoportego e Corte Contarina, tel. 041-523-7855).

## The Stand-Up Progressive Venetian Pub-Crawl Dinner

A tradition unique to Venice in Italy is a *giro di ombre* (pub crawl)— ideal in a city with no cars. My favorite Venetian dinner is a pub crawl. I've listed plenty of pubs in walking order for a quick or extended crawl below. If you've crawled enough, most of these bars make a fine one-stop, sit-down dinner. *Ombre* means shade, from the old days when a wine bar scooted with the shadow of the Campanile across St. Mark's Square.

Venice's residential back streets hide plenty of characteristic bars with countless trays of interesting toothpick-munchie food (*cicchetti*). This is a great way to mingle and have fun with the Venetians. Real *cicchetti* pubs are getting rare in these fast-food days, but locals appreciate the ones that survive.

Try fried mozzarella cheese, gorgonzola, calamari, artichoke hearts, and anything ugly on a toothpick. Ask for a *piatto misto* (mixed plate). Or try a plate of assorted appetizers for L10,000 (or more, depending on how hungry you are); ask for "*Un classico piatto di cicchetti misti da dieci mila lire*" (pron. oon KLAH-see-koh pee-AH-toh dee chee-KET-tee MEE-stee dah dee-AY-chee MEE-lah LEE-ray). Drink the house wines. A small glass of house red or white wine (*ombre rosso* or *ombre bianco*) or a small beer (*birrino*) costs about L2,000. *Vin bon*, Venetian for fine wine, may run you from L3,000 to L5,000 per little glass. Meat and fish (*pesce*: PAY-shay) munchies are expensive; veggies (*verdure*) are cheap, around L6,000 for a meal-sized plate. Bread sticks (*grissini*) are free for the asking. A good last drink is *fragolino*, the local sweet wine—*bianco* or *rosso*. A liter of house wine costs around L7,000. Bars don't stay open very late, and the *cicchetti* selection

## Venice Pub Crawl

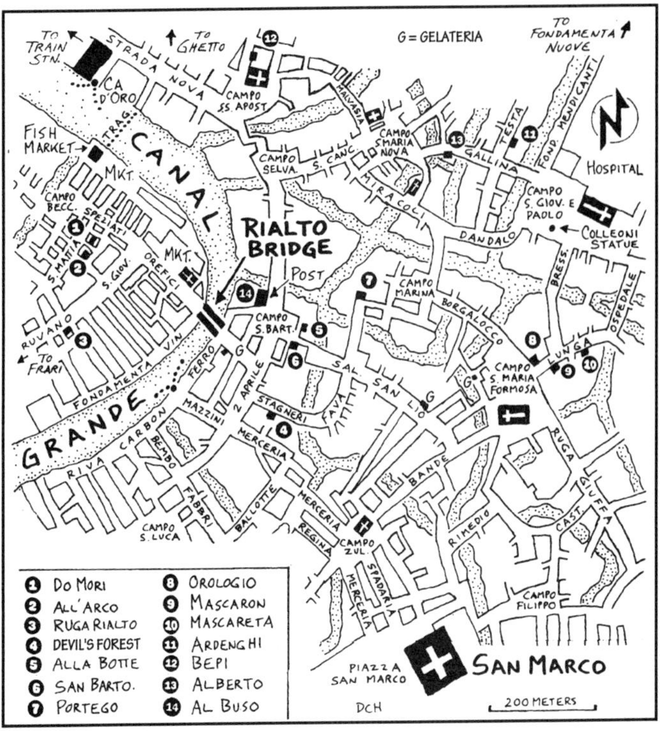
G = GELATERIA
TO TRAIN STN.
TO GHETTO
TO FONDAMENTA NUOVE
STRADA NOVA
CA D'ORO
CAMPO SS. APOST.
FISH MARKET
TRAG.
CANAL
MKT.
CAMPO BECC.
SPEZIALI
S. MATTIA
S. GIOV.
OREFICI
MKT.
RIALTO BRIDGE
POST
CAMPO SELVA
S. CANC.
CAMPO S. MARIA NOVA
MALVASIA
MIRACOLI
GALLINA
TESTA
FOND. MENDICANTI
HOSPITAL
CAMPO S. GIOV. E PAOLO
COLLEONI STATUE
DANDALO
CAMPO MARINA
BORGALOCCO
BRESS.
OSPEDALE
CAMPO S. BART.
RUVIANO
TO FRARI
FONDAMENTA VIN
FERRO
2 APRILE
SAL. SAN LIO
LUNGA
CAMPO S. MARIA FORMOSA
GRANDE
RIVA CARBON
MAZZINI
STAGNERI
FAVA
MERCERIA
BEMBO
FABBRI
BALLOTTE
BANDE
RUGA
GIUFFA
CAST.
RIMEDIO
CAMPO S. LUCA
REGINA
CAMPO ZUL.
SPADARIA
CAMPO FILIPPO
PIAZZA SAN MARCO
SAN MARCO
DCH
200 METERS
1 DO MORI
2 ALL'ARCO
3 RUGA RIALTO
4 DEVIL'S FOREST
5 ALLA BOTTE
6 SAN BARTO.
7 PORTEGO
8 OROLOGIO
9 MASCARON
10 MASCARETA
11 ARDENGHI
12 BEPI
13 ALBERTO
14 AL BUSO

is best early, so start your evening by 18:00. Most bars are closed on Sunday. You can stand around the bar or grab a table in the back—usually for the same price.

### Cicchetteria *West of the Rialto Bridge*

**Cantina Do Mori** is famous with locals (since 1462) and savvy travelers (since 1962) as a classy place for fine wine and *francobollo* (a spicy selection of 20 tiny sandwiches called "stamps"). Choose from the featured wines in the barrel on the bar. Order carefully, or they'll rip you off. From Rialto Bridge walk 200 meters down Ruga degli Orefici away from St. Mark's Square—then ask (Mon–Sat 17:00–20:30, closed Sun, stand up only, arrive early before *cicchetti* are gone, San Polo 429, tel. 041-522-5401). The rough-and-tumble **Cantina All' Arco** across the lane is worth a quick *ombre.*

**Antica Ostaria Ruga Rialto** is less expensive than Do Mori and offers tables, a busier/younger crowd, and a better selection of munchies (closed Mon, past the blue Chinese restaurant sign,

on corner of Ruga Vecchia S. Giovanni and Ramo del Sturion,
San Polo 692, tel. 041-521-1243).

These small restaurants, which serve meals and *cicchetti*
snacks, are a few steps from the  Rialto fish market: **Vini da
Pinto** faces the west entrance of the fish market on the small
square, Sestier de S. Polo (Tue–Sun 7:30–15:00, 17:30–21:00).
As you face Vini da Pinto, **Ostaria Sora al Ponte** is to your right,
on the bridge  (closed Mon), and **Cantina do Spade** is directly
behind Vini da Pinto (head around building to your left, take a
right through archway; closed Sun).

## Eating near Campo San Bartolomeo, East of the Rialto Bridge

**Osteria "Alla Botte" Cicchetteria** is an atmospheric place
packed with a young, local, bohemian jazz clientele. It's good for
a light meal or a *cicchetti* snack with wine (2 short blocks off
Campo San Bartolomeo in the corner behind the statue—down
Calle de la Bissa, notice the "day after" photo showing a debris-
covered Venice after the notorious 1989 Pink Floyd open-air
concert, tel. 041-520-9775).

If the statue on the Campo San Bartolomeo walked backward
20 meters, turned left, and went under a passageway, he'd hit
**Rosticceria San Bartolomeo.** This cheap—if confusing—self-
service restaurant on the ground floor has a likably surly staff
(good L9,000 pasta, great fried mozzarella *al* prosciutto for
L2,300, delightful fruit salad, and L2,000 glasses of wine, prices
listed on wall behind counter, no cover or service charge, daily
9:30–21:30, tel. 041-522-3569). Good but pricier meals are served
at the full-service restaurant upstairs. Take out or grab a table.

From Rosticceria San Bartolomeo, continue over a bridge
to Campo San Lio (a good landmark), go left at Hotel Canada,
and walk straight over another bridge into **Osteria Al Portego**
(at #6015). This fine, friendly, and local-style bar has plenty of
*cicchetti* (Mon–Fri 9:00–22:00, closed Sat–Sun, tel. 041-522-9038).
The *cicchetti* here can make a great meal. If pub crawling from
here, ask *"Dov'è Santa Maria di Formosa?"*

The **Devil's Forest Pub**, an air-conditioned bit of England
tucked away a block from the crowds, is—strangely—more Venetian
these days than the *tipico* places. Locals come here for good English
and Irish beer on tap, big salads (L12,000, lunch only), hot bar
snacks, and an easygoing ambience (no cover or service charge, fine
prices, backgammon and chess boards available-L3000, meals daily
12:00–15:30, bar snacks all the time, closed Sun in Aug, a block off
Campo San Bartolomeo on Calle dei Stagneri, tel. 041-520-0623).
Across the street, **Bora Bora Pizzeria** serves pizza and salads from
an entertaining menu (daily 12:00–15:00, 19:00–22:30, closed Wed
in winter, CC:VM, tel. 041-523-6583).

For a Grand Canal view, consider **Al Buso**, at the northeast end of the Rialto Bridge. Of the several restaurants that hug the canal near the Rialto, this is recommended by locals as offering the best value (daily 9:00–24:00, Ponte di Rialto 5338, tel. 041-528-9078).

### Eating near Campo Santa Maria di Formosa

Campo Santa Maria di Formosa is just plain atmospheric (as most squares with a Socialist Party office seem to be). For a balmy outdoor sit, you could split a pizza with wine on the square. **Bar all' Orologio** has a good setting and friendly service but mediocre "freezer" pizza (happy to split a pizza for pub crawlers, Mon–Sat 6:00–23:00, closed Sun). For a pizza snack on the square, cross the bridge behind the canalside *gelateria* and grab a slice to go from **Cip Ciap Pizza** (Wed–Mon 9:00–21:00, closed Tue; facing *gelateria*, take bridge to the right; Calle del Mondo Novo). Pub crawlers get a salad course at the fruit-and-vegetable stand next to the water fountain (open until about 19:30, closed Sun).

From Campo Santa Maria di Formosa, follow the yellow sign to "S.S. Giov e Paolo" down Calle Longa Santa Maria di Formosa and head down the street to **Osteria al Mascaron** (#5225, Gigi's bar, Mon–Sat 12:00–15:00, 19:00–23:00, best selection by 19:30, closed Sun). Gigi also runs **Enoteca Mascareta**, a wine bar, 30 meters farther down the street (#5183, Mon–Sat 18:00–01:00, closed Sun, tel. 041-523-0744). The piano sounds like they dropped it in the canal, but the wine was saved.

A *gelateria* is on the canal at Campo Santa Maria di Formosa (for more, see "Gelato," below).

### Cheap Meals

A key to cheap eating in Venice is bar snacks, especially stand-up mini-meals in out-of-the-way bars. Order by pointing. *Panini* (sandwiches) are sold fast and cheap at bars everywhere. Pizzerias are cheap and easy—try for a sidewalk table at a scenic location. For budget eating, I like small *cicchetti* bars (see "Pub-Crawl Dinner," above); for speed, value, and ambience, you can get a filling plate of local-style tapas at nearly any of the bars.

The **produce market** that sprawls for a few blocks just past the Rialto Bridge (best 8:00–13:00, closed Sun) is a great place to assemble a picnic. The nearby street, Ruga Vecchia, has good bakeries and cheese shops. Side lanes in this area are speckled with fine little hole-in-the-wall munchie bars.

The **Mensa DLF**, the public transportation workers' cafeteria, is cheap and open to the public (daily 11:00–14:30, 18:00–22:00). Leaving the train station, turn right on the Grand Canal, walk about 150 meters along the canal, up eight steps, and through the unmarked door.

### Gelato
**La Boutique del Gelato** is one of the best gelaterias in Venice (daily 10:00–21:00, closed Dec–Jan, 2 blocks off Campo Santa Maria di Formosa on corner of Salizada San Lio and Calle Paradiso, next to Hotel Bruno, #5727). A decent *gelateria* is canalside on Campo Santa Maria di Formosa.

For late-night gelato at Rialto, try **Michielangelo**, next to the McDonald's on Campo San Bartolomeo, on the St. Mark's side of the Rialto Bridge (daily 10:00–23:30, closed Wed in winter). At St. Mark's Square, the **Al Todaro** *gelateria* opposite the Doge's Palace is open late (daily 8:00–24.00, closed Mon in winter).

## Transportation Connections—Venice
**By train to: Verona** (hrly, 90 min), **Florence** (6/day, 3 hrs), **Dolomites** (8/day to Bolzano, 4 hrs with 1 transfer; catch bus from Bolzano into mountains), **Milan** (hrly, 3–4 hrs), **Rome** (6/day, 5 hrs, slower overnight), **Naples** (change in Rome, plus 2–3 hrs), **Brindisi** (3/day, 11 hrs), **Cinque Terre** (2 La Spezia trains go directly to Monterosso al Mare daily, 6 hrs, at 9:58 and 14:58), **Bern** (4/day, change in Milan, 8 hrs), **Munich** (5/day, 8 hrs), **Paris** (3/day, 11 hrs), **Vienna** (4/day, 9 hrs). Train and *couchette* reservations (about L35,000) are easily made at the American Express office near St. Mark's Square. Venice train info: tel. 147-888-088 or 041-785-570.

## NEAR VENICE: PADUA, VICENZA, VERONA, AND RAVENNA
While the Italian region of Veneto has much more to offer than Venice, few venture off the lagoon. Four important towns and possible side trips, in addition to the lakes and the Dolomites, make zipping directly from Venice to Milan (3-hr trip, hrly trains) a route strewn with temptation.

## Planning Your Time
The towns of Padua, Vicenza, Verona, and Ravenna are all, for various reasons, good stops. But none is an essential part of the best three weeks Italy has to offer. Of the towns discussed below, only Ravenna (2.5 hours from Padua or Florence) is not on the main Milan–Venice train line. Each town gives the visitor a low-key slice of Italy that complements the high-powered urbanity of Venice, Florence, and Rome. If you're Padua-bound, note that you need to reserve a day or two in advance to see the Scrovigni Chapel (see below). On Monday, most sights in Verona and Vicenza are closed.

High-speed town hopping between Venice and Bolzano or Milan (with 3-hour stops at Padua, Vicenza, and Verona) is a good day. Trains run frequently enough to allow flexibility and little wasted time.

## Temptations: Venice to Milan

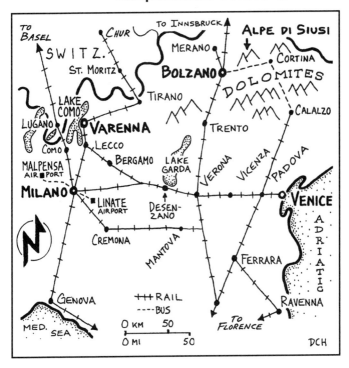

## PADUA (PADOVA)

Living under Venetian rule for four centuries seemed only
to sharpen Padua's independent spirit. Nicknamed "the brain
of Veneto," Padua has a prestigious university (founded 1222)
and was home to Galileo, Copernicus, Dante, and Petrarch.
The old town is a colonnaded time-tunnel experience, and
Padua's museums and churches hold their own in Italy's artistic
big league. Note that you need to reserve a day or two in
advance to see the Scrovigni Chapel with its great Giotto
paintings (see below).

    **Arrival in Padua:** From the train station TI, pick up a city
map and list of sights (Mon–Sat 9:15–19:00, Sun 9:00–12:00,
Oct–March Mon–Sat 9:15–5:45, Sun 9:00–12:00, tel. 049-875-
2077) and catch bus #8, #12, or #18 (tickets at bus ticket window,
far right of station as you leave) to Via Luca Belludi (next to
Piazza del Santo and the Basilica of St. Anthony). From here
walk through town via the old market square and the Scrovigni
Chapel and then back to the station.

## Sights—Padua

▲▲**Basilica of St. Anthony**—Friar Anthony of Padua, "Christ's perfect follower and a tireless preacher of the Gospel," is buried here. For 700 years his remains and this impressive church (started immediately after the death of the saint in 1231) have attracted pilgrims to Padua (daily 6:30–19:00, modest dress code enforced).

Start your visit at the information desk just inside the cloisters (daily 9:00–12:00, 15:00–18:00, very helpful, with an abundance of St. Anthony-related handouts). Wander around the cloisters and into the basilica. As you gaze past the crowds and through the incense haze at Donatello's glorious crucifix hanging over the altar you realize this is one important pilgrimage site.

Along with the *Crucifixion*, notice the Donatello statues of Mary and Padua's six patron saints on the high altar. Then pay a visit to the saint's tomb (left of the altar). Finally, visit the Chapel of the Reliquaries (behind the altar), where you can see St. Anthony's robe, vocal chords (discovered intact when his remains were examined in 1981), jaw...and "uncorrupted tongue" (discovered when the remains were examined in 1263).

Outside stands Donatello's much-admired equestrian statue (the first since ancient Roman times) of the Venetian mercenary General Gattamelata on Piazza del Santo. From here, walk 10 minutes into town down Via Sacra.

▲**Palazza della Ragione**—In the town center, between the Piazza della Erbe and the Piazza della Frutta, stands the 13th-century Palazza della Ragione, a huge covered produce market (lively in the morning, closed Sun). Ten minutes farther you reach the town's artistic wonder.

▲▲**Scrovigni Chapel (Cappella degli Scrovigni)**—This chapel (tourable by reservation only, see below) is surrounded by the ruins of a Roman amphitheater, a reminder that Padua was an important Roman town. But the sightseeing thrill here is the chapel wallpapered by Giotto's beautifully preserved cycle of more than 30 frescoes depicting scenes from the lives of Jesus and Mary. Painted around 1305 and considered by many to be the first piece of modern art, this work makes it clear: Europe was breaking out of the Middle Ages. It was radical for its real scenes, lively colors, light sources, emotion, and humanism.

You need a reservation to get inside. To protect the paintings from excess humidity, only a limited number of people are allowed in the chapel. Call 049-820-4550 a day or two before your visit (booking office open Mon–Fri 10:00–18:00). After you give your name and a phone number and choose a day and time, you'll be asked to show up one hour before your reserved time slot to pay cash for your tickets (L12,000, daily 9:00–19:00, last admission 18:40, no photos allowed in chapel). Although you'll have only 15 minutes inside the chapel, it's divine.

## Sleeping in Padua
**(L2,000 = about $1, country code: 39)**
**Hotel Piccolo Vienna** is small and near the station (D-L65,000, Db-L85,000, Via Beato Pellegrino 133, tel. 049-871-6331). **Hotel Verdi**, in the old center, is friendly and accommodating (S-L45,000, D-L65,000, bus #10 from station to Teatro Verdi, Via Dondi dell' Orologio 7, tel. 049-875-5744). The well-run **Ostello Città di Padova** has four-, six-, and 16-bed rooms (L27,000 per bed with sheets and breakfast, L28,000 in family rooms, bus #3, #8, #12, or #18 from the station, Via Aleardi 30, tel. 049-875-2219). Many budget travelers enjoy making this hostel a low-stress, low-price home base from which to tour Venice. I'd rather flip-flop it—sleeping in Venice and side-tripping to Padua, 30 minutes away by train.

# VICENZA
To many architects, Vicenza is a pilgrimage site. Entire streets look like the back of a nickel. This is the city of Palladio, the 16th-century Renaissance architect who gave us the Palladian style so influential in Britain (countless country homes). For the casual visitor, a quick stop offers plenty of Palladio—the last great artist of the Renaissance. Note that Vicenza's major sights are closed on Monday.

**Tourist Information**: The train station might have a TI (Aug–Oct only—if at all). You'll find the main TI at Piazza Matteotti 12 (Mon–Sat 9:00–13:00, 14:30–18:00, Sun 9:00–13:00, tel. 0444-320-854). At either TI, pick up a map.

**Arrival in Vicenza:** From the train station catch bus #1, #2, #4, #5, or #7 (L1,600, tickets at tiny kiosk across street in the bushes) to Piazza Matteotti in the city center.

## Sights—Vicenza
▲▲**Olympic Theater**—Palladio's last work is one of his greatest. Modeled after the theaters of antiquity, this is a festival of classical columns, statues, and an oh-wow stage bursting with perspective tricks. Begun in 1580, it's built of wood and stucco (L12,000 "Biglietto Unico" ticket includes entry to Santa Corona Archeological and Natural History Museum and the Paintings Gallery in Palazzo Chiericati, July–Aug Tue–Sun 9:00–19:00, Sept–June Tue–Sun 9:00–17:00, closed Mon; hours can vary depending on performances). One of the oldest indoor theaters in Europe and considered one of the world's best, it's still used.

▲**Church of Santa Corona**—A block away, this church was built in the 13th century to house a thorn from the crown of thorns given to the Bishop of Vicenza by the king of France (daily 8:30–12:00, 14:30–18:30). It has Giovanni Bellini's fine *Baptism of Christ* (c. 1500, put in a coin for light, to the left of the altar). Study the incredible inlaid marble and mother of pearl work on the high altar (1670) and the inlaid wood complementing that in the stalls of the choir (1485).

The cloisters holds the Archeological and Natural History Museum (July–Aug Tue–Sun 10:00–19:00, Sept–June 9:00–17:00). **Strolling Corso Palladio**—From the Church of Santa Corona, stroll down Vicenza's main drag, Corso Andrea Palladio, and see why they call Vicenza "Venezia on terra firma." A steady string of Renaissance palaces and Palladian architecture is peopled by Vicenzans (considered by their neighbors to be as uppity as most of their colonnades) and punctuated by upper-class *gelaterias.*

After a few blocks you'll see the commanding basilica standing (with its 82-meter-tall, 13th-century tower) over the Piazza dei Signori, which has been the town center since Roman times. It was young Palladio's proposal to redo Vicenza's dilapidated Gothic palace of justice in the neo-Greek style that established him as Vicenza's favorite architect. (This was not a church but a meeting place for local big shots.) The rest of his career was a one-man construction boom. The Loggia del Capitaniato, home of the Venetian governor (opposite the basilica) and one of Palladio's last works, gives you an easy chance to compare early Palladio (the basilica) with late Palladio (the loggia).

Finish your Corso Palladio stroll by walking to Piazzale Gasperi (where the PAM supermarket is a handy place to grab a picnic for the train ride), dip into the park on your right (with one last Palladio loggia), and then walk five minutes down Viale Roma back to the station. Trains leave about every hour toward Milan/Verona and Venice (less than an hour away). **Villa la Rotonda**—Thomas Jefferson's Monticello was inspired by Palladio's Rotonda, a private but sometimes tourable Palladian residence on the edge of Vicenza (L5,000 for grounds, mid-March–Sept Tue–Sun 10:00–12:00, 15:00–18:00, closed Mon; L10,000 includes interior—only open Wed 10:00–12:00, 15:00–18:00; everything closed Oct–mid-March, a 20-minute walk from station—best along bike path, bikes rentable at station).

## Sleeping in Vicenza
**(L2,000 = about $1, country code: 39)**
Hotel Vicenza is barely acceptable but is in the Palladian center of things (D-L130,000, Db-L180,000, Piazza dei Signori at Stradella dei Nodari, tel. & fax 0444-321-512). **Hotel Castello** is a tired, basic place on the train station end of the old town (Db-L180,000, CC:VMA, air-con, Contra Piazza Castello 24, tel. 0444-323-585, fax 0444-323-583). **Hotel Campo Marzio**, a four-star, American-style, modern place, faces a park on the main drag a few minutes' walk in front of the station (Db-L200,000–400,000, CC:VM, easy parking, air-con, elevator, Viale Roma 27, tel. 0444-545-700, fax 0444-320-495, e-mail: hcm@tradenet.it).

# VERONA

Romeo and Juliet made Verona a household word. But, alas, a visit here has nothing to do with those two star-crossed lovers. You can pay to visit the house falsely claiming to be Juliet's, with an almost believable balcony (and a courtyard slathered with tour groups), take part in the tradition of rubbing the breast of Juliet's statue to ensure finding a lover (or picking up the sweat of someone who can't), and even make a pilgrimage to what isn't "La Tomba di Giulietta." Despite the fiction, the town has been an important crossroads for 2,000 years and is therefore packed with genuine history. R and J fans will take some solace in the fact that two real feuding families, the Montecchi and the Capellos, were the models for Shakespeare's Montagues and Capulets. And, if R and J had existed and were alive today, they would recognize much of their "home town."

Verona's main attractions are its wealth of Roman ruins; the remnants of its 13th- and 14th-century political and cultural boom; its 21st-century, quiet, pedestrian-only ambience; and a world-class opera festival each July and August. After Venice's festival of tourism, Veneto's second city (in population and in artistic importance) is a cool and welcome sip of pure Italy, where Dumpsters are painted by schoolchildren as class projects. If you like Italy but don't need great sights, this town is a joy.

## Orientation

The most enjoyable core of Verona is along Via Mazzini between Piazza Brà and Piazza Erbe, Verona's market square since Roman times. Head straight for Piazza Bra—and stroll.

**Tourist Information:** Verona's TI offices are at the station (Mon–Sat 9:00–18:00, closed Sun, shorter hours off-season, tel. 045-800-0861, www.tourism.verona.it) and at Piazza Bra (daily 9:00–19:00 July–Aug, shorter hours off-season, facing the large yellow-white building, TI is across street to your right, tel. 045-806-8680). Pick up the free city map which contains a list of sights, hours, and walking tours. If you're staying the night, ask for the free *L'agenda di Verona*, the monthly entertainment guide (it's in Italian, but *concerto di musica classica* is darn close to English). Note: Virtually all sights are closed on Monday.

The Verona Card, which covers bus transportation and most of Verona's sights, isn't worth it for a short visit (L22,000/ 3 days, sold at museums, you'd need to to see 4–5 sights to make it pay). Juliet & Co. offers guided walks daily at 17:30 from May through October (L15,000, meet at Piazza Bra at equestrian statue of Vittorio Emanuele II, no reservation necessary, private tours possible, tel. & fax 045-810-3173, www.juliet.com). In July and August, Verona's opera festival brings crowds and higher hotel prices (tickets L42,000–290,000, Verdi's on for 2001—from *Aida* to *La Traviata*, box office tel. 045-800-5151, www.arena.it).

# Verona

| | | |
|---|---|---|
| ❶ HOTEL TORCOLO | ❺ LOCANDA CATULLO | ❾ BUS TO STATION |
| ❷ HOTEL CAVOUR | ❻ HOTEL AURORA | ❿ BUS FROM STATION |
| ❸ ALBERGO CASTELLO | ❼ YOUTH HOSTEL | |
| ❹ HOTEL EUROPA | ❽ PORTA BORSARI | |

**Arrival in Verona:** Arriving by train, get off at Verona's Porta Nuova station. The train station is modern but so cluttered with shops it's hard to get oriented. In the lobby, with your back to the tracks, lockers are on the far left (L3,000–5,000). To your far right, you'll find the baggage check (L5,000/12 hrs), and, if you search hard, you'll see the TI, tucked inside an office labeled "Centro Accoglienza e Informazioni."

The 15-minute walk from the station (on busy streets) to

Piazza Bra is miserable; take the bus. Directly in front of the
station are the buses. You need to buy a ticket before boarding
(L1,600, from *tabacchi* shop inside station or at white bus kiosk
outside at Platform A). Bus information will likely be posted in
English on the window of the bus kiosk (or ask, *Che numero per
centro?*, pron. kay NOO-may-roh pehr CHEN-troh). You'll probably have a choice of orange bus #11, #12, or #13, leaving from
Platform A. Validate your ticket on the bus by stamping it in the
machine in the middle of the bus (good for 60 min). Buses stop
on Piazza Bra, the square with the can't-miss-it Roman arena.
The TI is just a few steps beyond the bus stop.

Taxis pick up only at taxi stands (at train station and Piazza
Bra) and cost about L10,000 for a ride between the train station and
Piazza Bra. All sights of importance are within an easy walk through
the old town, which is defined by a bend in the river. Buses return
to the station from where Corso Porta Nuova hits Piazza Bra (just
outside city wall, under the big clock, on the right).

## Sights—Verona
**Arena**—This elliptical 140-by-120-meter amphitheater—the
third-largest in the Roman world—is well preserved, dates from
the first century A.D., and looks great in its pink marble. Over the
centuries, crowds of up to 25,000 spectators have cheered Roman
gladiator battles, medieval executions, and modern plays (including
the popular opera festival that takes advantage of the famous
acoustics every July and August). Climb to the top for a fine city
view (L6,000, Tue–Sun 8:00–18:00, closed Mon and at 15:00
during opera season, located on Piazza Bra).
**House of Juliet**—This bogus house is a block off Piazza Erbe
(detour right to Via Cappello 23). The tiny, admittedly romantic
courtyard is a spectacle in itself, with Japanese posing from the
balcony, Nebraskans polishing Juliet's bronze breast, and amorous
graffiti everywhere. The info boxes (L1,000 for 2) offer a good history. ("While no documentation has been discovered to prove the
truth of the legend, no documentation has disproven it either.") The
"museum" is only empty rooms and certainly not worth the L6,000
entry fee (tour it free via the security screen at the ticket desk).
▲**Piazza Erbe**—Verona's market square is a photographer's delight,
with pastel buildings corralling the stalls, fountains, pigeons, and
people that have come together here since Roman times. A fountain
has bubbled here for 2,000 years. Notice the Venetian Lion above,
reminding locals since 1405 of their conquerors.
▲▲**Evening** *Passeggiata*—For me the highlight of Verona is
the *passeggiata* (stroll)—especially in the evening—from the elegant
cafés of Piazza Bra through the old town on Via Mazzini (one of
Europe's many "first pedestrian-only streets") to the bustling and
colorful market square, Piazza Erbe.

**Introductory Old Town Walk**—This walk will take you from Piazza Erbe to the major sights and end at Piazza Bra. Allow an hour (including tower climb and dawdling).

From the center of Piazza Erbe, head toward the river on Via della Costa. The street is marked by an arch with a whale's rib suspended from it. When you pass through the arch, don't worry. The whale's rib has hung there a thousand years. According to legend, it will fall when someone who's never lied walks under it.

The street soon opens up to a square, **Piazza dei Signori**, which has a white statue of Dante center-stage. The pensive Dante seems to wonder why the tourists choose Juliet over him. Dante was granted exile in Verona by the Scaligeri family. With the whale's rib behind you, you're facing the brick, crenellated, 13th-century Scaligeri residence. Behind Dante is the yellowish 15th-century Venetian Renaissance–style Portico of the Counsel. In front of Dante (follow the white "WC" signs) is the 12th-century Romanesque **Palazzo della Ragione**. Go in the courtyard. For a grand view, you can climb to the top of the 13th-century Torre dei Lamberti (L5,000 for elevator, L4,000 for stairs, daily 9:30–17:00). There's no need to climb any farther than the view level just after you get out of the lift.

Exit the courtyard the way you entered and turn right, continuing down the whale-rib street. Within a block you'll find the strange and very **Gothic tombs** of the Scaligeri family, who were to Verona what the Medici family was to Florence.

Continue straight and then turn left on Via Sottoriva (paralleling the river). After passing behind an important church, Sant Anastasia (visit it later), you'll reach a small riverfront park which usually has a few modern-day Romeos and Juliets more interested in each other than the view. From the park you can see the Roman bridge, the **Ponte Pietra**, which survived nearly intact until World War II. Across the river, built into the hillside, is the **Teatro Romano**, the Roman theater, which stages Shakespeare plays every summer (only a little more difficult to understand in Italian than in olde English). If you're up for it, head for the bridge and consider climbing the stairs behind the theater for a great town view.

Return to the riverfront park and walk alongside it until you again reach the back of the church, Sant Anastasia, Verona's largest. Turn right immediately after the church on Via Don Bassi, to reach the church's entrance. (Verona's historic churches are all open Mon–Sat 9:30–18:00 and Sun 13:00–18:00, and charge L3,000; there's a L8,000 combo ticket covering all). With your back to the church's entrance, walk straight ahead on Corso Anastasia. In less than 10 minutes, you'll pass through a ghostly white, well-preserved first-century Roman gateway, **Porta Borsari.** Continue straight (the name of the street changes to Corso Cavour). In a little park next to the castle is a first-century Roman

triumphal arch, **Arco dei Gavi.** It was rebuilt in the 1900s after
being destroyed by French revolutionary troops in 1796. The
medieval castle next door, **Castelvecchio,** is now an art museum
with fine 16th- to 18th-century paintings (L6,000, free first Sun
of month, Tue–Sun 9:00–18:30, closed Mon).

From the castle, you have two good options. The castle's
drawbridge points the way to Via Roma, which takes you to Piazza
Bra and a well-deserved rest at a sidewalk café (Brek is good).

Or: A few blocks from the castle is the 12th-century **Basilica
of San Zeno Maggiore.** This offers not only a great example of
Italian Romanesque but also Mantegna's *San Zeno Triptych* and
a set of 48 paneled 11th-century bronze doors that are nicknamed
"the poor man's Bible." Pretend you're an illiterate medieval
peasant and do some reading.

## Sleeping and Eating in Verona
**(L2,000 = about $1, country code: 39, zip code: 37100)**
Several fine, family-run places are in the quiet streets just off
Piazza Bra, within 200 meters of the bus stop and well marked
with yellow signs. Prices can soar in July and August.

**Hotel Torcolo** provides 19 comfortable, air-conditioned
rooms in a good location near Piazza Bra (Sb-L98,000–125,000,
Db-L128,000–178,000, breakfast-L13,000–18,000 extra, prices
vary with season, CC:VMA, elevator, Vicolo Listone 3, tel. 045-
800-7512, fax 045-800-4058, Silvia Pomari).

**Hotel Cavour** is just off Piazza Bra (22 rooms, Db-L220,000–
270,000, depending on season and room size, breakfast-L16,000,
prices go soft in off-season, modern showers, air-con, Vicolo Chiodo
4, tel. 045-590-166, fax 045-590-508, SE).

**Hotel Europa** offers sleek, modern comfort in the same great
neighborhood (Db-L200,000 but L250,000 during opera, includes
breakfast, call a day ahead to check for discounts, CC:VMA, air-
con, elevator, Via Roma 8, 37121 Verona, tel.
045-800-2882, fax 045-800-1852, Giacomo SE and looks like
Verdi). Some of its 46 rooms are smoke free, a rarity in Italy.

**Albergo Al Castello,** on a busy street, is less atmospheric
(9 rooms, S-L85,000, Sb-L100,000, one D-L120,000, Db-L150,000,
includes breakfast, CC:VM, ceiling fans, Corso Cavour 43, tel. &
fax 045-800-4403, Katia SE).

**Locanda Catullo** is a cheaper, quiet, quirky, and paranoid
place deeper in the old town, with good basic rooms up three
flights of stairs (21 rooms, S-L70,000, D-L100,000, Db-L120,000,
no breakfast, left off Via Mazzini onto Via Catullo, down an alley
between 1D and 3A at Via Valerio Catullo 1, tel. 045-800-2786,
fax 045-594-717, SE).

**Hotel Aurora,** just off Piazza Erbe, is my favorite of all,
with a friendly family management, a terrace overlooking

the Piazza, and 19 fresh and newly renovated air-conditioned rooms (S-L120,000, Sb-L190,000, Db-L210,000, Tb-L270,000, includes buffet breakfast, CC:VMA, elevator, reserve with traveler's check or personal check for deposit, Piazza Erbe, 37121 Verona, tel. 045-594-717, fax 045-801-0860).

The **Verona youth hostel** is one of Italy's best hostels (8- to 10-bed rooms, L23,000 beds with breakfast, L14,000 dinners, Laundromat, some family rooms, camping possible, nonmembers welcome 1 night, bus #73 from station during the day or #90 at night and Sun, over the river beyond Ponte Nuovo at Salita Fontana del Ferro 15, tel. 045-590-360).

**Fast, cheap food on Piazza Bra:** For a quick and healthy bite with a great view of Verona's main square, eat at **Brek** (daily 11:30–15:00, 18:30–22:00, indoor/outdoor seating, cheap salad plates, Piazza Bra 20, tel. 045-800-4561).

## Transportation Connections—Verona
**By train to: Florence** (10/day, 3 hrs), **Milan** (hrly, 2 hrs), **Rome** (6/day, 6 hrs), **Bolzano** (hrly, 90 min). Hopping between **Verona, Padua, Vicenza,** and **Venice** couldn't be easier: All are 30 minutes apart on the Venice–Milan line (hrly, 3 hrs).

**Parking in Verona:** Drivers will find lots of free parking at the stadium or cheap long-term parking near the train station. The most central lot is behind the Arena on Piazza Cittadella (guarded, L1,000/hr). The town center is closed to regular traffic.

## RAVENNA
Ravenna is on the tourist map for one reason: its 1,500-year-old churches decorated with best-in-the-West Byzantine mosaics. Known in Roman times as Classe, the city was an imperial port for the large naval fleet. Briefly a capital of eastern Rome during its fall, Ravenna was taken by the barbarians. Then, in A.D. 539, the Byzantine emperor Justinian turned Ravenna into Byzantium's lieutenant in the west. Ravenna was a light in the Dark Ages. Two hundred years later the Lombards booted Byzantine out, and Ravenna melted into the backwaters of medieval Italy and stayed out of historical sight for a thousand years. Today the local economy booms with a big chemical industry, the discovery of offshore gas deposits, and the construction of a new ship canal. The bustling town center is Italy's most bicycle friendly (bike paths are in the middle of pedestrian streets, subtly indicated by white brick paving). Locals go about their business while busloads of tourists slip quietly in and out of town for the best look at the glories of Byzantium this side of Istanbul.

While not worth an overnight, it's only a 90-minute detour from the main Venice–Florence train line and worth the effort for those interested in old mosaics.

# Orientation

Central Ravenna is quiet, with a pedestrian-friendly core and more bikes than cars (bike rental at Coop San Vitale on Piazza Farini, on the left just as you exit the train station, tel. 0544-37031). On a quick visit to Ravenna, I'd see the basilicas, mausoleum, covered market, and Piazza del Popolo.

**Tourist Information:** The TI is a 20-minute walk (or a 5-minute pedal) from the train station (Mon–Sat 8:30–18:00, Sun 9:30–12:30, 14:30–17:30, Via Salara 8, tel. 0544-35404). For directions to the TI, see "Orientation Walk," below.

**Combo Tickets:** Many top sights can only be seen by purchasing a combo ticket (called *biglietto cumulativo*, L9,000, sold at the sights). It includes admission to the Basilica of San Vitale, St. Apollinare Nuovo, Spirito Santo, Battistero Neoniano, and the Cappella San Andrea. There are no individual admissions to these.

A different combo ticket (L10,000) includes admissions to the National Museum and Mausoleum of Teadorico. Pay an additional L2,000 to include the Sant' Appollinare in Classe. Unlike the other combo ticket mentioned above, you can buy individual admissions to the sights (National Museum-L8,000, daily 9:00–19:00; Mausoleum of Teadorico-L4,000, daily 9:00–19:00; and Sant' Appollinare in Classe-L4,000, Sun 13:00–19:00, Mon–Sat 9:00–19:00).

# Sights—Ravenna

**Orientation Walk**—A visit to Ravenna can be as short as a three-hour loop from the train station. From the station walk straight down Viale Farini to Piazza del Popolo. A right on Via IV Novembre takes you a block to the colorful covered market (Mercato Coperto, open Mon–Sat for picnic fixings 8:00–13:00, closed Sun). The TI is a block away (on Via Salaria 8). Ravenna's two most important sights, Basilica di San Vitale and the Mausoleum of Galla Placidia, are two blocks away down Via San Vitale. On the other side of Piazza del Popolo is the Basilica of St. Apollinare Nuovo, also worth a look. From there you're about a 15-minute walk back to the station.

**▲▲Basilica di San Vitale**—It's impressive enough to see a 1,400-year-old church. But to see one decorated in brilliant mosaics that still convey the intended feeling that "this peace and stability was brought to you by your emperor and God" is rare indeed. Study each of the scenes: the arch of apostles with a bearded Christ at their head, the lamb on the twinkly ceiling, the beardless Christ astride a blue earth behind the altar, and the side panels featuring Emperor Justinian, his wife Theodora, and their rigid and lavish courts. San Vitale can be seen as the last of the ancient Roman art and the first of the Christian era. This church was the prototype for Constantinople's Hagia Sofia, built 10 years later, and it

# Ravenna

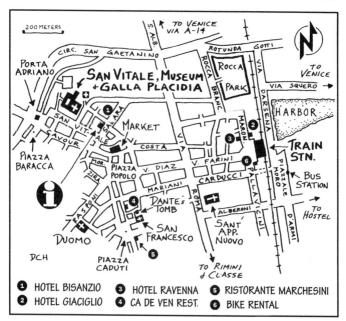

200 METERS

TO VENICE VIA A-14

PORTA ADRIANO

CIRC. SAN GAETANINO

ROTUNDA GOTTI

ROCCA PARK

TO VENICE

VIA SQUERO

SAN VITALE, MUSEUM + GALLA PLACIDIA

HARBOR

MARKET

COSTA

TRAIN STN.

PIAZZA BARACCA

PIAZZA POPOLO

V. DIAZ

V. FARINI

CARDUCCI

BUS STATION

MARIANI

DANTE'S TOMB

ALBERONI

TO HOSTEL

DUOMO

DCH

SAN FRANCESCO

SANT' APP. NUOVO

PIAZZA CADUTI

TO RIMINI & CLASSE

TO HOSTEL D'ARMI

**1** HOTEL BISANZIO    **3** HOTEL RAVENNA    **5** RISTORANTE MARCHESINI
**2** HOTEL GIACIGLIO    **4** CA DE VEN REST.    **6** BIKE RENTAL

inspired Charlemagne to build the first great church in northern
Europe in his capital of Aix-la-Chapelle, now present-day Aachen
(L6,000, L10,000 for combo ticket, see above, daily 9:00–19:00).
▲▲**Mausoleum of Galla Placidia**—Just across the courtyard
(and included in San Vitale admission) is this tiny, humble-looking
mausoleum, with the oldest—and to many, the best—mosaics in
Ravenna. The little light that sneaks through the thin alabaster
panels brings a glow and a twinkle to the very early Christian
symbolism (Jesus the Good Shepherd, Mark's lion, Luke's ox, John's
eagle, the golden cross above everything) that fills the little room.
Cover the light of the door with your hand to see the beardless
Christ as the Good Shepherd (L4,000, daily 9:00–19:00, reservations necessary March–May only, tel. 0544-219-938).
▲▲**Basilica of St. Apollinare Nuovo**—This austere sixth-
century church, in the typical early-Christian basilica form, has
two huge and wonderfully preserved side panels. One is a procession of haloed virgins, each bringing gifts to the Madonna and the
Christ Child. Opposite, Christ is on his throne with four angels,
awaiting a solemn procession of 26 martyrs (daily 9:30–19:00).
▲**Church of Sant' Apollinare in Classe**—Featuring great
Byzantine art, this church is a favorite among mosaic pilgrims

(Mon–Sat 9:00–19:00, Sun 13:00–19:00, tel. 0544-73643). It's five kilometers out of town. Catch bus #4 from the station or #44 from Piazza Caduti.

**Other Sights**—The **Basilica San Francesco** is worth a look for its simple interior and flooded, mosaic-covered crypt below the main altar (daily 7:30–12:00, 15:00–19:00). Nearby, the **Tomb of Dante** is the true site of his remains—the supposed tomb in Florence's Santa Croce Church is empty (daily 9:00–19:00).

**Overrated Sights**—The nearby beach town of Rimini is an overcrowded and polluted mess.

## Sleeping in Ravenna
### (L2,000 = about $1, country code: 39, zip code: 48100)
**Hotel Bisanzio** is a splurge in the city center (Sb-L120,000–170,000, Db-L220,000–270,000, Via Salara 30, tel. 0544-217-111, fax 0544-32539).

Two cheap hotels near the station are **Al Giaciglio** (S-L45,000, D-L65,000, Db-L80,000, Via R. Brancaleone 42, tel. & fax 0544-39403, SE) and **Hotel Ravenna** (S-L70,000, Sb-L80,000, D-L90,000, Db-L110,000, CC:VM, Via Varoncelli 12, tel. 0544-212-204, fax 0544-212-077).

The **youth hostel** is a 20-minute walk from the station (L24,000 dorm bed, L26,000/person in 4- to 6-bed family rooms, follow signs for Ostello Dante, Via Nicolodi 12, tel. & fax 0544-421-164, SE).

## Eating in Ravenna
The atmospheric **Ristorante-Enoteca Cá de Ven** offers plenty of pasta dishes and *piadina* (unleavened focaccia), the local specialty (Tues–Sun 11:00–14:00, 17:30–22:15, closed Mon, Via C. Ricca 24, 2-minute walk from Piazza del Popolo, tel. 0544-30163).

**Ristorante Marchesini** has a classy, delicious, self-serve menu that includes some great salads (Via Mazzini 6, 5 minutes from Piazza del Popolo, near Piazza Caduti, tel. 0544-212-309).

**Free Flow Bizantino**, inside the covered market, is another self-serve (Mon–Fri open lunch only). Or assemble a picnic at the market and enjoy your feast in the shady gardens of the **Rocca Brancaleone** fortress (5-minute walk from the station).

## Transportation Connections—Ravenna
**By train to: Venice** (3 hrs with transfer in Ferrara: Ravenna to Ferrara, every 2 hrs, 1 hr; Ferrara to Venice, hrly, 90 min), **Florence** (4 hrs with transfer in Bologna: Ravenna to Bologna, 8/day, 90 min; Bologna to Florence, hrly, 90 min). Train info: tel. 147-888-088.

# FLORENCE (FIRENZE)

Florence, the home of the Renaissance and birthplace of our modern world, is a "supermarket sweep," and the groceries are the best Renaissance art in Europe.

Get your bearings with a Renaissance walk. Florentine art goes beyond paintings and statues—there's food, fashion, and handicrafts. You can lick Italy's best gelato while enjoying some of Europe's best people watching.

## Planning Your Time

If you're in Europe for three weeks, Florence deserves a well-organized day. (Siena, an easy 75-minute bus ride away, has no awesome sights but is a more enjoyable home base.) For a day in Florence, see Michelangelo's *David*, tour the Uffizi Gallery (best Italian paintings anywhere), tour the underrated Bargello (best statues), and do the Renaissance ramble (explained below). Art lovers will want to chisel another day out of their itinerary for the many other Florentine cultural treasures. Shoppers and ice-cream lovers may need to do the same. Plan your sightseeing carefully. Mondays and afternoons can be sparse. While many spend several hours a day in lines, thoughtful travelers do not. Consider eating long and slow at lunch (it's hot out and prices are better). See any sights in the evening that you can.

## Orientation

The Florence we're interested in lies mostly on the north bank of the Arno River. Everything is within a 20-minute walk of the train station, cathedral, or Ponte Vecchio (Old Bridge). The less impressive but more characteristic Oltrarno (south

## Florence Schematic

bank) area is just over the bridge. The huge red-tiled dome of the cathedral (the Duomo) and its tall bell tower (Giotto's Tower) mark the center of historic Florence.

## Tourist Information

There are three TIs in Florence. The TI across the square from the train station can be plagued by long lines (Mon–Sat 8:30–19:00, Sun 8:30–13:00; off-season Mon–Sat 8:30–17:30, Sun 8:30–13:00, handy train schedule posted in lobby; with your back to tracks, TI is straight ahead, across square in wall near corner of church, look for "i" sign; Piazza Stazione, tel. 055-212-245). Note: In the station, avoid the Hotel Reservations "Tourist Information" window (marked Informazioni Turistiche Alberghiere) near the McDonald's; it's not a real TI but a hotel reservation business. The TI near Santa Croce Church is pleasant, helpful, and uncrowded (Mon–Sat 9:00–19:00, Sun 9:00–14:00, shorter hours off-season, Borgo Santa Croce 29 red, tel. 055-234-0444). Another winner is the TI three blocks north of the Duomo (Mon–Sat 8:15–19:15, Sun 8:30–18:30, shorter hours off-season, Via Cavour 1 red, tel. 055-290-832 or 055-290-833; international bookstore across street, see "Helpful Hints," below). TI Web site: www.firenze.turismo.toscana.it.

At the TI pick up a map, a current museum-hours listing (extremely important since hours are constantly in flux), and any information on entertainment. They even have a brochure on where to find public WCs in Florence. The free monthly *Florence Concierge Information* magazine lists museums plus lots that I

## Greater Florence

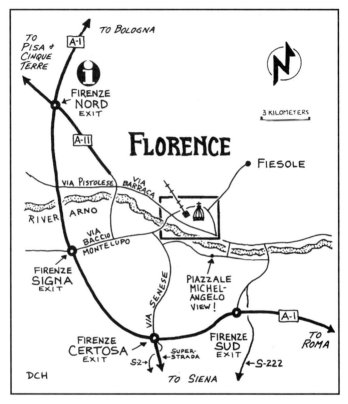

don't: concerts and events, markets, sporting events, church services, shopping ideas, bus and train connections, and an entire similar section on Siena. Get yours at the TI or from any expensive hotel (pick one up, as if you're staying there).

## Arrival in Florence

**By Train:** The station soaks up time and generates dazed and sweaty crowds. Try to get your tourist information and train tickets elsewhere. (You can get onward tickets and information at American Express—see "Helpful Hints," below.) With your back to the tracks, to your left are most of my recommended hotels, a 24-hour pharmacy (Farmacia Comunale, near McDonald's), city buses, and the entrance to the underground mall/ passage to Santa Maria Novella (but because the surface point near the church is frequented by pickpockets, stay above ground).

**By Car:** From the autostrada (north or south), take the Certosa exit (follow signs to Centro, at Porta Romana go to the left of the arch and down Via Francesco Petrarca). After driving and trying to park in Florence, you'll understand why Leonardo never invented the car. Cars flatten the charm of Florence. Don't drive in Florence and don't risk parking illegally (fines up to L300,000). The city has plenty of lots. For a short stay, consider the underground lot at the train station (L3,000/hr). The Fortezza da Basso is clearly marked in the center (L36,000/24 hrs). The least expensive lot is Parcheggio Parterre (Firenze Parcheggi, L15,000/24 hrs with hotel reservation). For parking information, call 055-234-0444.

## Helpful Hints

**Museums and Churches:** Hours of sights are certain to change without warning. Pick up the latest listing of museum hours at a TI, or you'll miss out on something you came to see. Visit everyone's essential sight, *David*, right off. In Italy a masterpiece seen and enjoyed is worth two tomorrow; you never know when a place will unexpectedly close for a holiday, strike, or restoration. The Uffizi has one- to two-hour lines on busy days (make reservations at least a day in advance before 18:30 when the ticket office closes, see Uffizi, under "Sights," below). Some museums close at 14:00 and stop selling tickets 30 minutes before that. The biggies (Uffizi and Accademia) close on Monday. The *Concierge Information* magazine thoughtfully lists which sights are open afternoons, Sundays, and Mondays (best attractions open Mon: Museo dell' Opera del Duomo, Giotto's Tower, Brancacci Chapel, Michelangelo's Casa Buonarroti, Dante's House, Science Museum, Palazzo Vecchio, and churches). In 2001, a combo ticket may cover the Accademia (*David*), Bargello, and the Medici Chapel (L25,000, available at participating sites). Churches usually close from 12:30 to 15:00 or 16:00. Local guidebooks are cheap and give you a map and a decent commentary on the sights.

**Theft Alert:** Florence has particularly hardworking thief gangs. They specialize in tourists and hang out where you do: near the train station, the station's underpass (especially where the tunnel surfaces), and major sights. American tourists—especially older ones—are considered the easiest targets.

**Medical Help:** For a doctor who speaks English, call 055-475-411 (reasonable hotel calls, cheaper if you go to clinic at Via L. Magnifico 59, 24-hour pharmacy at the train station). The TI has a list of English-speaking doctors.

**Addresses:** Street addresses list businesses in red and residences in black or blue (color coded on the actual street number and indicated by a letter following the number in printed addresses: n = black, r = red). *Pensioni* are usually black but can be either. The red and black numbers each appear in roughly

consecutive order on streets but bear no apparent connection
with each other.

**American Express:** Amex offers all the normal services but
is most helpful as an easy place to get your train tickets, reservations, supplements (all the same price as at station), or even just
information on train schedules. It's north of the Palazzo Vecchio
on Via Dante Alighieri 22 red (Mon–Fri 9:00–17:30, Sat 9:00–
12:30, CC:VMA!, tel. 055-50981).

**Long-Distance Telephoning:** Small newsstand kiosks
and dreary hole-in-the-wall phone shops all over town sell PIN
phone cards giving you cheap (3 minutes/$1) phone calls to the
United States.

**Books:** Feltrinelli International, a fine bookstore that
sells fiction and guidebooks in English, is a few blocks north of
the Duomo and across the street from the TI on Via Cavour
(Mon–Sat 9:00–19:30, Via Cavour 20 red). Paperback Exchange
also sells fiction and guidebooks (daily 9:00–19:30, shorter hours
in Aug, at corner of Via Fiesolana and Via dei Pilastri, 6 blocks
east of Duomo, tel. 055-247-8154).

**Tours: Walking Tours of Florence** offers a variety of tours
(up to 4 a day) Monday through Saturday featuring downtown
Florence, Uffizi highlights, or the countryside, presented by
informative, entertaining guides who are fluent in English
(L35,000 for 3-hr Original Florence walk, office open Mon–Sat
8:30–12:15, 14:15–18:00, Piazza Santo Stefano 2 black, a short
block north of Ponte Vecchio; go east on tiny Vicolo San Stefano,
in Piazza Santo Stefano go left to #2 and up the stairs; booking
necessary for Uffizi tour, private tours also available even on Sun,
tel. 055-264-5033 or cellular 0329-613-2730, www.florencewalk-
ingtours.com). Their office serves as the meeting point for the
tours (offered year-round, regardless of weather, maximum of 18,
extra guide available if more than 18 show up).

## Getting around Florence

I organize my sightseeing geographically and do it all on foot.
A L1,500 ticket gives you one hour on the buses, L2,500 gives
you three hours, and L6,000 gets you 24 hours (tickets not sold
on bus, buy in *tabacchi* shops or newsstands, validate on bus).
Minimum taxi ride: L7,000, or, after 22:00, L9,500 (rides in the
center of town should be charged as tarif #1). A taxi ride from
the train station to Ponte Vecchio costs about L15,000.

## A Florentine Renaissance Walk

Even during the Dark Ages people knew they were in a "middle
time." It was especially obvious to the people of Italy—sitting on the
rubble of Rome—that there was a brighter age before them. The
long-awaited rebirth, or Renaissance, began in Florence for good

# Florence

To Piazza Liberta
San Marco
ACCADEMIA
TRAIN STN.
BUS STN.
MERCATO CENTRALE
SAN LORENZO
MEDICI CHAPEL STREET MKT.
PIAZZA ANNUNZIATA
S. MARIA NOVELLA
MEDICI PALACE
LAUR. LIB.
DUOMO
BAPT.
CATHEDRAL MUSEUM
BARGELLO
AGLI
P. REP.
CORSO
CASA DI DANTE
Vivoli's
CASA BUONARROTI
ORSAN-MICHELE
PORTA ROSSA
COV. MKT.
RIVER
D. GRECI
S. CROCE
SANTA CROCE
PALAZZO VECCHIO
PAZZI CHAPEL
OLTRARNO
S. SPIRITO
PONTE VECCHIO
ARNO
PITTI PALACE
UFFIZI
BOBOLI GARDENS
FORTE BELVEDERE
DCH
PIAZZALE MICHELANGELO
★ PIAZZA SIGNORIA
View
G = GELATERIA
400 METERS

reason. Wealthy because of its cloth industry, trade, and banking; powered by a fierce city-state pride (locals would pee into the Arno with gusto, knowing rival city-state Pisa was downstream); and fertile with more than its share of artistic genius (imagine guys like Michelangelo and Leonardo attending the same high school)— Florence was a natural home for this cultural explosion.

Take a walk through the core of Renaissance Florence by starting at the Accademia (home of Michelangelo's *David*) and cutting through the heart of the city to Ponte Vecchio on the Arno River. (A 10-page, self-guided tour of this walk is outlined in my museum guidebook, *Rick Steves' Mona Winks*; otherwise, you'll find brief descriptions below.)

At the Accademia you'll look into the eyes of Renaissance man—humanism at its confident peak. Then walk to the cathedral (Duomo) to see the dome that kicked off the architectural Renaissance. Step inside the baptistery to view a ceiling covered with preachy, flat, 2-D, medieval mosaic art. Then, to learn what happened when art met math, check out the realistic 3-D reliefs on the doors. The painter, Giotto, designed the bell tower—an early example of how a Renaissance genius excelled in many areas. Continue toward the river on Florence's great pedestrian mall, Via de' Calzaiuoli (or "Via Calz"), which was part of the original grid plan given the city by the ancient Romans. Down a few blocks, compare medieval and Renaissance statues on the exterior of the Orsanmichele Church. Via Calz connects the cathedral with the central square (Piazza della Signoria), the city palace (Palazzo Vecchio), and the Uffizi Gallery, which contains the greatest collection of Italian Renaissance paintings in captivity. Finally, walk through the Uffizi courtyard—a statuary think tank of Renaissance greats—to the Arno River and Ponte Vecchio.

## Sights—On Florence's Renaissance Walk

▲▲▲**Accademia (Galleria dell' Accademia)**—This museum houses Michelangelo's *David* and powerful (unfinished) *Prisoners.* Eavesdrop as tour guides explain these masterpieces. More than any other work of art, when you look into the eyes of *David*, you're looking into the eyes of Renaissance man. This was a radical break with the past. Man was now a confident individual, no longer a plaything of the supernatural. And life was now more than just a preparation for what happened after you died.

The Renaissance was the merging of art and science. In a humanist vein, *David* is looking at the crude giant of medieval darkness and thinking, "I can take this guy." Back on a religious track (and speaking of veins), notice *David*'s large and overdeveloped right hand. This is symbolic of the hand of God that powered David to slay the giant...and enabled Florence to rise above its crude neighboring city-states.

Beyond the magic marble are two floors of interesting pre-Renaissance and Renaissance paintings, including a couple of dreamy Botticellis.

**Cost, Hours, Location**: L15,000 (ask about combo ticket that covers Bargello and Medici Chapel). Open Tue–Sun, 8:30–18:50, Sat until 22:00, closed Mon, shorter hours off-season (Via Ricasoli 60, tel. 055-238-8609).

**Nearby**: Piazza Santissima Annunziata, behind the Accademia, features lovely Renaissance harmony. Brunelleschi's Hospital of the Innocents (Spedale degli Innocenti, not worth going inside), with terra-cotta medallions by Luca della Robbia, was built in the 1420s and is considered the first Renaissance building.

▲▲**Duomo**—Florence's mediocre Gothic cathedral has the third-longest nave in Christendom (free, Mon–Wed and Fri–Sat 10:00–17:00, Thu 10:00–15:30, Sun 13:30–17:00, first Sat of month 10:00–15:30). The church's noisy neo-Gothic facade from the 1870s is covered with pink, green, and white Tuscan marble. Since nearly all of its great art is stored in the Museo dell' Opera del Duomo, behind the church, the best thing about the interior is the shade. The inside of the dome is decorated by one of the largest paintings of the Renaissance, a huge (and newly restored) *Last Judgment* by Vasari and Zuccari. The cathedral's claim to artistic fame is Brunelleschi's magnificent dome—the first Renaissance dome and the model for domes to follow. Ascend 463 steps and enjoy an inside look at the construction (L10,000, Mon–Fri 8:30–19:00, Sat 8:30–17:00, closed Sun, first Sat of month 8:30–15:20). When planning St. Peter's in Rome, Michelangelo said, "I can build a dome bigger, but not more beautiful, than the dome of Florence."

**Giotto's Tower**—Climbing Giotto's 82-meter-tall tower (or Campanile) beats climbing the neighboring Duomo's dome because it's 50 fewer steps, faster, not so crowded, and offers the same view plus the dome (L10,000, daily 8:30–19:30).

▲▲**Museo dell' Opera del Duomo**—The underrated cathedral museum, behind the church at #9, is great if you like sculpture. It has masterpieces by Donatello (a gruesome wood carving of Mary Magdalene clothed in her matted hair, and the *cantoria*, a delightful choir loft bursting with happy children) and della Robbia (another choir loft, lined with the dreamy faces of musicians praising the Lord). Look for a late Michelangelo *Pietà* (Nicodemus, on top, is a self-portrait), Brunelleschi's models for his dome, and the original restored panels of Ghiberti's doors to the baptistery. This is one of the few museums in Florence open on Monday (L10,000, Mon–Sat 9:30–18:30, Sun 8:00–14:00, tel. 055-230-2885).

▲**Baptistery**—Michelangelo said its bronze doors were fit to be the gates of Paradise. Check out the gleaming copies of Ghiberti's bronze doors facing the Duomo and the famous competition doors around to the right (north). Making a breakthrough in perspective, Ghiberti used mathematical laws to create the illusion of receding distance on a basically flat surface. Go inside Florence's oldest building and sit and savor the medieval mosaic ceiling. Compare that to the "new, improved" art of the Renaissance (L5,000 interior open Mon–Sat 12:00–18:30, Sun 8:30–13:30, bronze doors are on the outside so always "open"; original panels are in the Museo dell' Opera del Duomo).

▲**Orsanmichele**—Mirroring Florentine values, this was a combination church-granary. The glorious tabernacle by Orcagna takes you back (1359). Notice the grain spouts on the pillars inside. Also study the sculpture on its outside walls. You can see man stepping out of the literal and figurative shadow of the church in the great

Renaissance sculptor Donatello's *St. George* (free, daily 9:00–12:00, 16:00–18:00, closed first and last Mon of month, on Via Calzaiuoli; can be closed due to staffing problems, try going through the back door). Across the street is Museo Orsanmichele…

▲**Museo Orsanmichele**—For some peaceful time alone with the original statues that filled the niches of Orsanmichele, climb to the top of the church (entry behind church, across street). Be there during the few minutes at 9:00, 10:00, and 11:00 on weekdays when the door is open and art lovers in the know climb four flights of stairs to this little known museum, containing statues by Ghiberti, Donatello, and others (info in Italian, but picture guides on wall help you match art with artists). Upstairs is a tower room with city views. On Saturday and Sunday, the museum is wide open from 9:00 to 13:00 and 16:00 to 18:00 (free, closed first and last Mon of month; benches on both floors).

▲**Palazzo Vecchio**—This fortified palace, once the home of the Medici family, is a Florentine landmark. But if you're visiting only one palace interior in town, the Pitti Palace is better. The Palazzo Vecchio interior is wallpapered with mediocre magnificence, worthwhile only if you're a real Florentine art and history fan. The museum's most famous statues are Michelangelo's *Genius of Victory*, Donatello's static *Judith and Holerfernes*, and Verrocchio's *Winged Cherub* (a copy tops the fountain in the free courtyard at entrance, original inside).

Scattered throughout the museum are a dozen computer terminals with information in English on the Medici family, Palazzo Vecchio, and the building's architecture and art, including Michelangelo's *David* (with jerky animation showing how the original *David* was moved to the square in front of the Palazzo Vecchio). The computer info, combined with English descriptions labeling the art, make this otherwise-numbing museum more meaningful. Overeager to clock out, guards start turning off computer terminals 30 minutes before closing (L11,000, Sun 9:00–14:00, Mon–Wed and Fri–Sat 9:00–19:00, Thu 9:00–14:00, in summer open until 23:00 on Mon and Fri, buy ticket in office in second courtyard, then ascend stairs between first and second courtyard to reach museum; WC in second courtyard; tel. 055-276-8465). The gift shop sells Art Cubes (next to cash register) that can be manipulated into different paintings (L25,000, so cool they're probably sold out, but worth asking about; entrance to shop next to ticket office, no need to pay admission). A new "Secret Routes" tour takes you up hidden stairs to the Duke of Athens' private chambers and studio (L13,000, includes Palazzo Vecchio, book in advance; stop by Palazzo Vecchio or call 055-276-8224 between 9:30 and 12:00).

Even if you don't go to the museum, do step into the free courtyard (behind the fake *David*) just to feel the essence of the

Medici. Until 1873 Michelangelo's *David* stood at the entrance, where the copy is today. While the huge statues in the square are important only as the whipping boys of art critics and rest stops for pigeons, the nearby Loggia dei Lanzi has several important statues. Look for Cellini's bronze statue of Perseus (with the head of Medusa). The plaque on the pavement in front of the fountain marks the spot where Savonarola was burned in MCCCCXCVIII.

▲▲▲**Bargello (Museo Nazionale)**—This underrated sculpture museum is behind Palazzo Vecchio in a former prison that looks like a mini–Palazzo Vecchio. It has Donatello's painfully beautiful *David* (the very influential first male nude to be sculpted in a thousand years), works by Michelangelo, and rooms of Medici treasures cruelly explained in Italian only—mention that English descriptions would be wonderful (L8,000, daily 8:30–13:50 but closed first, third, and fifth Sun and second and fourth Mon of each month, Via del Proconsolo 4, tel. 055-238-8606).

▲▲▲**Uffizi Gallery**—The greatest collection of Italian paintings anywhere is a must, with plenty of works by Giotto, Leonardo, Raphael, Caravaggio, Rubens, Titian, and Michelangelo and a roomful of Botticellis, including his *Birth of Venus.* There are no official tours, so buy a book on the street before entering (or follow *Mona Winks*). Because only 600 visitors are allowed inside the building at any one time, during the day there's generally a very long wait. The good news: no Louvre-style mob scenes. The museum is nowhere near as big as it is great: Few tourists spend more than two hours inside. The paintings are displayed on one comfortable floor in chronological order from the 13th through 17th centuries.

Essential stops are (in this order) the Gothic altarpieces (narrative, prerealism, no real concern for believable depth); Giotto's altarpiece in the same room, which progressed beyond "totem-pole angels"; Uccello's *Battle of San Romano,* an early study in perspective (with a few obvious flubs); Fra Filippo Lippi's cuddly Madonnas; the Botticelli room, filled with masterpieces, including a pantheon of classical fleshiness and the small *La Calumnia,* showing the glasnost of Renaissance free-thinking being clubbed back into the darker age of Savonarola; two minor works by Leonardo; the octagonal classical sculpture room with an early painting of Bob Hope and a copy of Praxiteles' *Venus de Medici*—considered the epitome of beauty in Elizabethan Europe; Michelangelo's only surviving easel painting, the round *Holy Family;* Raphael's noble *Madonna of the Goldfinch;* Titian's voluptuous *Venus of Urbino;* and views from the café terrace at the end.

**Cost, Hours, Reservations:** L12,000, Tuesday through Sunday, 8:30 to 18:50, Saturday until 22:00, closed Monday (last entry 45 min before closing, take elevator or climb 4 long flights of stairs; Sat eve is least crowded).

Avoid the two-hour peak season midday wait by making a reservation. It's easy, slick, and costs only L2,000. Simply telephone during their office hours, choose a time, leave your name, and they'll give you a 15-minute entry time window and a five-digit confirmation number (call 055-294-883, Mon–Fri 8:30–18:30, Sat 9:00–12:00). You can reserve from months ahead to the day before (sometimes even on same day, but no guarantee). At the Uffizi, walk briskly past the 200-meter-long line to the special entrance for those with reservations (labeled in English "Entrance for Reservations Only"), give your name and number, pay (cash only), and scoot right in. You can reserve in advance for other museums—including the Bargello, Accademia (*David*), and Medici Chapel, though the only other one I'd consider reserving would be the Accademia.

If you haven't called ahead, you may be able to book directly at the Uffizi. Ask the clerk (who stands at the entrance for people with reservations) if you can make a reservation in person. He may direct you to the ticket office where you can secure a reservation for later in the day or the next day (depends on luck and availability).

Enjoy the Uffizi square, full of artists and souvenir stalls. The surrounding statues honor the earthshaking: artists, philosophers (Machiavelli), scientists (Galileo), writers (Dante), explorers (Amerigo Vespucci), and the great patron of so much Renaissance thinking, Lorenzo (the Magnificent) de Medici.

▲**Ponte Vecchio**—Florence's most famous bridge is lined with shops that have traditionally sold gold and silver. A statue of Cellini, the master goldsmith of the Renaissance, stands in the center, ignored by the flood of tacky tourism. Notice the "prince's passageway" above. In less secure times, the city leaders had a fortified passageway connecting the Palace Vecchio and Uffizi with the mighty Pitti Palace, to which they could flee in times of attack. This passageway, called the Vasari Corridor, is open to the persistent by request only (L12,000, Tue–Sat at 9:30, closed Mon, tel. 055-265-4321).

## More Sights—Central Florence

▲▲**Santa Croce Church**—This 14th-century Franciscan church, decorated by centuries of precious art, holds the tombs of great Florentines (free, Mon–Sat 8:00–18:30, Sun 15:00–17:30, in winter Mon–Sat 8:00–12:30, 15:00–17:30, Sun 15:00–17:30, modest dress code enforced, tel. 055-244-619). The loud 19th-century Victorian Gothic facade faces a huge square ringed with tempting touristy shops and littered with tired tourists. Escape into the church.

Working counterclockwise from the entrance you'll find the tomb of Michelangelo (with the allegorical figures of painting, architecture, and sculpture), a memorial to Dante (no body…he was banished by his hometown), the tomb of Machiavelli (the originator of hardball politics), a relief by Donatello of the Annunciation, and the tomb of the composer Rossini. To the right of the altar, step into the sacristy where you'll find the bit of St. Francis' cowl (he is supposed to have founded the church around 1290) and old sheets of music with the medieval and mobile C clef (two little blocks on either side of the line determined to be middle C). In the bookshop notice the photos high on the wall of the devastating flood of 1966. Beyond that is a touristy—but mildly interesting—"leather school." The chapels lining the front of the church are richly frescoed. The Bardi Chapel (far left of altar) is a masterpiece by Giotto featuring scenes from the life of St. Francis. On your way out you'll pass the tomb of Galileo (allowed in by the church long after his death). The neighboring Pazzi Chapel (by Brunelleschi) is considered one of the finest pieces of Florentine Renaissance architecture.

▲▲**Museum of San Marco**—One block north of the Accademia on Piazza San Marco, this museum houses the greatest collection anywhere of medieval frescoes and paintings by the early Renaissance master Fra Angelico. You'll see why he thought of painting as a form of prayer and couldn't paint a crucifix without shedding tears. Each of the monks' cells has a Fra Angelico fresco. Don't miss the cell of Savonarola, the charismatic monk who rode in from the Christian right, threw out the Medici, turned Florence into a theocracy, sponsored "bonfires of the vanities" (burning books, paintings, and so on), and was finally burned himself when Florence decided to change channels (L8,000, daily 8:30–13:50, Sat until 19:00, but closed the first, third, and fifth Sun and the second and fourth Mon of each month, tel. 055-238-8608).

▲**Medici Chapel (Cappella dei Medici)**—This chapel, containing two Medici tombs, is drenched in incredibly lavish High Renaissance architecture and sculpture by Michelangelo (L11,000, daily 8:30–17:00 but closed the second and fourth Sun and the first, third, and fifth Mon of each month, tel. 055-238-8602). Behind San Lorenzo on Piazza Madonna is a lively market scene that I find just as interesting. Take a stroll through the huge double-decker central market one block north.

**Science Museum (Museo di Storia della Scienza)**—This is a fascinating collection of Renaissance and later clocks, telescopes, maps, and ingenious gadgets. One of the most talked-about bottles in Florence is the one here containing Galileo's finger. English guidebooklets are available. It's friendly, comfortably cool, never crowded, and just downstream from the Uffizi (L12,000, Mon and Wed–Fri 9:30–17:00, Tue and Sat 9:30–13:00, closed Sun, Piazza dei Giudici 1, tel. 055-239-8876).

▲**Michelangelo's Home, Casa Buonarroti**—Fans enjoy Michelangelo's house, which has some of his early, much-less-monumental statues and sketches (L12,000, Wed–Mon 9:30–14:00, closed Tue, English descriptions, Via Ghibellina 70).

**Casa di Dante**—Dante's house is five rooms in an old building with little of substance to show but lots of photos relating to the life and work of Dante. Although it's well described in English, it's interesting only to his fans (L5,000, Mon and Wed–Sat 10:00–18:00, Sun 10:00–14:00, closed Tue, across the street and around the corner from Bargello, at Via S. Margherita 1).

**Church of Santa Maria Novella**—This 13th-century Dominican church is rich in art. Along with crucifixes by Giotto and Brunelleschi, there's every textbook's example of the early Renaissance mastery of perspective: *The Holy Trinity* by Masaccio (free, Mon–Sat 7:00–12:00, 15.00–18:00, Sat until 17:00, Sun 15:00–17:00).

A palatial perfumery is around the corner at 16 Via della Scala. Thick with the lingering aroma of centuries of spritzes, it started as the herb garden of the Santa Maria Novella monks. Well-known even today for its top-quality products, it is extremely Florentine. Pick up the history sheet at the desk and wander deep into the shop. From the back room you can peek at the S. M. Novella cloister, with its dreamy frescoes, and imagine a time before Vespas and tourists.

**Museum of Precious Stones (Museo dell' Opificio delle Pietre Dure)**—This unusual gem of a museum features mosaics of inlaid marble and semiprecious stones, along with oil-painting copies (L4,000, Mon–Sat 8:15–14:00, Tue until 19:00, closed Sun, Via degli Alfani 78, around corner from Accademia).

## Sights—Florence, South of the Arno River

▲▲**Pitti Palace**—From the Uffizi follow the elevated passageway (closed to non-Medicis) across the Ponte Vecchio bridge to the gargantuan Pitti Palace, which has five separate museums.

The **Palatine Gallery/Royal Apartments** features palatial room after chandeliered room, its walls sagging with paintings by the great masters. Its Raphael collection is the biggest anywhere (first floor, L14,000, Tue–Sun 8:30–18:50, Sat until 22:00, closed Mon, shorter hours off-season).

The **Modern Art Gallery** features Romanticism, neoclassicism, and Impressionism by 19th- and 20th-century Tuscan painters (second floor, L8,000, daily 8:30–13:50 but closed second and fourth Sun and first, third, and fifth Mon).

The **Grand Ducal Treasures**, or Museo degli Argenti, is the Medici treasure chest entertaining fans of applied arts with jeweled crucifixes, exotic porcelain, gilded ostrich eggs, and so on (ground floor, L4,000, same hours as Modern Art Gallery).

Behind the palace, the huge landscaped **Boboli Gardens** offer a shady refuge from the city heat (L4,000, Tue–Sun 9:00–18:30, until 19:30 June–Aug, until 16:30 in winter, closed first and last Mon of month).

▲**Brancacci Chapel**—For the best look at the early Renaissance master Massaccio, see his restored frescoes here (L6,000, Mon and Wed–Sat 10:00–17:00, Sun 13:00–17:00, closed Tue, cross Ponte Vecchio and turn right a few blocks to Piazza del Carmine). Since only a few tourists are let in at a time, seeing the chapel often involves a wait. The neighborhoods around here are considered the last surviving bits of old Florence.

▲**Piazzale Michelangelo**—Across the river overlooking the city (look for the huge statue of *David*), this square is worth the 30-minute hike, drive, or bus ride (either #12 or #13 from the train station) for the view of Florence and the stunning dome of the Duomo. After dark it's packed with local schoolkids feeding their dates slices of watermelon. Just beyond it is the stark and beautiful, crowd-free Romanesque San Miniato Church.

## Experiences—Florence

▲▲**Gelato**—Gelato is an edible art form. Italy's best ice cream is in Florence—one souvenir that can't break and won't clutter your luggage. But beware of scams at touristy joints on busy streets that turn a simple request of a cone into a L15,000 "tourist special." The **Gelateria Carrozze** is very good (daily in summer 11:00–01:00, closed Wed in winter, on riverfront 30 meters from Ponte Vecchio toward the Uffizi, Via del Pesce 3). **Gelateria dei Neri**—considered by many to be the best in central Florence—is worth finding. It's two blocks east of Palazzo Vecchio at Via Dei Neri 20 red (daily in summer 12:00–23:00, closed Wed in winter). **Vivoli's** is a longtime favorite (Tue–Sun 8:00–01:00, closed Mon, the last 3 weeks in Aug, and winter; opposite the Church of Santa Croce, go down Via Torta a block, turn right on Via Stinche; before ordering, try a free sample of their *riso*—rice). The Cinema Astro, across the street from Vivoli's, plays English/American movies in their original language (closed Mon).

## Shopping

Florence is a great shopping town. Busy street scenes and markets abound, especially near San Lorenzo, near Santa Croce, and on Ponte Vecchio (plus 3 blocks north of bridge at Mercato Nuovo—a covered market square). Leather (often better quality for less than the U.S. price), gold, silver, art prints, and tacky plaster "mini-*Davids*" are most popular. Prices are soft in the markets. Many spend entire days shopping. Shops usually have promotional stalls in the market squares. For ritzy Italian fashions, browse along Via de Tornabuoni, Via della Vigna Nuova, and Via Strozzi. Typical chain department stores are Coin (Mon–Sat 9:30–20:00, Sun 11:00–20:00, on Via Calzaiuoli, near Orsanmichele church) and Standa (Mon–Sat 9:00–19:55, closed Sun, at intersection of Via Panzani and Via del Giglio, near train station). For shopping ideas, ads, and a list of markets, see the *Florence Concierge Information* magazine described under "Tourist Information," above (free from TI and many hotels).

## Side Trips to Fiesole and Siena

For a candid peek at **Fiesole**—a Florentine suburb—ride bus #7 (3/hrly, from Piazza Adua, northeast side of the station and from Piazza San Marco) for about 25 minutes through neighborhood gardens, vineyards, orchards, and large villas to the last stop— Fiesole. Fiesole is a popular excursion from Florence because of its small eateries and its good views of Florence. Catch the sunset from the terrace just below the La Reggia restaurant; from the Fiesole bus stop, face the bell tower and take the very steep Via San Francisco on your left. You'll find the view terrace near the top of the hill.

Connoisseurs of peace and small towns who aren't into art or shopping (and who won't be seeing Siena otherwise) should consider riding the bus to **Siena** (75 minutes if you take the *"corse rapide"* via the autostrada). This can be a day trip or an evening trip. Siena is magic after dark. Confirm when the last bus returns. For more on Siena, see the chapter on Hill Towns of Central Italy.

## Sleeping in Florence
**(L2,000 = about $1, country code: 39)**

Sleep Code: **S** = Single, **D** = Double/Twin, **T** = Triple, **Q** = Quad, **b** = bathroom, **s** = shower only, **CC** = Credit Card (**V**isa, **M**aster-Card, **A**mex), **SE** = Speaks English, **NSE** = No English. Unless otherwise noted, breakfast is included (but usually optional). English is generally spoken.

The accommodations scene varies wildly with the season. Spring and fall are very tight and expensive, while mid-July through August are wide open and discounted. November through February is also generally empty. With good information and a phone call ahead, you can find a stark, clean, and comfortable double with breakfast for L120,000, with a private shower for L170,000 (less at the smaller places, such as the *soggiornos*). You get elegance for L200,000. Many places listed are old and rickety. I can't imagine Florence any other way. Rooms with air-conditioning cost around L200,000—worth the extra lire in the summer. Virtually all of the places are central, within minutes of the great sights.

Call direct to the hotel. Do not use the TI, which costs your host and jacks up the price. In slow times, budget travelers call around and find soft prices. Ask if you'll get a discount for paying in cash or for staying for three or more nights (or both). And ask if you can skip breakfast (these overpriced breakfasts are legally optional, though some hotels pretend otherwise).

Call ahead. I repeat, call ahead. Places will hold a room

# Florence Hotels and Restaurants

1 - HOTEL ACCADEMIA
2 - HOTEL MORANDI
3 - CASA RABATTI
4 - SOGGIORNO PEZZATI
5 - HOTEL ENZA
6 - SOGGIORNO MAGLIANI
7 - HOTEL LOGGIATO DEI SERVITI
8 - DUE FONTANE HOTEL
9 - HOTEL MONNA LISA & OBLATE
10 - SOGGIORNO LA PERGOLA
11 - PALAZZO CASTIGLIONI &
     HOTEL ALDOBRANDINI

12 - HOTEL BELLETTINI
13 - HOTEL BASILEA
14 - PENSIONE CENTRALE
15 - PICNIC SPOT IF NOT TOO HOT
16 - OSTERIA BELLEDONNE
17 - HOTEL PENDINI
18 - PENSIONE MAXIM
19 - HOTEL RITZ
20 - HOTEL ELITE
21 - ALBERGO MONTREALE
22 - PENSIONE SOLE

23 - PENSIONE BRETAGNA
24 - FLORENCE WALKING TOURS
25 - TORRE GUELFA, APOSTOLI
     & ALESSANDRA HOTELS
26 - TRATTORIA IL CONTADINO
27 - TRATTORIA DA GIORGIO
28 - GROTTA DI LEO
29 - TRATTORIA BURRASCA
30 - HYDRA PIZZERIA
31 - ROSTICCERIA GIULIANO
32 - OSTERIA SAPORI
33 - CANTINETTA VERRAZZANO

until early afternoon. If they say they're full, mention you're using this book.

**Laundromats**: The Wash & Dry Lavarapido chain offers long hours and efficient self-service Laundromats at several locations (daily 8:00–22:00, tel. 055-580-480). Close to recommended hotels: Via dei Servi 105 red (near *David*), Via del Sole 29 red and Via della Scala 52 red (between station and river), and Via dei Serragli 87 red (across the river). East of the station another handy modern launderette is just off Via Cavour at Via Guelfa 22 red (daily 8:00–22:00, 12 pounds wash and dry for L12,000).

## Sleeping between the Station and Duomo (zip code: 50123)

**Hotel Accademia** is an elegant two-star hotel with marble stairs, parquet floors, attractive public areas, 16 pleasant rooms, and a floor plan that defies logic (S with private bath down hall–L150,000, Sb-L160,000, Db-L230,000, Tb-L290,000, these discounted prices only with this book, CC:VMA, air-con, TV, tiny courtyard, Via Faenza 7, tel. 055-293-451, fax 055-219-771, www.accademiahotel.net, e-mail: info@accademiahotel.net).

**Hotel Bellettini** has 33 bright, cool, well-cared-for rooms with tile floors, inviting lounges, and a touch of class. Its five rooms in an annex two blocks away are three-star quality with all the comforts, but you need to come to the main hotel for breakfast (Sb-L150,000, Db-L200,000, Tb-L270,000, Qb-L340,000, CC:VMA, 5 percent discount with this book, buffet breakfast, air-con, free Internet access, Via de' Conti 7, tel. 055-213-561, fax 055-283-551, www.firenze.net/hotelbellettini, e-mail: hotel.bellettini@dada.it).

**Residenza Dei Pucci**, a block north of the Duomo, has 12 tastefully decorated rooms—in soothing earth tones—with good furniture and tweed carpeting. Just opened last year, it's fresh and bright. The suite has a huge view of the dome (Db-L230,000, Db suite-L315,000, these discounted prices good only with this book, includes breakfast—served in room, CC:VM, treats and beverages available in afternoon, Via dei Pucci 9, tel. 055-281-886, fax 055-264-314, SE).

**Palazzo Castiglioni**, newly opened, offers six grand rooms with all the conveniences in a 19th-century palazzo package. Most rooms are spacious, several have frescoes, and all make a fine splurge (Db-L320,000, Db suite-L400,000, includes breakfast, CC:VM, air-con, elevator, Via del Giglio 8, tel. 055-214-886, fax 055-274-0521, e-mail: torre.guelfa@flashnet.it, Giancarlo and Sabina).

**Pensione Centrale**, a happy and traditional-feeling place, is indeed central. Run by aristocratic Marie Therese Blot, spunky Margherita, and Franco, you'll feel right at home

(18 rooms, D-L170,000, Db-L200,000 with an "American" breakfast, CC:VMA, quiet, some air-con rooms, often filled with American students, elevator, Via de' Conti 3, tel. 055-215-761, fax 055-215-216). They sometimes send people to a nearby, noisier pension; confirm that your reservation is for this place.

**Hotel Aldobrandini**, a good budget choice, has 15 decent, clean, affordable rooms, with the San Lorenzo market at its doorstep and the entrance to the Medici Chapel a few steps away (Ss-L80,000, Sb-L100,000, D-L120,000, Db-L150,000, includes breakfast, CC:VM, noisy in front, quieter rooms in back, lots of stairs, Piazza Madonna Degli Aldobrandini 8, tel. 055-211-866, fax 055-267-6281, e-mail: welcome@srl.com).

## Sleeping near the Central Market
### (zip code: 50129)

**Hotel Basilea** features a rare ground-floor lobby and offers predictable three-star, air-conditioned comfort in its 38 modern rooms (Db-L200,000–280,000 depending on season, CC:VM, elevator, terrace, free e-mail service, Via Guelfa 41, at intersection with Nazionale—a busy street, ask for rooms in the back, tel. 055-214-587, fax 055-268-350, e-mail: basilea@dada.it).

**Casa Rabatti** is the ultimate if you always wanted to be a part of a Florentine family. It's simple, clean, friendly, and run with motherly warmth by Marcella and her husband Celestino, who speak minimal English (4 rooms, D-L85,000, Db-L100,000, L40,000 per bed in shared quad or quint, prices good with this book, no breakfast, no sign other than on doorbell, 5 blocks from station, Via San Zanobi 48 black, tel. 055-212-393).

**Soggiorno Pezzati Daniela** is another quiet little place with six homey rooms (Sb-L78,000, Db-L105,000, Tb-L150,000, Qb-L180,000, no breakfast, marked only by small sign near door, Via San Zanobi 22, tel. 055-291-660, fax 055-287-145, e-mail: 055291660@iol.it, Daniela SE). If you get an Italian recording when you call, hang on—your call is being transferred to a cell phone.

**Hotel Enza** rents 16 quirky rooms. While Eugenia's chihuahua, Tricky, is tiny, her rooms are spacious (S-L80,000, Sb-L85,000, D-L100,000, Ds-L120,000, Db-L135,000, T-L135,000, Tb-L175,000, family loft, no breakfast, CC to reserve but pay cash, Via San Zanobi 45 black, tel. 055-490-990, fax 055-473-672).

Central and humble **Soggiorno Magliani** feels and smells like a great-grandmother's place (7 rooms, S-L60,000, D-L80,000, double-paned windows don't quite keep out street noise, near corner of Via Guelfa and Via Reparata, Via Reparata 1, tel. 055-287-378, run by a friendly family duo, Vincenza and English-speaking daughter Cristina).

## Sleeping East of the Duomo

The first two listings are near the Accademia, on Piazza Annunziata (zip code: 50122).

**Hotel Loggiato dei Serviti**, at the most prestigious address in Florence on the most Renaissance square in town, gives you Renaissance romance with a place to plug in your hair dryer (29 rooms, Sb-L250,000, Db-L380,000, family suites from L500,000, book a month ahead during peak season, discounts in Aug, CC:VMA, elevator, square noisy at night, Piazza S.S. Annunziata 3, tel. 055-289-592, fax 055-289-595, e-mail: loggiato_serviti@italyhotel.com, SE). Stone stairways lead you under open-beam ceilings through this 16th-century monastery's elegant public rooms. The cells, with air-conditioning, TVs, mini-bars, and telephones, wouldn't be recognized by their original inhabitants.

**Le Due Fontane Hotel** faces the same great square but fills its old building with a smoky, 1970s, business-class ambience. Its 57 air-conditioned rooms are big and comfortable (Sb-L190,000, Db-L260,000, Tb-L370,000, buffet breakfast, CC:VMA, phones, TVs, elevator, they're trying to make third floor nonsmoking, Piazza S.S. Annunziata 14, tel. 055-210-185, fax 055-294-461, SE).

At **Hotel Morandi alla Crocetta**, a former convent, you're enveloped in a 16th-century cocoon. Located on a quiet street, with period furnishings throughout the hotel, parquet floors, and wood-beamed ceilings, it draws you in (Sb-L160,000, Db-L270,000, CC:VM, Via Laura 50, a block off Piazza S.S. Annunziata, tel. 055-234-4747, fax 055-248-0954, www.hotelmorandi.it, e-mail: welcome@hotelmorandi.it).

**Hotel Monna Lisa**, my only four-star listing in this neighborhood, is an art-filled convent-turned-palace with an elegant garden, palatial public spaces, and professional service. It's steeped in history. Judging from the guest book, its visitors are happy to have paid the ransom (30 rooms, Db-L370,000 most of the year but L550,000 mid-March–mid-July and Sept–Oct, CC:VMA, air-con, parking, 3 blocks east of Duomo at Borgo Pinti 27, tel. 055-247-9751, fax 055-247-9755, www.monnalisa.it, e-mail: monnalis@ats.it).

The **Oblate Sisters of the Assumption** run a small hotel in a Renaissance building with a dreamy garden and a quiet, institutional feel (S-L65,000, D-L120,000, Db-L130,000, big L25,000 dinners, elevator, Borgo Pinti 15, 50121 Firenze, tel. 055-248-0582, fax 055-234-6291, NSE).

**Soggiorno La Pergola** is a homey, air-conditioned place with 14 rooms, some with kitchenettes (Db-L150,000–190,000, Qb-L200,000–250,000 depending on season, Via della Pergola 23, tel. & fax 055-700-896).

## Sleeping on or near Piazza Repubblica
### (zip code: 50123)

These are the most central of my accommodations recommendations, though given Florence's walkable core, nearly every hotel can be considered central.

**Hotel Pendini**, a three-star hotel with 42 elegant rooms (8 with views of the square), is popular and central, overlooking Piazza Repubblica (Sb-L150,000–200,000, Db-L200,000–280,000 depending on season, CC:VMA, elevator, fine lounge and breakfast room, air-con, Via Strozzi 2, reserve ASAP, tel. 055-211-170, fax 055-281-807, e-mail: pendini@dada.it).

**Pensione Maxim**, right on Via Calz, is a big, institutional-feeling place as close to the sights as possible. Its halls are narrow, but the 26 rooms are comfortable and well maintained (Sb-L150,000, Db-L170,000, Tb-L225,000, Qb-L280,000, with breakfast, add L10,000 per person per day for air-con June–Sept, CC:VMA but pay first night in cash, Internet access, phones, elevator, no curfew, Via dei Calzaiuoli 11, tel. 055-217-474, fax 055-283-729, www.firenzealbergo.it/home/hotelmaxim, e-mail: hotmaxim@tin.it, Paolo and Nicola Maioli).

**Soggiorno Battistero**, next door to the Baptistery, has seven simple, airy rooms, most with urban noise but great views overlooking the Baptistery and square. You're in the heart of Florence (S-L80,000, D-L120,000, Db-L150,000, Tb-L180,000, breakfast extra—served in room, Internet access, CC:VM, Piazza San Giovanni 1, third floor, tel. 055-295-143, fax 055-268-189, www.venere.it/firenze/battistero, e-mail: battistero@dada.it, run by Italian Luca and American wife Kelly).

## Sleeping South of the Train Station near Piazza Santa Maria Novella
### (zip code: 50123)

From the station, follow the Galleria S.M. Novella tunnel (with back to tracks, outside on the left) to Piazza Santa Maria Novella, a pleasant square by day that becomes a little sleazy after dark. *Note: Theft alert in the tunnel, where the tunnel surfaces, and at night.* The square is handy—only three blocks from the cathedral and near a good launderette (Lavarapido, daily 8:00–22:00, Via della Scala 52 red) and cheap restaurants (on Via Palazzuolo, see below).

**Hotel Pensione Elite**, with eight comfortable rooms and a charm rare in this price range, is a fine basic value run warmly by Maurizio and Nadia (Ss-L90,000, Sb-L120,000, Ds-L130,000, Db-L150,000, breakfast-L10,000, at south end of square with back to church, go right to Via della Scala 12, second floor, tel. & fax 055-215-395, SE).

The nearby **Albergo Montreal** is OK for backpackers, with 18 clean, airy, characterless, although renovated, rooms

(S-L75,000, Db-L120,000, Tb-L160,000, mention this book when reserving to get these prices, no breakfast, Via della Scala 43, tel. 055-238-2331, fax 055-287-491, e-mail: info@hotelmontreal.com, SE).

**Pensione Sole**, a clean, cozy, family-run place with seven bright, modern rooms, is just off Santa Maria Novella toward the river (Db-L120,000–130,000, no breakfast; air-con, phone, elevator, Via del Sole 8, third floor, tel. & fax 055-239-6094, friendly Anna NSE).

### Sleeping near Arno River and Ponte Vecchio (zip code: 50123)

**Pensione Bretagna** is an Old World–elegant place. It's run by the helpful, English-speaking Antonio, Maura, and Sara. Imagine eating breakfast under a painted, chandeliered ceiling overlooking the Arno River (S-L80,000, Ss-L90,000, Sb-L100,000, D-L130,000, Ds-L145,000, Db-L175,000, Tb-L220,000, Qb-L245,000, including optional L5,000 breakfast, family deals, prices special with this book through 2001, CC:VMA, air-con, elevator, just past Ponte San Trinita, Lungarno Corsini 6, tel. 055-289-618, fax 055-289-619, e-mail: hotelpens.bretagna@agora.stm.it). They also run Althea, a cheaper place with nicer rooms, near Piazza San Spirito in the Oltrarno neighborhood (Db-L120,000, no breakfast, no reception desk, call Bretagna to book).

**Hotel Torre Guelfa** is topped with a fun medieval tower with a panoramic rooftop terrace and a huge living room. Its 16 rooms vary wildly in size (Sb-L180,000, small Db-L250,000, Db-L290,000–300,000). Number 15, with a private terrace—L350,000—is worth reserving several months in advance (elevator, air-con, a couple blocks northwest of Ponte Vecchio, Borgo S.S. Apostoli 8, tel. 055-239-6338, fax 055-239-8577, http://home.venere.it/firenze/torreguelfa, e-mail: torre.guelfa@flashnet.it, Giancarlo, Carlo, and Luigi all SE).

**Residenza Apostoli**, in the same building, is bright, spacious, and modern, with parquet floors and 12 air-conditioned rooms all buried in a very old building on a quiet street one block off the river (Sb-L190,000–200,000, Db-L200,000–250,000 depending on season, breakfast in room, CC:VM, 10 percent discount with this book, stay-awhile TV lounge, levator, Borgo Santi Apostoli 8, tel. 055-284-837, fax 055-268-790, run by Mirella).

**Hotel Pensione Alessandra** is an old 16th-century, peaceful place with 25 big rooms (S-L120,000, Sb-L190,000, D-L190,000, Db-L250,000, T-L250,000, Tb-L330,000, Q-L280,000, Qb-L370,000, includes breakfast, CC:VMA, most rooms have air-con, 2 have views, Borgo S.S. Apostoli 17, tel. 055-283-438, fax 055-210-619, www.hotelalessandra.com).

**Hotel Ritz** is a grand, riverside, four-star place with all the comforts, (Db-L200,000–320,000, Lungarno della Zecca Vecchia 24, 50122 Firenze, tel. 055-234-0650, fax 055-24-0863, e-mail: ritz@dada.it).

## Sleeping in Oltrarno, South of the River (zip code: 50125)

Across the river in the Oltrarno area, between the Pitti Palace and Ponte Vecchio, you'll still find small traditional crafts shops, neighborly piazzas, and family eateries. The following places are a few minutes' walk from Ponte Vecchio.

**Hotel La Scaletta** is elegant, friendly, and clean, with a dark, cool, labyrinthine floor plan, lots of Old World lounges, and a romantic and panoramic roof terrace. Owner Barbara, her son Manfredo, and daughters Bianca and Diana run this well-worn but loved place. If Manfredo is cooking dinner, eat here (S-L100,000, Sb-L180,000, D-L190,000, Db-L210,000–240,000, Tb-L250,000–270,000, Qb-L280,000–300,000, higher price is for quieter rooms in back, L10,000–20,000 discount if you pay cash, CC:VM, air-con in 3 rooms and fans in others, elevator, bar, Via Guicciardini 13 black, 150 meters south of Ponte Vecchio, tel. 055-283-028, fax 055-289-562, www.lascaletta.com, e-mail: lascaletta.htl@dada.it). Reserve by phone, confirm by fax, then send a personal or traveler's check.

**Hotel Silla**, a classic three-star hotel with 36 cheery, spacious, pastel, and modern rooms, is a fine value. It faces the river and overlooks a park opposite the Santa Croce Church (Db-L290,000, includes breakfast, CC:VMA, elevator, air-con, Via dei Renai 5, 50125 Florence, tel. 055-234-2888, fax 055-234-1437, www.hotelsilla.it, e-mail: hotelsilla@tin.it, SE).

**Pensione Sorelle Bandini** is a ramshackle, 500-year-old palace on a perfectly Florentine square, with cavernous rooms, museum-warehouse interiors, a musty youthfulness, cats, a balcony lounge-loggia with a view, and an ambience that, for romantic bohemians, can be a highlight of Florence. Mimmo or Sr. Romeo will hold a room until 16:00 with a phone call (D-L172,000, Db-L200,000, T-L240,000, Tb-L290,000, includes breakfast, elevator, Piazza Santo Spirito 9, tel. 055-215-308, fax 055-282-761).

**Soggiorno Pezzati Alessandra** is a warm and friendly place renting five great rooms in the Oltrarno neighborhood (Sb-L78,000, Db-L105,000, Tb-L150,000, Qb-L180,000, no breakfast, Via Borgo San Frediano 6, tel. 055-290-424, fax 055-264-6742, e-mail: alex170169@libero.it, Alessandra). If you get an Italian recording when you call, hang on —your call is being transferred to a cell phone.

**Istituto Gould** is a Protestant Church–run place with 33 clean but drab rooms with twin beds and modern facilities (S-L55,000, Sb-L65,000, D-L78,000, Db-L86,000, Tb-L114,000,

## Florence's Oltrarno Neighborhood

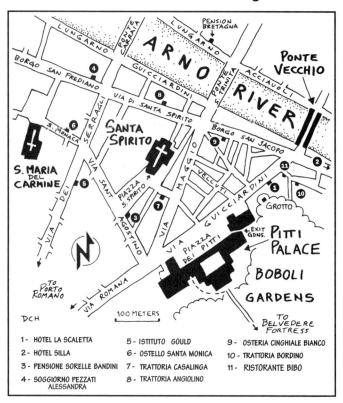

1 - HOTEL LA SCALETTA
2 - HOTEL SILLA
3 - PENSIONE SORELLE BANDINI
4 - SOGGIORNO PEZZATI ALESSANDRA
5 - ISTITUTO GOULD
6 - OSTELLO SANTA MONICA
7 - TRATTORIA CASALINGA
8 - TRATTORIA ANGIOLINO
9 - OSTERIA CINGHIALE BIANCO
10 - TRATTORIA BORDINO
11 - RISTORANTE BIBO

L37,000 in quads, L33,000 in quints, no breakfast, quieter rooms in back, Via dei Serragli 49, tel. 055-212-576, fax 055-280-274, e-mail: gould.reception@dada.it). You must arrive when the office is open (Mon–Fri 9:00–13:00, 15:00–19:00, Sat 9:00–13:00, no check-in Sun).

**Ostello Santa Monica**, a cheap hostel, is a few blocks south of Ponte Alla Carraia, one of the bridges over the Arno (L26,000 beds, 10-bed rooms, breakfast extra, 01:00 curfew, Via Santa Monica 6, tel. 055-268-338, fax 055-280-185).

## Sleeping Away from the Center
**Hotel Ungherese**, warmly run by Sergio and Rosemary, is good for drivers. It's northeast of the city center (near Stadio, en route to Fiesole), with easy, free street parking and quick bus access (#11 and #17) into central Florence (Sb-L120,000, Db-L210,000, these

discounted prices available with this book, pay cash for additional
7 percent discount, rooms are 20 percent less off-season, includes
breakfast, CC:VM, most rooms air-con, Via G. B. Amici 8, tel. &
fax 055-573-474, www.prato.dada.it/ungherese, e-mail: hotel
.ungherese@dada.it, NSE). It has great singles and a backyard
garden terrace (ask for a room on the garden). On the downside,
no restaurants are nearby (eat in Florence).

**Villa Camerata**, classy for an IYHF hostel, is on the outskirts
of Florence (L25,000 per bed with breakfast, 4- to 12-bed rooms,
no reservations, show up 9:00–13:00, ride bus #17 to Salviatino
stop, Via Righi 2, tel. 055-601-451).

# Eating in Florence
To save money and time for sights, you can keep meals fast and
simple, eating in one of the countless self-service places and
pizzerias or just picnicking (try juice, yogurt, cheese, and a roll
for L10,000). Or consider the following.

## Eating in Oltrarno, South of the River
For a change of scene, I'd eat across the river in Oltrarno. Here
are a few good places just over Ponte Vecchio and on or near
Piazza Santo Spirito.

A block south of Ponte Vecchio is the unpretentious and
happy Piazza San Felicita, with two great restaurants to consider.
**Ristorante Bibo** serves *"cucina tipica Fiorentina"* with smart and
friendly service, an air-conditioned interior, and leafy candlelit
outdoor seating (good L28,000 3-course meal, CC:VMA, reserve
for outdoor seating, Fri–Wed 11:00–15:00, 19:00–24:00, closed
Thu, Piazza San Felicita 6 red, tel. 055-239-8554). The cozier
**Trattoria Bordino**, just up the street, is similar, serving fine
Florentine cuisine (L40,000 dinners, cheaper options, Mon–Sat
12:00–14:30, 19:30–22:30, closed Sun, Via Stracciatella 9 red).

Piazza Santo Spirito is a classic Florentine square (and therefore touristy) with two classy and popular little restaurants offering
good local cuisine every night of the week, indoor and on-the-
square seating (reserve for on-the-square), moderate prices, and
impersonal service: **Borgo Antico** (Piazza Santo Spirito 6 red,
tel. 055-210-437) and **Osteria Santo Spirito** (Piazza Santo
Spirito 16 red, tel. 055-238-2383).

The **Ricchi Caffè**, next to Borgo Antico, has fine gelati and
shaded outdoor tables across the street. Notice how plain the
facade of the Brunelleschi church facing the square is. Then step
inside, grab a coffee, and ponder the many proposals on how it
might be finished.

**Trattoria Casalinga** is an inexpensive standby. Famous for
its home cooking, it's now filled with tourists rather than locals.
But it sends them away full, happy, and with lire left for *gelato*

(closed Sun, plus all of Aug, just off Piazza Santo Spirito, near the church at Via dei Michelozzi 9 red, tel. 055-218-624).

Consider **Osteria del Cinghiale Bianco** (Borgo S. Jacopo 43 red, air-con, closed Tue–Wed, tel. 055-215706), **Trattoria Angiolino** (closed Mon, Via Santo Spirito 36 red, tel. 055-239-8976), or other inviting places along Via Santo Spirito.

## Eating North of the River

### Eating near Santa Maria Novella and the Train Station
**Osteria Belledonne** is a crowded and cheery hole-in-the-wall serving great food at good prices. I loved the meal but had to correct the bill—read it carefully (Mon–Fri 12:00–14:30, 19:00–22:30, closed Sat–Sun, Via delle Belledonne 16 red, tel. 055-238-2609). **Ristorante La Spada**, nearby, is another local favorite serving typical Tuscan cuisine with less atmosphere and more menu (L23,000 lunch special, air-con, near Via della Spada at Via del Moro 66 red, tel. 055-218-757).

Twin chow houses for local workers offer a L17,000, hearty, family-style, fixed-price menu with a bustling working-class/budget-Yankee-traveler atmosphere (Mon–Sat 12:00–14:30, 18:15–21:30 or 22:00, closed Sun, 2 blocks south of train station): **Trattoria il Contadino** (Via Palazzuolo 69 red, tel. 055-238-2673) and **Trattoria da Giorgio** (across the street at Via Palazzuolo 100 red). Arrive early or wait.

The touristy **La Grotta di Leo** (a block away) has a cheap, straightforward menu and edible food and pizza (daily 11:00–01:00, Via della Scala 41 red, tel. 055-219-265).

### Eating near the Central and San Lorenzo Markets
For mountains of picnic produce or just a cheap sandwich and piles of people watching, visit the huge, multistoried Central Market—**Mercato Centrale** (Mon–Sat 7:00–14:00, closed Sun), a block north of the San Lorenzo street market.

**Trattoria la Burrasca** is a small, inexpensive place serving local-style dishes in a characteristic setting (Fri–Wed 12:00–15:00, 19:00–22:00, closed Thu, Via Panicale 6 black, at north corner of Central Market, tel. 055-215-827).

**Hydra Pizzeria Spaghetteria**, two blocks south, is brighter and more modern (closed Tue off-season, CC:VM, across from entrance of Medici Chapel, amid San Lorenzo street market, Canto de' Nelli 38 red, tel. 055-218-922).

### Eating near Palazzo Vecchio
The cozy **Rosticceria Giulano Centro**, a few blocks east of the Palazzo Vecchio, serves fine food to go or enjoy there (Tue–Sat 8:00–15:30, 17:00–21:30, closed Sun–Mon, Via Dei Neri 74 red).

**Osteria Vini e Vecchi Sapori** is a colorful hole-in-the-wall serving traditional food, including plates of mixed sandwiches (L1,500 each), half a block north of the Palazzo Vecchio (Tue–Sun 9:30–22:30, closed Mon, Via dei Magazzini 3 red, facing the bronze equestrian statue in Piazza della Signoria, go behind its tail to your left).

**Cantinetta dei Verrazzano** is a long-established bakery/café/wine bar serving elegant sandwich plates and hot focaccia sandwiches in an elegant old-time setting (until 21:00, closed Sun, just off Via Calzaiuoli on a side street across from Orsanmichele at Via dei Tavolini 18, tel. 055-268-590).

For a reasonably priced pizza with a Medici-style view, consider one of the pizzerias on Piazza della Signoria.

## Transportation Connections—Florence

**By train to: Assisi** (3/day, 2 hrs, more frequent with transfers, direction: Foligno), **Orvieto** (6/day, 2 hrs), **Pisa** (2/hrly, 1 hr), **La Spezia** (for the Cinque Terre, 2/day direct, 2 hrs, or change in Pisa), **Venice** (7/day, 3 hrs), **Milan** (12/day, 3–5 hrs), **Rome** (hrly, 2.5 hrs), **Naples** (2/day, 4 hrs), **Brindisi** (3/day, 11 hrs with change in Bologna), **Frankfurt** (3/day, 12 hrs), **Paris** (1/day, 12 hrs overnight), **Vienna** (4/day, 9–10 hrs). Train info: tel. 147-888-088.

**Buses:** The SITA bus station, a block west of the Florence train station, is user-friendly (but remember, bus service drops dramatically on Sunday). Schedules are posted everywhere with TV monitors indicating imminent departures. You'll find buses to: **San Gimignano** (hrly at :40 past the hour, 1.75 hrs), **Siena** (hrly at :10 past the hour, 75-min *corse rapide* fast buses, faster than the train, avoid the 2-hr *diretta* slow buses), and the **airport** (hrly, 15 min). Bus info: tel. 055-214-721 from 9:30 to 12:30; some schedules are in the *Florence Concierge Information* magazine.

## PISA

Pisa was a regional superpower in her medieval heyday (11th, 12th, and 13th centuries), rivaling Florence and Genoa. Its Mediterranean empire, which included Corsica and Sardinia, helped make it a wealthy republic. But the Pisa fleet was beaten (in 1284, by Genoa), and its port silted up, leaving the city high and dry, with only its Field of Miracles and its university keeping it on the map.

Pisa's three important sights (the cathedral, the baptistery, and the bell tower) float regally on the best lawn in Italy. Even as the church was being built, the Piazza del Duomo was nicknamed the Campo dei Miracoli, or Field of Miracles, for the grandness of the undertaking. The style throughout is Pisa's very own "Pisan Romanesque," surrounded by Italy's tackiest ring of souvenir stands. This spectacle is tourism at its most crass. Wear gloves.

The big news for 2001 is that the tower is supposed to reopen on June 17, if it's deemed safe and stable. To ascend, you'll have to reserve in advance and the price will likely be high (maybe L50,000). For the latest, call either of Pisa's TIs (phone numbers below) or check www.turismo.toscana.it.

## Planning Your Time

Seeing the tower and the square and wandering through the church are 90 percent of the Pisan thrill. Pisa is a touristy quickie. By car it's a headache. By train it's a joy. Train travelers may change trains in Pisa anyway. Hop on the bus and see the tower. Since you can't climb the tower (at least until June), a look doesn't take very long and is worthwhile. Sophisticated sightseers stop more for the Pisano carvings in the cathedral and baptistery than for a look at the tipsy tower. There's nothing wrong with Pisa, but I'd stop only to see the Field of Miracles and get out. By car it's a 45-minute detour from the freeway.

## Orientation

**Tourist Information:** One TI is at the train station (daily 8:00–20:00 in summer; in winter 9:00–17:00 and possibly closed Sun; to your left as you exit station, tel. 050-42291) and another is near the Leaning Tower (same hours as station TI, outside the medieval wall, hidden behind souvenir stands in a nook of the wall, about 100 meters to the left of the gate before you enter the Field of Miracles, tel. 050-560-464).

## Arrival in Pisa

**By Train:** To get to the Field of Miracles from the station, you can walk (25–30 min, get free map from TI at station, they'll mark the best route on your map), take a taxi (L10,000, at taxi stand at station or call 541-600), or catch a bus. The latest information on the bus route to the Field of Miracles is posted in the train information office in Pisa's station lobby (or ask at TI). Even though thousands of travelers come to Pisa every year just to see the tower, Pisa frequently changes the bus number and route to its most famous sight. Currently, you take bus #3 (3/hrly, 10 min, leaves from in front of station, across the street—at the big hotel). Buy a L1,500 ticket from the *tabacchi*/magazine kiosk in the station's main hall or at any *tabacchi* shop (good for 1 hr, round-trip OK, 15-minute ride one-way). Confirm the bus route number or take a long tour of Pisa's suburbs. The correct bus will let you off in front of the gate to the Field of Miracles. To return to the station, catch the bus from across the street (confirm the stop with a local or at either TI).

You can store your bag at Pisa's train station in lockers (which take coins or bills in a complicated process; choice of L3,000, L4,000, and L5,000 sizes) or faster at the pricier *deposito bagaglio* counter (L5,000, 12 meters beyond lockers, tucked into a bleak corner).

**By Car:** To get to the Leaning Tower, follow signs to the Duomo or the Campo dei Miracoli, located on the north edge of town. Drivers (coming from the Pisa Nord autostrada exit) don't have to mess with the city center (although you will have to endure some terrible traffic). There's no option better than the L2,000-per-hour pay lot just outside the town wall a block from the tower.

## Prices

Pisa has a scheme to get you into its neglected secondary sights. The various combo tickets cost: L10,000 for any two sights; L13,000 for two monuments plus the cathedral; L15,000 for four monuments—not including the cathedral; and L18,000 for the works (cathedral, baptistery, Camposanto cemetery, Museo dell' Opera del Duomo, and Museo delle Sinopie). In comparison, the cathedral is a bargain (L3,000). You can buy your ticket at the usually crowded ticket office (behind tower and cathedral entrance), or easier at the Camposanto cemetery, Museo dell' Opera del Duomo, or Museo delle Sinopie (near Baptistery, almost suffocated by souvenir stands); note that you can buy a ticket, say, just for the cathedral at any of these points.

## Sights—Pisa

▲▲**Leaning Tower**—This most famous example of Pisan Romanesque architecture was leaning even before its completion. Notice how the architect, for lack of a better solution, kinked up the top section. The 294 tilted steps to the top are closed while engineers work to keep the bell tower from toppling. The formerly clean and tidy area around the tower is now a construction zone. Steam pipes drying out the subsoil and huge weights are working together to stop the leaning (but not straighten out the tower). The tower is slated to reopen on June 17, 2001, allowing visitors (who have reserved in advance) to clamber to the top (for about L50,000). For the latest, call the TI or check www.turismo.toscana.it.

▲▲**Cathedral**—The huge Pisan Romanesque church (known as the Duomo), with its carved pulpit by Giovanni Pisano, is artistically more important than its more famous bell tower (L3,000, summer: Mon–Sat 10:00–19:40, Sun 13:00–19:40; closes Mon–Sat at 17:40 in spring and fall, at 16:40 in winter). Shorts are OK as long as they're not short shorts. Big backpacks are not allowed, nor is storage provided (but ticket taker might let you leave bag at entrance).

**Baptistery**—The baptistery, the biggest in Italy, is interesting for its great acoustics (daily 9:00–17:40, until 16:40 in winter, located in front of cathedral). If you ask nicely and leave a tip, the ticket taker uses the place's echo power to sing haunting harmonies with himself. The pulpit, by Nicolo Pisano (1260), inspired Renaissance

# Pisa

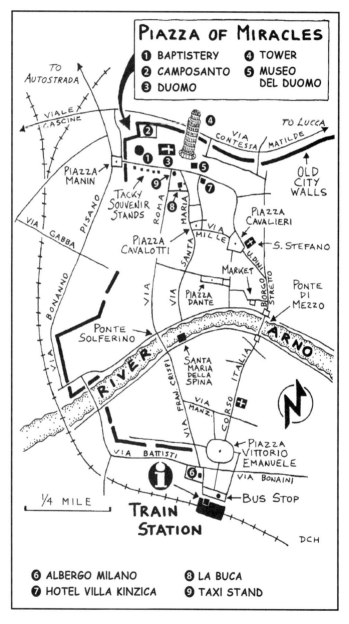

**PIAZZA OF MIRACLES**
- ❶ BAPTISTERY
- ❷ CAMPOSANTO
- ❸ DUOMO
- ❹ TOWER
- ❺ MUSEO DEL DUOMO

TO AUTOSTRADA

VIALE CASCINE

TO LUCCA

VIA CONTESSA MATILDE

PIAZZA MANIN

PISANO

TACKY SOUVENIR STANDS

VIA GABBA

BONANNO

ROMA

SANTA MARIA

PIAZZA CAVALOTTI

VIA MILLE

OLD CITY WALLS

PIAZZA CAVALIERI

U.DINI

S. STEFANO

MARKET

PONTE DI MEZZO

BORGO STRETTO

VIA

VIA

PIAZZA DANTE

PONTE SOLFERINO

RIVER

ARNO

VIA FRAN CRISPI

SANTA MARIA DELLA SPINA

VIA MANZ.

ITALIA

VIA

CORSO

N

VIA BATTISTI

PIAZZA VITTORIO EMANUELE

VIA BONAINI

① ← BUS STOP

¼ MILE

**TRAIN STATION**

DCH

- ❻ ALBERGO MILANO
- ❼ HOTEL VILLA KINZICA
- ❽ LA BUCA
- ❾ TAXI STAND

art to follow, but the same artist's pulpit and carvings in Siena were just as impressive to me—in a more enjoyable atmosphere. Notice that even the baptistery leans about five feet.

**Other Sights**—The much-advertised **Panoramic Walk on the Wall**, which includes just a small section of the medieval wall (entrance near baptistery, at Porta Leone), isn't worth your time or L4,000. Skip the **Camposanto** cemetery bordering the cathedral square, even if its "Holy Land dirt" does turn a body into a skeleton in a day (daily 9:00–17:40, until 16:40 in winter). The **Museo delle Sinopie**, housed in a 13th-century hospital, features the sketchy frescoes which were preparatory work for the frescoes in the cemetery (daily 9:00–17:40, until 16:40 in winter, across street from Baptistery entrance).

For Pisan art, see the **Museo dell' Opera del Duomo**, featuring treasures of the cathedral: from sculptures (12th–14th century), paintings, and silverware to ancient Egyptian, Etruscan, and Roman artifacts (daily 9:00–17:40, until 16:40 in winter, housed behind tower, Piazza Arcivescovado 18). The **Museo Nazionale di San Matteo**, in a former convent, displays 12th to 15th century sculptures, illuminated manuscripts, and paintings by Martini, Ghirlandaio, Massaccio, and others (L12,000, Tue–Sat 9:00–19:00, Sun 9:00–13:00, closed Mon, on the river near Piazza Mazzini at Lungarno Mediceo).

Walking between the station and Field of Miracles shows you a student-filled, classy, Old World town with an Arnoscape much like its rival upstream. A **fruit market** is pinched and squeezed into Piazza Vettovaglie Monday through Saturday (7:00–18:00, near river, between station and tower). The **flea market** attracts itchy shoppers Wednesday and Saturday mornings on Via del Brennero (just outside of wall, about 6 blocks east of tower).

## Sleeping and Eating in Pisa
### (L2,000 = $1, country code: 39)

Consider **Albergo Milano**, near the station, offering 10 spacious rooms with faded—but clean—bedspreads (D-L90,000, Db-L120,000, breakfast extra, CC:VM, air-con, Via Mascagni 14, tel. 050-23162, fax 050-44237, e-mail: hotelmilano@csinfo.it). For a splurge, try **Hotel Villa Kinzica**, with 34 modern rooms within a block of the Field of Miracles—ask for a room with a view of the tower (Db-L180,000, CC:VM, elevator, most rooms air-con, attached restaurant, Piazza Arcivescovado 2, tel. 050-560-419, fax 050-551-204). For a quick lunch or dinner, the pizzeria/trattoria **La Buca**—just a block from the tower—has a good reputation among locals (Sat–Thu 12:00–15:30, 19:00–23:00, closed Fri, CC:VM, at Via Santa Maria and Via G. Tassi, tel. 050-560-660).

## Transportation Connections—Pisa

**By train to:** **Florence** (hrly, 1 hour), **La Spezia** (hrly, 1 hr, most trains heading to Torino and Ventimiglia stop in La Spezia; small trains run from La Spezia to Cinque Terre), **Siena** (change at Empoli: Pisa–Empoli, hrly, 30 min; Empoli–Siena, hrly, 1 hr). Even the fastest trains stop in Pisa, and you might be changing trains here whether you plan to stop or not. Train info: tel. 147-888-088.

## Route Tips for Drivers

**To Florence and Siena:** The drive from Pisa to Florence is that rare case where the non-autostrada highway (free, more direct, and at least as fast) is a better deal than the autostrada. When departing for Florence, San Gimignano, or Siena, follow the blue "*superstrada*" signs (green signs are for the autostrada) for the SS road (along the city wall east from the tower—away from the sea) for Florence (and later Siena).

**To the Cinque Terre:** From Pisa, catch the Genova-bound autostrada. The white stuff you'll see in the mountains as you approach La Spezia isn't snow—it's Carrara marble, Michelangelo's choice for his great art. From Pisa to La Spezia takes about an hour.

# HILL TOWNS OF CENTRAL ITALY

Break out of the Venice-Florence-Rome syndrome. There's more to Italy! Experience the slumber of Umbria, the texture of Tuscany, and the lazy towns of Lazio. For starters, here are a few of my favorites.

Siena seems to be every Italy connoisseur's pet town. In my office, whenever Siena is mentioned, someone moans, "Siena? I luuuv Siena!" San Gimignano is the quintessential hill town, with Italy's best surviving medieval skyline. Assisi—visited for its hometown boy, St. Francis, who made very good—is best after dark. Orvieto, one of the most famous hill towns, is an ideal springboard for a trip to tiny Civita. Stranded alone on its pinnacle in a vast canyon, Civita's the most lovable.

## Planning Your Time

Siena, the must-see town, has the easiest train and bus connections. On a quick trip, consider spending three nights in Siena (with a whole-day side trip into Florence and a day to relax and enjoy Siena). Whatever you do, enjoy a sleepy medieval evening in Siena. After an evening in Siena, its major sights can be seen in half a day. San Gimignano is an overrun, pint-sized Siena. Don't rush Siena for San Gimignano (with less than 24 hours for Siena, skip San Gimignano).

Assisi has half a day of sightseeing and another half a day of wonder. While a zoo by day, it's a delight at night.

Orvieto, an easy train stop, is worth a short visit and provides the carless traveler with the best launchpad for a trip to Civita.

Civita di Bagnoregio is the great pinnacle town. A night in Bagnoregio (via Orvieto bus) with time to hike to the town and spend three hours makes the visit worthwhile.

## Hill Towns of Central Italy

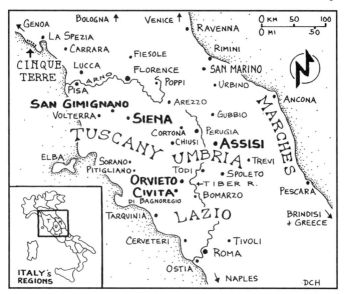

## SIENA

Seven hundred years ago, Siena was a major military power in a class with Florence, Venice, and Genoa. With a population of 60,000, it was even bigger than Paris. In 1348 a disastrous plague weakened Siena. Then, in the 1550s, her bitter rival, Florence, really salted her, making Siena forever a nonthreatening backwater. Siena's loss became our sightseeing gain, as its political and economic irrelevance pickled it purely Gothic. Today Siena's population is still 60,000, compared to Florence's 420,000.

Siena's thriving historic center, with red-brick lanes cascading every which way, offers Italy's best Gothic city experience. Most people do Siena, just 50 kilometers south of Florence, as a day trip, but it's best experienced after dark. While Florence has the blockbuster museums, Siena has an easy-to-enjoy soul: Courtyards sport flower-decked wells, alleys dead-end at rooftop views, and the sky is a rich blue dome. Right off the bat, Siena becomes an old friend.

For those who dream of a Fiat-free Italy, pedestrians rule in the old center of Siena. Sit at a café on the red-bricked main square. Take time to savor the first European city to eliminate automobile traffic from its main square (1966) and then, just to be silly, wonder what would happen if they did it in your city.

## Hill Towns: Public Transportation

To GENOVA    To MILAN    To VENICE
CINQUE·
TERRE →
LA
SPEZIA
FLORENCE    BOLOGNA    FERRARA
LUCCA
PISA →    EMP.    RAVENNA
SAN.    POGG.    TEREN·
GIM.    TOLA    RIMINI
CORTONA    PESARO
ELBA    SIENA →    PERUGIA    FALCONARA
CHIUSI →    ASSISI    FOSSATO
ORVIETO    TODI
CIVITA    FOLIGNO    ANCONA
DI    SPOLETO
BAGNOREGIO    VITERBO
ORTE    DCH
ROMA    PESCARA
ANZIO    NAPLES
*NOT TO SCALE*

N

KEY:    — RAIL  --- BUS  ···· SHIP
● GOOD OVERNIGHT STOPS

## Orientation

Siena lounges atop a hill, stretching its three legs out from Il
Campo. This main square, the historic meeting point of Siena's
neighborhoods, is pedestrians only. And most of those pedestrians
are students from the local university. Everything I mention is
within a 15-minute walk of the square. Navigate by landmarks,
following the excellent system of street-corner signs. The typical
visitor sticks to the San Domenico–Il Campo axis.

Siena is one big sight. Its essential individual sights come in
two little clusters: the square (city hall, museum, tower) and the
cathedral (baptistery, cathedral museum with its surprise viewpoint). Check these sights off and you're free to wander.

**Tourist Information:** Pick up a free town map from the
main TI on Il Campo (#56, look for the yellow "Change" sign—
bad rates, good information, Mon–Sat 8:30–19:30, mid-Nov–
mid-March Mon–Sat 8:30–14:00, 15:00–19:00, tel. 0577-280-551,
www.siena.turismo.toscana.it). The little TI at San Domenico is
for hotel promotion only and and sells a Siena map for L1,000.
For a longer stay, consider buying the combo ticket (*biglietto*

*cumulativo*) for L29,000 that covers nine sights, including the Museo Civico, Santa Maria della Scala, Museo dell' Opera, Baptistery, Piccolomini Library (in cathedral), and more (valid for 7 days, sold at participating sites).

**Local Guide:** Roberto Bechi, a hardworking Sienese guide, specializes in off-the-beaten-path tours of Siena and the surrounding countryside. Married to an American (Patti) and having run restaurants in Siena and the U.S., Roberto communicates well with Americans. His passions are Sienese culture, Tuscan history, and local cuisine. Book well in advance for full-day tours (ranging in cost from $60–90 per person). Half days ($30–50 per person) cannot be pre-booked during high season, but may be available at the last minute (tel. & fax 0577-704-789, www.zaslon.si/roberto, e-mail: tourrob@tin.it; for U.S. contact, fax Greg Evans at 540/434-4532).

## Arrival in Siena

**By Train:** At Siena's train station, buy a L1,400 bus ticket from the blue machine near the door (exact change needed), or, easier, from the Bus Ticket Office across from the machine (daily 5:50–19:30, ask for city map—it's free and just a bus route map, but helps get you started). Then cross the square (and street) and board any bus heading for Piazza Gramsci, Piazza del Sale, or Stufa Secco (buses leave about every 7 minutes, fewer on Sun). Day-trippers can store luggage at the *deposito bagagli* at the train station (L3,000). The cost of a taxi from the station to your hotel is about L15,000. Siena taxi numbers: at the station (tel. 0577-44504) and elsewhere (tel. 0577-49222).

To get to Siena's train station from the center of Siena, catch a bus at Piazza del Sale or Stufa Secco; note that bus stops are not usually marked by a sign but by a yellow rectangle and the word "bus" marked on the pavement. Confirm with the driver that the bus is going to the *stazione* (stat-zee-OH-nay). Remember to purchase your ticket in advance from a *tabacchi* shop.

**By Bus:** Some buses arrive at the train station (see "Arrival By Train," above), others at Piazza Gramsci (a few blocks from city center), and some stop at both. You can store baggage underneath Piazza Gramsci in Sotopassaggio la Lizza (L5,000, daily 7:00–19:30, no overnight).

**By Car:** Drivers coming from the autostrada take the Porta San Marco exit and follow the "Centro" then "Stadio" signs (stadium, soccer ball). The soccer-ball signs take you to the stadium lot (Parcheggio Stadio, L2,500/hr, L24,000/day) at the huge, bare-brick San Domenico Church. The Fortezza lot nearby charges the same. Or park in the lot underneath the railway station. You can drive into the pedestrian zone (a pretty ballsy thing to do) only to drop bags at your hotel. You can park free in the lot below the Albergo Lea, in white-striped spots behind Hotel Villa Liberty, and behind the Fortezza. (The signs showing a street cleaner and a day of the week indicate which day the street is cleaned; there's a L200,000 tow-fee incentive to learn the days of the week in Italian.)

## Sights—Siena's Main Square

▲▲▲**Il Campo**—Siena's great central piazza is urban harmony at its best. Like a people-friendly stage set, its gently tilted floor fans out from the tower and city hall backdrop. It's the perfect invitation to loiter. Think of it as a trip to the beach without sand or water. Il Campo was located at the historic junction of Siena's various competing districts, or *contrada*, on the old marketplace. The brick surface is divided into nine sections, representing the council of nine merchants and city bigwigs who ruled medieval Siena. At the square's high point, look for the Fountain of Joy, the two naked guys about to be tossed in, and the pigeons politely waiting their turn to gingerly tightrope down slippery snouts to slurp a drink. At the base of the tower, the Piazza's chapel was built in 1348 as a thanks to God for ending the Black Plague (after it killed more than a third of the population). The market area behind the city hall, a wide-open expanse since the Middle Ages, originated as a farming area within the city walls to feed the city in times of siege (now the Wednesday morning market is held here).

To say Siena and Florence have always been competitive is an understatement. In medieval times a statue of Venus stood on Il Campo (where the Fountain of Joy is today). After the plague hit Siena, the monks blamed this pagan statue. The people cut it to pieces and buried it along the walls of Florence.

▲**Museo Civico**—The Palazzo Pubblico (City Hall), at the base of the tower, has a fine and manageable museum housing a good sample of Sienese art. In the following order you'll see the Sala Risorgimento, with dramatic scenes of Victor Emmanuel's unification of Italy (surrounded by statues that don't seem to care); the chapel, with impressive inlaid wood chairs in the choir; and the Sala del Mappamondo, with Simone Martini's *Maesta* (Enthroned Virgin) facing the faded *Guidoriccio da Fogliano* (a mercenary providing a more concrete form of protection). Next is the Sala della Pace—where the city's fat cats met. Looking down on the oligarchy during their meetings were two interesting frescoes showing the effects of good and bad government. Notice the whistle-while-you-work happiness of the utopian community ruled by the utopian government (in the better-preserved fresco) and the fate of a community ruled by politicians with more typical values (in a terrible state of repair). The message: Without justice there can be no prosperity. The rural view out the window is essentially the view from the top of the big stairs—enjoy it from here (L12,000, combo ticket with tower-L18,000, daily March–Oct 10:00–17:00,

# Siena

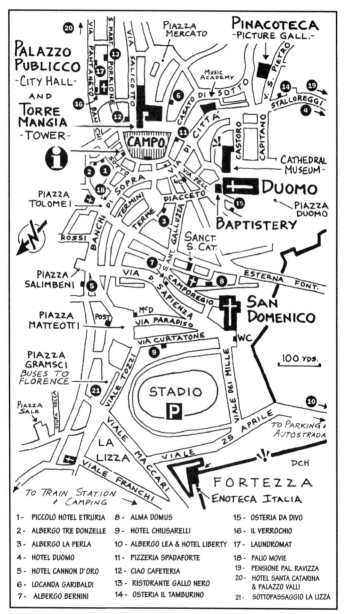

| | | |
|---|---|---|
| 1 - PICCOLO HOTEL ETRURIA | 8 - ALMA DOMUS | 15 - OSTERIA DA DIVO |
| 2 - ALBERGO TRE DONZELLE | 9 - HOTEL CHIUSARELLI | 16 - IL VERROCHIO |
| 3 - ALBERGO LA PERLA | 10 - ALBERGO LEA & HOTEL LIBERTY | 17 - LAUNDROMAT |
| 4 - HOTEL DUOMO | 11 - PIZZERIA SPADAFORTE | 18 - PALIO MOVIE |
| 5 - HOTEL CANNON D'ORO | 12 - CIAO CAFETERIA | 19 - PENSIONE PAL. RAVIZZA |
| 6 - LOCANDA GARIBALDI | 13 - RISTORANTE GALLO NERO | 20 - HOTEL SANTA CATARINA & PALAZZO VALLI |
| 7 - ALBERGO BERNINI | 14 - OSTERIA IL TAMBURINO | 21 - SOTTOPASSAGGIO LA LIZZA |

July–Sept 10:00–23:00, Nov–Jan 10:00–16:00, last entry 45
minutes before closing, tel. 0577-292-111). Leave Mauro Civai
(the director of this museum) a polite note requesting that a little
English information be shared with his paying guests.

▲**City Tower (Torre del Mangia)**—Siena gathers around its
city hall, not its church. It was a proud republic, and its "declara-
tion of independence" is the tallest secular medieval tower in Italy,
the 100-meter-tall Torre del Mangia (named after a hedonistic
watchman who consumed his earnings like a glutton consumes
food; his chewed-up statue is in the courtyard, to the left as you
enter). Its 300 steps get pretty skinny at the top, but the reward
is one of Italy's best views (L10,000, combo ticket with Museo
Civico-L18,000, daily 10:00–19:00, until 20:30 mid-July–mid-
Aug, closed in rain, sometimes long lines, limit of 30 towerists
at a time, avoid midday crowd).

▲**Pinacoteca (National Picture Gallery)**—Siena was a power
in Gothic art. But the average tourist, wrapped up in a love affair
with the Renaissance, hardly notices. This museum takes you on
a walk through Siena's art, chronologically from the 12th through
the 15th centuries. For the casual sightseer, the Sienese art in the
city hall and cathedral museums is adequate. But art fans enjoy this
opportunity to trace the evolution of Siena's delicate and elegant
art (L8,000, Sun–Mon 8:30–13:15, Tue–Sat 8:15–19:15, plus
possibly 20:30–23:30 on Sat in summer, tel. 0577-281-161). From
the Campo, walk out Via di Città to Piazza di Postierla and go
left on San Pietro.

## Sights—Siena's Cathedral Area

▲▲▲**Duomo**—Siena's cathedral is as Baroque as Gothic gets.
The striped facade is piled with statues and ornamentation; the
interior is decorated from top to bottom. The heads of 172 popes
peer down from the ceiling over the fine inlaid art on the floor.
This is one busy interior.

To orient yourself in this *panforte* of Italian churches, stand
under the dome and think of the church floor as a big clock.
You're the middle, and the altar is high noon: you'll find the
*Slaughter of the Innocents* roped off on the floor at 10:00, Pisano's
pulpit between two pillars at 11:00, Bernini's chapel at 3:00, two
Michelangelo statues (next to snacks, shop, and WC) at 7:00, the
library at 8:00, and a Donatello statue at 9:00. Take some time
with the floor mosaics in the front. Nicola Pisano's wonderful
pulpit is crowded with delicate Gothic storytelling from 1268.
To understand why Bernini is considered the greatest Baroque
sculptor, step into his sumptuous *Cappella della Madonna del Voto*.
This last work in the cathedral, from 1659, is enough to make a
Lutheran light a candle. Move up to the altar and look back at the
two Bernini statues: St. Jerome playing the crucifix like a violinist

lost in beautiful music, and Mary Magdalene in a similar state of spiritual ecstasy. The Piccolomini altar is most interesting for its two Michelangelo statues (the lower big ones). Paul, on the left, may be a self-portrait. Peter, on the right, resembles Michelangelo's more famous statue of Moses. Originally contracted to do 15 statues, Michelangelo left the project early (1504) to do his great *David* in Florence. The Piccolomini Library—worth the L2,000 entry—is brilliantly frescoed with scenes glorifying the works of a pope from 500 years ago. It contains intricately decorated, illuminated music scores and a Roman copy of three Greek graces (library open Sun 14:30–19:30, Tue–Sat same as church hours, below). Donatello's bronze statue of St. John the Baptist, in his famous rags, is in a chapel to the right of the library (church open daily 9:00–19:30 but Sun 10:15–13:30 is reserved for worship only, Nov–mid-March 10:00–13:00, 14:30–17:00, modest dress required).

▲▲**Santa Maria della Scala**—This renovated old hospital (opposite the Duomo entrance) displays a rich treasury and a lavishly frescoed hall. The frescoes in the Pellegrinaio Hall show medieval Siena's innovative health care and social welfare system in action (c. 1442, wonderfully described in English). Downstairs are statues from the *Fountain of Gaia* by Jacopo della Quercia (L10,000, daily 10:00–18:00, until 23:00 Fri–Sat in summer, off-season 11:00–16:30). The chapel just inside the door to your left is free (English description inside chapel entrance).

▲**Baptistery**—Siena is so hilly that there wasn't enough flat ground on which to build a big church. What to do? Build a big church and prop up the overhanging edge with the baptistery. This dark and quietly tucked-away cave of art is worth a look (and L3,000) for its cool tranquility and the bronze panels and angels—by Ghiberti, Donatello, and others—adorning the pedestal of the baptismal font (daily mid-March–Sept 9:00–19:30, Oct 9:00–18:00, Nov–mid-March 10:00–13:00, 14:30–17:00).

▲▲**Cathedral Museum (Museo dell'Opera e Panorama)**—Siena's most enjoyable museum, on the Campo side of the church (look for the yellow signs), was built to house the cathedral's art. The ground floor is filled with the cathedral's original Gothic sculpture by Giovanni Pisano (who spent 10 years here carving and orchestrating the decoration of the cathedral in the late 1200s) and a fine Donatello *Madonna and Child.* Upstairs to the left awaits a private audience with Duccio's *Maesta* (Enthroned Virgin). Pull up a chair and study one of the great pieces of medieval art. The flip side of the *Maesta* (displayed on the opposite wall), with 26 panels—the medieval equivalent of pages—shows scenes from the Passion of Christ. Climb onto the "Panorama dal Facciatone." From the first landing, take the skinnier second spiral for Siena's surprise view. Look back over the Duomo and consider this:

When rival republic Florence began its grand cathedral, proud Siena decided to build the biggest church in all Christendom. The existing cathedral would be used as a transept. You're atop what would have been the entry. The wall below you, connecting the Duomo with the museum of the cathedral, was as far as Siena got before a plague killed the city's ability to finish the project. Were it completed, you'd be looking straight down the nave—white stones mark where columns would have stood (L6,000, worthwhile L5,000 40-minute audioguide, daily mid-March–Sept 9:00–19:30, Oct 9:00–18:00, Nov–mid-March 9:00–13:30, tel. 0577-283-048).

## Sights—Siena's San Domenico Area
**Church of San Domenico**—This huge brick church is worth a quick look. The bland interior fits the austere philosophy of the Dominicans. Walk up the steps in the rear for a look at various paintings from the life of Saint Catherine, patron saint of Siena. Halfway up on the right you'll see a wooden bust of Saint Catherine and her finger in a case. And in the adjacent chapel, you'll see her actual head (free, daily April–Oct 7:00–12:55, 15:00–18:30, Nov–March 9:00–12:55, 15:00–18:00).

**Sanctuary of Saint Catherine**—A few downhill blocks toward the center from San Domenico (follow signs to the Santuario di Santa Caterina), step into Catherine's cool and peaceful home. Siena remembers its favorite hometown girl, a simple, unschooled, but almost mystically devout girl who, in the mid-1300s, helped get the pope to return from France to Rome. Pilgrims have come here since 1464. Since then, architects and artists have greatly embellished what was probably a humble home (her family worked as wool dyers). Enter through the courtyard and walk to the far end. The chapel on your right was built over the spot where Saint Catherine received the stigmata while praying. The chapel on your left used to be the kitchen. Go down the stairs next to the chapel/kitchen to reach the saint's room. Once a bare cell, it's been frescoed, coffered, and honored beyond recognition. Much of the art throughout the sanctuary depicts scenes from the saint's life (free, daily 9:00–12:30, 14:30–18:00, winter 9:00–12:30, 15:30–18:00, Via Tiratoio).

## Siena's Palio
In the Palio, the feisty spirit of Siena's 17 *contrada* (neighborhoods) lives on. These neighborhoods celebrate, worship, and compete together. Each even has its own historical museum. *Contrada* pride is evident any time of year in the colorful neighborhood banners and parades. (If you hear distant drumming, run to it for the medieval action.) But *contrada* pride is most visible twice a year— on July 2 and August 16—when they have their world-famous Palio di Siena. Ten of the 17 neighborhoods compete (chosen by

lot), hurling themselves with medieval abandon into several days of trial races and traditional revelry. On the big day, Il Campo is stuffed to the brim with locals and tourists, as the horses charge wildly around the square in this literally no-holds-barred race. Of course, the winning neighborhood is the scene of grand celebrations afterward. The grand prize: simply proving your *contrada* is numero uno. All over town, sketches and posters depict the Palio. This is not some folkloristic event. It's a real medieval moment. If you're packed onto the square with 15,000 people who each really want to win, you won't see much, but you'll feel it. While the actual Palio packs the city, you could side trip in from Florence to see horse-race trials each of the three days before the big day (usually at 9:00 and 19:45).

▲**Palio al Cinema**—This 20-minute film helps recreate the craziness of the Palio. See it at the Cinema Moderno in Piazza Tolomei, two blocks from the Campo (L10,000, L8,000 or 2 for L15,000 with this book, Mon–Fri 9:30–17:30, Sat 9:30–15:30, maybe until 17:30 on Sat July–Aug, English showings generally hourly at :30 past the hour, closed Sun, tel. 0577-289-201). Call or drop by to confirm when the next English showing is scheduled—there are usually nine each day.

## Shopping
Shops line Via Banchi di Sopra, the *passeggiata* route (see "Nightlife," below). For a department store, try Upim on Piazza Mateotti (Mon–Sat 9:30–19:50, closed Sun). The large, colorful scarves/flags, each depicting the symbol of one of Siena's 17 different neighborhoods, are easy-to-pack souvenirs, fun for decorating your home (L10,000 apiece, sold at souvenir stands).

## Nightlife
Join the evening *passeggiata* (peak strolling time is 19:00) along Via Banchi di Sopra with gelato in hand. **Nannini's** at Piazza Salimbeni has fine gelato (daily 11:00–24:00).

The **Enoteca Italiana** is a good wine bar in a cellar in the Fortezza (Mon 12:00–20:00, Tue–Sat 12:00–01:00, closed Sun, sample glasses in 3 different price ranges: L3,000, L5,000, L10,000, bottles and snacks available, CC:VM, tel. 0577-288-497).

## Sleeping in Siena
### (L2,000 = about $1, country code: 39, zip code: 53100)
Sleep Code: **S** = Single, **D** = Double/Twin, **T** = Triple, **Q** = Quad, **b** = bathroom, **t** = toilet only, **s** = shower only, **CC** = Credit Card (**V**isa, **M**asterCard, **A**mex), **SE** = Speaks English, **NSE** = No English. Breakfast is generally not included. Have breakfast on Il Campo or in a nearby bar.

Finding a room is tough during Easter or the Palio in early

July and mid-August. Call ahead any time of year, as Siena's few budget places are listed in all the budget guidebooks. While day-tripping tour groups turn the town into a Gothic amusement park in midsummer, Siena is basically yours in the evenings and off-season. Nearly all listed hotels lie between Il Campo and the Church of San Domenico. About a third of the listings don't take credit cards. If "CC:VM" isn't mentioned in a listing, they don't take plastic, no matter how earnestly you ask. Cash machines are plentiful on the main streets.

The TI lists private homes that rent rooms for around L60,000 per person. Some are central, and some require a stay of several days (tel. 0577-280-551).

Siena has two modern, self-service **Laundromats**: Lavarapido Wash and Dry (daily 8:00–21:00, Via di Pantaneto 38) and Onda Blu (daily 8:00–22:00, Via del Casato di Soto 17).

## Sleeping near Il Campo

Each of these first listings is forgettable but inexpensive and just a horse wreck away from one of Italy's most wonderful civic spaces.

**Piccolo Hotel Etruria**, a good bet for a hotel with 19 decent rooms but not much soul, is just off the square (S-L70,000, Sb-L80,000, Db-L130,000, Tb-L165,000, Qb-L210,000, breakfast-L8,000, CC:VMA, with your back to the tower, leave Il Campo to the right at 2:00, Via Donzelle 1–3, tel. 0577-288-088, fax 0577-288-461, e-mail: hetruria@tin.it).

**Albergo Tre Donzelle** is a plain, institutional place next door to Piccolo Hotel Etruria that makes sense only if you think of Il Campo as your terrace (S-L60,000, D-L85,000, Db-L110,000, CC:VMA, Via Donzelle 5, tel. 0577-280-358, fax 0577-223-933, Senora Iannini SE).

**Hotel Cannon d'Oro,** a few blocks up Via Banchi di Sopra, is spacious and group friendly (30 rooms, Sb-L112,000, Db-L137,000, Tb-L181,000, these discounted prices promised through 2001 with this book, family deals, breakfast-L10,000, CC:VMA, Via Montanini 28, tel. 0577-44321, fax 0577-280-868, e-mail: cannonsi@tin.it, Maurizio and Debora SE).

**Locanda Garibaldi** is a modest, very Sienese restaurant/ *albergo*. Gentle Marcello wears two hats, as he runs a fine, busy restaurant downstairs and seven pleasant rooms up a funky metal staircase (Db-L120,000, Tb-L150,000, family deals, takes reservations only a few days in advance, half a block downhill off the square at Via Giovanni Dupre 18, tel. 0577-284-204, NSE).

**Albergo La Perla** is a funky, jumbled, 13-room place. Its narrow maze of hallways, stark rooms, old bedspreads, miniscule bathrooms, and laissez-faire environment works for backpackers (Sb-L80,000, Db-L110,000, Tb-L150,000, a block off the square on Piazza Independenza at Via della Terme 25, tel. 0577-47144).

Attilio and his American wife, Deborah, take reservations only a day or two ahead. Ideally, call the morning you'll arrive.

**Splurges**: **Hotel Duomo** is the best in-the-old-town splurge, a classy place with 23 spacious, elegant rooms (Sb-L200,000, Db-L250,000, Tb-L330,000, Qb-L360,000, includes breakfast, CC:VMA, air-con, picnic-friendly roof terrace, free parking, follow Via di Città, which becomes Via Stalloreggi, to Via Stalloreggi 38, 10-minute walk to Il Campo, tel. 0577-289-088, fax 0577-43043, www.hotelduomo.it, e-mail: hduomo@comune.siena.it, Stefania SE). If you arrive by train, take a taxi (L15,000); if you drive, go to Porta San Marco and follow the signs to the hotel, drop off your bags, and then park in nearby "Il Campo" lot.

**Pensione Palazzo Ravizza** has an aristocratic feel and a peaceful garden. Classy and friendly, it's a 10-minute walk from Il Campo (Db-L380,000–550,000, includes breakfast and dinner, cheaper mid-Nov–Feb, CC:VMA, elevator, back rooms face open country, good restaurant, parking, Via Pian dei Mantellini 34, tel. 0577-280-462, fax 0577-221-597).

### Sleeping near San Domenico Church

These hotels are listed in order of closeness to Il Campo—maximum 10-minute walk. The first two enjoy views of the old town and cathedral (which sits floodlit before me as I type) and are the best values in town.

**Albergo Bernini** makes you part of a Sienese family in a modest, clean home with nine fine rooms. Friendly Nadia and Mauro welcome you to their spectacular view terrace for breakfast and picnic lunches and dinners. Mauro, an accomplished accordionist, might play "Happy Birthday" if you say it's your birthday (Sb-L95,000, D-L110,000, Db-L130,000, breakfast-L12,000, less in winter, midnight curfew, on the main San Domenico–Il Campo drag at Via Sapienza 15, tel. & fax 0577-289-047, www.albergobernini.com, e-mail: hbernin@tin.it, their son, Alessandro, SE).

**Alma Domus** is ideal—unless nuns make you nervous, you need a double bed, or you plan on staying out past the 23:30 curfew (no mercy given). This quasi hotel (not a convent) is run with firm but angelic smiles by sisters who offer clean and quiet rooms for a steal and save the best views for foreigners. Bright lamps, quaint balconies, fine views, grand public rooms, top security, and a friendly atmosphere make this a great value. The check-out time is strictly 10:00, but they will store your luggage in their secure courtyard (Db-L105,000, Tb-L130,000, Qb-L160,000, breakfast-L11,000, ask for view room—*con vista*, elevator, from San Domenico walk downhill with the church on your right toward the view, turn left down Via Camporegio, make a U-turn at the little chapel down the brick steps to

Via Camporegio 37, tel. 0577-44177 and 0577-44487, fax 0577-47601, NSE).

**Hotel Chiusarelli**, a proper hotel in a beautiful building with a handy location, comes with lots of traffic noise at night—ask for a quieter room in the back (50 rooms, S-L102,000 without breakfast; the following include a big buffet breakfast: S-L130,000, Db-L190,000, Tb-L255,000, suites available, CC:VMA, air-con, pleasant garden terrace, across from San Domenico at Viale Curtatone 15, tel. 0577-280-562, fax 0577-271-177, e-mail: chiusare@tin.it, SE).

**Albergo Lea** is a sleepable place in a residential neighborhood a few blocks away from the center (past San Domenico) with easy parking (11 rooms, S-L100,000, Db-L160,000, Tb-L185,000 Qb-L200,000, cheaper in winter, includes breakfast, rooftop terrace, CC:VMA, Viale XXIV Maggio 10, tel. & fax 0577-283-207, e-mail: hotellea@libero.it, SE). **Hotel Villa Liberty** has 18 big, bright, comfortable rooms (S-L140,000, Db-L220,000, includes breakfast, CC:VMA, only one room with twin beds, elevator, bar, air-con, TVs, courtyard, etc., facing the fortress at Viale V. Veneto 11, tel. 0577-44966, fax 0577-44770, SE).

## Sleeping Farther from the Center, near Porta Romana

**Splurges: Hotel Santa Caterina** is a three-star, 18th-century place best for drivers who need air-conditioning. It's peaceful with a delightful garden, and professionally run with real attention to quality (Sb-L185,000, small Db-L185,000, Db-L230,000, Tb-L290,000, mention this book to get these prices, includes breakfast, CC:VMA, request quiet garden side, fridge in room, parking-L10,000/day—request when you reserve, 100 meters outside Porta Romana at Via E.S. Piccolomini 7, tel. 0577-221-105, fax 0577-271-087, e-mail: hsc@sienanet.it, Stefania SE). Easy parking and shuttle bus (Mon–Sat 4/hrly, Sun 2/hrly) to town center. A taxi to/from the station runs L15,000.

**Palazzo di Valli**, with 11 big, peaceful rooms, a fine TV lounge, and a garden, is 800 meters beyond Porta Romana (the Roman gate). It's a straight shot into town on the shuttle bus (Mon–Sat 4/hrly, Sun 2/hrly) and it feels like it's in the country (Db-L250,000 with breakfast for travelers with this book in 2001, CC:VMA, parking, Via E.S. Piccolomini, tel. 0577-226-102, fax 0577-222-255, Camarda family). From the autostrada exit at Siena Sud in the direction of Porta Romana.

**Cheaper Options:** The homespun **Casa Laura** has five clean, well-maintained rooms, some with brick-and-beam ceilings (Db-L160,000, breakfast-L15,000 for 2, CC:VM, Via Roma 3, tel. 0577-226-061 fax 0577-225-240, e-mail: labenci@tin.it).

Siena's **Guidoriccio Youth Hostel** has 120 cheap beds, but, given the hassle of the bus ride and the charm of downtown Siena at night, I'd skip it (office open 15:00–01:00, L24,000 beds in doubles, triples, and dorms with sheets and breakfast, bus #10 from train station or bus #15 from Piazza Gramsci, Via Fiorentina 89 in Stellino neighborhood, tel. 0577-52212, SE).

## Eating in Siena

Budget eaters look for *pizza al taglio* shops, scattered throughout Siena, selling pizza by the slice. Picnickers enjoy the open-air market on Wednesday morning (Piazza Mercato, just behind Il Campo).

Sienese restaurants are reasonable by Florentine and Venetian standards. Even with higher prices, lousy service, and lower-quality food, consider eating on Il Campo—a classic European experience. **Pizzeria Spadaforte**, at the edge of the Campo, has a decent setting, mediocre pizza, and tables steeper than its prices (daily 12:00–16:00, 19:30–22:30, CC:VM, to the far right of city tower as you face it, tel. 0577-281-123). At the bottom of the Campo, a **Ciao** cafeteria offers easy self-service meals, no ambience, and no views. The crowded **Spizzico**, a pizza counter in the front half of Ciao, serves huge, inexpensive quarter pizzas; people take the pizza, trays and all, out on the Campo for a picnic (daily 12:00–15:00, 19:00–21:00, nonsmoking section—*non fumatori*—in back, CC:VM only in cafeteria, to left of city tower as you face it).

For authentic Sienese dining at a fair price, eat at **Locanda Garibaldi**, down Via Giovanni Dupre at #18, within a block of Il Campo (L27,000 menu, Sun–Fri opens at 12:00 for lunch and 19:00 for dinner, arrive early to get a table, closed Sat). Marcello does a nice little L5,000 *piatto misto dolce*, featuring several local desserts with sweet wine.

**Ristorante Gallo Nero**, a friendly "grotto" for authentic Tuscan cuisine, is a good student-type place. This "black rooster" serves a mean *ribollita* (hearty Tuscan bean soup) and offers a L40,000 "medieval menu" (L28,000 Tuscan menu, daily 12:00–15:30, 19:00–24:00, CC:VMA, 3 blocks down Via del Porrione from the Campo at #65, tel. 0577-284-356). A block away, **Il Verrochio** serves a decent L22,000 menu (CC:VM, Logge del Papa 1).

**Osteria il Tamburino** is friendly, small, and intimate and serves up tasty meals (Mon–Sat 12:00–14:30, 19:00–20:30, closed Sun, CC:VM, follow Via di Città off Campo, becomes Stalloreggi, Via Stalloreggi 11, tel. 0577-280-306).

**Antica Osteria Da Divo** is the place for a fine L80,000 meal. The kitchen is creative, the food is fresh and top notch, and the ambience is candlelit. You'll get a basket of exotic fresh breads. The "black pearls"—with a truffle sauce—are sumptuous. The lamb goes baaa in your mouth. And the chef is understandably proud of his desserts (daily 12:00–14:30, 19:00–22:00, CC:VMA, facing baptistery door, take the far right, reserve for summer eves, Via Franciosa 29, tel. 0577-284-381).

**Osteria la Chiacchera**, while touristy, is an atmospheric, tasty, and affordable hole-in-the-brick-wall (daily 12:00–14:30, 19:00–24:00, CC:VM, below Pension Bernini at Costa di San Antonio 4, reservations wise, tel. 0577-280-631).

**Le Campane**, two blocks off the Campo, is also good (indoor/outdoor seating, CC:VM, a few steps off Via di Città at Via delle Campane 6, tel. 0577-284-035).

Snack with a view from a balcony overlooking the Campo. Survey these three places from the Campo to see which has a free table: **Gelateria Artigiana** (perhaps Siena's best ice cream), **Bar Paninoteca** (sandwiches, closed Mon), or **Bar Barbero d'Oro** (*panforte*—L3,500/100 grams—and cappuccino, best balcony, closed Sun), all of which are on Via di Città.

**Sienese Sweets**: All over town, Prodotti Tipici shops sell Sienese specialties. Siena's claim to caloric fame is its *panforte*, a rich, chewy concoction of nuts, honey, and candied fruits that impresses even fruitcake haters (although locals prefer a white macaroon-and-almond cookie called *ricciarelli*).

## Transportation Connections—Siena

**By bus to: Rome** (6/day, 3 hrs, by Sena bus, arrives at Rome's Tiburtina station), **Assisi** (3/day, 2 hrs, by Sena bus; 1 goes direct to Assisi, the other 2 go to S. Maria Angeli, from here catch a local bus to Assisi, 2/hrly, 20 min), **San Gimingano** (hrly, 1 hr, by Train bus), **Florence** (2/hrly, 1.25–2 hrs, by Train bus). Schedules get sparse on Sunday.

Buses depart Siena from Piazza Gramsci, the train station, or both. Confirm when you buy your ticket. You can buy tickets for the confusingly named Train (pron. TRAH-een) buses or Sena buses at the train station (Train bus office: Mon–Sat 5:50–19:30; for Sena, buy tickets at *tabacchi* shop unless they've opened a new office in the station), or even easier and more central, at Sottopassaggio La Lizza under Piazza Gramsci (Train bus office: daily 5:50–19:30, tel. 0577-204-246, toll-free 800-373-760; Sena bus office: Mon–Sat 7:45–19:45, Sun 15:15–19:45, tel. 0577-283-203).

Sottopassaggio La Lizza has a cash machine (neither office accepts credit cards), luggage storage (L5,000, daily 7:00–19:30), posted bus schedules, TV monitors (listing imminent departures), and expensive WCs. The fastest buses are marked "*corse rapide,*" the *diretto* makes a few stops, and the misnamed *accellerata* stops everywhere. These milk-run buses are much slower but more scenic, offering an interesting glimpse of small-town and rural Tuscany.

If you plan to depart Siena after the bus offices close, either buy a ticket in advance from a nearby *tabacchi* shop, or on the bus from the driver (this is discouraged, but possible).

Buses run from Siena to **Viterbo** for Civita connections (usually 1/day, departs Siena in aftenoon); get tickets in Siena at the train station or at Balzana Viaggi travel agency (Via Montanini 73, near Piazza Gramsci, tel. 0577-285-013).

**By train to:** Florence (9/day, 1.75 hrs, last one at 21:00).

# SAN GIMIGNANO

The epitome of a Tuscan hill town, with 14 medieval towers still standing (out of an original 72!), San Gimignano is a perfectly preserved tourist trap so easy to visit and visually pleasing that it's a good stop. In the 13th century, back in the days of Romeo and Juliet, towns were run by feuding noble families. They'd periodically battle things out from the protective bases of their respective family towers. Pointy skylines were the norm in medieval Tuscany. But in San Gimignano, fabric was big business, and many of its towers were built simply to hang dyed fabric out to dry.

While the basic three-star sight here is the town of San Gimignano itself, there are a few worthwhile stops. From the town gate, shop straight up the traffic-free town's cobbled main drag to Piazza del Cisterna (with its 13th-century well). The town sights cluster around the adjoining Piazza del Duomo. Thursday is market day (8:00–13:00), but, for local merchants, every day is a sales frenzy.

**Tourist Information**: The TI is in the old center on Piazza Duomo (daily March–Oct 9:00–13:00, 15:00–19:00, Nov–Feb 9:00–13:00, 14:00–18:00, changes money, tel. 0577-940-008, www.sangimignano.com, e-mail: prolocsg@tin.it). To see virtually all of the city's sights, consider a L20,000 combo ticket (covers Collegiata, Torre Grossa, Museo Civico, archaeological museum, and more).

## Sights—San Gimignano

The **Collegiata**, with the round windows and wide steps, is a Romanesque church filled with fine Renaissance frescoes (L6,000, Mon–Fri 9:30–19:30, Sat 9:30–17:00, Sun 13:00–17:00).

You can climb the city's tallest tower, **Torre Grossa** (L8,000, 60 meters tall, March–Oct daily 9:30–19:20; Nov–Feb Sat–Thu 10:30–16:20, closed Fri), but the free *rocca* (castle), a short hike behind the church, offers a better view and a great picnic perch, especially at sunset.

The **Museo Civico**, in Piazza Popolo, has a classy little painting collection with a 1422 altar piece by Taddeo di Bartolo honoring Saint Gimignano. You can see him with the town in his hands surrounded by events from his life (L7,000, L12,000 combo ticket with Torre Grossa, same hours as Torre Grossa).

## Sleeping and Eating in San Gimignano
**(L2,000 = about $1, country code: 39, zip code: 53037)**
**Carla Rossi** offers rooms—most with views—throughout the town (Db-from L100,000, Via di Cellole 81, tel. & fax 0577-955-041, cellular 036-8352-3206, www.appartamentirossicarla.com). For a listing of private rooms, stop by or call **Associazione Strutture Extralberghiere** (Db-L100,000, no breakfast, Piazza della Cisterna, tel. 0577-943-190). **Osteria del Carcere** has good food and prices (Via del Castello 13, just off Piazza della Cisterna, tel. 0577-941-905). Shops guarded by wild boar statues sell boar by the gram; carnivores buy some boar (*cinghiale*—cheen-GAH-lay), cheese, bread, and wine and enjoy a picnic in the garden by the castle.

## Transportation Connections—San Gimignano
**To: Florence** (hrly buses, 75 min, change in Poggibonsi; or catch the frequent 20-min shuttle bus to Poggibonsi and train to Florence), **Siena** (hrly buses, 90 min, change in Poggibonsi to bus or train), **Volterra** (6 buses/day, 2 hrs, change in Poggibonsi and Colle di Val d'Elsa). Bus tickets are sold at the bar just inside the town gate. San Gimignano has no baggage-check service.

**Drivers:** You can't drive within the walled town of San Gimignano, but a car park awaits just a few steps outside.

## ASSISI
Around the year 1200, a simple friar from Assisi challenged the decadence of church government and society in general with a powerful message of nonmaterialism, simplicity, and a "slow down and smell God's roses" lifestyle. Like Jesus, Francis taught by example. A huge monastic order grew out of his teachings, which were gradually embraced (some would say co-opted) by the church. Clare, St. Francis' partner in poverty, founded the Order of the Poor Clares. Catholicism's purest example of simplicity is now glorified in beautiful churches. In 1939 Italy made Francis and Clare its patron saints.

Francis' message of love and sensitivity to the environment has a broad and timeless appeal. But any pilgrimage site will be commercialized, and the legacy of St. Francis is Assisi's basic industry. In summer the town bursts with flash-in-the-pan Francis fans and Franciscan knickknacks. Those able to see past the tacky friar mementos can actually have a "travel on purpose" experience. Most visitors are day-trippers. Assisi after dark is closer to a place Francis could call home.

## Orientation
Assisi, crowned by a ruined castle, is beautifully preserved and rich in history. The 1997 earthquake did more damage to the tourist industry than to the local buildings. But it's back to business as

# Assisi

**1** ALBERGO ITALIA

**2** HOTEL BELVEDERE

**3** CAMERE ANNALISA

**4** HOTEL IDEALE

**5** ALBERGO DUOMO

**6** HOTEL FORTEZZA

**7** SRA. GAMBACORTA'S STORE

**8** LA PALLOTTA ROOMS

**9** LA PALLOTTA REST.

**10** HOTEL SOLE & PRIORI

**11** HOTEL UMBRIA

**12** HOTEL ASCESI

*NOT TO SCALE...
PIAZZA COMUNE TO:*
- *BASILICA = 10 MIN. WALK DOWNHILL*
- *ROCCA MAGGIORE = 10 MIN. WALK UPHILL*
- *ROCCA MINORE = 15 MIN. WALK UPHILL*

usual for 2001, and that quake should be of no concern to anyone planning a visit.

**Tourist Information:** The TI is in the center of town on Piazza del Comune (Mon–Sat 8:00–14:00, 15:30–18:30, Sun 9:00–13:00, tel. 075-812-534), along with the Roman temple of Minerva, a Romanesque tower, banks, a finely frescoed pharmacy, the Pinacoteca (with obscure Umbrian art, not worth the admission for most), and a Roman Forum (see "Sights," below). Market day is Saturday on Piazza Mateotti.

**Arrival in Assisi:** Buses connect Assisi's train station (near Santa Maria degli Angeli) with the old town center (L1,200, 2/hrly, 5 km), stopping at Piazza Unita d'Italia (near Basilica of St. Francis), Largo Properzio (near Basilica of St. Clare), and Piazza Matteotti (top of old town). Buses usually leave from both the station and Piazza Matteotti at :10 and :40 past the hour. Taxis into town run about L16,000 to L20,000 (there are legitimate extra charges for luggage and night service, but beware: many taxis rip off tourists with tarif #2; the meter should be set on tarif #1, L5,000 drop). You can check bags at the train station (L5,000) but not in town. Drivers just coming in for the day should follow the signs to Piazza Matteotti's wonderful underground parking garage at the top of the town (which comes with bits of ancient Rome in the walls, L1,500/hr, open 7:00–21:00, until 23:00 in summer).

**Travel Agency:** You can get bus and train tickets within a block of the Basilica of St. Clare at Agenzia Viaggi Stoppini (Corso Mazzini 31, tel. 075-812-597).

**Local Guide:** Anne Robichaud, an American Elderhostel lecturer who has lived in Italy since 1975, offers personalized tours of Assisi and all the Umbrian hill towns, focusing on history, art, crafts, folklore, contemporary culture, and even cooking lessons—your choice ($260/half day, $380/full day, mention book when you reserve to get these discounted prices, families welcome, lunch in her home an optional extra for full-day tours—minimum 4 people, book well in advance, tel. 075-802-334—best from 6:30–7:30 and 21:00–23:00, fax 075-813-698, e-mail: arobichaud@tecnonet.it). Thanks to Anne for her help with the following walk.

## Assisi Welcome Walk

There's much more to Assisi than St. Francis and what all the blitz tour groups see. This self-guided short walk, rated ▲▲, covers the town from Piazza Matteotti at the top, down to the Basilica of St. Francis at the bottom. To get to Piazza Matteotti, ride the bus from the train station (or Piazza Unita d'Italia) to the last stop, or drive your car there (underground parking with Roman ruins).

**The Roman Arena:** Start 50 meters beyond Piazza Matteotti (at intersection at far end of parking lot, away from the city center—see map). A lane, named Via del Teatro Romano, leads to a cozy circular neighborhood built around a Roman arena. Assisi was an important Roman town. Circle the arena counterclockwise (if a chain is stretched across the road, it's to keep cars out, not you). Imagine how colorful the town laundry must have been in the last generation when the women of Assisi gathered here to do their wash. Adjacent to the laundry is a small rectangular pool filled with water; above it are the coats of arms of the town's leading families. Twenty meters farther, hike up the steps to the top of the hill for an aerial view of the oval arena. The Roman stones have long been absorbed into the medieval architecture. It was Roman tradition to locate the arena outside of town...which this was. Continue on. The lane leads down to a city gate.

**Umbrian view:** Leave Assisi at the Porta Perlici for a commanding Umbrian view. This state is called the "green heart of Italy": the geographical center of the country and only state completely landlocked by other Italian states. Enjoy the greens: silver green on the valley floor (olives), emerald green 10 meters below you (grape vines), and deep green on the hillsides (evergreen oak trees). Also notice the Rocca Maggiore (big castle), a fortress providing townsfolk a refuge in times of attack and, behind you,

the Rocca Minore (little castle). Now walk back to Piazza
Matteotti. Go to the opposite end of this piazza, to the corner
(at bend in road) closest to the city center. Down a small road,
you'll see the big dome of San Rufino. Walk down this road
(Via del Torrione) to the church. Stand in front of the church;
its square bell tower is on your left.

**Church of San Rufino:** While Francis is Italy's patron saint,
Assisi's is Rufino, the town's first bishop (in the third century, he
was martyred and buried here). The church is 12th-century
Romanesque with a neoclassical interior. As you enter, look left
(under the bell tower) at the Roman cistern (behind the black iron
fence)—the town's water source when under attack. Both Francis
and Clare were baptized in this church. Traditionally, the children
of Assisi are still baptized right here.

**Medieval Architecture:** Follow the sign down Via Dono
Doni toward St. Clare. After 20 meters, hike down the steps on
the right. At the bottom notice the pink limestone pavement. The
medieval town survives. The pointed arches (built over doorways)
indicate that the buildings date from the 12th through the 14th
century. The vaults that turn lanes into tunnels are reminders of
medieval urban expansion (mostly 15th century). While the population grew, people wanted to live protected within the walls, so
Assisi became more dense. Medieval Assisi had five times the
population density of today's Assisi. Notice the floating gardens.
Assisi has a flowering balcony competition each June. When you
arrive at the street, turn left, going slightly uphill, then jog right,
following the sign down to the Basilica of St. Clare.

**Basilica of St. Clare (Santa Chiara):** Dedicated to the
founder of the order of the Poor Clares, this Umbrian Gothic
church is simple, in keeping with the Poor Clares' dedication to
a life of contemplation. (For description, see "Sights," below.)

**Another Umbrian View:** Belly up to the viewpoint in front of
the basilica. On the left is the convent of St. Clare; below you, the
olive grove of the Poor Clares since the 13th century; and, in the
distance, a grand Umbrian view. Assisi overlooks the richest and
biggest valley in otherwise hilly and mountainous Umbria. The
municipality of Assisi has 29,000, but only 1,000 live in the old town.
The lower town grew up with the coming of the railway in the
19th century. In the haze, the blue-domed church is St. Mary of the
Angels (Santa Maria degli Angeli, see description below), the cradle
of the Franciscan order, marking the place St. Francis lived and
worked. This church, a popular pilgrimage sight today, is the first
Los Angeles. Think about California. The Franciscans named L.A.
(after this church), San Francisco, and even Santa Clara.

**Artisans:** From Via Santa Chiara you can see three arches.
The arch next to the church dates from 1265. (Beyond that, the
Porta Nuova, from 1316, marks the final expansion of Assisi.)

Toward the city center (on Via Santa Chiara, the high road), an arch indicates the site of the Roman wall. Forty meters before this arch, pop into the souvenir shop at #1b. The plaque over the door explains that the old printing press (a national monument now, just inside the door) was used to make fake documents for Jews escaping the Nazis in 1943 and 1944. The shop is run by a couple of artisans: the man makes frames out of medieval Assisi timbers; the woman makes the traditional Assisi or Franciscan cross-stitch. Just past the gate, the Lisa Assisi shop (at Corso Mazzini 25b) has a delightful bargain basement with surviving bits of a 2000-year-old mortarless Roman wall. Cooks love the La Pasteria natural products shop at Corso Mazzini 18b (across from entrance of Hotel Sole). Here you can peruse Umbrian wines, herbs, pâtés, and truffles and sample an aromatic "fruit infusion." Ahead at Corso Mazzini 14d, the small shop (Poiesis) sells olive-wood carvings. Drop in. It's said that St. Francis made the first nativity scene to help teach the Christmas message. That's why you'll see so many of these in Assisi. Even today, nearby villages are enthusiastic about their "living" manger scenes. Ahead of you, the columns of the Temple of Minerva mark the Piazza del Comune (described below). Walk there. Sit at the fountain for a few minutes of people watching—don't you love Italy? Within 200 meters of this square, on either side, were the medieval walls. Imagine a commotion of 5,000 people confined within these walls. No wonder St. Francis needed an escape for some peace and quiet. I'll meet you over at the temple.

**Roman Temple/Christian Church:** Assisi has always been a spiritual center. The Romans went to great lengths to make this Temple of Minerva a centerpiece of their city. Notice the columns cutting into the stairway. It was a tight fit here on the hilltop. The stairs went down probably triple the distance you see today. The store facing the temple has a basement with the original pavement stones of the Roman square. There was a church of Santa Maria *sopra* (over) Minerva here in the ninth century. The bell tower is 13th century. Pop inside. Today's church interior is 17th-century Baroque. Flanking the altar are the original Roman temple floor stones. You can even see the drains for the bloody sacrifices that took place here. Behind the statues of Peter and Paul, the original Roman embankment peeks through.

The Keramos store (filled with typical ceramics and textiles) welcomes "shoppers" into its classy basement, where the actual Roman pavement is artfully incorporated into the shop. A few doors back toward the fountain, step into the 16th-century vaults from the old fish market. Notice the Italian flair for design. Even a smelly fish market was finely decorated. The art style is "grotesque"—literally a painting in a grotto. This was painted in the early 1500s, a few years after Columbus brought turkeys back from the New World. The turkeys painted here may just be that bird's European debut.

**Church of San Stefano:** From the main square, hike past the temple up the high road, Via San Paolo. After 200 meters a sign directs you down a lane to San Stefano, which used to be outside the town walls in the days of St. Francis. Legend is that its bells miraculously rang on October 3, 1226, the day St. Francis died. Surrounded by cypress, fig, and walnut trees, it's a delightful bit of offbeat Assisi. Step inside. This is the typical rural Italian Romanesque church—no architect, just built by simple stone masons who put together the most basic design. The lane zigzags down to Via San Francesco. Turn right and walk under the arch toward the Basilica of St. Francis.

**Via San Francesco:** This was the main drag leading from the town to the basilica holding the body of St. Francis. Francis was a big deal even in his own day. He died in 1226 and was made a saint in 1228—the same year the basilica's foundations were laid— and his body was moved in by 1230. Assisi was a big-time pilgrimage center, and this street was a booming place. Notice the fine medieval balcony just below the arch. A few meters farther down (on the left), cool yourself at the fountain. The hospice next door was built in 1237 to house pilgrims. Notice the three faces of its fresco to survive: Jesus, Francis, and Clare.

## Sights—Assisi

▲▲▲**Basilica of St. Francis (Basilica de San Francesco)**—In 1226 St. Francis was buried (with the outcasts he had stood by) outside of his town on the "hill of the damned." Now called the "Hill of Paradise," this is one of the artistic highlights of medieval Europe. It's frescoed from top to bottom by the leading artists of the day: Cimabue, Giotto, Simone Martini, and Pietro Lorenzetti. A 13th-century historian wrote, "No more exquisite monument to the Lord has been built."

From a distance you see the huge arcades "supporting" the basilica. These were 15th-century quarters for the monks. The arcades lining the square leading to the church housed medieval pilgrims.

There are three parts to the church: the upper basilica, the lower basilica, and the saint's tomb (below the lower basilica). In the 1997 earthquake, the lower basilica (with nine-foot-thick walls) was undamaged. The upper basilica (with three-foot-thick walls and bigger windows) was damaged. After restoration was completed in November 1999, the entire church was reopened to visitors (free, daily 6:30–19:00, relic chapel in lower basilica closes at 18:30, tel. 075-819-0084, e-mail: assisisanfrancesco@krenet.it). Note: Modest dress is required (no sleeveless tops or shorts for men or women).

The Basilica of St. Francis—a theological work of genius—
can be difficult for the 21st-century tourist/pilgrim to appreciate.
Since the basilica is the reason most visit Assisi, and the message
of St. Francis has even the least devout blessing the town Vespas,
I've designed a *Mona Winks*–type tour with the stress on the
place's theology rather than art history. It's adapted from the
excellent little *The Basilica of Saint Francis—A Spiritual Pilgrimage*,
by Goulet, McInally, and Wood (L6,000 in bookshop).

Start at the lower entrance in the courtyard. The information
center (daily 9:30–12:15, 14:00–18:00, tel. 075-819-0084) is opposite the entry to the lower basilica. At the doorway of the lower
basilica, look up and see St. Francis (in a small gold triangle), who
greets you with a Latin inscription (arching over the doorway).
Sounding a bit like John Wayne, he says the equivalent of "Slow
down and be joyful, pilgrim. You've reached the Hill of Paradise,
and this church will knock your spiritual socks off." Start with the
tomb (turn left into the nave, midway down the nave to your right
are stairs marked *"Tomba"*). Grab a pew right in front of his tomb.

**The message:** Francis' message caused a stir. He traded a life
of power and riches for one of obedience, poverty, and chastity.
The Franciscan existence (Brother Sun, Sister Moon, and so on)
is a space where God, man, and the natural world frolic harmo-
niously. Franciscan friars, known as the "Jugglers of God," were a
joyful part of the community. In an Italy torn by fighting between
towns and families, Francis promoted peace and the restoration of
order. (He set an example by reconstructing a crumbled chapel.)
While the Church was waging bloody Crusades, Francis pushed
ecumenism and understanding. Even today the leaders of the
world's great religions meet here for summits.

This rich building seems to contradict the teachings of the poor
monk it honors, but it was built as an act of religious and civic pride
to remember the hometown saint. It was also designed, and still
functions, as a pilgrimage center and a splendid classroom.

**The tomb:** In medieval times, pilgrims came to Assisi
because St. Francis was buried here. Holy relics were the "ruby
slippers" of medieval Europe. They gave you power—got your
prayers answered and helped you win wars—and ultimately helped
you get back to your eternal Kansas. Assisi made no bones about
promoting the saint's relics but hid his tomb for obvious reasons
of security. Not until 1818 was the tomb opened to the public.
The saint's remains are above the altar in the stone box with the
iron ties. His four closest friends are buried in the corners of the
room. Opposite the altar, up four steps in between the entrance
and exit, notice the small gold box behind the metal grill; this
contains the remains of Francis' rich Roman patron, Jacopa dei
Settesoli. Climb back to the lower nave.

**The lower basilica** is appropriately Franciscan, subdued and

Romanesque. The nave was frescoed with parallel scenes from
the lives of Christ and Francis—connected by a ceiling of stars.
Unfortunately, after the church was built and decorated, the popu-
larity of the Franciscans meant side chapels needed to be built.
Huge arches were cut out of some scenes, but others survive. In
the fresco directly above the entrance to the tomb, Christ is being
taken down from the cross (just the bottom half of his body can be
seen, to the left), and it looks like the story is over. Defeat. But in
the opposite fresco (above the tomb's exit), we see Francis preaching to the birds, reminding the faithful that through baptism, the
message of the Gospel survives.

These stories directed the attention of the medieval pilgrim
to the altar, where, through the sacraments, he met God. The
church was thought of as a community of believers sailing toward
God. The prayers coming out of the nave (*navis*, or ship) fill the
triangular sections of the ceiling—called *vele*, or sails—with spiritual wind. With a priest for a navigator and the altar for a helm,
faith propels the ship.

Stand behind the altar (toes to the bottom step) and look up.
The three scenes in front of you are, to the right, "Obedience"
(Francis wearing a yoke); to the left, "Chastity" (in a tower of
purity held up by two angels); and straight ahead, "Poverty." Here
Jesus blesses the marriage as Francis slips a ring on Lady Poverty.
In the foreground two "self-sufficient" merchants (the new rich of
a thriving North Italy) are throwing sticks and stones at the bride.
But Poverty, in her patched wedding dress, is fertile and strong,
and even those brambles blossom into a rosebush crown.

Putting your heels to the altar and bending back like a drum
major, look up at Francis, who traded a life of earthly simplicity
for glory in heaven. Now, turn to the right and march...

In the corner, steps lead down into the relic chapel. Circle
the room clockwise. You'll see the silver chalice and plate Franc
is used for the bread and wine of the Eucharist (in small dark
windowed case set into wall, marked *Calice con Patena*). Francis
believed that his personal possessions should be simple, but the
items used for worship should be made of the finest materials. In
the display case in the corner is a small section of the "hair cloth"
worn by Francis as penitence. In the next corner is the tunic and
slippers Francis wore during his last days. Next find a prayer (in a
fancy silver stand) that St. Francis wrote for Brother Leo, signed
with his tau cross. Next is a papal document (1223) legitimizing
the Franciscan order and assuring his followers that they were
not risking a (deadly) heresy charge. Finally, see the tunic
lovingly patched and stitched by followers of the five-foot,
four-inch-tall St. Francis.

Return up the stairs to the lower basilica. You're in the tran-
scept. This church brought together the greatest Sienese (Martini

and Lorenzetti) and Florentine (Cimabue and Giotto) artists of the day. Look around at the painted scenes. In 1300 this was radical art—believable homespun scenes, landscapes, trees, real people. Study the crucifix (by Giotto) with the eight sparrowlike angels. For the first time, holy people are expressing emotion: One angel turns her head sadly at the sight of Jesus, and another scratches her hands down her cheeks, drawing blood. Mary, previously in control, has fainted in despair. The Franciscans, with their goal of bringing God to the people, found a natural partner in Europe's first modern painter, Giotto.

To see the Renaissance leap, look at the painting to the right. This is by Cimabue—it's Gothic, without the 3-D architecture, natural backdrop, and slice-of-life reality of the Giotto work. Cimabue's St. Francis is considered by some to be the earliest existing portrait of the saint. To the left, at eye level, enjoy the Martini saints and their exquisite halos.

Francis' friend, "Sister Death," was really not all that terrible. In fact, Francis would like to introduce you to her now (above and to the right of the door leading into the relic chapel). Go ahead, block the light and meet her. I'll wait for you upstairs, in the courtyard. By the way, monks in robes are not my idea of easy-to-approach people, but the Franciscans are still God's jugglers (and most of them speak English).

From the courtyard, climb the stairs to the **upper basilica**. The upper basilica, built later than the lower, is brighter, Gothic (the first Gothic church in Italy, 1228), and nearly wallpapered by Giotto. This gallery of frescoes by Giotto and his assistants shows 28 scenes from the life of St. Francis.

Look for these scenes:

• **A common man spreads his cape before Francis** (imme-diately to right of altar) out of honor and recognition to a man who will do great things. Symbolized by the rose window, God looks over the 20-year-old Francis, a dandy imprisoned in his selfishness. A medieval pilgrim fluent in symbolism would under-stand this because the Temple of Minerva (which you saw today on Assisi's Piazza del Comune) was a prison at that time. The rose window, which never existed, is symbolic of God's eye.

• **Francis offers his cape to a needy stranger** (next panel). Prior to this act of kindness, Francis had been captured in battle, held as a prisoner of war, and then released.

• **Francis is visited by the Lord in a dream** (next panel) and told to leave the army and go home.

• **Francis relinquishes his possessions** (two panels down), giving his dad his clothes, his credit cards, and even his time-share condo on Capri. Naked Francis is covered by the bishop, symboliz-ing his transition from a man of the world to a man of the church.

• **The pope has a vision** (next panel) of a simple man

propping up his teetering church. This led to the papal acceptance of the Franciscan reforms.

• **Christ appears to Francis** being carried by a seraph—a six-winged angel (other side of church, fourth panel from the door). For the strength of his faith, Francis is given the marks of his master, the "battle scars of love"...the stigmata. Throughout his life Francis was interested in chivalry; now he's joined the spiritual knighthood.

• **Francis preaches to the birds** (to the right of the exit). Francis was more than a nature lover. The birds, of different species, represent the diverse flock of humanity and nature, all created and loved by God and worthy of each other's love.

Before you leave, look at the ceiling above the altar and front entrance to see large tan patches; these careful repairs were made after the basilica was damaged in the 1997 earthquake. It's a blessing that so many of the frescoes remain.

Near the outside of the upper basilica is the Latin pax (peace) and the Franciscan tau cross in the grass. Tau, the last letter in the Hebrew alphabet, is symbolic of faithfulness to the end. Francis signed his name with this simple character. Tau and pax. (For more pax, take the high lane back to town, up to the castle, or into the countryside.)

▲**Basilica of Saint Clare (Basilica di Santa Chiara)**—Dedicated to the founder of the order of the Poor Clares, this Umbrian Gothic church is simple, in keeping with the Poor Clares' dedication to a life of contemplation. The church was built in 1265, and the huge buttresses were added in the next century. The interior's fine frescoes were whitewashed in Baroque times. The Chapel of St. George, on the right (actually an earlier church incorporated into this one), has the crucifix that supposedly spoke to St. Francis, leading to his conversion in 1206. In the back of that chapel are some important Franciscan relics, including Clare's robe. Stairs lead from the nave down to the tomb of Saint Clare. The attached cloistered community of the Poor Clares has flourished for 700 years (church open 7:00–12:00, 14:00–19:00, Sun until 18:00).

For a change of pace, dip into the wondrous mechanical, water-powered manger scene of Silvano Gionbolina (Via Sermei 2b, opposite flying buttresses of church).

**Roman Forum (Foro Romano)**—For a look at Assisi's Roman roots, tour the Roman Forum, which is actually under the Piazza del Comune. The floor plan is sparse, the odd bits and pieces obscure, but it's well explained in English, and you can actually walk an ancient Roman road (L4,000, daily 10:00–13:00, 15:00–19:00).

▲**Rocca Maggiore**—The "big castle" offers a good look at a 14th-century fortification and a fine view of Assisi and the Umbrian countryside (L5,000, daily 10:00–19:30, closes earlier off-season). If you're counting lire, the view is just as good from outside the castle, and the interior is pretty bare. For a picnic with the same birdsong and views that inspired St. Francis, leave all the tourists and hike to the Rocca Minore (small castle) above Piazza Matteotti.

▲▲**Santa Maria degli Angeli**—This huge church, towering above the buildings below Assisi, was built around the tiny but historic Porziuncola Chapel. When the pope gave Francis his blessing, he was given this *porziuncola,* or "small portion"—a little land with a fixer-upper chapel—from which Francis and his followers established their order. As you enter St. Mary of the Angels, notice the sketch on the door showing the original little chapel with the monks' huts around it and Assisi before it had its huge basilica. Francis lived here after he founded the Franciscan Order in 1208, and this was where he consecrated St. Clare as the Bride of Christ. The other "sights" in the church (a chapel on the spot where Francis died, the rose garden, a museum that has a few monastic cells upstairs) are most interesting to pilgrims (daily 7:00–18:30, Nov–April 7:00–12:00, 14:00–sunset).

Orange city buses run between Santa Maria degli Angeli and Assisi, with a stop en route at the train station (2/hrly, can buy ticket at *tabacchi* for L1,200 or on bus for L2,000). If you're using public transportation, this church is most easily visited either on your way to Assisi (arriving in Assisi by train, catch bus from station for short 8-minute ride to church, buses loop back to station and continue to Assisi center; facing the church, the stop is to your left, alongside church) or as you leave Assisi (departing from Assisi, catch bus to church, may need to transfer at train station, some buses—such as the one to Siena—leave from the church; facing the church, the stop is on your left across the street).

## Sleeping in Assisi
**(L2,000 = about $1, country code: 39, zip code: 06081)**
Sleep Code: **S** = Single, **D** = Double/Twin, **T** = Triple, **Q** = Quad, **b** = bathroom, **t** = toilet only, **s** = shower only, **CC** = Credit Card (**V**isa, **M**asterCard, **A**mex), **SE** = Speaks English, **NSE** = No English.

The town accommodates large numbers of pilgrims on religious holidays. Finding a room any other time should be easy. See map on page 174 for hotel locations.

**Albergo Italia** is clean and simple, with great beds and delightful owners. Some of its 13 rooms overlook the town square (Ss-L39,000, D-L55,000, Db-L69,000, T-L66,000, Tb-L90,000, Qb-L100,000, CC:VM, no breakfast, just off Piazza del Comune's fountain at Vicolo della Fortezza 2, tel. 075-812-625, fax 075-804-3749, Paola SE).

**Hotel Belvedere**, which offers 16 comfortable rooms and good views, is run by friendly Enrico and his American wife, Mary (Db-L130,000, breakfast-L10,000, elevator, 2 blocks past Basilica of St. Clare at Via Borgo Aretino 13, tel. 075-812-460, fax 075-816-812, e-mail: assisihotelbelvedere@hotmail.com, SE). Their attached restaurant is good.

**Camere Annalisa Martini** is a cheery home swimming in vines and roses in the town's medieval core. Annalisa speaks English and enthusiastically accommodates her guests with a picnic garden, a washing machine (small load-L5,000), a refrigerator, and six homey rooms (S-L38,000, Sb-L40,000, D-L60,000, Db-L65,000, Tb-L90,000, Qb-L100,000, 3 rooms share 2 bathrooms, no breakfast, 1 block below Piazza del Comune, then left on Via S. Gregorio to #6, tel. & fax 075-813-536).

**Hotel Ideale** is on the top edge of town, overlooking the valley, and has 12 bright, modern rooms, view balconies, a peaceful garden, free parking, and an English-speaking welcome (Sb-L90,000, Db-L150,000, includes big-for-Italy breakfast, CC:VMA, most rooms with views, Piazza Matteotti 1, tel. 075-813-570, fax 075-813-020, e-mail: hotelideale@libero.it, sisters Lara and Ilaria SE). **Hotel Ascesi**, run by the same family, has an inviting little lobby, nine fine rooms, and a tiny terrace, located within a block of the Basilica of St. Francis (Sb-L65,000, Db-L95,000, breakfast-L7,500, CC:VM, air-con, Via Frate Elia 5, walk up from Piazza Unita d'Italia, take a left on Frate Elia, then a quick right on miniscule alley—Vicolo Venanzo, tel. & fax 075-812-420, e-mail: hotelideale@libero.it). Both of these hotels—at the top and bottom of town—are close to bus stops (and parking lots), handy if you're packing lots of luggage.

**Albergo Il Duomo** is tidy and *tranquillo* on a stair-step lane one block up from San Rufino (9 rooms, S-L50,000, Sb-L55,000, D-L62,000, Db-L72,000, breakfast-L8,000, saggy beds, CC:VM, Vicolo S. Lorenzo 2, tel. 075-812-742, fax 075-812-762, e-mail: ilduomo@krenit.it, Carlo SE).

**Hotel La Fortezza** is a simple, modern, and quiet place with seven rooms (Db-L95,000, Tb-L130,000, Qb-L150,000 CC:VMA, a short climb above Piazza del Comune at Vicolo della Fortezza 19b, tel. 075-812-993, fax 075-819-8035, www.lafortezzahotel.com, SE).

**La Pallotta**, a recommended restaurant (see "Eating" below), offers seven clean, bright rooms. Rooms #12 and #18 have views (Db-L90,000, CC:VMA, view terrace, Via San Rufino 4, go up short flight of stairs outside building to reach entrance, tel. & fax 075-812-307, e-mail: pallotta@tecnonet.it).

**Signora Gambacorta** rents several decent rooms and has a roof terrace on a quiet lane (Via Sermei 9) just above St. Chiara. There is no sign or reception desk, so you'll need to check in at her shop a half block east of Piazza Comune at San Gabriele 17—look for the sign "Bottega di Gambacorta" (S-L35,000, Db-L70,000, 2-night stays preferred, no breakfast; store is open

Mon–Wed and Sat 8:00–13:00, 16:30–20:00, Thu 8:00–13:00, closed Sun—if you can't arrive when store is open, call when you arrive, tel. 075-812-454, fax 075-813-186, www.umbrars.com/gambacorta, e-mail: geo@umbrars.com, NSE). She also has an apartment for stays of at least four nights (L150,000/night for up to 5 people, kitchen, no breakfast).

**Hotel Sole** is well located, with 35 spacious, comfortable rooms in a 15th-century building (Sb-L75,000, Db-L120,000, Tb-L140,000, breakfast-L10,000, CC:VMA, half its rooms are in a newer annex across the street, some rooms have views and balconies, elevator in annex, 100 meters before Basilica of St. Clare, Corso Mazzini 35, tel. 075-812-373, fax 075-813-706, e-mail: sole@tecnonet.it, NSE).

**Hotel Umbra**, the best splurge in the center, feels like a quiet villa in the middle of town (25 rooms, Sb-L130,000, Db-L170,000–200,000, depending upon season and size of room, Tb-L210,000, includes breakfast, CC:VMA, air-con, peaceful garden and view terrace, most rooms have views, good restaurant, very quiet, 100 meters below Piazza di Comune at Via degli Archi 6, tel. 075-812-240, fax 075-813-653, e-mail: humbra@mail.caribusiness.it, family Laudenzi).

**Hotel Dei Priori** is a three-star, palace-type place in the old center with big, quiet rooms that have all the comforts (Db-L190,000–210,000, deluxe Db-L250,000–270,000, includes breakfast, CC:VMA, elevator, air-con, Corso Mazzini 15, tel. 075-812-237, fax 075-816-804, www.assisihotel.net, e-mail: hpriori@edisons.it).

Francis probably would have bunked with the peasants in Assisi's **Ostello della Pace** (L25,000 beds in 4- to 8-bed rooms, Qb-L30,000 apiece, includes breakfast, dinner-L15,000, laundry, a 15-minute walk below town at Via di Valecchie 177, at San Pietro stop on the station–town bus, tel. & fax 075-816-767, SE).

## Eating in Assisi

For a fine Assisian perch and good regional cooking, relax on a terrace overlooking Piazza del Comune at **Taverna dei Consoli** (L25,000 4-course menu, also à la carte, Thu–Tue 12:00–14:30, 19:00–21:30, closed Wed, CC:VM, across from Albergo Italia, tel. 075-812-516, friendly owner Moreno SE and recommends the *bruschetta*, *stringozzi*—noodles, *agnello*—lamb, and *cinghiale*—boar).

**La Pallotta**, a local favorite run by a friendly, hardworking family, offers excellent regional specialties, such as *piccione* (pigeon), *coniglio* (rabbit), and more (L27,000 menu, Wed–Mon 12:15–14:30, 19:15–21:30, closed Tue, CC:VM, a few steps off Piazza del Comune, through gate across from temple/church, Vicolo della Volta Pinta, tel. 075-812-649).

**Osteria Piazzetta Dell Erba** is a fun, little family-run place a block above Piazza del Comune serving good, basic Umbrian specialties next to the Gambacorta grocery (closed Mon, CC:VM, Via San Gabriele dell' Addolorata, tel. 075-815-352). **Pizzeria/ Tavola Calda Dal Carro** is similar, popular, and friendly (good pizzas and L22,000 menu, closed Wed, Vicolo di Nepis 2, tel. 075-815-249).

**Ristorante San Francesco** is the place to splurge for dinner (Thu–Tue 12:00–14:30, 19:30–20:00, closed Wed, CC:VM, facing basilica at Via San Francesco 52, tel. 075-812-329).

## Transportation Connections—Assisi

**To train to: Rome** (4/day, 2 hrs), **Florence** (5/day, 2.5 hrs, more with transfers at Terontola and Cortona), **Orvieto** (4/day, 2 hrs). Train info: tel. 147-888-088.

**By bus to: Siena** (1/day, 2 hrs, L16,000, departs in morning from Santa Maria degli Angeli church near Assisi train station), **Florence** (1/day, departs Assisi's Porta San Pietro very early in morning, 2.75 hrs), **Rome** (3/day, 3 hrs, first bus departs Assisi's Porta San Pietro in early afternoon, arrives at Rome's Tiburtina station).

## ORVIETO

Umbria's grand hill town, while no secret, is still worth a quick look. Just off the freeway, with three popular claims to fame (its cathedral, Classico wine, and ceramics), it's loaded with tourists by day and quiet by night. Drinking a shot of wine in a ceramic cup as you gaze up at the cathedral lets you experience Orvieto all at once.

Ride the back streets of Orvieto into the Middle Ages. The town sits majestically on a big chunk of tufa. Streets lined with buildings made from the exhaust-stained volcanic stuff seem to grumble Dark Ages.

Piazza Cahen is a key transportation hub at the entry to the hilltop town. It has a ruined fortress with a garden, a commanding view, and the Pozzo San Patrizio, an impressive, although over-priced, double helix well carved into tufa rock.

**Tourist Information:** The TI is at Piazza Duomo 24 on the cathedral square (Mon–Fri 8:15–14:00, 16:00–19:00, Sat 10:00–13:00, 16:00–19:00, Sun 10:00–12:00, 16:00–18:00, tel. 0763-341-772). The TI sells a "Carta Unica" (L20,000) that covers entry to the Archaeological Museum, Underground Orvieto Tours, and other sights, plus your public transportation (bus and funicular) for one day.

**Arrival in Orvieto:** A handy funicular/bus shuttle takes visitors quickly from the train station and car park to the top of the town (4/hrly, L1,600 ticket includes Piazza Cahen–Piazza Duomo minibus transfer, where you'll find everything that

# Orvieto

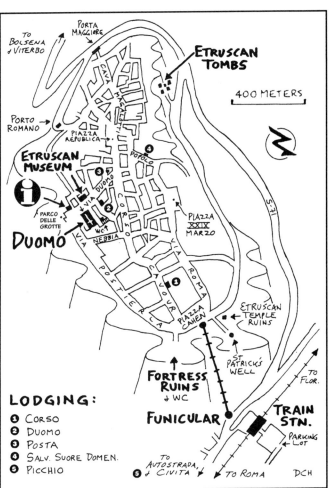

**LODGING:**
- ① Corso
- ② Duomo
- ③ Posta
- ④ Salv. Suore Domen.
- ⑤ Picchio

matters; or L1,200 for funicular only—best choice if you're staying at Hotel Corso; funicular runs Mon–Sat 7:15–20:30, Sun 8:00–20:30).

Buy your ticket at the entrance to the funicular (look for *"biglietteria"* sign) or at the train station *tabacchi* shop across the street. At the top of the funicular, get on the waiting orange bus. The shuttle bus drops you at the TI (last stop, in front of Duomo). Drivers park at the base of the hill at the huge, free lot behind the

Orvieto train station (follow the "P" and "funicolare" signs) or at the pay lot to the right of Orvieto's cathedral (L1,500 for first hour, L1,000/hrly thereafter).

## Sights—Orvieto

▲▲**Duomo**—Orvieto's cathedral has Italy's most striking facade (from 1330). Grab a gelato (to the left of the church) and study this fascinating mass of mosaics and sculpture (daily 7:30–12:45, 14:30–19:15, closes at 18:15 March and Oct, closes at 17:15 Nov–Feb). Inside the cathedral notice how the downward-sloping floor diminishes the perspective, giving it the illusion of being shorter than it is. Notice also the alabaster windows.

To the right of the altar, the Chapel of St. Brizio features Luca Signorelli's brilliantly lit and recently restored frescoes of the Apocalypse. Step into the chapel and you're surrounded by vivid scenes showing the Preaching of the Antichrist, the End of the World, the Resurrection of the Bodies, the Last Judgment, and a gripping pietà. For a bonus, check out Fra Angelico's painting of Jesus, the angels, and the prophets on the ceiling. This room is Orvieto's artistic must-see (get L3,000 ticket at the TI or the shop across the square; chapel sometimes free 7:30–10:00—drop by to check, only 24 people allowed in chapel at a time, closed on Sun). A good book about the chapel is Dugald McLellan's *Signorelli's Orvieto Frescoes*.

Public toilets are just off the square, down the stairs from the left transept. To find the viewpoint park, face the cathedral and go right (past parking lot) for a one-minute walk.

**Archaeological Museum (Museo Civico)**—Across from the entrance of the cathedral is a fine Etruscan art museum combined with a city history museum (L8,000, daily 9:30–18:00; Oct–March Tue–Sun 10:00–13:00, 14:30–17:00).

**Underground Orvieto Tours (Parco delle Grotte)**—Guides weave a good archaeological history into an hour-long look at about 100 meters of caves (L10,000, tours daily at 11:00, 12:15, 16:00, and 17:15 from TI, tel. 0763-344-891 or the TI). Orvieto is honeycombed with Etruscan and medieval caves. You'll see only the remains of an old olive press, two impressive 40-meter-deep Etruscan well shafts, and the remains of a primitive cement quarry, but if you want underground Orvieto, this is the place to get it.

## Sleeping in Orvieto
**(L2,000 = about $1, country code: 39, zip code: 05018)**
Here are five places in the old town and one in a more modern neighborhood near the station.

**Hotel Corso** is small, clean, and friendly, with comfy, modern rooms, some with balconies and views (Sb-L110,000, Db-L150,000, 10 percent discount if you show this book, buffet breakfast-L12,500, CC:VM, elevator, air-con at no extra charge, garage on the main street up from funicular toward Duomo at Via Cavour 339, tel. & fax 0763-342-020).

**Hotel Virgilio** is a decent hotel with bright and modern— if overpriced—rooms shoehorned into an old building ideally located on the main square facing the cathedral (Sb-L120,000, Db-L175,000, includes breakfast, send personal or traveler's check for first night's deposit, CC:VM, elevator, noisy church bells, Piazza Duomo 5, tel. 0763-341-882, fax 0763-343-797, SE). They also have a cheaper *dependencia*—a double and quad in a one-star hotel a few doors away (Db-L110,000, Qb-L200,000).

**Hotel Duomo** is a funky, brightly colored, Old World place with 17 not-quite-clean rooms and a great location (renovated for 2001, Db-maybe L100,000, a block from Duomo, behind *gelateria* at Via di Maurizio 7, tel. 0763-341-887, fax 0763-341-105).

**Hotel Posta** is a five-minute walk from the cathedral into the medieval core. It's a big, old, formerly elegant but well-cared-for-in-its-decline building with a breezy garden, a grand old lobby, and spacious, clean, plain rooms with vintage rickety furniture and springy beds (20 rooms, S-L60,000, Sb-L70,000, D-L80,000, Db-L100,000, breakfast-L10,000, Via Luca Signorelli 18, tel. & fax 0763-341-909).

The sisters of the **Istituto Salvatore Suore Domenicane** rent 15 spotless twin rooms in their heavenly convent (Sb-L55,000, Db-L90,000, 2-night minimum, breakfast-L5,000, just off Piazza del Populo at Via del Populo 1, tel. & fax 0763-342-910).

**Hotel Picchio** is a concrete-and-marble place, more comfortable but with less character than others in the area. It's in the lower, plain part of town, 300 meters from the train station (S-L35,000, Sb-L60,000, D-L65,000, Db-L85,000, Tb-L105,000, ask for the Rick Steves discount; some rooms with air-con, fridge, and phone; Via G. Salvatori 17, 05019 Orvieto Scalo, tel. 0763-301-144 or 0763-90246, family run by Marco and Picchio). A trail leads from here up to the old town.

## Transportation Connections—Orvieto

**By train to: Rome** (14/day, 75 min, consider leaving your car at the large car park behind the Orvieto station), **Florence** (14/day, 90 min), **Siena** (10/day, 2–3 hrs, change in Chiusi).

**By bus to Bagnoregio:** It's a 50-minute, L3,000 bus ride (departures in 2000 from Orvieto's Piazza Cahen on blue Cotral bus: 9:10, 12:40, 13:55, 15:45, 17:40, and 18:35, each bus stops at Orvieto's train station five minutes later, runs daily except Sun, buy tickets on bus or from "café snack bar" at station, confirm return times with the conductor, tel. 0763-792-237). If the bus is empty, develop a relationship with your driver. He may let you jump out in Lubriano for a great photo of distant Civita.

## Orvieto Area

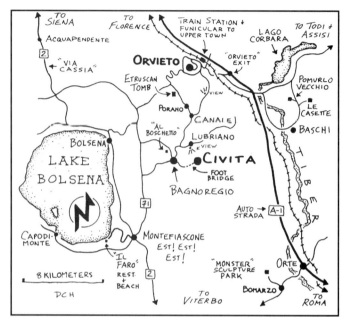

# CIVITA DI BAGNOREGIO

Perched on a pinnacle in a grand canyon, the traffic-free village of Civita is Italy's ultimate hill town. Curl your toes around its Etruscan roots.

Civita is terminally ill. Only 15 residents remain, as, bit by bit, it's being purchased by rich big-city Italians who escape here. Apart from its permanent (and aging) residents and those who have weekend homes here, there is a group of Americans—introduced to the town through a small University of Washington architecture program—who have bought into the rare magic of Civita. When the program is in session, 15 students live with residents and study Italian culture and architecture.

Civita is connected to the world and the town of Bagnoregio by a long pedestrian bridge. While Bagnoregio lacks the pinnacle-town romance of Civita, it is a pure and lively bit of small-town Italy. It's actually a healthy, vibrant community (unlike Civita, the suburb it calls "the dead city"). Get a haircut, sip a coffee on the square, walk down to the old laundry (ask, *"Dov'è la lavanderia vecchia?"*). A lively market fills the parking lot each Monday.

From Bagnoregio, yellow signs direct you along its long, skinny spine to its older neighbor, Civita. Enjoy the view as you walk up the bridge to Civita. Be prepared for the little old ladies of Civita, who have become aggressive at getting lire out of visitors—tourists are their only source of support. Off-season Civita, Bagnoregio, and Al Boschetto (see "Sleeping," below) are all deadly quiet—and cold. I'd side trip in quickly from Orvieto or skip the area altogether.

## Civita Orientation Walk

Civita was once connected to Bagnoregio. The saddle between the separate towns eroded away. Photographs around town show the old donkey path, the original bridge. It was bombed in World War II and replaced in 1965 with the new bridge you'll climb today. The town's hearty old folks hang on the bridge's hand railing when fierce winter weather rolls through.

Entering the town you'll pass through a cut in the rock (made by Etruscans 2,500 years ago) and under a 12th-century Romanesque arch. This was the main Etruscan road leading to the Tiber Valley and Rome.

Inside the town gate on the left notice the old laundry (in front of the WC). On the right a fancy door and windows lead to thin air. This was the facade of a Renaissance palace—one of five that once graced Civita. It fell into the valley riding a chunk of the ever-eroding rock pinnacle. Today the door leads to a remaining chunk of the palace—complete with Civita's first hot tub—owned by the "Marchesa," a countess who married into Italy's biggest industrialist family.

Poke through the museum next door and check out the viewpoint around the corner near the long-gone home of Civita's one famous son, Saint Bonaventure, known as the "second founder of the Franciscans."

Now wander to the town square in front of the church, where you'll find Civita's only public phone, bar, and restaurant—and a wild donkey race on the first Sunday of June and the second Sunday of September. The church marks the spot where an Etruscan temple, and then a Roman temple, once stood. The pillars that stand like giants' bar stools are ancient—Roman or Etruscan.

Go into the church and find Anna. She'll give you a tour, proudly pointing out frescoes and statues from "the school of Giotto" and "the school of Donatello," a portrait of the patron saint of your teeth (notice the scary-looking pincers), and an altar dedicated to Marlon Brando (or St. Ildebrando). Tip her and buy your postcards from her.

The basic grid street plan of the ancient town survives. Just around the corner from the church, on the main street, is Rossana and Antonio's cool and friendly wine cellar. Pull up a stump and let them or their children, Arianna and Antonella, serve you *panini* (sandwiches), *bruschetta* (garlic toast with optional tomato topping),

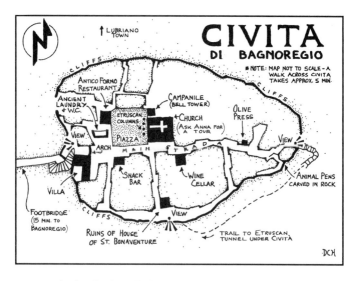

wine, and a local cake called *ciambella*. Climb down into the cellar
and note the traditional wine-making gear and the provisions for
rolling huge kegs up the stairs. Tap on the kegs in the cool bottom
level to see which are full.

The rock below Civita is honeycombed with ancient cellars
(for keeping wine at the same temperature all year) and cisterns
(for collecting rainwater, since there was no well in town). Many
of these date from Etruscan times.

Explore farther down the street but remember, nothing is
abandoned. Everything is still privately owned. After passing an
ancient Roman tombstone on your left, you'll come to Vittoria's
Antico Mulino, an atmospheric collection of old olive presses
(donation requested, give about L1,500). Her sons Sandro and
Felice, running the local equivalent of a lemonade stand, toast
delicious *bruschetta* on weekends and holidays. Choose your
topping (chopped tomato is super) and get a glass of wine for a
fun, affordable snack.

Farther down the way, Maria (for a donation of about L1,500)
will show you through her garden with a grand view (Maria's
Giardino) and share historical misinformation (she says Civita
and Lubriano were once connected).

At the end of town the main drag peters out, and a trail leads
you down and around to the right to a tunnel that has cut through
the hill under the town since Etruscan times. It was widened in the
1930s so farmers could get between their scattered fields easier.

Evenings on the town square are a bite of Italy. The same
people sit on the same church steps under the same moon, night

after night, year after year. I love my cool late evenings in Civita. If you visit in the cool of the morning, have cappuccino and rolls at the small café on the town square.

Whenever you visit, stop halfway up the donkey path and listen to the sounds of rural Italy. Reach out and touch one of the monopoly houses. If you know how to turn the volume up on the crickets, do so.

## Sleeping in Civita and Bagnoregio
### (L2,000 = about $1, country code: 39, zip code: 01022)

When you leave the tourist crush, life as a traveler in Italy becomes easy, and prices tumble. Finding a room is easy in small-town Italy.

Franco, who runs Civita's only restaurant, **Antico Forno**, rents three remodeled rooms on Civita's main square. Call a minimum of one day in advance. Franco will meet you at the base of the bridge to beam up your luggage (Db-L120,000, D-L100,000, the more expensive rooms overlook the square, L20,000 more for optional half pension, CC:VM, Piazza Del Duomo Vecchio, 01022 Civita di Bagnoregio, tel. 0761-760-016, cellular 034-7611-5426, e-mail: fsala@pelagus.it, Franco Sala SE).

For information about a fully furnished and equipped two-bedroom **Civita apartment** with a terrace and cliffside garden that's rentable May through October ($700/week, $2,200/month, one-week minimum Sat to Sat), call Carol Watts in Kansas (tel. 785/539-0815, evenings).

**Hotel Fidanza**, in Bagnoregio near the bus stop, is tired but decent and the only hotel in town. Of its 25 rooms, #206 and #207 have views of Civita (Sb-L90,000, Db-L120,000, breakfast-L10,000, attached restaurant, Via Fidanza 25, Bagnoregio/Viterbo, tel. & fax 0761-793-444).

Just outside Bagnoregio is **Al Boschetto**. The Catarcia family speaks no English. Have an English-speaking Italian call for you (Sb-L65,000, D-L85,000, Db-L95,000, breakfast-L6,000, CC:V, Strada Monterado, Bagnoregio/Viterbo, tel. 0761-792-369, walking and driving instructions below). Most rooms, while very basic, have private showers (no curtains, slippery floors—be careful not to flood the place; sing in search of your shower's resonant frequency). The Catarcia family (Angelino, his wife Perina, sons Gianfranco and Domenico, daughter-in-law Giuseppina, and the grandchildren) offer a candid look at rural Italian life. Meals are sometimes hearty, and the men are often tipsy (can pose a problem for women). If the men invite you down deep into the gooey, fragrant bowels of the cantina, be warned: The theme song is *"Trinka Trinka Trinka,"* and there are no rules unless the female participants set them. The Orvieto bus drops you at the town gate. (Remember, no bus service at all on Sunday.) Al Boschetto is a 15-minute walk out of town past the old arch (follow "Viterbo" signs); turn left at the pyramid monument and right at the first fork (follow "Montefiascone" sign). Civita is a pleasant 45-minute walk (back through Bagnoregio) from Al Boschetto.

**Casa San Martino,** in the village of Lisciano Niccone (near Cortona and Perugia), is a 250-year-old farmhouse run as a B&B by American Italophile Lois Martin. Using this comfortable hill-top countryside as a home base, those with a car can tour Assisi, Orvieto, and Civita. While Lois reserves the summer for one-week stays, she'll take guests staying a minimum of three nights for the rest of the year (Db-$140, 10 percent discount with this book, includes breakfast, views, pool, washer/dryer, house rental available, Casa San Martino 19, Lisciano Niccone, tel. 075-844-288, fax 075-844-422). When she's booked, she refers people to her neighbors Ernestina and Gisbert Schwanke, who rent a charming two-bedroom apartment for less than Lois' (minimum 4-night stay, San Martino 36, tel. & fax 075-844-309, SE).

**For drivers only:** Outside the village of Baschi is the out-standing **Agriturismo Le Cassette**, with rooms in several restored stone farmhouses clustered around a grassy lawn and a swimming pool with a fabulous view of the green Umbrian land-scape (Db-L160,000, includes breakfast and home-cooked dinner, minimum 1-week stays preferred July–Aug, tel. 0744-957-645, fax 0744-950-500, www.argoweb.it/agriturismo_pomurlovecchio, e-mail: pomurlovecchio@tiscalinet.it, run by charming Minghelli family, Daniela speaks "a leetle" English). The same family also owns **Pomurlo Vecchio**, a 12th-century tower house with three rooms a few kilometers away (same prices and phone numbers).

## Eating in and near Civita

In Civita, try **Trattoria Antico Forno**, which serves up pasta at affordable prices (daily for lunch at 12:30 and dinner at 19:30, on the main square, also rents rooms, tel. 0761-760-016).

**Hostaria del Ponte** offers light, creative cuisine at the car park at the base of the bridge to Civita (Tue–Sat 12:30–16:00, 19:30–24:00, Sun 12:30–16:00, closed Mon, great view terrace, tel. 0761-793-565).

In Bagnoregio, check out **Ristorante Nello il Fumatore** (closed Fri, on Piazza Fidanza). You'll get country cooking—such as bunny—served at **Al Boschetto,** just outside Bagnoregio (see "Sleeping," above).

## Transportation Connections—Bagnoregio

**To Civita:** It's a 30-minute walk. Taking the shuttle bus from Bagnoregio (10-min ride, first bus at 7:45, last at 17:50, 2/hrly except during 13:00–15:00 siesta) still involves a 15-minute walk up the pedestrian bridge from the bus stop.

**To Orvieto:** Public buses (8/day, 50 min) connect Bagnoregio to the rest of the world via Orvieto (2000 departures from Bagnoregio: 5:30, 6:35, 6:55, 9:30, 10:15, 13:00, 13:35, 14:25, 16:40, 17:20, runs daily except Sun, see "Connections—Orvieto," above). While there's no official baggage-check service in Bagnoregio, I've arranged with Laurenti Mauro, who runs the Bar Enoteca just outside the Bagnoregio old-town gate, to let you leave your bags there (open 6:00–24:00 with a short lunch break, closed Thu, from the Orvieto bus stop walk downhill and turn right on first street). Pay him L2,000 per bag or buy breakfast there.

**Driving from Orvieto to Bagnoregio:** Orvieto overlooks the autostrada (and has its own exit). The shortest way to Civita from the freeway exit is to turn left (below Orvieto) and follow the signs to Lubriano and Bagnoregio. The more winding and scenic route takes 20 minutes longer: From the freeway, pass under hill-capping Orvieto (on your right, signs to Lago di Bolsena, on Viale I Maggio); take the first left (direction: Bagnoregio), winding up past great Orvieto views through Canale, and through farms and fields of giant shredded wheat to Bagnoregio, where the locals (or rusty old signs) will direct you to Al Boschetto, just outside town. Either way, just before Bagnoregio, follow the signs left to Lubriano and pull into the first little square by the church on your right for a breathtaking view of Civita. Then return to the Bagnoregio road. Drive through Bagnoregio (following yellow "Civita" signs) and park at the base of the steep pedestrian bridge leading up to the traffic-free, 2,500-year-old, canyon-swamped pinnacle town of Civita di Bagnoregio.

# More Hill Towns

Italy is spiked with hill towns. **Perugia**, big and reeking with history, is famous for its fragrant Perugina candy factory and its well-known university for sweet-toothed foreigners bent on learning Italian. **Cortona** is smaller and has a fine youth hostel (tel. 0575-601-765). **Todi** is nearly untouristed. **Pienza**, a Renaissance-planned town, and **Montepulciano**, with its dramatic setting, are also worth the hill town–lover's energy and time. **Sorano** and **Pitigliano** have almost no tourism. **Bevagna**, near Assisi, is as dazed as its town fool, who stands between the twin dark Romanesque churches on its main square. Paranoid **Orte** filled its tufa perch so completely that there's no room for charm, and traffic circulates on a single, skinny, one-way lane. You'll see Orte, Orvieto's poor cousin, from the freeway 30 minutes north of Rome (consider La Ciocciola B&B, Db-L170,000, Seripola, 01028 Orte, tel. & fax 0761-402-734). Wine lovers flock to **Montalcino** for its wonderful Brunello, best enjoyed in the atmospheric *enoteca* built inside the fortress. Train travelers often use the town of **Chiusi** as a home base for the hill towns. The region's trains (to Siena, Orvieto, Assisi) go through or change at this hub, and there are several reasonable hotels near the station.

# THE CINQUE TERRE

The Cinque Terre (CHINK-wuh TAY-ruh), a remote chunk of the Italian Riviera, is the traffic-free, lowbrow, underappreciated alternative to the French Riviera. There's not a museum in sight. Just sun, sea, sand (well, pebbles), wine, and pure unadulterated Italy. Enjoy the villages, swimming, hiking, and evening romance of one of God's great gifts to tourism. For a home base, choose among five villages, each of which fills a ravine with a lazy hive of human activity—calloused locals, sunburned travelers, and no Vespas. While the place is now well discovered (and has its own Web site: www.cinqueterre.it), I've never seen happier, more relaxed tourists. Vernazza is my favorite home base.

The area was first described in medieval times as "the five castles." Tiny communities grew up in the protective shadows of the castles ready to run inside at the first hint of a Turkish "Saracen" pirate raid. Many locals were kidnapped and ransomed or sold into slavery somewhere far to the east. As the threat of pirates faded, the villages grew, with economies based on fish and grapes. Until the advent of tourism in this generation, the towns were very remote. Even today, traditions survive, and each of the five villages comes with a distinct dialect and proud heritage. The region has just become a UNESCO World Heritage Site and a national park, and its natural and cultural wonders will be carefully preserved.

Now that the Cinque Terre is a national park, there are plans to charge entry fees. Starting March 1, hikers and overnight visitors will pay L5,000 for a pass (at train stations, hotels, and possibly booths at trailheads; includes hiking map). When you arrive, see if your hotel offers free passes for guests (if not, buy pass at hotel or back at station). The fees will be used for trail repair. The pass

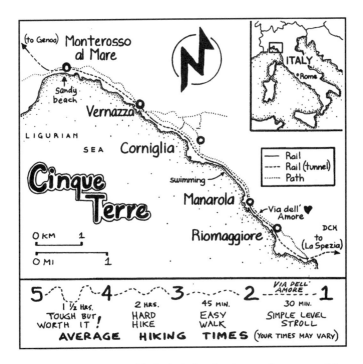

covers your entire visit. To include local train travel, get a combination pass (L10,000/1 day, L20,000/3 days, L30,000/week). Look for the latest on www.ricksteves.com/update.

Over the next decade, Italy has quiet plans for the Cinque Terre. For the sake of tranquility, a new train line will be built inland for the noisy fast trains, leaving the Cinque Terre tracks for just the pokey milk-run trains.

Sadly, a few ugly, noisy Americans are giving tourism a bad name here. Even hip young locals are put off by loud, drunk tourists. They say (and I agree) the Cinque Terre is a special place. It deserves a special dignity. Party in Viareggio but be mellow in the Cinque Terre. Talk softly. Help keep it clean. In spite of the tourist crowds, it's still a real community, and we are guests.

## Planning Your Time

The ideal minimum stay is two nights and a completely uninterrupted day. The Cinque Terre is served by the milk-run train from Genoa and La Spezia. Speed demons arrive in the morning, check their bags in La Spezia, take the five-hour hike through all five towns, laze away the afternoon on the beach or rock of their choice, and zoom away on the overnight train to somewhere back in the real world. But be warned: The Cinque Terre has a strange way of messing up your momentum.

The towns are each just a few minutes apart by hourly train or boat. There's no checklist of sights or experiences; just a hike, the towns themselves, and your fondest vacation desires. Study this chapter in advance and piece together your best day, mixing hiking, swimming, trains, and a boat ride. For the best light and coolest temperatures, start your hike early.

Market days perk up the towns (8:00–13:00, Tue in Vernazza, Wed in Levanto, Thu in Monterosso, and Fri in La Spezia— near train station).

## Getting around the Cinque Terre

**By Train:** The city of La Spezia is the gateway to the Cinque Terre. In La Spezia's train station, the milk-run Cinque Terre train schedule is posted at the information window, and the La Spezia TI hands out the schedule for free. Also ask about the nifty "Footpaths Along The Cinque Terre" brochure/map (daily in summer 9:00–13:00, 15:00–18:00; winter Mon–Sat 9:00–13:00, 14:00–17:00, Sun 9:00–13:00; look for "i" on platform, tel. 0187-718-997).

Buy your L2,300 ticket and take the half-hour train ride into the Cinque Terre town of your choice. Once in the villages, you'll get around cheapest by train but more conveniently and scenically by boat.

Cinque Terre Train Schedule: Since the train is the Cinque Terre lifeline, many shops and restaurants post the current schedule (train info tel. 0187-817-458). Pick up a photocopied schedule—it'll come in handy.

Trains leave La Spezia for the Cinque Terre villages (last year's schedule) at 7:17, 8:10, 10:00, 11:23, 12:40, 13:20, 14:16, 15:00, 16:32, 17:19, 18:16, 19:16, 21:09, and 23:05.

Trains leave Monterosso al Mare for La Spezia (departing Vernazza about 10 minutes later, last year's schedule) at 6:30, 7:06, 8:07, 9:04, 10:16, 11:00, 12:13, 13:05, 13:43, 14:08, 15:12, 16:15, 17:23, 18:24, 19:14, 20:07, and 23:31.

Do not rely on these train times. Check the current posted schedule and then count on half the trains being 15 minutes or so late (unless you're late, in which case they are right on time).

To orient yourself, remember that directions are "*per* [to] Genoa" or "*per* La Spezia," and any train that stops at any of the villages other than Monterosso will stop at all five. (Note that many trains leaving La Spezia skip them all or stop only in Monterosso.) The five towns are just minutes apart by train. Know your stop. After leaving the town before your destination, go to the door to slip out before mobs pack in. Since the stations are small and the trains are long, you might need to get off the train deep in a tunnel, and you might need to open the door yourself.

New for 2001, the train stations should be staffed at all five Cinque Terre towns. They sell train tickets, the national park entry pass (L5,000), and the combination pass, which covers the park fee and train travel on the Cinque Terre (L10,000/1 day, L20,000/3 days, and L30,000/week).

It's cheaper to buy individual tickets to travel between the towns. Since a one-town hop costs the same as a five-town hop (L1,900) and every ticket is good for six hours with stopovers, save money and explore the region in one direction on one ticket. Stamp the ticket at the station machine before you board.

The combination pass, which includes the national park entry fee, isn't a great value. Since the trains are so inexpensive, you'll save money if you pay for the national park entry (L5,000) and your train travel separately. Don't spend one of your valuable rail-pass flexi-days on the cheap Cinque Terre.

**By Boat:** From Easter to late October (through Nov if weather is good), a daily boat service connects Monterosso, Vernazza, Manarola, Riomaggiore, and Portovenere. This provides a scenic way to get from town to town and survey what you just hiked. It's also the only efficient way to visit the nearby resort of Portovenere (the alternative is a tedious train/bus connection via La Spezia). In good weather, the boats are more reliable than the trains. Boats go about hourly, from 10:00 until 18:00 (about L5,000 per single hop or L20,000 for an all-day pass to the Cinque Terre towns, L30,000 to add Portovenere, buy tickets at little stands at each town's harbor, tel. 0187-777-727). A more frequent boat service connects Monterosso and Vernazza (tel. 0187-817-452). Schedules are posted at docks, harbor bars, and hotels. If you're in a jam, Gianni in Monterosso runs a taxi boat service (cellular 033-9761-0022).

**By Foot:** A scenic trail runs along the coast, connecting each of the five Cinque Terre towns (see "Hiking," below).

# VERNAZZA

With the closest thing to a natural harbor—overseen by a ruined castle and an old church—and only the occasional noisy slurping up of the train by the mountain to remind you of the modern world, Vernazza is my Cinque Terre home.

The action is at the harbor, where you'll find a kids' beach, plenty of sunning rocks, outdoor restaurants, a bar hanging on the edge of the castle (great for evening drinks), and a tailgate-party street market every Tuesday morning. In the summer, the beach becomes a soccer field where teams fielded by local bars and restaurants provide late night entertainment. In the dark, locals fish off the promonotory, using glowing bobs that shine in the waves.

The town's 500 residents, proud of their Vernazzan heritage, brag that "Vernazza is locally owned. Portofino has sold out."

## Vernazza

NARROW ROAD!
(TO AUTOSTRADA)

P  BANK · POST · BAR
SORRISO'S ANNEX

TO
CEMETERY
TEL.    PENSION
SORRISO        LA TORRE REST.
TRAIL TO
CORNIGLIA

TUNNEL    TRAIN    TUNNEL
STN.
TO/PER
MONTEROSSO
& GENOVA                              TO / PER
LA SPEZIA + PISA

BLUE MARLIN
BAR + LAUNDRY
BAKERY                    "MAIN STRADA"
(A.K.A. VIA ROMA)

TRAIL TO                  PIZZA         BARS, RESTAURANTS,
MONTEROSSO      ALBERGO          FARMACIA   GROC. STORES + TEL
BARBARA    GROC.   TRAT.
+ PIVA

SUNNING     CHURCH     PIAZZA          GELATI
+ SWIMMING              MARCONI   TRAT.            FRANZI
GIANNI           ROOMS
KIDS BEACH

HARBOR                        CASTLE

TO
MONTEROSSO                         BAR/       CASTELLO
BREAKWATER    SHOWERS    REST.      RESTAURANT
(GREAT VIEW!)

L I G U R I A N              SUNNING
+ SWIMMING         STATI
S E A         DOCK              UNITI

✳ **NOTE:** MAP NOT TO
SCALE- TRAIN STN. TO BREAK-
WATER IS A 5 MINUTE WALK.
☰ = STEPPED                      (BUT DON'T RUSH IT!)
ALLEYS        DCH

Fearing the change it would bring, keep-Vernazza-small proponents stopped the construction of a major road into the town and region. Families are tight and go back centuries; several generations stay together. Leisure time is devoted to the *passeggiata*—strolling lazily together up and down the main street. Sit on a bench and study the passersby. Then explore the characteristic alleys called *carugi*. In October the cantinas are draped with drying grapes. In the winter the population shrinks, as many people move to more comfortable big-city apartments.

A steep five-minute hike in either direction from Vernazza gives you a classic village photo op (for the best light, head toward Corniglia in the morning, toward Monterosso in the evening). Franco's Bar, with a panoramic terrace, is at the tower on the trail toward Corniglia.

Vernazza has ATMs and two banks (center and top of town). The Blue Marlin bar (run by Franco and Massimo) offers Internet access and a self-service laundry (L9,000 wash, L9,000 dry, super-easy machines with automatic detergent and English instructions, buy tokens at adjacent bar daily except Thu, laundry open daily 8:00–22:00, Via Roma 49, 30 meters below train station).

At least at this moment, the Vernazza train station is staffed (daily 7:00–20:00), stores luggage, and can help you find a room when you arrive (tel. 0187-812-533, NSE). Accommodations are listed at the end of this chapter.

Vernazza honors its patron saint, St. Margaret, on July 20 with a religious festival.

## Sights—Vernazza

▲▲**Vernazza Top-Down Orientation Walk**—Walk uphill until you hit the parking lot—with a bank, a post office, and a barrier that keeps all but service vehicles out. The tidy new square is called Fontana Vecchia, after a long-gone fountain. Older locals remember the river filled with townswomen doing their washing. Begin your saunter downhill to the harbor.

Just before the "Pension Sorriso" sign you'll see the ambu-lance barn (big brown wood doors) on your right. A group of volunteers is always on call for a dash to the hospital, 30 minutes away in La Spezia. Opposite that is a big empty lot next to Pension Sorriso. Like many landowners, Sr. Sorriso had plans to expand, but the government said no. The old character of these towns is carefully protected.

Across from Pension Sorriso is the honorary clubhouse for the ANPI (members of the local WWII resistance). Only five ANPI old-timers survive. Cynics consider them less than heroes. After 1943 Hitler called up Italian boys over 15. Rather than die on the front for Hitler, they escaped to the hills. Only to remain free did they become "resistance fighters."

A few steps farther you'll see a monument (marble plaque in wall to your left) to those killed in World War II. Not a family was spared. Study this: Soldiers *"morti in combattimento"* fought for Mussolini, some were deported to Germania, and "partisans" were killed later fighting against Mussolini.

The tiny monorail *trenino* (as you're facing plaque, look up on the wall on your right) is parked quietly here except in September and October, when it's busy helping locals bring down the grapes. The path to Corniglia leaves from here (it runs above plaque, starting at your left). Behind you is a tiny square playground, dec-orated with three millstones, which no longer grind local olives into oil. From here, Vernazza's tiny river goes underground.

In the tunnel under the railway tracks, you'll see a door marked "Croce Verde" (Green Cross). Posted on the other side of the tunnel is the "P.A. Croce Verde Vernazza," the list of volunteers ready for ambulance duty each day of the month.

The train tracks are above you. The second set of tracks (nearer harbor) was recently renovated to lessen the disruptive noise; locals say it made no difference.

Follow the road downhill. Until the 1950s, Vernazza's river ran open through the center of town from here to the *gelateria*.

Wandering through this main business center you'll pass many locals doing their *vasca* (laps) past the entrepreneurial Blue Marlin bar (about the only nightspot in town) and the tiny Chapel of Santa Marta (the small stone building with iron grillwork over the window, across from Bar Il Baretto), where Mass is celebrated only on special Sundays. Next you'll see a grocery, *gelateria*, bakery, pharmacy, another grocery, and another *gelateria*.

On the left, in front of the second *gelateria*, an arch leads to what was a beach and where the river used to flow out of town. Continue on down to the harbor square and breakwater. Vernazza, with the only natural harbor of the Cinque Terre, was established as the only place boats could pick up the fine local wine. (It's named for a kind of wine.) Peek into the tiny street behind the Vulnetia restaurant with the commotion of arches. Vernazza's most characteristic side streets, called *carugi*, lead up from here. The trail (above the church toward Monterosso) leads to the classic view of Vernazza (best photos just before sunset).

▲▲▲**The Burned-Out Sightseer's Visual Tour of Vernazza**—Sit at the end of the harbor breakwater (perhaps with a glass of local white wine or something more interesting from Bar Capitano—borrow the glass, they don't mind), face the town, and see . . .

**The harbor:** In a moderate storm you'd be soaked, as waves routinely crash over the *molo* (breakwater, built in 1972). The train line (to your left), constructed 130 years ago to tie a newly united Italy together, linked Turin and Genoa with Rome. A second line (hidden in a tunnel at this point) was built in the 1960s. The yellow building was Vernazza's first train station. You can see the four bricked-up alcoves where people once waited for trains. Vernazza's fishing fleet is down to three small fishing boats (with the net spools); the town's restaurants buy up everything they catch. Vernazzans are more likely to own a boat than a car. In the '70s tiny Vernazza had one of the top water polo teams in Italy, and the harbor was their "pool." Later, when a real pool was required, Vernazza dropped out of the league.

**The castle:** On the far right, the castle, which is now a grassy park with great views, still guards the town (L2,000, daily 10:00–19:30, from harbor, take stairs by Trattoria Gianni and follow signs to Castello restaurant, tower is a few steps beyond, see the photo and painting gallery rooms). It's called *Belforte*, or "loud screams," for the warnings it made back in pirating days. The lowest deck is great for a glass of wine (follow the rope to the

Belforte Bar, open until 24:00, closed Tue; inside the submarine-strength door, a photo of a major storm shows the entire tower under a wave). The highest umbrellas mark the recommended Castello restaurant (see "Eating," below).

**The town:** Vernazza has two halves. *"Sciuiu,"* on the left (literally "flowery"), is the sunny side, and *"luvegu,"* on the right (literally "dank"), is the shady side. The houses below the castle were connected by an interior arcade—ideal for fleeing attacks. The pastel colors are regulated by a commissioner of good taste in the community government. The square before you is locally famous for some of the region's finest restaurants. The big red central house, the 12th-century site where Genoan warships were built, used to be a kind of guardhouse.

**Above the town:** The small tower above the "guardhouse," another part of the city fortifications, reminds us of Vernazza's importance in the Middle Ages, when it was an important ally of Genoa (whose arch enemies were the other maritime republics of Pisa, Amalfi, and Venice). Franco's Bar, just behind the tower, welcomes hikers finishing, starting, or simply contemplating the Corniglia–Vernazza hike with great town views. Vineyards fill the mountainside beyond the town. Notice the many terraces. Someone calculated that the vineyard terraces of the Cinque Terre have the same amount of stonework as the Great Wall of China. Wine production is down nowadays, as the younger residents choose less physical work. But locals still work their plots and proudly serve their family wine. A single steel train line winds up the gully behind the tower. This is for the vintner's *trenino*, the tiny service train.

**The church, school, and city hall:** Vernazza's Ligurian Gothic church, built with black stones quarried from Punta Mesco (the distant point behind you), dates from 1318. The gray-and-red house above and to the left of the spire is the local elementary school (which about 25 children attend). High school is in the "big city," La Spezia. The red building to the right of (and below) the schoolhouse is the former monastery and present city hall. Vernazza and Corniglia function as one community. Through most of the 1990s, the local government was Communist. In 1999 they elected a coalition of many parties working to rise above ideologies and simply make Vernazza a better place. Finally, on the top of the hill, with the best view of all, is the town cemetery, where most locals plan to end up.

## Cinque Terre Hiking and Swimming
▲▲▲**Hiking**—All five towns are connected by good trails. Experience the area's best by hiking from one end to the other. The entire 11-kilometer hike can be done in about four hours, but allow five for dawdling. While you can detour to dramatic hill-top sanctuaries (one trail leads from Vernazza's cemetery uphill),

I'd keep it simple by following the easy red-and-white-marked low trails between the villages. A good L7,000 hiking map (sold everywhere, not necessary for this described walk) covers the expanded version of this hike, from Porto Venere through all five Cinque Terre towns to Levanto, and more serious hikes in the high country.

Since I still get the names of the Cinque Terre towns mixed up, I think of the towns by number: Riomaggiore (town #1), Manarola (#2), Corniglia (#3), Vernazza (#4), and resorty Monterosso (#5).

**Riomaggiore–Manarola (20 min):** Facing the front of the train station in Riomaggiore (town #1), go up the stairs to the right, following signs for the Via dell' Amore. The film-gobbling promenade—wide enough for baby strollers—leads down the coast to Manarola. While there's no beach here, stairs lead down to sunbathing rocks.

**Manarola–Corniglia (45 min):** The walk from the Manarola (#2) to Corniglia (#3) is a little longer and a little more rugged than that from #1 to #2.

Ask locally about the more difficult six-mile inland hike to Volastra. This tiny village, perched between Manarola and Corniglia, offers great views and the Five-Terre wine co-op; stop by the Cantina Sociale. If you take this high road between Manarola and Corniglia, allow two hours; in return, you'll get sweeping views and a closer look at the vineyards.

**Corniglia–Vernazza (90 min):** The hike from Corniglia (#3) to Vernazza (#4)—the wildest and greenest of the coast—is most rewarding. From the Corniglia station and beach, zigzag up to the town. Ten minutes past Corniglia toward Vernazza you'll see the well-hung Guvano beach far below (see below). The trail leads past a bar and picnic tables, through lots of fragrant and flowery vegetation, and scenically into Vernazza.

**Vernazza–Monterosso (90 min):** The trail from Vernazza (#4) to Monterosso (#5) is a scenic up-and-down-a-lot trek. Trails are rough (and some readers report "very dangerous") but easy to follow. Camping at the picnic tables midway is frowned upon. The views just out of Vernazza are spectacular.

▲**Swimming**—Wear your walking shoes and pack your swim gear. Each beach has showers (no shampoo, please) that may work better than your hotel's. Underwater sightseeing is full of fish; goggles are sold in local shops. Here's a beach review:

**Riomaggiore**: The beach is rocky but clean and peaceful and has a diving center (follow the roped path from the harbor 100 meters to the left; shower at beach).

**Manarola**: Manarola has no sand but the best deepwater swimming of all. The first "beach" with a shower, ladder, and wonderful rocks (with daredevil high divers) is my favorite.

The second (follow paved path around the point) has tougher access and no shower but feels more remote and pristine.

**Corniglia**: This hilltop town has a rocky man-made beach below its station. It's clean and uncrowded, and the beach bar has showers, drinks, and snacks.

The nude Guvano (GOO-vah-noh) beach (between Corniglia and Vernazza) made headlines in Italy in the 1970s as clothed locals in a makeshift armada of dinghies and fishing boats retook their town beach. But big-city nudists still work on all-around tans in this remote setting. From the Corniglia train station (follow the road north, go over the tracks, then zigzag below the tracks, follow signs to the tunnel in the cliff), travelers buzz the intercom, and the hydraulic *Get Smart*–type door is opened from the other end. After a 15-minute hike through a cool, moist, and dimly lit unused old train tunnel, you'll emerge at the Guvano beach—and be charged L5,000 (L4,000 with this guidebook). The beach has drinking water, but no WC. A steep (free) trail leads from the beach up to the Corniglia–Vernazza trail. The crowd is Italian counterculture: pierced nipples, tattooed punks, hippie drummers in dreads, and nude exhibitionist men. The ratio of men to women is about three to two. About half the people on the pebbly beach keep their swimsuits on.

**Vernazza**: The village has a sandy children's cove, sunning rocks, and showers by the breakwater. There's a ladder on the breakwater for deepwater access. The tiny *acque pendente* (waterfall) cove which locals call their *laguna blu*, between Vernazza and Monterosso, is accessible only by small hired boat.

**Monterosso**: The town's beaches, immediately in front of the train station, are easily the Cinque Terre's best and most crowded. It's a sandy resort with everything rentable...lounge chairs, umbrellas, paddleboats, and usually even beach access. Beaches are free only where you see no umbrellas.

## Cinque Terre Towns

(Note: Readers of this book fill Vernazza. For this reason you might prefer to stay in one of these towns with fewer Americans. See "Sleeping," below, for accommodations for each town.)

▲▲**Riomaggiore (town #1)**—The most substantial nonresort town of the group, Riomaggiore is a disappointment from the train station. But walk through the tunnel next to the train tracks (or ride the elevator through the hillside to the top of town) and you land in a fascinating tangle of pastel homes leaning on each other as if someone stole their crutches. There's homemade gelato at the Bar Central on main street, and, if Ivo is there, you'll feel right at home. When Ivo closes, the gang goes down to the harborside with a guitar.

Riomaggiore's TI is inside the train station (Mon–Sat

# Riomaggiore and Manarola

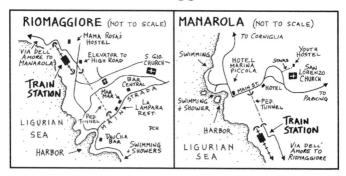

14:30–17:30, sometimes also mornings, tel. 0187-920-633). A little orange electric bus shuttles locals and tourists up and down Riomaggiore's steep main street (free with park pass, 2/hrly, just flag it down); a larger blue bus helps out in the morning.

If you arrive in Riomaggiore by train (rather than boat), here's an easy loop trip through town that maximizes views and minimizes walking uphill. From the station, take the elevator up to the top of town (free, entrance just before railway tunnel). At the top, follow the walkway—with spectacular sea views—around the cliff. Ignore the steps marked "Marina Sea Coast" (harbor). Instead, continue on the path; it's a five-minute, fairly level walk to the church. Continue past the church and then take either the stairs or the road down to Via Columbo, Riomaggiore's main street. Stroll down Via Columbo past the colorful, small shops. (The flower boxes blocking the road can be electrically pulled back on a track to let the little electric bus get past.) When Via Columbo dead-ends, on your left you'll find the stairs down to the harbor, boat dock, and a short 100-meter trail to the beach (*spiaggia*). To your right is the tunnel, running alongside the tracks, that takes you directly to the station. Either take a train or hop a boat (from the harbor) to your next destination.

For hikes from Riomaggiore, consider the cliff-hanging trail that leads from the beach to a hilltop botanical garden and old WWII bunkers. Another climbs scenically to the Madonna di Montenero sanctuary high above the town. Riomaggiore also has a diving center (scuba, snorkeling, boats, Via San Giacomo, tel. 0187-920-011).

Riomaggiore honors its patron saint, John the Baptist, on June 24 with a procession.

▲**Manarola (town #2)**—Like town #1, #2 is attached to its station by a 200-meter-long tunnel. Manarola is tiny and picturesque, a tumble of buildings bunny-hopping down its ravine

## Corniglia and Monterosso

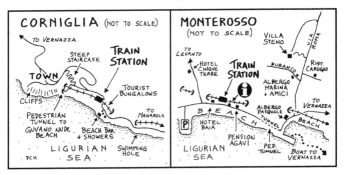

to the fun-loving harbor. Notice how the I-beam crane launches the boats. As you face the harbor, a hillside is to your right, dotted with a bar in the middle. It's Punta Bonfiglio, an entertaining park/game area/bar with the best view playground on the coast. The gate at the top of the hillside is the entrance to the cemetery. From here you can get poster-perfect views of Manarola (2-minute walk from the harbor on path to Corniglia).

Within Manarola, a little electric bus shuttles people between main street and the parking lot (free with park pass, 2/hrly, just flag it down). In the middle of town, across from the railway tunnel, you'll see Bar Aristide, which shows outdoor movies in August by hanging a screen over part of the tunnel entrance. At the top of the town you'll find great views, the church, and a cluster of accommodations, including a super hostel (see "Sleeping," below).

On August 10, Manarola holds a religious festival for its patron saint, St. Lawrence.

▲▲**Corniglia (town #3)**—From the station a footpath zigzags up 370 stairs to the only town of the five not on the water (electric bus planned for 2001, free with park pass). Originally settled by a Roman farmer who named it for his mother, Cornelia (which is how Corniglia is pronounced), its ancient residents produced a wine so famous that vases found at Pompeii touted its virtues. Today its wine is still its lifeblood. Follow the pungent smell of ripe grapes into an alley cellar and get a local to let you dip a straw into her keg. Remote and less visited, Corniglia has fewer tourists, cooler temperatures, a windy belvedere (on its promontory), a few restaurants, and plenty of private rooms for rent. Continue past the train station (toward Manarola) to find Corniglia's beach.

The festival of St. Peter and St. Paul, patron saints of Corniglia, is on June 29.

▲▲▲**Vernazza (town #4)**—See beginning of chapter.

▲▲**Monterosso al Mare (town #5)**—This is a resort with cars, hotels, rentable beach umbrellas, and crowds. The town is split into the old and new, connected by a tunnel. The train station is in the new town, along with the TI (daily Mon–Sat 9:30–12:30, 15:30–17:30, closed Mon and Nov–Easter, exit station and go left a few doors, tel. 0187-817-506), several recommended accommodations, and a statue—*Il Gigante*. This 14-meter-tall statue, which once held a shell and trident, looks as if it were hewn from the rocky cliff, but it's made of reinforced concrete, and dates from the beginning of the 20th century.

The old town contains Old World charm, small crooked streets, and nearly hourly boats to Vernazza and points beyond. From the breakwater (and the new town), you can see all the towns of the Cinque Terre (though just a "corner" of Riomaggiore).

You can easily take the short tunnel between the new and old towns, but hikers will prefer the trail. It's like a mini–Cinque Terre trail, combining scenery and greenery, a world away from the resort town below. Heading from the station to the old town, take the path to the right of the tunnel entrance. The path leads to views of a German WWII bunker below on the rocks (worth seeing, but not worth climbing down to). Continuing on the path gets you into the old town. Or, at the point where you see the bunker, take the path up to the top of the hill (where you'll see a statue of St. Francis), and up farther still through the woods to reach a gate leading to a church with a Van Dyck painting of the Crucifixion (accommodations next to church, see "Sleeping," below). Then take the trail down into the old town. (Reversing this, if you're going from the old town to the new town, take the trail to the right of the tunnel entrance). Allow a total of a half hour if you include the church and gawking at the views.

Monterosso celebrates a number of festivals: Lemon Festival (May 26), Corpus Domini (June 17, a procession passes on carpet of flowers), Festival of St. John the Baptist (June 24), Ascension of Mary (Aug 15, a holiday throughout Italy), Maria Nascente ("Rising Mary," Sept 8, fair with handicrafts), and the intriguing Walnut Festival (near end of Sept, ancient games played with walnuts).

## Cinque Terre Cuisine 101

A few menu tips: *Accuighe* (pron. ah-CHOO-gay) are anchovies, a local specialty—always served the day they're caught. If you've always hated anchovies (the harsh, cured-in-salt American kind), try them fresh here. *Tegame alla Vernazza* is the most typical main course: anchovies, potatoes, tomatoes, white wine, oil, and herbs. *Pansotti* is ravioli with ricotta and spinach, often served with a hazelnut sauce...delightful. While antipasto is cheese and salami in Tuscany, here you'll get *antipasti di mare*, a big plate of mixed fruits of the sea and a fine way to start a meal. For many, splitting this and a pasta dish is plenty. Try the fun local dessert: "grandmother's cake" with a glass of *sciacchetrà* for dunking (see "Wine," below).

▲▲**Pesto**—This is the birthplace of pesto. Basil, which loves the temperate Ligurian climate, is mixed with cheese (half *Parmigiano* cow cheese and half pecorino sheep cheese), garlic, olive oil, and pine nuts and then poured over pasta. Try it on spaghetti, *trenette*, or *trofie* (made of flour with a bit of potato, designed specifically for pesto). Many also like pesto lasagna. If you become addicted, small jars of pesto are sold in the local grocery stores.

▲▲**Wine**—The *vino delle Cinque Terre*, famous throughout Italy, flows cheap and easy throughout the region. It is white—great with the local seafood. D.O.C. is the mark of top quality. For a sweet, sherrylike wine, the local *sciacchetrà* wine is worth the splurge (L5,000 per glass, often served with a cookie). While 10 kilos of grapes yield seven liters of local wine, *sciacchetrà* is made from near-raisins, and 10 kilos of grapes make only 1.5 liters of *sciacchetrà*. The word means "push and pull"...push in lots of grapes, pull out the best wine. If your room is up a lot of steps, be warned: *sciacchetrà* is 18 percent alcohol, while regular wine is only 11 percent. In the cool, calm evening, sit on the Vernazza breakwater with a glass of wine and watch the phosphorescence in the waves. While red wine is sold as Cinque Terre wine, it's a fantasy designed to please the tourists.

## Sleeping and Eating on the Cinque Terre
**(L2,000 = about $1, country code: 39)**
Sleep Code: **S** = Single, **D** = Double/Twin, **T** = Triple, **Q** = Quad, **b** = bathroom, **t** = toilet only, **s** = shower only, **CC** = Credit Card (**V**isa, **M**asterCard, **A**mex), **SE** = Speaks English, **NSE** = No English. Breakfast is included only in real hotels.

If you're trying to avoid my readers, stay away from Vernazza. Rich, sun-worshiping softies (who prefer firm reservations for hotels with private bathrooms) like Monterosso. Wine lovers and mountain goats prefer Corniglia. Budget travelers sleep cheap in Riomaggiore. Sophisticated Italians and Germans choose Manarola.

While the Cinque Terre is too rugged for the mobs that ravage the Spanish and French coasts, it's popular with Italians, Germans, and Americans in the know. Hotels charge the most and are packed on Easter, in August, and on summer Fridays and Saturdays. August weekends are worst. But L50,000 beds in private rooms abound throughout the year. Outside of August weekends, you can land a comfortable L100,000 double in a private home on any day by just arriving in town (ideally by noon) and asking around at bars and restaurants or simply approaching locals on the street. This seems scary, but it's true.

For the best value, visit three private rooms and snare the best. Going direct cuts out a middleman and softens prices.

Plan on paying cash. Private rooms are generally bigger and more comfortable than those offered by the pensions.

If you want the security of a reservation, make it long in advance for a hotel (small places generally don't take reservations made weeks ahead). If you don't get a reply to your faxed request for a room, assume the place is fully booked.

### Sleeping in Vernazza
### (zip code: 19018)

Vernazza, the essence of the Cinque Terre, is my favorite. There are three pensions and piles of private rooms for rent. Anywhere you stay here will require some climbing. Night noises can be a problem if you're near the station or the church bell tower. Address letters to 19018 Vernazza, Cinque Terre, La Spezia.

**Albergo Barbara**, on the harbor square, is run by kindly Giuseppe and his Swiss wife, Patricia. Their nine, clean, modern rooms share three public showers and WCs (S-L70,000–90,000 depending on season, D without view-L80,000, D with small view-L85,000, D with big view-L100,000, bunky family Q-L130,000, 2-night stay preferred, loads of stairs, fans, closed Dec–Jan, Piazza Marconi 30, call to reserve instead of fax, tel. & fax 0187-812-398, cellular 032-8221-9688, SE). The big doubles on the main floor come with grand harbor views and are the best value (top-floor doubles have small windows and small views). The office is on the top floor of the big, red, vacant-looking building facing the harbor.

**Trattoria Gianni** rents 23 small rooms just under the castle. The funky ones are artfully decorated à la shipwreck and are up lots of tight, winding, spiral stairs, and most have tiny balconies and grand views. The new, comfy rooms lack views but have modern bathrooms and a superscenic, cliff-hanger private garden. Marisa (who doles out smiles like a rich gambler on a losing streak) requires a two-night minimum and check-in before 16:00 (S-L65,000, D-L90,000, sinks and bathrooms down the hall; Db-L120,000, Tb-L150,000, CC:VMA but 10 percent discount for cash, Piazza Marconi 5, closed Jan–Feb, tel. & fax 0187-812-228, tel. 0187-821-003). Pick up your keys at Trattoria Gianni's restaurant/reception on the harbor square and hike up the stairs to #41 (funky, *con vista mare*) or #47 (new, *nuovo*) at the top. As a matter of principle, no English is spoken here. (Note: My tour company books this place 50 nights of the season.) Telephone three days in advance and leave your first name and time of arrival.

**Pension Sorriso** knows it's the only real pension in town. Don't expect an exuberant welcome. Prices include breakfast and an obligatory dinner (D-L180,000, Db-L200,000, cash only, 50 meters up from station, minimal views, closed Nov–Feb, tel. 0187-812-224, fax 0187-821-198, some English spoken). While train sounds rumble through the front rooms of the main building, the annex up the street is quieter.

**Affitta Camere** are the best values in Vernazza. The town is honeycombed year-round with pleasant, rentable private rooms and apartments with kitchens (cheap for families). They are reluctant to reserve rooms far in advance. It's easiest to call a day or two in advance or simply show up by morning and look around. All are comfortable and inexpensive (L30,000–50,000 per person, depending on the view and plumbing). Some are lavish with killer views, and cost the same as a small dark place on a back lane over the train tracks. Little or no English is spoken at these places. Any main-street business has a line on rooms for rent.

**Filippo Camere** has eight sharp, new rooms run by dreadlocked Filippo and his mother, Rita (Db-L100,000, 2 rooms have views, Via A. Del Santo 62—take stairs across street from phone booths by railroad tracks, tel. 0187-812-244).

**Tonino Basso** rents four pleasant rooms near the post office at the top of town—with bath, without views (Db-L120,000, tel. 0187-821-264, tel. & fax 0187-821-260, cellular 0335-269-436, when you arrive, call cellular number from train station—phones at bottom of stairs—and Tonino will meet you; or the Gambero Rosso restaurant at harbor can find him—but then you'll have to backtrack to get to rooms).

**Mike and Franca Castiglione**, who speak New Yorkish, rent a room with a small private garden with a grand sea view (Via Carratino 16, turn left at pharmacy, climb Via Carattino to #16, tel. 0187-812-374). Farther up the same street, consider **Affitta Camere da Anna-Maria** (D-L80,000, Db-L100,000 with view or terrace, Via Carattino 64, tel. 0187-821-082).

The woman at the grocery store near the harbor can check if **Giuseppina's Villa** is available—a modern, deluxe apartment without a view (Db-L80,000, Qb-L140,000, Via S. Giovanni Battista 7, tel. 0187-812-026).

**Martina Callo** rents three fine rooms overlooking the square up miles of steps near the church tower (Db-L110,000, room #1-Db with harbor view, room #2-Qb is huge family room with no view, room #3-Db with great view terrace, prices drop to L90,000 Nov–March, heating in winter, ring bell at Piazza Marconi 26, tel. & fax 0187-812-365, e-mail: roomartina@supereva.it).

**Franca Maria Dimartino** rents two comfortable rooms overlooking the harbor square (Db-L90,000–130,000, Qb-L160,000–200,000 depending on season, only a few steps up from harbor, Piazza Marconi 30, tel. 0187-812-002).

**Pizzeria Vulnetia** on the harbor rents two rooms, one with a view (Db-L120,000, Qb with terrace and view-L240,000, no reservations taken, just show up at restaurant—opens for lunch at

12:30 but doors open much earlier, closed Mon, Piazza Marconi 29, tel. 0187-821-193).

**Working Holiday:** Consider the work camp offered by Protect the Landscape of Vernazza (run by the city of Vernazza and the Italian Environmental Impact Assessment Center in Milan). You pay about L750,000 and do three days of work (such as repairing walls and trails and picking grapes depending on the season). In return, you get room and board in Vernazza plus guided tours in English (tel. 02-7601-5672, fax 02-782485, www.protectvernazza.org).

## Eating in Vernazza

If you're into Italian cuisine, Vernazza's restaurants are worth the splurge. All take pride in their cooking and have similar prices. At about 20:00 wander around and compare the ambience.

The **Castello**, run by gracious and English-speaking Monica, her husband Massimo, kind Mario, and the rest of her family, serves great food with great views just under the castle (Thu–Tue 12:00–15:00 for lunch, 15:00–19:00 for drinks and snacks, 19:00–22:00 for dinner, closed Wed and Nov–April, tel. 0187-812-296).

Four fine places fill the harborfront with happy eaters: **Gambero Rosso**, considered Vernazza's best restaurant, feels classy and costs only a few thousand lire more than the others (Tue–Sun 12:00–15:00, 19:00–22:00, closed Mon and Nov–March, Piazza Marconi 7, tel. 0187-812-265). **Trattoria del Capitano** might serve the best food for the lire (Thu–Tue 12:00–15:00, 19:00–22:30, closed Wed except in Aug, closed Dec–Jan, Paolo speaks English). **Trattoria Gianni** is also good, especially for seafood (daily 12:30–15:00, 18:30–22:00 in July–Aug, otherwise closed Wed). **Pizzeria Vulnetia** serves the best harborside pizza (Tue–Sun 12:30–15:00, 19:00–23:00, closed Mon, Piazza Marconi 29).

**Trattoria da Sandro** mixes Genovese and Ligurian cuisine with friendly service but no view (Wed–Mon 12:00–15:00, 19:00–22:00, closed Tue, CC:VM, just below train station, Via Roma 60, tel. 0187-812-223). The more offbeat and intimate **Trattoria da Piva** may come with late-night guitar strumming (Tue–Sun 12:00–15:30, 19:00–01:00, closed Mon, Via Carattino 6, around corner from pharmacy).

For great food, a grand view, and perfect peace, hike to Franco's **Ristorante "La Torre"** for a dinner at sunset (Wed–Mon 20:00–21:30, closed Tue, on trail toward Corniglia, tel. 0187-821-082).

The main street is creatively finding tourist needs and filling them. The **Blue Marlin** bar offers a good selection of sandwiches, salads, and *bruschetta*. Try the bakery and bars for good focaccia and pizza by the slice. Grocery stores make inexpensive sandwiches to order (Mon–Sat 7:30–13:00, 17:00–19:30, Sun 7:30–13:00).

The town's two *gelaterias* are good. Most harborside bars will let you take your glass on a breakwater stroll.

**Breakfast:** Locals take breakfast about as seriously as flossing. A cappuccino and a pastry or a piece of focaccia does it. The two harborfront bars offer the most ambience; the Ananas Bar often decorates the foam on a cup of cappuccino with an artistic design (can either sit down at their indoor or outdoor tables, or, even cheaper, get your cappuccino to go, sit on a harborfront picnic bench, then return the cup). The bakery is open early and makes ham and cheese on toast. Many tourists start their day at the Blue Marlin. Consider their L12,000 special breakfast: ham and cheese focaccia, tiny slices of three local pastries, juice, and cappuccino (Fri–Wed 7:00–24:00, closed Thu, just below station, tel. 0187-821-149).

## Sleeping and Eating in Riomaggiore
### (zip code: 19017)

Riomaggiore has organized its private room scene better than its neighbors. Several agencies within a few meters of each other on the main drag (with regular office hours, English-speaking staff, and e-mail addresses) manage a corral of local rooms for rent. Expect lots of stairs.

**Edi's Rooms** is open daily from 8:00 to 20:00 and has a line on 10 fine rooms and 20 apartments (Db-L80,000, Qb-L160,000, CC:V, some with views—especially the apartments, Via Colombo 111, tel. & fax 0187-920-325, tel. 0187-760-842, e-mail: edi-vesigna@iol.it).

**Mar Mar Rooms**, run by Mario Franceschetti, has pleasant rooms and a mini-hostel (L40,000 dorm beds, Db-L90,000–100,000, bunky family deals, can request kitchen and balcony, CC:VMA, Internet access and small self-service laundry in office, 30 meters above train tracks on the main drag next to Lampara restaurant, Via Malborghetto 8, tel. & fax 0187-920-932, e-mail: marmar5t@tin.it). Mar Mar also rents kayaks (double kayaks L15,000/hr, cheaper by the half day).

**Michielini Anna** rents four clean, decent apartments with kitchens and no views (L50,000 per person June–Sept, otherwise L40,000 per person, CC to reserve but please pay cash, cheaper for longer stays, 2 nights preferred June–Sept, across from Bar Central at Colombo 143, tel. 0187-920-950 for friendly Daniela who speaks good English, tel. & fax 0187-920-411 for solo-Italiano-speaking mother, e-mail: anna.michielini@tin.it, another e-mail: michielinis@yahoo.it).

**Luciano and Roberto Fazioli** have five apartments, nine rooms, and a basic 11-bed mini-hostel (L30,000–40,000 for dorm bed, D-L70,000, Db-L120,000, apartments-L50,000–100,000 per person, prices increase with view and demand, Via Colombo 94, tel. 0187-920-904 or 0187-920-822).

At **Bar Central**, friendly Ivo and Alberto can help you find a room (Via Colombo 144, tel. 0187-920-208, e-mail: barcentr@tin.it). Ivo lived in San Francisco, fills his bar with only the best San Francisco rock, and speaks great English. His Bar Central, a good stop for breakfast, cheeseburgers, and Internet access, is a shady place to relax with other travelers. It's the only lively late-night place in town. And there's prizewinning gelato next door.

**Hotel**: If you want a real hotel, consider **Villa Argentina**. It's near the top of town, with 15 crisply clean modern rooms, fine balconies (for 9 rooms), and sea views. The little electric bus which shuttles people (and their luggage) twice hourly between the top and bottom of town makes this hotel an option even for train travelers (Db-L200,000, breakfast extra, no CC, Via de Gasperi 37, go through tunnel from station, wait for bus, tel. 0187-920-213, fax 0187-920-213, www.emmeti.it/hvillaargentina).

**Hostel**: **Youth Hostel Mama Rosa** is a hard-to-forget slum that gives vagabonds a reason to bond. It's run by Rosa Ricci (an aggressively friendly character who snares backpackers at the train station), her husband Carmine (a.k.a. "Papa Rosa"), and their English-speaking son, Silvio. It's a jumble of bunk beds with the ambience of a YMCA locker room (L30,000–40,000 beds in 9 coed, poorly ventilated dorms, meager washroom, no curfew, 20 meters in front of station—angle left as you exit station and then enter courtyard, no sign, Via T. Signovini 673G, just show up without a reservation—the earlier the better, no telephone). This is one of those rare places where perfect strangers become good friends with the slurp of spaghetti, and wine supersedes the concept of ownership—organize and cook a co-op dinner.

**Eating**: Eat well at **Ristorante La Lampara**. Check out the *frutti di mare* pizza, the *trenete al pesto*, and my favorite 5-Terre pasta experience: the aromatic *spaghetti al cartoccio*—spaghetti with mixed seafood cooked in foil (L25,000 tourist menu, Wed–Mon 12:00–15:30, 18:00–24:00, CC:VMA, closed Tue, on Via Colombo just above tracks, tel. 0187-920-120). Groceries and delis (such as Il Bomber) on Via Columbo sell food to go including pizza slices (picnic at the harbor). While the late-night action is at Ivo's Bar Central, take a walk down to the harborside **Dau Cila** bar for jazz, nets, and mellow *limoncino* (a drink of lemon juice, sugar, and pure alcohol—a.k.a. *limoncello* elsewhere in Italy).

## Sleeping in Manarola
### (zip code: 19010)

Manarola has plenty of private rooms. Ask in bars and restaurants. Otherwise you'll find a modern three-star place halfway up the main drag, a cluster of great values around the church at the peaceful top of town a five-minute hike above the train tracks, and a salty old place on the harbor.

Up the hill, the utterly normal **Albergo ca' d'Andrean** is quiet, comfortable, modern, and very hotelesque, with 10 big, sunny rooms and a cool garden oasis complete with lemon trees (Sb-L95,000, Db-L120,000, breakfast-L9,000, closed Nov, Via A. Discovolo 101, tel. 0187-920-040, fax 0187-920-452, Simone SE).

**Affitta Camere de Baranin** rents eight airy, refreshing rooms (Db-L100,000–120,000, Internet access, includes breakfast, CC to reserve but please pay cash, climb stairway against wall beyond church square—with your back to the church, stairway is at 7:00, follow sign to Trattoria dal Billy, Via Rollandi 29, tel. & fax 0187-920-595, www.baranin.com, Sara and Silvia SE).

**La Torretta** has two compact apartments with kitchens, four doubles, and a single, all attractively designed by the young English-speaking architect/manager Gabriele Baldini (Sb-L40,000–60,000, Db-L70,000–90,000, apartment for 2 people-L90,000–120,000, extra bed-L30,000, prices vary with season, breakfast-L10,000, views, big garden, with your back to church, it's at 10:00—look left across the square toward the sea, Piazza della Chiesa, Vico Volto 14, tel. & fax 0187-920-327, check Web for deals involving their Tuscan mountain villa, www.cinqueterre.net/torretta/, e-mail: torretta@cdh.it).

**Casa Capellini** rents four rooms (D-L80,000, L70,000 for 2 or more nights, Db-L90,000, L80,000 for 2 or more nights; the *alta camera* on the top, with a kitchen, private terrace, and knock-out view-L110,000, L100,000 for 2 or more nights, 2 doors down the hill from the church, with your back to the church, it's at 2:00, Via Ettore Cozzani 12, tel. 0187-920-823 or 0187-736-765, NSE).

**Ostello 5-Terre,** Manarola's modern and well-run hostel, stands like a Monopoly hotel behind the church square. It's smart to reserve at least two weeks in advance in high season (one week in off-season). You book with your credit card number; if you cancel with less than three days' notice, you'll be charged (June–mid-Sept: beds-L30,000, Qb-L120,000, off-season: beds-L25,000, Qb-L100,000, closed mid-Jan–mid-Feb, CC:VMA, 48 beds in 4- to 6-bed rooms, office closed 13:00–17:00, rooms closed 10:00–17:00, curfew-01:00, open to anyone of any age, laundry, Internet access, elevator, breakfast and dinner, great roof terrace with showers and sunsets, Via B. Riccobaldi 21, tel. 0187-920-215, fax 0187-920-218, www.cinqueterre.net/ostello/, e-mail: ostello@cdh.it). They rent bikes, kayaks, and snorkeling gear.

**Marina Piccola** has 10 bright, modern rooms on the water, so they figure a warm welcome is unnecessary (Db-L130,000 for 1-day stays, otherwise half-pension required at L120,000 per person, CC:VMA, Via Discovolo 192, tel. 0187-920-103, fax 0187-920-966, e-mail: marijes@tin.it).

## Sleeping in Corniglia
### (zip code: 19010)

Perched high above the sea on a hilltop, this town has plenty of private rooms (generally Db-L100,000). There is a slim chance someone will be waiting for stray travelers at the station with a car to run you up to their place in the town—otherwise, prepare for a 15-minute uphill hike. From the station, you reach the town by either a long road or many stairs. At the top of the stairs, turn left to reach the town (if you've taken the road, just stay on the road). The main drag is Via Fieschi, stretching to the tip of the promontory and its viewpoint park.

For this first listing, take the road (rather than the stairs) up from the station. **Domenico Spora** has 10 rooms scattered throughout town, all with views and private bath (Db-L100,000, Qb-L200,000, Via Villa 19, tel. 0187-812-293, NSE). Her place is about three-fourths of the way up the hill from the station.

For the following listings, take the stairs leading up from the station (turn left to reach the center). These are listed in the order you'll encounter them as you walk up Via Fieschi. At the main square, you'll see **La Lanterna** bar, which rents a dozen rooms (Db-L100,000, tel. 0187-812-291). Continue up Via Fieschi. Detour right—up the stairs—on Via Solferino to find #34 for **Pelligrini** (3 rooms, tel. 0187-812-184). Return to Via Fieschi. Next comes **Villa Sandra** (Db-L90,000, Via Fieschi 212, tel. 0187-812-384), followed by...

**Louisa Christiana** rents a great apartment with three doubles and a big comfy living room/kitchen with view terrace on the tiny soccer court at the top of the town (Db-L100,000, grand apartment for 2 people-L200,000, for 4 people-L220,000, for 6 people-L250,000, Via Fieschi 215, tel. 0187-812-345 or English-speaking daughter Cristiana at Bar Matteo on Via Fieschi, below main square, tel. 0187-812-236; daughter rents small apartment for L110,000). Finally, near the town promontory, you'll see the door for **Signora Silvana** (Via Fieschi 220, tel. 0187-513-830) and next door, **Maria Guelfi** (Via Fieschi 222, tel. 0187-812-178); both offer rooms at this scenic cliff-hanging edge of town.

**Villa Cecio** is more of a hotel (on the main road 200 meters toward Vernazza, views, tel. 0187-812-043).

## Sleeping in Monterosso
### (zip code: 19016)

Monterosso al Mare, the most beach-resorty of the five Cinque Terre towns, offers maximum comfort and ease. There are plenty of hotels and rentable beach umbrellas, shops, and cars. The TI (Pro Loco) can find you a L50,000-per-person double (pricier for a single) in a private home (below the station, Mon–Sat 10:00–12:00, 15:30–17:30, Sun 10:00–12:00, tel. 0187-817-506).

Monterosso is 30 minutes off the freeway (exit: Carrodano). Parking is easy in the huge beachfront guarded lot (L12,000/day). Via Roma at the top of the old town has banks, a post office, and a self-serve laundry. Another self-serve laundry in the old town is more central (daily 9:00–12:00, 15:00–21:00, Via Mazzini 4, off Via Roma).

The following hotel listings are in the order you'll see them as you leave the station heading right (5 hotels) or left (the rest of the hotels). My favorite is Hotel Villa Steno, listed near the end.

Turn right leaving the station to the central, waterfront **Hotel Baia** (Db-L250,000, includes breakfast, CC:VMA, elevators, balconies, request view—same price, Via Fegina 88, tel. 0187-817-363, fax 0187-817-512).

Consider the newly remodeled **Hotel Punta Mesco** (Db-L150,000, Tb-L180,000, no views, exit right from station, take first right, Via Molinelli 35, tel. 0187-817-495, www.cinqueterre .it/belvedere) or the cheaper **Affitta Camere Villa Mario** (5 rooms, Db-L120,000, exit right from station, take second right, Via Padre Semeria 28, tel. & fax 0187-818-030).

**Hotel Cinque Terre**, a slick new building with 54 similar rooms, is often the last to fill (Db-L240,000–260,000, includes breakfast, skip dinner deal, closed Nov–March, CC:VM, reconfirm reservations, easy parking, exit right from station, walk along waterfront, turn right at Via IV Novembre, 300 meters off beach, Via IV Novembre 21, tel. 0187-817-543, fax 0187-818-380, Giovanna and Vittorio). Next door is . . .

**Villa Adriana**, run by brusque Austrian nuns, has 55 decent, clean rooms divided between a 19th-century villa and an adjacent, modern annex. With a strict 23:00 curfew, a lofty setting (up off the street with a tropical garden as its front yard), and a religious, institutional atmosphere, it's peaceful (Db-L180,000–200,000, includes breakfast, extra for optional half-pension, CC:VM, double and twins available, some views, attached chapel, parking, Via IV Novembre 23, reception at back of building, tel. 0187-818-109, fax 0187-818-128, SE).

Turn left out of the station to the bright, airy **Pension Agavi** (8 rooms, Db-L140,000–160,000, refrigerators, Fegina 30, tel. 0187-817-171, fax 0187-818-264, cellular 0336-258-467, spunky Hillary SE). The tunnel then leads to the old town.

**Albergo Pasquale** is the first hotel you'll see as you exit the tunnel. Run by the same family who own Hotel Villa Steno (see listing below), this is a decent place with more comfort than character. It's just a few steps from the beach. The air-conditioning (used with closed windows) minimizes train noise (Db-L210,000, Tb-L250,000, Qb-L280,000, includes breakfast, CC:VMA, L20,000 discount per room per night if you pay cash and show this book, readers get a free glass of the local sweet wine—

*sciacchetrà*—at check-in, Via Fegina 4, tel. 0187-817-550 or
0187-817-477, fax 0187-817-056, e-mail: pasquale@pasini.com,
Felicita and Marco SE).

The next two places push half-pension during peak season:
the fancy, nicer **Albergo degli Amici** (36 rooms, Db-L160,000–
170,000 with breakfast, cheaper without breakfast, Db with half-
pension-L240,000—technically not required but encouraged
July–Aug, CC:VMA, air-con, no views from rooms, peaceful
above-it-all view garden with "sun beds"—lawn chairs with
movable sun shades, Via Buranco 36, tel. 0187 817-544, fax
0187-817-424) and **Albergo Marina** (23 rooms, Db with required
half-pension-L200,000–240,000, CC:VM, elevator, some air-con,
garden with lemon trees, next door at Via Buranco 40, tel. & fax
0187-817-242 or 0187-817-613). To get to the Amici and Marina
from the old town harbor, go to the left of the arcaded building
with the bell tower; for the next listing go to the right of the
arcaded building up Via Roma.

**Ristorante al Carugio** rents 10, no-view rooms in an apartment flat at the no-character top end of town (Db-L120,000,
CC:VM, office at Via S. Pietro 15—just off Via Roma, rooms at
Via Roma 100, tel. & fax 0187-817-453). **Hotel La Colonnina**,
a comfy, modern place on a sleepy side street, usually takes only
long-term reservations but rents fine rooms to those who call a
day in advance (Db-L160,000, no breakfast, elevator, garden, Via
Zuecca 6, tel. 0187-817-439). Near the harbor playground is a
square with a statue of Garibaldi; Via Zuecca is directly behind him.

Farther on is the best place in town: the lovingly managed
**Hotel Villa Steno**, featuring great view balconies, private gardens
off some rooms, TVs, telephones, air-conditioning, and the
friendly help of English-speaking Matteo. Of his 16 rooms, 12
have view balconies (Sb-L140,000, Db-L210,000, Tb-L250,000,
Qb-L280,000, includes hearty buffet breakfast, CC:VMA, L20,000
discount per room per night if you pay with cash and show this
book, Internet access, 10-minute hike from the station to the
top of the old town at Via Roma 109, tel. 0187-817-028 or 0187-
818-336, fax 0187-817-354, www.pasini.com, e-mail: steno
@pasini.com). Readers get a free glass of the local sweet wine,
*sciacchetrà*, when they check in—ask. The Steno has a tiny parking
lot (free, but call to reserve a spot).

**For the hardy:** The religious **Convento dei Cappuccini**
rents 14 spartan rooms, named after monks, on the hill above the
tunnel that connects the old and new parts of town. Their terrace,
overlooking the garden and a long stretch of coastline, has a
tremendous panoramic view. But it's a steep hike (D-L140,000,
all twins, attached church and cloister, either call when you arrive
or reserve 2–3 days in advance, honor your reservation or fear the
afterlife, tel. 0187-817-531, truly NSE). From the station, go

through the tunnel, then take a hairpin left. Zigzag up the side of the hill until you reach the gate, church (Chiesa Cappuccin), and *convento* (15-minute walk from station).

### Eating in Monterosso
**Ristorante Belvedere** is a good bet for good value in the old town (Wed–Mon 12:00–14:30, 19:00–22:00, closed Tue, CC:VM, right on the harbor, across from Albergo Pasquale). Lots of shops and bakeries sell pizza and focaccia, which make an easy picnic at the beach. **Il Frantoia** makes tasty pizza to go (Via Gioberti 1, off Via Roma in old town). For a splurge in the new town, try **Il Pirata** (closed Wed, reserve in advance—even if only a half hour in advance—because they have just a few tables, CC:VM, Via Molinelli 8, exit right from train station, take first right, tel. 0187-817-536).

## Transportation Connections—Cinque Terre
The five towns of the Cinque Terre are on a milk-run train line described earlier in this chapter. Hourly trains connect each town with the others, La Spezia, and Genoa. While a few of the milk-run trains go to more distant points (Milan or Pisa), it's faster to change in La Spezia or Monterosso to a bigger train. Train info tel. 0187-817-458 or 147-888-088.

**From La Spezia by train to: Rome** (10/day, 4 hrs), **Pisa** (hrly, 1 hr), **Florence** (hrly, 2.5 hrs, change at Pisa), **Milan** (hrly, 3 hrs, possible change in Genoa), **Venice** (2 direct 6-hr trains/day).

**From Monterosso by train to: Venice** (2/day, 6 hrs), **Milan** (3/day, 3 hrs), **Genova** (9/day, 1.25 hrs), **Turin** (5/day, 3.25 hrs), **Pisa** (3/day, 1.5 hrs), **Sestri Levante** (hrly, 15 min, most trains to Genova stop here), **La Spezia** (nearly hrly, 20 min), **Levanto** (nearly hrly, 6 min).

## Driving in the Cinque Terre
**Milan to the Cinque Terre (130 miles):** Drivers speed south by autostrada from Milan, skirt Genoa, and drive along some of Italy's most scenic and impressive freeways toward the port of La Spezia. The road via Parma is faster but less scenic.

It's possible to snake your car down the treacherous little road into the Cinque Terre and park above the town, but you're likely to park a mile above the town. Don't even try this on weekends or in August, when Italian day-trippers clog the region. Monterosso has a big, guarded beachfront parking lot that fills only on August weekends (L12,000/day). There is no adequate parking near Vernazza (park in Levanto or Monterosso and take the train to Vernazza). Riomaggiore has a huge but expensive garage and an orange shuttle bus to get you into town. Manarola also has parking and a shuttle bus to the center. To drive to Monterosso or

Vernazza, exit the autostrada at Uscita Carrodano west of La Spezia. To drive to Riomaggiore, leave the freeway at La Spezia.

You can park your car near the train station in La Spezia. Spots on Via Paleocapa below the station are free for long stays. Confirm that parking is OK and leave nothing inside to steal. The "Autorimessa Stationi" garage immediately below the station can store your car for about L20,000 per day.

## TOWNS NEAR THE CINQUE TERRE

La Spezia, a gateway to the Cinque Terre, is simply a place to stay if you can't find a room in the Cinque Terre (20–30 minutes away). Levanto has a long beach and a scenic trail to Monterosso (2.5-hour hike, or easier, 6 minutes by train). Sestri Levante, on a narrow peninsula flanked by beaches, is for sun seekers (15 min by train from Cinque Terre). Santa Margherita, 75 minutes by train from the Cinque Terre, is more of a real town, with actual sights, beaches, and easy connections with Portofino (by trail, bus, or boat).

## LA SPEZIA

When all else fails, you can stay in a noisy, bigger town like La Spezia. While a quick train ride into the fanciful Five-Terre, La Spezia feels like work-a-day Italy.

The TI is at the station (daily 9:00–13:00, 15:00–18:00 in summer; Mon–Sat 9:00–13:00, 14:00–17:00, Sun 9:00–13:00 in winter, look for "i" on platform, tel. 0187-718-997).

Sights are slim. On Friday morning a huge open-air market sprawls along Via Garibaldi (about 6 blocks from station). The Museo Amedeo Lia displays Italian paintings and statues from the 13th to 18th centuries (L12,000, Tue–Sun 10:00–18:00, closed Mon, 10-minute walk from station at Via Prione 234, tel. 0187-731-100).

### Sleeping in La Spezia
**(L2,000 = about $1, country code: 39, zip code: 19122)**
The first three hotels are within a block of the train station; the fourth is a five-minute walk from the station. The last is for drivers only. Only the first has air-conditioning.

The grand, old, but newly restored **Hotel Firenze e Continentale** has 68 rooms with all the classy comforts (Db-L200,000, maybe L180,000 in slow time, includes buffet breakfast, CC:VMA, air-con, some nonsmoking rooms, elevator, no parking, Via Paleocapa 7, tel. 0187-713-200, fax 0187-714-930, SE). **Hotel Venezia**, across the street, has a plain lobby but its 22 rooms are pleasant and modern (Db-L170,000, CC:VM, elevator, Via Paleocapa 10, tel. & fax 0187-733-465, NSE). **Albergo Parma**, tight, bright, and bleachy clean, with TVs in the rooms, is located just below the station, down the stairs (D-L80,000, Db-L95,000, CC:VM, Via Fiume 143, 19100 La Spezia, tel. 0187-743-010, fax 0187-743-240, some English spoken). **Hotel Astoria**, with 56 decent rooms, has a lobby and breakfast room as large as a school cafeteria. It's a fine backup if the hotels nearer to the station are full (Db-L170,000–190,000, includes breakfast, elevator, Via Roma 139, take street left of Albergo Parma—Via Milano, go 3 blocks and turn left on Via Roma, tel. 0187-714-655, fax 0187-714-425).

**Il Gelsomino**, for drivers only, is a small B&B in the hills above La Spezia (3 rooms, D-L120,000, Db-L140,000, Tb-L160,000, views, Via dei Viseggi 9, tel. & fax 0187-704-201, run by Carla Massi).

# LEVANTO

Graced with a sandy beach, Levanto is packed in summer. The rest of the year, it's just a fine town, with less charm and fewer tourists than the Cinque Terre towns. Levanto has a new section (gridded-street plan) and a twisty old town (bisected by a modern street), along with a few pedestrian streets, a castle (not tourable), and a scenic, no-wimps-allowed hike to Monterosso (2.5 hrs).

It's a 10-minute walk from the train station to the TI; pick up a map (summer Mon–Sat 9:00–13:00, 14:00–18:00, Sun 9:00–13:00, shorter hours off-season, route is well signed, Piazza Cavour, tel. 0187-808-125).

Enjoy the beach (half the beach is free, half requires admission fee). Stroll the old town around Piazza del Popolo. Until 10 years ago, the town market (*mercato*) was held at the 13th-century loggia in the square. Go uphill to the church (the striped Chiesa di S. Andrea), past part of the old medieval wall, to the castle. Beyond the castle you'll find the trail to Monterosso (2.5 hrs, follow signs to Punta Mesco—the tip of the peninsula).

For picnic supplies, try Levanto's modern, covered *mercato* (Mon–Sat 9:00–13:00, fish and produce market). On Wednesday morning, the open-air market fills the street in front of the *mercato* (this street, "only" 10 years old, hasn't yet been officially named).

To get to the Cinque Terre, take the boat (2/day, stops at every Cinque Terre town except Corniglia, Easter–Oct) or the train (nearly hrly, 6 minutes to Monterosso).

## Sleeping in Levanto
**(L2,000 = about $1, country code: 39, zip code: 19015)**
In the popular beach town, a number of hotels require half-pension (breakfast and dinner) in summer.

**Albergo Primavera** has 17 comfortable rooms—10 with terraces but no views—just a half a block from the beach (Db-L170,000, Db with half-pension-L240,000, half-pension is technically required in July–Aug but they're flexible, buffet breakfast, closed Nov–Jan, CC:VM, Via Cairoli 5, tel. 0187-808-023, fax 0187-801-588, friendly staff speaks a little English). **Hotel**

**Europa**, not quite as friendly or central, is a backup (22 rooms, Db-L160,000, terrace, Via Dante Alighieri 41, tel. 0187-808-126, fax 0187-808-594, e-mail: albeurop@tin.it).

For a major splurge (which includes dinner), consider **Hotel Stella Maris**, an 18th-century palazzo with original furnishings: chandeliers, frescoed ceilings, and massive beds and armoires. The rooms on the busy street are bigger and grander than the two quieter rooms in the back (Db with required half-pension-L360,000, cheaper rooms in modern annex also include half-pension: Db-L260,000, CC:VM, Via Marconi 4, a few steps from Piazza Cavour and TI, tel. 0187-808-258, fax 0187-807-351, www.hotelstellamaris.it).

## SESTRI LEVANTE

This peninsular town is squeezed as skinny as a hot dog between its two beaches. A pedestrian road (Corso Columbo) runs down the middle of the peninsula, lined with shops selling pizza to go, pastries, and beach paraphernalia. The rocky, forested bluff at the end of the peninsula is inaccessible to the public (it's the huge backyard of the fancy Hotel Castelli). Market day is Saturday at Piazza Aldo Moro (8:00–13:00).

The best, quick visit from the station starts with a trip to the TI to get a map (daily 9:30–12:30, 15:00–18:00, shorter hours off-season; go straight out of station on Via Roma, turn left at fountain in park, TI at next square—Piazza S. Antonio 10; tel. 0185-457-011). From the TI, look across the piazza to see Corso Columbo, the pedestrian street. Stroll this street until nearly the end (about 5 minutes). Just before you get to the large white church at the end, turn off for either beach (the free public beach, Baia del Silencio, is on your left). Or head uphill behind the church to the Castelli for a drink at their view café (so-so view, reasonably priced drinks, café is at end of parking lot to your right). On the way up the hill you'll pass the evocative arches of a ruined chapel, bombed during WWII.

Most people are here for the sun. The beaches are named after the bays (*baias*) they border. The bigger beach, Baia delle Favole, is divided up most of the year (April–Oct) into sections that you pay to enter. The fees, which can soar up to L45,000 in August, generally include chairs, umbrellas, and fewer crowds. There are several small free sections: at the ends and in the middle (look for *libere* signs). The town's other beach, Baia del Silencio, is narrow, virtually all free, and packed, providing a good chance to see Italian families at play. There isn't much more to do than unroll a beach towel and join in.

Sestri Levante is easy to reach by train, just 15 minutes away from Monterosso (hrly connections with Monterosso, nearly hrly with other Cinque Terre towns).

## Sleeping in Sestri Levante
**(L2,000 = about $1, country code: 39, zip code: 16039)**
**Hotel Due Mari** has three stars, 29 elegant rooms, and a rooftop terrace with a stunning view of both beaches. For this splurge, reserve months in advance (Db-L195,000–220,000 depending on view, Db with half-pension required in July–Aug-L300,000, CC:VM, some air-con, elevator, garden, take pedestrian street to end, hotel is behind church, free parking, Vico del Coro 18, tel. 0185-42695, fax 0185-42698, SE). **Hotel Helvetia**, overlooking Baia del Silencio, is another good three-star bet (24 rooms, Db-L220,000–280,000 depending on view, CC:VM, large view terrace, Via Cappuccini 43, tel. 0185-41175, fax 0185-457216, www.hotelhelvetia.it, SE).

**Hotel Elisabetta**, less central and cheaper, has comfortable rooms on a busy street at the end of Baia delle Favole (Db-L100,000–150,000 depending on season, CC:VM, Via Novara 7, tel. 0185-41128, fax 0185-487-206, NSE).

**Hotel dei Fiori** has 15 basic rooms across Piazza S. Antonio from the TI (Db-L100,000–125,000, includes breakfast, CC:VM, Via Nazionale 12, tel. & fax 0185-41147, NSE).

# SANTA MARGHERITA LIGURE
If you need the movie star's Riviera, park your yacht at Portofino. Or you can settle down in the nearby and more personable Santa Margherita Ligure (15 minutes by bus from Portofino and 75 minutes by train north of the Cinque Terre). While Portofino's velour allure is tarnished by snobby residents and a nonstop traffic jam in peak season, Santa Margherita tumbles easily downhill from its huggable train station. The town has a fun resort character with a breezy promenade.

On a quick day trip, walk the beach promenade, see the small old-town section, and catch the bus (or boat) to Portofino to see what all the fuss is about. With more time, Santa Margherita makes an enjoyable overnight stop.

**Tourist Information**: The TI gives out maps and books rooms (daily 9:00–12:30, 15:00–18:00, less off-season, Via XXV Aprile 2B, tel. 0185-287-485, www.apttigullio.liguria.it).

**Arrival by Train**: From the station, take the stairs (marked "Mare," meaning "sea") down to the harbor. The harborfront promenade is as wide as the skimpy beach (the real beach is a 10-minute walk farther on).

To get to the pedestrian-friendly old town and the TI, take a right at the first square (Piazza Veneto). To get to the TI, continue straight, then angle left on Via XXV Aprile. Or, for the old town, turn left on Via Torino, which opens almost immediately onto Piazza Caprera, a square with a church and fruit vendors (Mon–Sat) in the midst of pedestrian streets.

## Sights—Santa Margherita Ligure
If you need a sight more than a beach, try **Villa Durazzo**, a 17th-century building with a lavish interior (L5,000, summer: Tue–Sun 9:00–18:00, winter: Tue–Sun 9:30–12:30, 14:30–16:30, closed Mon, guided tour mandatory, English sometimes possible—ask) set in a grand **garden** (free, daily 9:00–19:00 in summer, until 17:00 in winter, Piazzale San Giacomo 3, several blocks uphill and inland from harborfront square, tel. 0185-205-449). The castle overlooking the promenade will likely be open to tourists in 2001.

At the **fish market**, fishing boats unload their catch at 17:00 daily except Sunday, and in the morning the fish market bustles with smelly sales and earnest customers (closed Sun, on Via Marconi, on harbor, just past castle). The **open air market**, a commotion of clothes and produce, is held every Friday morning on Salita S. Giacomo (between the castle and harbor).

## Getting to Portofino
From Santa Margherita, Portofino is an easy day trip by bus, boat, or foot (Portifino TI, Via Roma 35, tel. 0185-269-024). Catch **bus** #82 from Santa Margherita's train station or at bus stops along the harbor (L1,700, 2–3/hrly, 15 min, buy tickets at bar at station, at bus kiosk at Piazza Veneto—open daily 7:10–21:40, or at any shop that displays a *Biglietti Bus* sign). The **boat** makes the trip hourly with more class and without the traffic jams (dock is off Piazza Martiri della Libertà, a 2-minute walk from Piazza Veneto). Hikers call the 1.5-hour Santa Margherita–Portofino **hike** one of the best on the Riviera (start at Via Maragliano several blocks past the castle).

## Sleeping in Santa Margherita Ligure
**(L2,000 = about $1, country code: 39, zip code: 16038)**
**Hotel Fasce** is a hardworking place with 18 bright rooms and a happy clientele (Sb-L148,000, Db-L165,000, Tb-L220,000, Qb-L260,000, includes breakfast, CC:VM, free round-trip train tickets to Cinque Terre for 3-night stays, free parking, free bikes, English newspapers, roof garden, laundry service-L30,000, a 10-minute walk from the station at Via Bozzo 3, taxi from station runs about L20,000, tel. 0185-286-435, fax 0185-283-580, www.hotelfasce.it, run by Jane Fasce—an Englishwoman—and her husband Aristide).

**Hotel Fiorina**, with 55 airy rooms decorated in a light-and-dark color scheme, is on a busy square with quieter rooms in the back. It's family run with pride and care (Db-L160,000 with breakfast, Db-L130,000 without breakfast, CC:VM, fans in every room, sun terrace—no view, Piazza Mazzini 26, 2 blocks inland from pedestrian Piazza Caprera, tel. 0185-287-517, fax 0185-281-855, e-mail: fiorinasml@libero.it, SE).

At the **Hotel Nuova Riviera**, a stately old villa, the Sabini family offers 12 nonsmoking rooms (Db-L160,000, Tb-L210,000,

Qb-L260,000, discount of L10,000 per day if you pay cash, CC:VM, includes breakfast, dinner optional, cramped parking, peaceful garden, 10-minute walk from the station; walking or driving, follow signs to hospital, on Piazza Mazzini see hotel signs, Via Belvedere 10, tel. & fax 0185-287-403, http://space.tin.it /viaggi/gsabin/, e-mail: gisabin@tin.it, son Gian Carlo SE). Their annex is cheaper (3-night minimum, D-L120,000, T-L170,000, Q-L200,000, includes breakfast, cash only). Note that if you cancel your reservations, you'll be billed for one night.

These three hotels, which are near (or at) the train station, all come with train noise: **Hotel Terminus**, with 24 rooms right at the station, works hard to keep its customers satisfied (Db-L160,000, includes huge breakfast, CC:VMA, terrace, good meals, some view rooms, ask for room away from tracks, tel. 0185-286-121, fax 0185-282-546, Angelo SE). **Nuovo Hotel Garden** is tucked away down a side street. From its comfortable rooms to its restaurant (for guests only), the quality is high (Db-L105,000–205,000 depending on season, CC:VM, terrace, a block from train station—instead of taking the stairs down to harbor, face stairs and go right—away from station, Via Zara 13, tel. 0185-285-398, fax 0185-290-439, SE). Next door, **Hotel Conte Verde** rents 33 rooms of varying quality and prices. The cheaper rooms are decent, but if you've got the money, it's worth springing for a nicer room. Ask if a room with a big terrace is available (D-L85,000–135,000, Db-L125,000–200,000, garden, big public areas, parking extra, Via Zara 1, tel. 0185-287-139, fax 0185-284-211, e-mail: cverde@zeus.omninet.it, SE).

# MILAN
# (MILANO)

For every church in Rome, there's a bank in Milan. Italy's second city and the capital of Lombardy, Milan is a hardworking, fashion-conscious, time-is-money city of 2 million. Milan is a melting pot of people and history. Its industriousness may come from the Teutonic blood of its original inhabitants, the Lombards, or from the region's Austrian heritage. Milan is Italy's industrial, banking, TV, publishing, and convention capital. The economic success of modern Italy can be blamed on this city of publicists and pasta power lunches.

As if to make up for its shaggy parks, blocky fascist architecture, and recently bombed-out feeling (World War II), its people are works of art. Milan is an international fashion capital with a refined taste. Window displays are gorgeous. Even the cheese comes gift wrapped.

Three hundred years before Christ, the Romans called this place Mediolanum, or "the central place." By the fourth century A.D. it was the capital of the western half of the Roman Empire. It was from here that Emperor Constantine issued the Edict of Milan, legalizing Christianity. After some barbarian darkness, medieval Milan rose to regional prominence under the Visconti and Sforza families. By the time of the Renaissance it was called "the New Athens" and was enough of a cultural center for Leonardo to call home. Then came 400 years of foreign domination (Spain, Austria, France, more Austria). Milan was a center of the 1848 revolution against Austria and helped lead Italy to unification in 1870.

Mussolini left a heavy fascist touch on the city's architecture (such as the central train station). His excesses also led to the WWII bombing of Milan. But Milan rose again. The 1959

Pirelli Tower (the skinny skyscraper in front of the station) was a trendsetter in its day. Today Milan is pedestrian friendly, with a great transit system and inviting, people-friendly pedestrian zones.

Many tourists come to Italy for the past. But Milan is today's Italy, and no Italian trip is complete without seeing it. While it's not big on the tourist circuit, Milan has plenty to see.

And seeing Milan is not difficult. My coverage focuses on the old center. Nearly all the sights and hotels covered are within a 10-minute walk of the cathedral (Duomo), which is one straight 10-minute shot on the Metro from the train station. Milan, no more expensive than other Italian cities, is well organized and completely manageable.

## Planning Your Time

OK, it's a big city, so you probably won't linger. But with two nights and a full day you can gain an appreciation for the town and see the major sights. (Note that about half of Milan's sights close on Monday.) With 36 hours, I'd sleep in Milan and focus on the center. Tour the Duomo and La Scala museum, hit what art you like (Brera Gallery, Michelangelo's last *Pietà*, Leonardo's *Last Supper*—now requires reservations), browse through the elegant shopping area and the Galleria, and try to see an opera. Technology buffs like the Science and Technology Museum, while medieval art buffs dig the city's very old churches. People watchers and pigeon feeders could spend an entire vacation never leaving sight of the Duomo.

Since Milan is a cold Italian plunge, and most flights to the United States leave Milan early in the morning, you may want to start your Italian trip softly by going directly from Milan to Lake Como (1-hour train ride to Varenna) or the Cinque Terre (4 hours to Vernazza). Then spend a night or two in Milan at the end of your trip before flying home.

**Three-hour tour:** If you're just changing trains in Milan (as sooner or later you will), consider this blitz tour: Check your bag at the station, pick up a city map at the station TI, ride the subway to the Duomo (in front of the train station, follow yellow line 3 direction "*per* San Donato" 4 stops to "Duomo"), peruse the square, explore the cathedral's rooftop and interior, have a scenic coffee in the Galleria, spin on the Taurus, see the opera museum at La Scala (closed 12:30–14:00), and return by subway to the station (yellow line 3, direction "Zara"). Art fans might make time for the Duomo's museum, Leonardo (if you have reservations, Metro: Cadorna), or the Michelangelo (no reservations necessary, Metro: Cairoli).

## Orientation

**Tourist Information:** Milan has two TIs. One is in the central train station (Mon–Sat 9:00–19:00, Sun 9:00–12:30, 13:30–18:00, tel. 02-7252-4360). At track level (with your back to the tracks) look for the sign "APT Tourist Information" near the blinking orange-and-white *T*. The TI is tucked away down a corridor next to a Telecom telephone center.

The other TI is on Piazza Duomo (Mon–Fri 8:30–20:00, Sat 9:00–13:00, 14:00–19:00, Sun 9:00–13:00, 14:00–17:00, closes 1 hour earlier Oct–April, tel. 02-7252-4301). As you face the church it's to your right in a skinny three-story building.

At either TI, confirm your sightseeing plans and pick up the free "Milan is Milan" map (with lots of extra info, a handy close-up of the city center) and the classy *Museums in Milan* booklet (with latest museum hours). For events, concerts, and films in English, ask for the free *Hello Milano* monthly newspaper (www .hellomilano.it) or the less-helpful *Milano Mese* (events are listed in Italian by category rather than date). The 80-page *Where, When, How* booklet—useful but overkill for most short visits—details several self-guided walking tours, and provides a listing of sights, shopping ideas, bookstores, restaurants, nightlife, sports events, and much more (L3,000).

The TI sells a Welcome Card packet for L15,000 which includes a 24-hour transit pass (good on Metro, trams, and buses), a coupon booklet good for discounts on their city bus tour and several museums, a CD of opera music, and an unnecessary vinyl pouch. This is a decent value if you want the CD.

While I've listed enough sights to keep you hectic for two days, there's much more to see in Milan. Its many thousand-year-old churches make it clear that Milan was an important beacon in the Dark Ages. The TI, the *Where, When, How* booklet, and other local guidebooks can point you in the right direction if you have more time.

## Arrival in Milan

**By Train:** The huge, sternly decorated, Fascist-built train station is a city and a sight in itself. You'll get off the train and enter the lobby at track level; another floor is downstairs.

· Orient from the track-level lobby with your back to the tracks. On your right: train information (daily 7:00–21:00, validate rail-passes here at refund window, tel. 147-888-088), baggage check (L5,000/12 hrs), and a 24-hour pharmacy (*farmacia*, look for green neon cross). On your left are cash machines (near track 14) and the TI (see above, look for blinking orange *T*). Out the side exit on the left: airport shuttle buses (to Malpensa and Linate, run by STAM).

From the track level, go downstairs straight ahead to find train-ticket windows, Hertz/Avis/Europcar offices, and a great and huge supermarket/cafeteria that's hidden away (daily 7:30–24:00, after you descend stairs from track-level lobby, go right and enter Pellini bar, snake your way through the cafeteria to the SuperCentrale market, also called Supermercato Sigma). Just outside the front of the station is the taxi stand (figure on L20,000 to Duomo) and escalators which take you down into the Metro system.

Warning: Locals call the change offices in the train station *ladri auttorizzati* (authorized thieves). Ignore them and their 10 percent commission. Use a cash machine (from track 14, enter the lobby—you'll find a Bancomat cash machine to your left and another across the hall) or exit the station straight ahead and cross the square to Banca Commerciale Italiana (Mon–Fri 8:30–13:30, 15:00–16:30).

For most quick visits, the giant city is one simple axis from the train station to the Duomo. To get downtown go straight into the Metro (look for red *M*) and buy a L1,500 ticket (from the underground ticket office at the Metro stop—with all prices in English over the window, or from a machine—coins or bills). Follow signs for line 3 (yellow), direction "S. Donato." To return to the station, take the yellow line 3, direction "Zara." After one trip on the Metro you'll dream up other excuses to use it.

**By Car:** Driving is bad enough in Milan to make the L40,000/ day fee for a downtown garage a blessing. If you're driving, do Milan (and Lake Como) before or after you rent. If you have a car, use the well-marked suburban *parcheggi* (parking lots), which offer affordable and safe parking at city-edge subway stations.

**By Plane:** Frequent shuttle trains and buses run between Milan's airports and the central train station. For details, see "Transportation Connections," below.

## Helpful Hints
**Theft Alert:** Be on guard. Milan's thieves target tourists. At the station and around the Duomo, thieves roam dressed as beggars, sometimes in gangs of three too-young-to-arrest children. Watch out for ragged people carrying newspaper and cardboard. If you're ripped off, ask the police to fill out a report; it's necessary if you plan to file a claim with your insurance company (Polizia, Piazza San Sepolcro, behind Pinacoteca Ambrosiana, near Duomo, tel. 02-806051). For lost or stolen credit cards or traveler's checks, contact Visa in Italy at 800-877-232; MasterCard at 800-68086; or American Express at 800-864-046 (for credit cards) or 800-72000 (for traveler's checks).

**U.S. Consulate:** Monday–Friday 8:30–5:30, Via Principe Amedeo 2, tel. 02-290-351.

**Scheduling:** Monday is a terrible sightseeing day, since most museums are closed. August is rudely hot and muggy. Locals who can, vacate, leaving the city pretty quiet. Those visiting in August find many shops closed, nightlife sleepy, and hotels empty and discounted (or closed entirely). I've indicated which recommended hotels offer air-conditioning—worth the money for a summer visit.

**Buying Train Tickets:** You can buy train tickets and reserve *couchettes* for the station price without the station lines near the Duomo at CIT (Mon–Fri 9:00–19:00, Sat 9:00–13:00, 14:00–18:00, closed Sun, must place order at least 30 minutes before closing, CC:VM, in the center of Galleria Vittorio Emanuele, tel. 02-8637-0228) or American Express (Mon–Fri 9:00–12:30, 14:30–17:00, pay cash or use Amex credit card, up Via Verdi from La Scala, Via Brera 3, tel. 02-7200-3694).

**Bookstore**: Of the many bookstores in Milan, the biggest and handiest is Libreria Feltrinelli, under the Galleria Vittorio Emanuele. The books in English—fiction and guidebooks— are at opposite ends of the store (daily 9:00–23:00, Aug 10:00–23:00, CC:VM, store is huge but entrances are subtle: either enter at Ricordi Mediastore next to McDonald's in center of Galleria and go downstairs, or enter through Autogrill restaurant on Piazza Duomo, also sells maps, tel. 02-8699-6903). The American Bookstore is at Via Camperio 16 (near Sforza Castle, tel. 02-878-920).

**Street Market:** Milan's most popular flea market is Fiera di Senigallia, which spills down Viale D'Annunzio every Saturday from 8:30 to 17:00 (Metro: San Agostino, walk down Viale Papiniano—where market starts—to D'Annunzio—where it gets bigger); be wary of pickpockets at any street market.

## Getting around Milan

Use Milan's great subway system. The clean, spacious, fast, and easy three-line Metro zips you anywhere you may want to go. Transit **tickets** are good for one subway ride followed by 75 minutes of bus or tram travel (L1,500 at newsstands, at machines in the station: push green *"rete urbana di Milano"* button; note that some machines sell only the L1,500 ticket—just feed in the money). Other options include: a *carnet* (L14,000 for 10 rides; you get 5 tickets that can be used twice—flip over to use a second time; these can be shared), the **24-hour pass** (L5,000, worthwhile if you take 4 rides; can usually cover a journey the following morning since it's a 24-hour rather than a 1-day pass), and a **48-hour pass** (L9,000). Transit info: toll-free tel. 800-016857 (underground office at Duomo stop, open Mon–Sat 8:00–19:45, www.atm.mi.it).

I've keyed sightseeing to the subway system. While most sights are within a few blocks of each other, Milan is an exhausting city for walking. You'll rarely wait more than five minutes for a subway train, and the well-marked trams can be useful (especially to the *Last Supper*).

Small groups go cheap and fast by **taxi** (metered, drop charge L6,000 and L1,300 per km, often easier to walk to a taxi stand than flag one down).

## Milan Metro

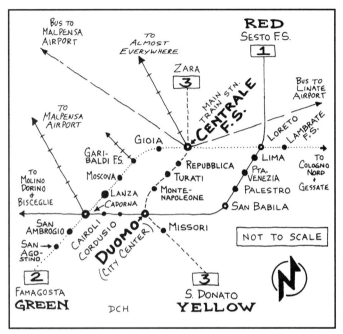

## Tours of Milan

**Bus Tours**—Consider the three-hour **Autostradale** city bus tour, which includes visits to the La Scala museum, Sforza Castle, and, best of all, Leonardo's *Last Supper* (L60,000, discounted to L50,000 with TI's Welcome Card, includes entry fees—a good value, CC:VM, departs Tue–Sun at 9:30 from Piazza Duomo at Via Marconi, runs year-round, book at TI on Piazza Duomo, tel. 02-7252-4301). The **Ciao Milano** vintage tram, which does a circle-8 trip around the city, isn't worth L30,000 for the transportation, because Milan's sights cluster in the center (3/day, multilingual tour, you can hop on and off but what's the point, departs Piazza Duomo at roughly 11:00, 13:00, and 15:00, tel. 02-805-5323). **Walking Tour**—The TI offers a walking tour on Mondays only (the day the city bus tour doesn't run), covering the Duomo, Galleria Vittorio Emanuele, and the La Scala Museum (L25,000, 3 hrs, in English, runs year-round, book at TI, tel. 02-7252-4301).

## Sights—Milan's Cathedral and Museum

▲▲**Duomo**—The cathedral, the city's centerpiece, is the fourth-largest church in Europe—after the Vatican's, London's, and

# Milan

Sevilla's. (Get the most out of your visit by starting with the adjacent museum, located just outside the church, directly across from the south transept, and described below.)

Back when Europe was fragmented into countless tiny kingdoms and dukedoms, the dukes of Milan wanted to impress their counterparts in Germany and France. Their goal: to earn Milan recognition and respect from both the Vatican and the kings and princes of northern Europe by building a massive, richly ornamented cathedral. Even after Renaissance domes were in vogue elsewhere in Italy, Milan's cathedral stayed on Gothic target. The dukes—thinking northerners would relate better to Gothic— loaded it with pointed arches and spires. For good measure, the cathedral was built not of stone but of marble—pink marble of Candoglia from top to bottom—rafted to Milan from a quarry 70 kilometers away.

At 160 meters long and 93 meters wide, with fifty-two 30- meter-tall sequoia pillars inside and more than 2,000 statues, the place seats 12,000 worshippers. If you do two laps, you've done your daily walk. Built from 1386 to 1810, this construction project originated the Italian phrase meaning "never ending": "like building a cathedral." It started Gothic (best seen in the apse behind the altar) and was finished under Napoleon. While a good example of the flamboyant, or "flamelike," overripe final stage of Gothic, architectural harmony is not its forte. Make a circuit simply to enjoy the giant stained-glass windows trying to light the cavernous interior (church free, L6,000 for 1-hr audioguide, daily 7:00–19:00, enforced dress code: no shorts or bare shoulders for anyone of any age, Metro: Duomo). For most, the treasury (*tesoro*) isn't worth the time or the L2,000. The west front (wonderful late in the day, with the sun low in the sky) was finished in the early 1800s under Napoleon. Notice the lower part is actually neoclassical.

The rooftop is the most memorable part of a Duomo visit. You'll wander through a fancy forest of spires with great views of the city, the square, and—on clear days—even the Swiss Alps. And overlooking everything: the 13-foot-tall gilt Virgin Mary, 100 meters above the ground (climb the stairs for L6,000; or ride the elevator for L9,000, L12,000 combo ticket includes elevator and Duomo museum; daily mid-Feb–mid-Nov 9:00–17:45, mid-Nov–mid-Feb 9:00–16:15, enter outside from the north transept; clue: in Europe old churches face roughly east).

▲▲**Museo del Duomo**—To really understand Milan's cathedral, visit the cathedral museum first (L10,000, the L12,000 combo ticket includes elevator to Duomo rooftop, daily 9:30–12:30, 15:00–18:00, located in Ducal Palace next to south side of Duomo, Piazza Duomo 14, Metro: Duomo). Here's a tour:

**Room 1:** After you buy your ticket, look up. Greeting you, as he did pilgrims 500 years ago, is God the Father, made of wood, wrapped in copper, and gilded. In 1425 this covered the keystone connecting the tallest arches directly above the high altar.

**Room 2:** Meet St. George. Among the oldest cathedral statues, it once stood on the highest spire and shows nearly 600 years of pollution and aging. Some think this is the face of Duke Visconti—the man who started the cathedral. The museum is filled with originals like this. On the right, finger a raw piece of *marmo di Candoglia*—the material of the church, spires, and statues. The duke's family gave the entire Candoglia quarry to the church for all the marble it would ever need.

**Room 3:** In this room (which used to be the stable for the Duke's horses), you can see that Gothic was an international style. Gothic craftsmen, engineers, and artists roamed across Europe to work on huge projects like Milan's. The statues in this room show the national differences: Peter (near the door, showing off his big keys) is Italian...expressive face—made even more expressive by his copper-button pupils. The smaller statues behind glass are German and French—more stern and statuesque. Pope Martino

V, on the far wall, celebrated the first mass in the cathedral in 1418. Enjoy a close look at the stained-glass windows. The grotesque gargoyles (originals) served two purposes: to scare away evil spirits and to spew rainwater away from the building.

**Room 5:** A lit panel shows how the church was built in stages from 1386 to 1774. Building resumed only when the community had the money.

**Room 6:** The brick backdrop reminds us what the church would have looked like if not for the dandy with the rolled-up contract in his hand. That's Galeazzo Sforza, donating his marble quarry to the church.

**Room 7:** The crucifix (again, copper sheet gilded with real gold nailed onto wood) is 900 years old. It hung in the church that stood here before as well as today's cathedral.

**Room 8:** These statues, from around 1500, are originals. Copies now fill their niches in the church.

**Room 9:** Five hundred years ago, this sumptuous Flanders-style tapestry hung from the high altar. Note the exquisite detail. In the hall, more fancy fabric—this one is silk, silver, and gold embroidery. These were all gifts from big shots hoping to gain favor with the Church.

**Room 10:** The sketchy red cartoons were designs for huge paintings (see photographs opposite) that still hang between the columns in the winter. Notice the inlaid 16th-century marble floor. The black and red marble is harder. Go ahead, wear down the white a little more.

**Room 12:** Turn left and circle the room clockwise.

A. The terra-cotta in this room is clay—worked in a creative frenzy and then baked. Study the quick design below the careful marble originals. And notice what 300 years of acidic pigeon droppings does to marble.

B. The statues in this room (c. 1600), sculpted 100 years later than the statues in room 8, are therefore more expressive.

C. The painting of the saint in the black robe shows (in the background) the 13th-century original church's facade with today's church—before spires—behind it.

D. Crespi's monochrome painting of the *Creation of Eve* came first (1628). From that the terra-cotta model was made (1629), and this served as the model for the marble statue that still stands above the center door on the church's west portal (1643). Three other sets line the wall.

E. Opposite *Eve*, see the *Dance of Angels* and its terra-cotta model. Compare the two and *Sant' Uguccione*, behind you.

**Room 13:** Standing like a Picasso is the original (1772) iron frame for the statue of the Virgin Mary that still crowns the Cathedral's tallest spire. In 1967 a steel replacement was made for the 33 pieces of gilded copper bolted to the frame. The wood face of Mary (in the corner) is the original mold for Mary's cathedral-crowning copper face.

**Room 15:** At the modern doors with the thin pink marble windows, turn right into a tunnel-like hall. On the left you'll see a painting of the earlier church, competition designs proposing possible facades for the cathedral, and a photo of the actual west portal. On the right: the evolution of the church and the Ducal Palace (which you're in now).

**Room 16:** This huge wooden model of the cathedral was the actual model—necessary in that precomputer age—used in the 16th century by the architects and engineers to build the church. The more recent facade wasn't used. Climb around the back to see the spire-filled rooftop, which you'll explore later if you like. Later rooms are more technical, showing the recent restoration work and the stabilization and reinforcement of the main pylons. To exit, retrace your steps.

## Sights—Milan

Compared to Rome and Florence, Milan's art is mediocre, but the city does have unique and noteworthy sights. To maximize your time, use the Metro and note which places stay open through the siesta. I've listed sights in a logical geographical order.

▲**Piazza Duomo**—The piazza is a classic European scene. Professionals scurry, label-conscious kids loiter, young thieves peruse. For that creepy-crawly, pigeons-all-over-you experience, buy a bag of seed. The Duomo Center is a modern mall with a megamusic store, a one-hour photo service, a decent Spizzico pizzeria, and the handy Ciao cafeteria. For a fine view of the Duomo and the piazza, climb the steps (unless strewn with litter and derelicts) to the balcony above the TI. Behind the Duomo is a tidy, pedestrian shopping zone along Vittorio Emanuele II.

Within a block of the Duomo are a few interesting glimpses of old Milan. The center of medieval Milan was Piazza Mercanti, now just a small square opposite the front of the Duomo. It's a strangely peaceful place today, with a fine smattering of old-time Milano architecture.

▲**Via Speronari**—A block off Piazza Duomo, this is one of Milan's oldest streets and the most charming street in the center. Via Speronari—named for the spurs once made and sold here— is worth a wander. Start at the recommended Hotel Speronari, formerly a dorm for monks from the church across the street. The classy Vino Vino wine shop next door welcomes tasters (L3,000/glass). The sign next door—*"L'Ortolan Pusae Vecc de Milan"*—brags in the old Milanese language that this is the oldest fruit and veggie store in the city. The Princi bakery next door is understandably popular. Its brioches are rarely more than a few minutes old. In the back, a busy *tavola calda* serves locals a quick,

fresh, and tasty hot meal (around L8,000 per plate, pay for a
*"piatto misto"* at the cashier, get a mixed plate of what looks good,
and grab a stool).

When you hit Via Torino, go 20 meters to the left into the
**Church of Santa Maria presso San Satiro** (daily 7:30–11:30,
15:30–18:00). It was the scene of a temper tantrum in 1242,
when a losing gambler vented his anger by hitting the baby Jesus
in the Madonna-and-Child altarpiece. Blood "miraculously"
spurted out, and the beautiful little church has been on the
pilgrimage trail ever since. While I've never seen any blood, I'd
swear I've seen a 3-D background behind the basically flat altar
(a trompe l'oeil illusion by Bramante).

▲▲**Galleria Vittorio Emanuele**—Milan is symbolized by its
great four-story, glass-domed arcade on the cathedral square.
Here you can turn an expensive cup of coffee into a good value with
Europe's best people watching (or enjoy the same view for peanuts
from the strategically placed McDonald's). Stand under the central
dome and enjoy the art above. For good luck, locals step on the
irresistible testicles of the mosaic Taurus on the floor's zodiac
design. Two local girls explained to me that it works better if you
spin. Find the poor bull and just observe for a few minutes . . . it's a
very cute scene. Also under the Galleria dome is the CIT travel
agency (sells train tickets and *couchettes*; see "Helpful Hints," above)
and a cluster of SIP public phone booths.

▲▲**La Scala Opera House and Museum**—From the Galleria
you'll see a statue of Leonardo. He's looking at a plain but famous
neoclassical building, possibly the world's most prestigious opera
house, Milan's Teatrale alla Scala. La Scala opened in 1778 with
an opera by Antonio Salieri (of *Amadeus* fame). While seats are
expensive, anyone can have a peek into the grand theater from
a box connected to the museum (no photos allowed). Opera
buffs love the museum's extensive collection of things that mean
absolutely nothing to the MTV crowd: Verdi's top hat, Rossini's
eyeglasses, Toscanini's baton, Fettucini's pesto, and original
scores, busts, portraits, and death masks of great composers and
musicians (L6,000, May–Oct daily 9:00–12:30, 14:00–17:30,
Nov–April open same hours but closed Sun, last entry 30 min
before closing, Metro: Duomo, tel. 02-805-3418).

**Opera**: While schedules vary, the opera season is December
to July, and ballet and classical concerts are held from September
to November. La Scala Opera House and its box office are
closed in August (from Sept–July, box office open daily
12:00–18:00, to find box office, face theater, go left around
building until nearly at the back, look for *biglietteria* sign, on
Via Filodrammatici, CC:VM, tel. 02-7200-3744—live, tel. 02-
860-775—automated booking, or book online at La Scala's
fine Web site: www.lascala.milano.it, show time usually 20:00).

Tickets generally go on sale two months before a performance. The expensive seats sell out quickly. At noon on the day of the show, any remaining seats (usually in the affordable, sky-high gallery) are sold at a 50 percent discount at the box office and on the Internet (Web sales cease 1 hour before show time). Due to safety regulations, standing-room spots are no longer available.

▲**World-Class Window-Shopping**—The "Quadrilateral," the elegant, high-fashion shopping area around Via Montenapoleone, is worth a wander (except in Aug, when most shops close). In this land where cigarettes are still chic, the people watching is as fun as the window-shopping. Via Montenapoleone and the pedestrian-ized Via Spiga are the best streets. From La Scala, walk up Via Manzoni to the Metro stop at Montenapoleone, browse down Montenapoleone to Piazza San Babila, then (for less expensive shopping thrills) walk down the pedestrians-only Corso Vittorio Emanuele II to the Duomo. Rinascente is a Bon Marche-type department store with reasonable prices and a good selection of toys (Mon–Sat 9:00–22:00, Sun 10:00–20:00, faces north side of Duomo on Piazza Duomo).

**Museum of Milan (Civico Museo di Milano)**—This museum offers a quick walk through wall-sized pages of Milan's past, partly illustrated by maps and paintings from the 17th to 19th centuries. I found the period from 1914 to 1945—the rise and fall of fascism—particularly interesting (free, Tue–Sun 9:00–13:00, 14:00–18:00, closed Mon, Via S. Andrea 6, Metro: Montenapo-leone, tel. 02-7600-6245).

▲**Brera Art Gallery**—Milan's top collection of paintings (Italian, 14th–20th centuries) is world class, but it can't top Rome's or Florence's. Established in 1809 to house Napoleon's looted art, it fills the first floor above an art college. On the ground level wan-der past the nude *Napoleon* (by Canova) in the courtyard and straight through the art school to a great, cheap cappuccino machine.

From the courtyard climb the stairway following signs to "Pinacoteca" (L8,000, L12,000 if there's an exhibition, Tue–Sun 8:30–19:30, maybe June–Sept Sat until 23:00, closed Mon, last entry 45 min before closing, shorter hours Nov–April, Via Brera 28, Metro: Lanza, tel. 02-722-631).

The gallery's highlights include works by Gentile da Fabriano (room IV), the Bellini brothers and Mantegna (his textbook example of feet-first foreshortening, *The Dead Christ*, room VI), Crivelli (for someone new, in room XXI), Raphael (*Wedding of the Madonna*, room XXIV), and Michelangelo Merisi (a.k.a. Caravaggio, *Supper at Emmaus*, room XXIX).

▲**Risorgimento Museum**—You'll learn the interesting story (if you speak Italian or befriend a bored and talkative English-speaking guard) of Italy's rocky road to unity: from Napoleon (1796) to the victory in Rome (1870). It's just around the block from the Brera

Gallery at Via Borgonuovo 23 (free, Tue–Sun 9:00–13:00, 14:00–18:00, closed Mon, Metro: Montenapoleone).

**Poldi Pezzoli Museum**—This classy house of art features top Italian paintings of the 15th through the 18th centuries, old weaponry, and lots of interesting decorative arts, such as a roomful of old sundials and compasses (L10,000, or L14,000 combo ticket with Bagatti Valsecchi Museum, Tue–Sun 10:00–18:00, closed Mon, not a word of English, Via Manzoni 12, Metro: Montenapoleone, tel. 02-794-889).

**Bagatti Valsecchi Museum**—This unique 19th-century collection of Italian Renaissance furnishings was assembled by two aristocratic brothers who spent a wad turning their home into a Renaissance mansion (L10,000, half price on Wed, Tue–Sun 13:00–17:00, closed Mon, good English descriptions, Via Santo Spirito 10, Metro: Montenapoleone).

▲**Sforza Castle (Castello Sforzesco)**—This immense, much-bombed-and-rebuilt brick fortress is exhausting at first sight. It can only be described as heavy. But its courtyard has a great lawn for picnics and siestas, and its free museum is filled with interesting medieval armor, furniture, early Lombard art, an Egyptian collection, and, most important, Michelangelo's unfinished *Rondanini Pietà*. Michelangelo died while still working on this piece, which hints at the elongation of the Mannerist style that would follow. This is a rare opportunity to enjoy a Michelangelo with no crowds (free, daily 9:30–17:30, study posted diagram at castle entrance to find the museum—marked #12 on diagram, on the right at the beginning of second courtyard, photos OK without flash, Metro: Cairoli, tel. 02-6208-3940). A big park—with a couple of cheap eateries—sprawls behind the fortress.

▲**Leonardo da Vinci's** *Last Supper* **(Cenacolo)**—You'll need a reservation to see this Renaissance masterpiece in the refectory of the church of Santa Maria delle Grazie. Because of Leonardo's experimental use of oil rather than the normal fresco technique, deterioration began within six years of its completion. The church was bombed in World War II, but—miraculously, it seems—the *Last Supper* survived. The 21-year restoration project is complete. In a big, vacant, whitewashed room you'll see faded pastels and not a crisp edge. The feet under the table look like negatives. But the composition is dreamy—Leonardo captures the psychological drama as the Lord says "One of you will betray me," and the apostles huddle in stressed-out groups of three wondering, "Lord, is it I?" Notice Judas with his 30 pieces of silver, looking pretty guilty.

Reservations are mandatory. To minimize the humidity problem—even though the damage has already been done—25 tourists are allowed in every 15 minutes for just 15 minutes. Prior to your appointment time, you wait in several rooms, while doors close behind you and open up slowly in front of you. Information posted on Leonardo is mainly in Italian. Most of the English translation (a timeline of Leonardo's life) is posted where, if you read it, you give up some of your 15 minutes; consider skipping it to spend time with Leonardo. For a reservation, call 028-942-1146 (or from the U.S., call 011-39-028-942-1146) a minimum of three days in advance for a weekday visit and at least a week ahead for a weekend visit. Long-range planners can book up to three or four months in advance (L12,000 plus L2,000 reservation fee). Hours of booking office: Monday through Friday 9:00 to 18:00, Saturday 9:00 to 14:00, closed Sunday.

Hours of *Last Supper*: Tuesday through Sunday 8:15 to 18:45 (last visit), July through September also open Saturday until 22:15 (last visit), in winter Tuesday through Sunday 9:00 to 18:15 (last visit), always closed Monday. You'll be asked to show up 30 minutes before your scheduled time. Consider the L5,000 15-minute audioguide (L8,000 with 2 headphones).

To get to Santa Maria delle Grazie, you can either take the Metro to Cadorna (plus a 5-minute walk), or, even better, hop on tram #24 from Via Mazzini (catch it in front of Rolex store at intersection of Via Dogana and Via Mazzini, just off Piazza Duomo) which drops you off in front of the church.

People who show up without a reservation can sometimes get in (even if "Sold Out" sign is posted). You'll be told that entry is by reservation only—but if fewer than 25 people show up for a particular time slot, you can get lucky. Still, for guaranteed entry, it's best to call ahead. Note that the city bus tour (see "Tours of Milan," above) includes entry to *Last Supper*.

▲**National Leonardo da Vinci Science and Technology Museum (Museo Nazionale della Scienza e Tecnica)**—The spirit of Leonardo lives here. Most tourists visit for the hall of Leonardo designs illustrated in wooden models, but Leonardo's mind is just as easy to appreciate by paging through a coffee-table edition of his notebooks in any bookstore. The rest of this immense collection of industrial cleverness is fascinating, with plenty of push-button action (and few English descriptions): trains, radios, old musical instruments, computers, batteries, telephones, chunks of the first transatlantic cable, and on and on (L12,000, Tue–Fri 9:30–16:50, Sat–Sun 9:30–18:30, closed Mon, Via San Vittore 21, bus #50 from Duomo, or Metro: San Ambrogio, tel. 02-485-551).

**Pinacoteca Ambrosiana**—Newly reopened after seven years of work, they forgot that non-Italians may visit. The only English words are in the price list at the turnstile—ask if there are any plans to add English descriptions to the art. While a prestigious collection, there are few recognizable names for most tourists except for the impressive drawing Raphael used as a design for his School of Athens in the Vatican (L12,000, small English guidebook for L12,000 covers museum's highlights, Tue–Sun

10:00–17:30, last ticket sold at 16:30, closed Mon, a couple of blocks from Piazza Duomo at Piazza Pio XI, tel. 02-806-921). **Nightlife**—For evening action, check out the arty, student-oriented Brera area in the old center and Milan's formerly bohemian, now gentrified "Little Venice," the Navigli neighborhood. Specifics change so quickly that it's best to rely on the entertainment information in periodicals from the TI. **Soccer**—The Milanese claim their soccer team is the best in Europe. For a dose of Europe's soccer mania (which many believe provides a necessary testosterone vent to keep Europe out of a third big war), catch a match in Milan. Games are held in the 85,000-seat Meazza stadium most Sunday afternoons, September through June (tickets L20,000–75,000, sold at several downtown outlets, tel. 02-4870-7123, Metro: Lotto—no kidding, or tram #24 from Duomo directly to stadium—last stop).

# Sleeping in Milan
**(L2,000 = about $1, country code: 39)**
Sleep Code: **S** = Single, **D** = Double/Twin, **T** = Triple, **Q** = Quad, **b** = bathroom, **t** = toilet only, **s** = shower only, **CC** = Credit Card (**V**isa, **M**asterCard, **A**mex), **SE** = Speaks English, **NSE** = No English.

I have tried to minimize traffic noise problems in my listings. All are within a few minutes' walk of Milan's subway system. With Milan's fine Metro you can get anywhere in town in a flash. Anytime in April, September, and October, the city can be completely jammed by conventions; summer is usually wide open. Hotels cater more to business travelers than to tourists. Everyone speaks at least some English.

### Sleeping near the Duomo
The Duomo area is thick with people watching, reasonable eateries, and the major sightseeing attractions. From the central train station to the Duomo, it's just four stops on a direct Metro line (yellow line 3, direction "S. Donato") to Metro: Duomo. There is no self-service laundry in the center.

**Hotel Speronari** is perfectly located, safe, and fairly quiet, with 32 bright, clean rooms on a great pedestrian street full of delis and food shops. Enjoy a free cappuccino upon arrival. Note that this is a one-star hotel. If you want an elevator, air-conditioning, and more comfort, please choose any of the pricier hotels listed below. (S-L80,000, Ss-L95,000, D-L120,000, Db-L160,000, T-L155,000, Tb-L215,000, Qb-L240,000, these discounted prices promised through 2001 with this book—speak up, CC:VM but L5,000 off per person per night if you pay cash, lots of stairs, no breakfast, ceiling fans, 200 meters off Piazza Duomo, Via Speronari 4, 20123 Milano, tel. 02-8646-1125,

# Milan Center

1. ELEVATOR TO ROOF
2. STAIRS TO ROOF
3. CIT TRAVEL AGENCY, TEL. CENTER, McD's & TAURUS
4. HOTEL SPERONARI
5. OPERA TICKETS
6. LONDON HOTEL
7. HOTEL GIULIO CESARE
8. HOTEL GRAND DUCA DI YORK
9. HOTEL SANTA MARTA
10. HOTEL GRITTI
11. HOTEL ROVELLO
12. STAR HOTEL
13. HOTEL NUOVO
14. ANTICA LOCANDA MERCANTI
15. ODEON GELATERIA
16. PECK GROCERY & HOTEL SPADARI
17. PECK ROSTICCERIA
18. PECK SNACK BAR
19. CIAO RISTORANTE
20. PIZZERIA DOGANA
21. PIZZERIA CALAFURIA UNIONE
22. REST. FAMILIARE CIMBRACCOLA
23. TRATTORIA MILANESE
24. PIZZERIA DOLLARO
25. BIG BANKS
26. PINACOTECA AMBROSIANA

fax 02-7200-3178, run by the friendly Isoni family: father
Paolo and John Paolo, Maurizio, Carolina, and Fara.) For breakfast, I like the Chicco D'Oro Bar across the intersection (from
7:00, closed Sun), or grab a fresh brioche at the Princi bakery
next door to have with your coffee in the Speronari lobby. If
you're flying out of Malpensa airport, they can get you there
via car much cheaper than a taxi—which charges L150,000
(2 people-L80,000, 3 people-L100,000, 4 people-L120,000,
request 1 day in advance).

**Hotel Grand Duca di York** is a real hotel with 33 simple
rooms and lavish public spaces oddly stuck in the middle of banks
and big-city starkness three blocks southwest of Piazza Duomo
(Sb-L180,000, Db-L270,000, Tb-L300,000, includes breakfast,
CC:VMA, air-con, elevator, closed Aug, near Metro: Piazza
Cordusio at Via Moneta 1, 20123 Milano, tel. 02-874-863,
fax 02-869-0344, SE).

**Hotel Santa Marta** is a shiny little hotel on a small street
with 15 fresh, tranquil, and spacious rooms (Db-L230,000 most
of year but L300,000 during conventions and as low as L190,000,
includes breakfast, CC:VM, air-con, elevator, closed Aug, Via
Santa Marta 4, 20123 Milano, tel. 02-804-567, fax 02-8645-2661,
e-mail: htls.marta@tiscalinet.it).

**Hotel Gritti**, facing a peaceful square just off Via Torino, is
a bright, classy, professionally run three-star hotel that comes
with a sleepy dog, Boris (48 rooms, Sb-L176,000, Db-L253,000,
Tb-L363,000, includes big breakfast, same price all seasons, open
year-round, family deals, CC:VMA but 10 percent off with cash,
elevator, air-con, two blocks southwest of Piazza Duomo, Piazza
S. Maria Beltrade 4, 20123 Milano, tel. 02-801-056, fax 02-8901-
0999, e-mail: hotel.gritti@iol.it, SE).

**Hotel Nuovo**, which is one step above a youth hostel, has
renovated some of its 36 rooms. It's central on a noisy square
east of the Duomo near a pedestrian street (D-L80,000–100,000,
Db-L150,000, CC:VM, no breakfast, some air-con, TV and
phones in room, request third floor for less noise, no public
space, Piazza Beccaria 6, tel. 02-8646-4444, fax 02-7200-1752,
Joseph SE).

**Splurge:** The **Hotel Spadari** is for art lovers. Designed by
a Milanese artist, the furnishings of the 39 rooms—the V-shaped
headboards, billowing drapes, big paintings, and even the designer
doors—are striking but tasteful. Well located, the hotel is in the
midst of the three Peck eateries (see below), just two blocks from
Piazza Duomo (standard Db-L400,000–500,000, the standards
are great, no need for pricier suites, includes breakfast, CC:VM,
quiet for a hotel in the center, open year-round, Via Spadari 11,
tel. 02-7200-2371, fax 02-861-184, www.spadarihotel.com, e-mail:
spadari@tin.it).

## Sleeping between La Scala and Sforza Castle

**London Hotel** is a fine little 30-room hotel with all the comforts on a side street. It's run by the friendly Gambino family (S-L140,000, Sb-L160,000, D-L200,000, Db-L250,000, Db in July-L200,000, T-L230,000 Tb-L310,000, breakfast-L12,000, CC:VM but 10 percent off with cash except during special events, elevator, TVs, phones, air-con, closed Aug, near Metro: Cairoli at Via Rovello 3, 20121 Milano, tel. 02-7202-0166, tel. & fax 02-805-7037, e-mail: hotel.london@traveleurope.it, Tanya and Licia SE).

**Hotel Giulio Cesare** (across the street from London Hotel) is bigger, basic, and impersonal but quiet and comfortable (Sb-L180,000, Db-L300,000, CC:VMA, air-con, Via Rovello 10, 20121 Milano, tel. 02-7200-3915, fax 02-7200-2179, www .hotelgiuliocesare.com).

**Antica Locanda dei Mercanti** feels like a library in heaven, well located and seriously quiet (no TVs, lots of books). It lacks public spaces and a breakfast area, but comes with fresh flowers in each of its 10 rooms (standard Db-L230,000, master Db-L300,000, Db with air-con and terrace-L400,000, optional L15,000 breakfast served in room, CC:VM, fans, elevator, no young children, no sign—only a name on doorbell at their address—Via San Tomaso 6, Metro: Cordusio, tel. 02-805-4080, fax 02-805-4090, www.locanda.it, e-mail: locanda@locanda.it).

**Hotel Star** is a comfortable 30-room place with fancy modern plumbing (Sb-L200,000, Db-L290,000, includes big breakfast, CC:VMA, air-con, fridge, Via dei Bossi 5, tel. 02-801-501, fax 02-861-787, www.starhotel.it).

**Hotel Rovello** has three stars and 10 quiet, high-ceilinged rooms, some with hardwood floors and wood-beamed ceilings (Db-L320,000, prices can drop dramatically for same-day requests—call from station, CC:VM, breakfast, elevator, air-con, Via Rovello 18, 20121 Milano, tel. 02-8646-4654, fax 02-7202-3656, e-mail: htlrovel@tin.it).

## Sleeping near the Train Station

For pure convenience and price, this is a handy, if dreary, area. The neighborhood between the train station and Corso Buenos Aires, in spite of its shady characters in the park and its 55-year-old prostitutes after dark, is reasonably safe. Many soulless business hotels have desperately discounted prices for those who just drop in during slow times. Just walk down Via Scarlatti (leave the station's upper hall—with your back to the tracks—to the left). Decent options include **"The Best" Hotel** (19 rooms, Sb-L110,000, Db-L160,000, CC:VM, reconfirm reservations, Via B. Marcello 83, tel. 02-2940-4757), **Hotel Andreola** (4-star business hotel with occasional door-breaker prices, Via Scarlatti 24, tel. 02-670-9141), **Hotel Valley** (small, dark, inexpensive,

Via Soperga 19, tel. 02-669-2777), and **Hotel Virgilio** (inexpensive business hotel, Via P.L. da Palestrina 30, tel. 02-669-1337).

# Eating in Milan

This is a fast-food city, but fast food in a fashion capital isn't a burger and fries. The bars, delis, *rosticcerie*, and self-service cafeterias cater to people with plenty of taste and more money than time. You'll find delightful eateries all over town (but many close in Aug for vacation). Free munchies appear late in the afternoon in most bars. A L3,000 beer (if you're either likable or discreet) can become a light meal.

Breakfast is a bad value in hotels and fun in bars. It's OK to quasi-picnic. Bring in a banana (or whatever) and order a toasted ham-and-cheese *panino* (*calda* = hot/toasted) or croissant with your cappuccino.

### *Eating near the Duomo and Recommended Hotels*

**Peck** consists of three very classy places located within a block of each other and two blocks of the Duomo. Glide aristocratically—as people who shopped here 100 years ago did—through Peck's gourmet grocery (Mon 15:00–19:30, Tue–Sat 8:45–19:30, closed Sun, Via Spadari 9, fancy wine downstairs, fancy coffee shop upstairs). Peck's elegant *rosticcería* sells local cuisine by weight to go; have a superb picnic dinner in your hotel room (order by the *etto*—100-gram unit, one-tenth of a kilo, or quarter pound, Tue–Fri 8:45–14:30, 16:00–19:30, Sat 8:00–13:15, 15:45–19:30, Sun 8:00–13:00, closed Mon, nearby at Via C. Cantu, off Via Orefici). At the **Peck Snack Bar**, order at the bar, take the bill to the cashier, pay, pick up your food, and find a stool surrounded by the local office crowd (Mon–Sat 7:30–21:00, closed Sun, free appetizers with drink at bar, pasta-L9,000, veggies-L7,000, off Via Orefici at Via Victor Hugo 4).

For a low-stress, affordable meal on Piazza Duomo, eat at **Ciao**, a shiny, modern, second-floor self-serve cafeteria (daily 11:30–15:00, 18:30–23:00, pasta-L5,500, meatier courses-L12,000, view tables from top "terrace" floor, easy public WC). Other Ciao restaurants are on Via Dante (just off Piazza Cordusio, outdoor seating on pedestrian-only street) and on Piazza San Babila (at end of pedestrian street—Corso Vittorio Emanuele II—behind Duomo; self-serve cafeteria is at the back). Fast-food cheapskates enjoy the best people watching in Milan inside the Galleria at **McDonald's** (salad/pasta plate and tall OJ for L10,000).

For a fun adventure, assemble an elegant dinner picnic by hitting the colorful shops on Via Speronari (off Via Torino, a block southwest of Piazza Duomo, classy *rosticcerie*, cheese, bread, and produce shops).

**Pizzeria Dogana** offers L12,000 pizzas and indoor/outdoor seating (closed Mon and Aug, a block from the Duomo at Via Dogana 3). Worth the two-blocks-farther walk, the local favorite, **Ristorante Pizzeria Calafuria Unione**, serves tasty L12,000 pizzas in a nonsmoking room (Mon–Sat 11:00–15:00, 19:00–24:00, closed Sun and Aug, near where Via Falcone hits Via dell' Unione at Via dell' Unione 8, tel. 02-866-103).

At **Ristorante Familiare della Cimbraccola** the atmosphere is more memorable than the food. Stefanini Arnaldo, with his imaginary mother in the kitchen (she's 85 and still prepares through the afternoon), throws his entire menu at his guests— a series of uninspired appetizers, pastas, and entrées; endless wine, water, coffee, and *grappa* (fire water); and three desserts—all for L30,000. The food is Tuscan and plain. After six or eight courses you'll get a big plate of meats. The walls are plastered with model ships, pipes, dusty paper money, and pins for each hungry client on a U.S. map (Mon–Sat 19:00–22:30, closed Sun and Aug, an olive toss off Via Dante, midway between Duomo and Fortress at Via S. Tomaso 8, tel. 02-869-2250).

**Trattoria Milanese**, a classy family-run place, is ideal for a L60,000 splurge. It has an enthusiastic and local clientele (the restaurant didn't even bother to get a phone until 1988). Expect a Milanese ambience, traditional cuisine, and surly waiters (opens at 19:30, reservations necessary after 20:30, closed Tue and Aug, pasta-L15,000, meat-L25,000, Via Santa Marta 11, 5-minute walk from the Duomo near Piazza Borromei, tel. 02-8645-1991).

**Ristorante/Pizzeria Al Dollaro** is a mod, happy place with well-fed locals (Mon–Sat 12:00–15:00, 19:00–23:00, closed Sun and Aug, air-con, smoke-free section, 4 blocks south of the Duomo at Via Paolo da Cannobio 11, tel. 02-869-2432).

Floodlit Mary gazes down from the top of the Duomo on the **Odeon Gelateria** for good reason (next to McDonald's on Piazza Duomo, facing the Duomo, open nightly until 01:00).

# Transportation Connections—Milan

**By train to: Venice** (departures :05 after each hour, 3 hrs), **Florence** (hrly, 3 hrs, also check schedule for trains going to Rome and Naples—these stop in Florence), **Genoa** (hrly, 2 hrs), **Rome** (hrly, 4.5 hrs), **Brindisi** (4/day, 10–12 hrs), **Cinque Terre** (hrly, 3–4 hrs to La Spezia, some direct trains to Monterosso, sometimes changing in Genoa; trains from La Spezia to the villages go nearly hrly), **Varenna** on Lake Como (the small line to Lecco/Sondrio/ Tirano leaves every 2 hours for the 1-hour trip to Varenna— maybe 8:15, 9:15, 12:15, 14:16, 16:15, 18:00, 19:10, 20:15), **Como** (around :25 after each hour, 30 min, ferries go from Como to Varenna until 19:00). Train info: tel. 147-888-088.

**International destinations: Amsterdam** (4/day, 14 hrs), **Barcelona** (2 changes, 17 hrs—before paying extra for Pablo

Casals express, consider flying), **Bern** (7/day, 3 hrs), **Frankfurt** (5/day, 9 hrs), **London** (2/day, 18 hrs), **Munich** (5/day, 8 hrs), **Nice** (5/day, 7–10 hrs), **Paris** (4/day, 7 hrs), **Vienna** (4/day, 14 hrs).

## Milan's Airports

To get flight information for either airport or the current phone number of your airline, call 027-485-2200 (www .sea-aeroportimilano.it).

**Malpensa:** Most international flights land at the cozy Malpensa airport, 45 kilometers northwest of Milan. Customs guards fan you through, and even the sniffing dog seems friendly. The airport has a bank (Banca di Milano, daily 8:00–20:00, fine rates), a TI (daily 8:00–18:00, tel. 02-5858-1192), and a bus/ train information office (consider buying train tickets and checking departure times for train trips from Milan). Buy a phone card and confirm your hotel reservation.

The Malpensa Express train zips travelers between Malpensa and central Milan's Cadorna station (it's both a Metro stop and a small train station), closer to the Duomo than the central train station (L15,000, sometimes discounted to L9,000 for Alitalia and KLM passengers, 40 min, 2/hrly, departing airport at :15 and :45 past the hour, departing Cadorna at :20 and :50 past the hour, runs from about 6:00 to 24:00, no railpasses, tel. 02-27763 or 02-8447-7500, www.malpensaexpress.com). Purchase your ticket before you board or pay L5,000 extra to buy it on the train.

A shuttle bus connects Malpensa twice hourly with Milan's central train station (L14,000, 50 min, from Piazza Luigi di Savoia at east side of Milan's train station the bus runs 5:30–22:00, from airport 7:00–22:15, tel. 02-8447-5001).

Taxis into Milan cost L150,000 ($75).

**Linate:** Most European flights fly into Linate, eight kilo- meters east of Milan. The airport has a bank (Banca Popolare di Milano, just past customs, decent rates) and a TI (daily 8:30–20:00, tel. 02-7020-0443). Linate is linked with the central train station by STAM buses (Piazza Luigi di Savoia on east side of Milan's central station, buy L5,000 tickets from driver, 2/hrly, runs 5:40–21:00, tel. 02-6698-4509); from the station, take the Metro or a taxi to your hotel. Taxis from Linate to the Duomo cost L35,000 ($18).

**Between Malpensa and Linate:** A shuttle bus runs hourly between the airports (L18,000, 75 min).

# LAKE COMO
# (LAGO DI COMO)

Commune with nature where Italy is welded to the Alps, in the lovely Italian Lakes District. The million-lire question is: Which lake? For the best mix of accessibility, scenery, and offbeatness, Lake Como is my choice. And the sleepy midlake town of Varenna is the handiest base of operations. Here you'll get a complete dose of Italian-lakes wonder and aristocratic-old-days romance. Bustling Milan, just an hour away, doesn't even exist. Now it's your turn to be *chiuso per ferie* (closed for vacation).

Lake Como, lined with elegant, 19th-century villas, crowned by snowcapped mountains, and buzzing with ferries, hydrofoils, and little passenger ships, is a good place to take a break from the intensity and obligatory turnstile culture of central Italy. It seems half the travelers you'll meet have tossed their itineraries into the lake and are actually relaxing.

Today the hazy, lazy lake's only serious industry is tourism. Thousands of lakeside residents travel daily to nearby Lugano, in Switzerland, to find work. The lake's isolation and flat economy have left it pretty much the way the 19th-century Romantic poets described it.

## Planning Your Time
If relaxation's not on your agenda, Lake Como shouldn't be either. Even though there are no essential activities, plan for at least two nights so you'll have an uninterrupted day to see how slow you can get your pulse.

Lake Como is Milan's quick getaway, and the charming little village of Varenna is the gateway. With its handy connections to Milan and midlake destinations, Varenna is my favorite home base.

# Lake Como

## Arrival in Varenna

I zip directly by train from Milan to Varenna, set up, and limit my activities to midlake (Varenna and Bellagio). From Milan's central station, catch a train heading for Sondrio or Tirano (often confused with Torino—wrong city). Be certain your train stops in Varenna; look at the fine print on the *Partenze* (departures) schedule posted at Milan's train station to make sure Varenna is listed. Trains leave about hourly (at :15 past each hour). Sit on the left for maximum lake-view beauty. Get off at Varenna-Esino. (Note that the name Varenna-Esino appears only at the station. Train schedules list simply Varenna. Same place.)

You can also get to Varenna from Milan via the town of Como. Trains take you from Milan to Como (50-minute rides usually leaving at :25 past each hour), where you can catch a boat for the two-hour ride (L10,000) up the lake to Varenna.

# Varenna

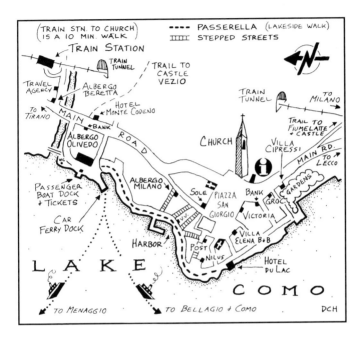

(TRAIN STN. TO CHURCH IS A 10 MIN. WALK)

---- PASSERELLA (LAKESIDE WALK)
Ⅲ STEPPED STREETS

N

TRAIN STATION

TRAIN TUNNEL
TRAVEL AGENCY
ALBERGO BERETTA
HOTEL MONTE CODENO
TO TIRANO
MAIN
ROAD
BANK
ALBERGO OLIVEDO
WC

TRAIL TO CASTLE VEZIO

TRAIN TUNNEL
TO MILANO
TRAIL TO FIUMELATTE + CASTLE
VILLA CIPRESSI
CHURCH
MAIN RD.
TO LECCO

PASSENGER BOAT DOCK + TICKETS
CAR FERRY DOCK
ALBERGO MILANO
SOLE
PIAZZA SAN GIORGIO
BANK
VICTORIA
GARDENS
GROC.
TO LECCO

HARBOR
POST
NILUS
VILLA ELENA B+B
HOTEL DU LAC

L A K E        C O M O

TO MENAGGIO          TO BELLAGIO + COMO          DCH

## Getting around Lake Como

**By Boat:** Lago di Como is well served by boats and hydrofoils. The lake service is divided into three parts: north-south from Como to Colico; midlake between Varenna, Bellagio, Menaggio, and Cadenabbia (Villa Carlotta); and the southeastern arm to Lecco. Unless you're going through Como you'll probably limit your cruising to the midlake service (boat info: tel. 031-579-211 or toll free 800-551-801). Boats go about hourly between Varenna, Menaggio, and Bellagio (L4,700 per hop, 15 min).

Passengers pay the same for car or passenger ferries but 50 percent more for the enclosed, stuffy, speedy, but less scenic hydrofoil. The free schedule (at TI, hotel, or boat dock) lists times and prices. Stopovers aren't allowed, and there's no break for round-trips, so buy a ticket for each ride. The one-day, L13,000 midlake pass saves you money if you make three rides.

Boat schedule literacy tips: *Feriale* = workdays, Monday–Saturday. *Festivo* = Sunday and holidays. *Partenze da* = departing from. *Autotraghetto* = car ferry. *Aliscafo* = hydrofoil. *Battello* = passenger-only ferry.

**By Car:** With the parking problems, constant traffic jams, and expensive car ferries, this is no place to drive if you don't need to. While you can easily drive around the lake, the road is narrow, congested, and lined by privacy-seeking walls, hedges, and tall fences. It costs L16,500 to take your car onto a ferry. And parking is rarely easy where you need it, especially in Bellagio. Park in Varenna and cruise. White lines (near Varenna's ferry dock and south of the monastery) indicate free parking; blue lines mean metered parking (L1,500/hr, 2 hrs max, overnight plus 2 hrs is OK); and yellow, residents only.

## Sights—Lake Como

▲▲▲**Varenna**—This town of 800 people is the best of all lake worlds. Easily accessible by train, on the less-driven side of the lake, Varenna has a romantic promenade, a tiny harbor, narrow lanes, and its own villa. It's the right place to savor a lakeside cappuccino or *aperitivo*. There's wonderfully little to do here. This place is quiet at night. The *passerella* (lakeside walk) is adorned with caryatid lovers pressing silently against each other in the shadows.

Varenna's TI is on the main square to the right of the church (Pro Varenna, Tue–Sat 10:00–12:30, 15:30–18:30, Sun 10:00–12:30, Nov–April only Sat–Sun 10:00–12:30, tel. 0341-830-367, www.varennaitaly.com). Two banks, a cash machine, and a small post office (Mon–Fri 8:00–13:30, Sat 8:00–11:30) are also on the main square.

If you need a beach, you'll find a tiny one if you leave the main square through the archway (to the right of Hotel Victoria) and go straight down the stairs. In 2001, the government may "install" a new beach near the dock, replacing the original beach flooded out years ago by stormy weather.

A steep trail leads to Varenna's ruined hilltop castle, Castello di Vezio—start at the stairs to the left of the Hotel Monte Codeno and figure on 30 minutes one-way (L4,000, daily 10:00–18:00 in summer, closed when rainy, spring and fall open only Sat–Sun 10:00–18:00, closed Oct–April, tel. 033-546-5186). The castle comes with a fine café at its entrance and a peaceful, traffic-free, one-chapel town.

The town of **Fiumelatte**, a kilometer south of Varenna, was named for its milky river. It's the shortest river in Italy at 277 meters (800 feet) and runs—like most of the local tourist industry—only April through September. The "La Sorgente del Fiumelatte" brochure, available at Varenna's TI, lays out a walk from Varenna to the Fiumelatte to the castle and back. It's a 30-minute hike to the source (*sorgente*) of the milky river (at Varenna's monastery, take high road, drop into peaceful cemetery, and climb steps to wooded trail leading to peaceful and refreshing cave where river appears). For a longer lakeside hike, ask about the *Sentiera di Viadante* (hike one-way up the lake and return by train).

Two manicured lakeside gardens—Villa Cipressi and the

adjacent monastery—are tourable for a L5,000 combo ticket available at Villa Cipressi or the monastery (L3,000 for one garden only, March–Oct daily 9:00–18:00).

For bus and boat tours, consider Varenna's travel agency, I Viaggi del Tivano, next to Albergo Beretta below the train station. They book planes, trains, and automobiles and can offer half-day and day-long tours of the region (Mon–Fri 8:30–12:00, 15:00–19:00, Sat 9:00–12:00, CC:VM, Via per Esino 3, tel. 0341-814-009, e-mail: sberet@tin.it, helpful Silvia SE).

▲**Bellagio**—The self-proclaimed "Pearl of the Lake" is a classy combination of tidiness and Old World elegance. If you don't mind that "tramp in a palace" feeling, it's a fine place to surround yourself with the more adventurous of the posh travelers and shop for ties and umbrellas. The heavy curtains between the arcades keep the visitors and their poodles from sweating.

Steep-stepped lanes rise from the harborfront. While Johnny Walker and jewelry sell best at lake level, the locals shop up the hill. Piazza Chiesa, near the top of town, has a worth-a-look church and the TI (Mon and Wed–Sat 9:00–12:00, 15:00–18:00, closed Sun and Tue, tel. 031-950-204, e-mail: prombell@tin.it). If you need a destination, you can tour the Villa Serbelloni Park— overlooking the town—with a guide (L9,000, 2 tours daily April– Oct, 90 min, ask at TI).

For something offbeat, clink glasses with Tony the Wine King. He runs a wild little cantina behind the camera shop near the car-ferry dock (daily 11:00–13:30, 15:00–19:30, Salita Genaz- zini 3, tel. 031-950-935). Tony, who speaks a little English, greets you with a smile, an empty glass, and 10 or 15 open bottles of wine and booze to taste. The tasting's free. After 56 years in his cantina, he looks darn good.

The administrative capital of the midlake region, Bellagio is located where the two southern legs of the lake split off. For an easy break in a park with a great view, wander right on out to the crotch. Meander past the rich and famous Hotel Villa Serbelloni, past the little Ortofrutta market (get fruit and juice for the view- point, Tue–Sat 8:00–12:30, 14:30–18:30), and walk five minutes to the Punta Spartivento, literally "the point that divides the wind." You'll find a Renoir atmosphere complete with a bar/restaurant, a tiny harbor, and a chance to sit on a park bench and gaze north past Menaggio, Varenna, and the end of the lake to the Swiss Alps.

For another stroll, head south from the car-ferry dock down the tree-shaded promenade. Ten minutes later, you'll hit Bellagio's beach.

For more active entertainment, consider a downhill mountain- bike run. Cavalcalario Club carts you uphill, then lets you go (L55,000–65,000 includes bike rental, several itineraries, reservations necessary, tel. & fax 031-964-814, www.bellagio-mountains.it).

## Bellagio

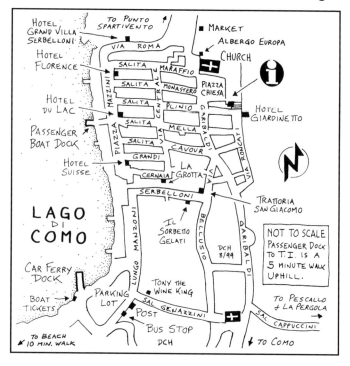

Bellagio has two docks a few minutes' walk apart—the northern dock is for the passenger-only ferry (*battello*) and the hydrofoil (*aliscafo*), and the southern dock is for the car ferry, which also takes foot passengers (*autotraghetto*). To make sure you're waiting at the right dock for the boat you want to take, check the boat schedule carefully (posted near dock, free brochure from kiosk at dock). The schedule is divided into three different schedules: *battello* (passengers only), *aliscafo* (passengers in a hurry), and *autotraghetto* (passengers and cars). If you have questions, ask at the kiosk near either dock.

▲**Menaggio**—Menaggio has more urban bulk than its neighbors. Since the lake is too dirty for swimming, consider its fine public pool. This is the starting point for a few hikes. Only 25 years ago these trails were used by cigarette smugglers, sneaking at night from Switzerland back into Italy with tax-free cigarettes. The hostel (see "Sleeping," below) has information about catching the bus to trailheads on nearby Mount Grona. The hostel also rents bikes for a 40-kilometer, four-hour bike trip: Pedal 15 level kilometers from the hostel to Argegno, catch the lift to 2,500-foot-high Pigra (L5,000 with bike), and coast scenically back to Lake Lugano and then 10 kilometers along the traffic-filled road home to Menaggio. This physically demanding ride can be scary because of traffic.

**Villa Carlotta**—This is the best of Lake Como's famed villas (L12,000, April–Sept daily 9:00–18:00, Oct daily 9:00–12:00, 14:00–16:30, closed Nov–March, tel. 034-440-405). I see the lakes as a break from Italy's art, but if you're in need of a place that charges admission, Villa Carlotta offers an elegant neoclassical interior, a famous Canova statue, and a garden (its highlight, best in spring). If you're touring one villa on the lake, this is the best. Nearby Tremezzo and Cadenabbia are pleasant lakeside resorts an easy walk away. Boats serve all three places.

**Isola Comacina**—This remote little island (just south of Bellagio) offers peace, ancient church foundations, goats, sheep, and a million-lire view of Lago di Como. It takes 30 minutes to walk around the island but longer to savor it. Bring a picnic or try the snack bar at the dock. Look for trips to Isola Comacina on the Colico-Como schedule (listed in Lago di Como boat timetable brochure, free at ticket booths at ferry docks). The *isola* is accessible from Varenna (1 hr), Menaggio (45 min), or Bellagio (30 min). Check return times carefully (Como-Colico direction) and don't miss your boat. Usually only one trip a day each way works out for a visit.

**Como**—On the southwest tip of the lake, Como has a good, traffic-free old town, an interesting Gothic/Renaissance cathedral, and a pleasant lakefront with a promenade (TI tel. 031-330-0111). It's an easy walk from the boat dock to the train station (from Milan in 30 minutes, usually leaving at :25 past each hour). Boats leave Como about hourly for midlake (ferries-L12,600, 2 hrs; hydrofoils-L18,100, 1 hr; tel. 031-579-211).

## Sleeping and Eating on Lake Como
### (L2,000 = about $1, country code: 39)
Sleep Code: **S** = Single, **D** = Double/Twin, **T** = Triple, **Q** = Quad, **b** = bathroom, **t** = toilet only, **s** = shower only, **CC** = Credit Card (**V**isa, **M**asterCard, **A**mex), **SE** = Speaks English, **NSE** = No English.

The area is tight in August, snug in July, and wide open most of the rest of the year. Many places close in winter. All places listed are family run and have lake-view rooms, and some English is spoken. If you're expecting friendliness, especially during peak season, you'll be disappointed. Enjoy the view. View rooms are given (sometimes for no extra cost) to those who telephone reservations and request a *"camera con vista."* If ever I were to kill, it would be here . . . for the view. Prices get soft off-season (Nov–May). The Varenna TI can find private rooms.

## Sleeping in Varenna
### (zip code: 23829)

**Albergo Olivedo**, facing the ferry dock, is a tidy, elegant, old hotel with old-time furniture and squeaky hardwood floors. Many rooms have glorious little lake-view balconies. It's a fine place to hang out and watch the children, boats, and sun come and go (prices vary with season and views: S-L50,000–105,000, D-L110,000–130,000, Db-L130,000–170,000, includes breakfast, some lumpy mattresses, closed mid-Nov–mid-Dec, tel. & fax 0341-830-115, www.olivedo.it, e-mail: olivedo@tin.it, hardworking Laura SE). In May, June, July, and September, half-pension (dinner) is required—and rarely regretted—with the best rooms (L40,000 per person for a tasty dinner).

**Albergo Milano**, located right in the old town, is great. Friendly but non-English speaking Amelia obviously loves serving people. Each of the eight rooms is comfortable and comes with super plumbing (Db-L170,000, or L200,000 with breakfast, discounts for 3-night stays, CC:VMA, Via XX Settembre 29, tel. & fax 0341-830-298, U.S. fax 781/634-0094, www.varenna.net, e-mail: hotelmilano@varenna.net, son Giovanni SE). Lakeside rooms 1 and 2 are small and have royal balconies (best in sunny weather). Lakeside rooms 5 and 6 are bigger but have small balconies. This place whispers *luna di miele* (honeymoon).

**Hotel Monte Codeno**, with 11 pleasant rooms and no views, is on the main road between the train station and lake (2 Sb-L110,000, Db-L150,000, includes breakfast buffet, CC:VMA, attached restaurant serves fresh fish and a curious L35,000 "Rick Steves" menu, Via della Croce 2, tel. 0341-830-123, fax 0341-815-227, e-mail: ferrcas@tin.it, Marina Castelli SE). Ask about their apartments (as low as L150,000 for 2 people, up to L360,000 for 6 people, good for families). At any of their accommodations, prices drop for three-night stays.

**Albergo Beretta**, on the main road a block below the station, has 10 decent rooms, several with balconies (D-L90,000, Db-L115,000, breakfast-L10,000, CC:VMA, room #9 has best view, coffee shop on ground floor, Via per Esino 1, tel. & fax 0341-830-132, e-mail: hotelberetta@iol.it, Tosca NSE, daughter Julia SE).

**Villa Elena**, a grandmotherly, low-energy place on the main square, offers the best budget beds in town. English-speaking Signora Vitali rents her four rooms at the same price—room #1 has a bathroom and view terrace; the others don't even have sinks (Db-L80,000 with fine breakfast, L70,000 without, the vine-covered facade on Piazza San Giorgio near Via San Giovanni, tel. 0341-830-575). **Albergo del Sole**, a restaurant on the same square, will likely offer six rooms in 2001 (Piazza San Giorgio 17, tel. 0341-815-218, NSE).

**Larger Hotels:** Of the following hotels, the first is the best value. **Villa Cipressi**, in a huge, quiet garden, is a sprawling, centuries-old mansion with 35 classy rooms and a garden people pay to see (Sb-L135,000, Db-L170,000, Db with view-L190,000, Qb suite-L300,000, extra bed-L55,000, includes breakfast, CC:VM, garden access, elevator, Via IV Novembre 18, tel. 0341-830-113, fax 0341-830-401, SE). If you're looking for elegance, this beats Albergo Milano.

Both of Varenna's four-star hotels offer view terraces, some balconies, and suites (at an additional cost). Close to the lake, **Hotel du Lac** is stylish and sleek, with air-conditioning (Db-L310,000, add about L40,000 for view, includes breakfast, CC:VM, Via del Prestino 4, tel. 0341-830-238, fax 0341-831-081, SE). **Hotel Victoria**, on the main square, has more Old World character and lacks air-conditioning, but has a big view garden that tumbles down toward the lake (43 rooms, Db-L240,000, add L60,000 for view, includes breakfast, CC:VM, possibly a pool for 2001, Piazza San Giorgio 5, tel. 0341-81511, fax 0341-830-722, SE).

### Eating in Varenna
**On the waterfront:** The **Albergo Olivedo's** restaurant serves fine food near the ferry dock (L40,000–60,000 meals, daily 12:15–14:00, 19:15–21:15, CC:VM). **Vecchia Varenna** on the harbor is romantic and respected but pricey (L70,000 meals, daily 12:30–14:00, 20:00–22:00, closed Mon–Tue in winter, CC:VM). For the same great view but much cheaper eating, the harborfront **Nilus Bar** serves dinner crepes, salads, and hot sandwiches with a smile (daily 12:00–23:00, Dec–Feb only Sat–Sun). For cold, sweet, and fruity treats, check out the harborfront **La Frulleria/Il Gelato.**

**On Piazza San Giorgio:** The **Ristorante del Sole** serves tasty Naples-style pizzas at Piazza San Giorgio 17 (L9,000–15,000, daily 12:00–14:30, 19:00–22:00, closed Wed in winter, garden in back, tel. 0341-815-218). Also on the main square, **Victoria Grill** (under the fancy Hotel Victoria) has a classier ambience and serves good, well-priced meals and pizza (daily 12:00–14:00, 19:00–22:00, closed Mon in winter, CC:VM). The two grocery stores, nearly next door and just off the main square, have all you need for a classy balcony or breakwater picnic dinner (daily 7:30–12:30, 15:30–19:30).

### Sleeping and Eating in Bellagio
### (zip code: 22021)
The first five are on the waterfront.

**Hotel Suisse**, next to the fancy places, has simple rooms, hardwood floors, fine bathrooms, unpredictable beds, and some great views and balconies (Db-L140,000 with this book in 2001, breakfast-L16,000, CC:VMA, Piazza Mazzini 8, tel. 031-950-335, fax 031-951-755, e-mail: hsuisse@tiscalinet.it).

**Hotel du Lac**, a good splurge, comes with 48 rooms, a roof

garden, and old-time elegance with no loss of comfort (Sb-
L170,000, Db-L300,000, includes breakfast, view rooms cost
the same as viewless rooms, CC:VM, parking-L20,000, air-con,
TVs, mini-bars, closed Nov–March, Piazza Mazzini 32, tel.
031-950-320, fax 031-951-624, www.bellagiohoteldulac.com,
e-mail: dulac@tin.it, Leoni family SE).

**Hotel Florence**, a few doors away and 150 years old, is
family run and similar, with hardwood, pastels, and a rich touch
of Old World elegance (30 rooms, Db-L260,000–350,000 depending on view and balcony, Db suite-L400,000–450,000, includes
breakfast, CC:VMA, closed Nov–March, elevator, hand-held
showers only, tel. 031-950-342, fax 031-951-722, www.bellagio
.co.nz, e-mail: hotflore@tin.it, Ketzlar family SE). Enjoy live jazz
in the Florence Bar on Sunday nights.

**Hotel Metropole**, a tired but grand old place, dominates
the waterfront with 42 reasonably comfortable rooms and plush
public spaces (Db-L180,000, L200,000 with lake view, CC:VMA,
elevator, fridge, tel. 031-950-409, fax 031-951-534).

**Grand Hotel Villa Serbelloni**, a famous 19th-century
palace, comes with history, doormen, two pools (inside and out),
a garden, and elite clientele (83 rooms, standard Db-L241,000,
deluxe Db-L433,000, executive double-L542,000, pricier rooms
have views, CC:VM, air-con and all the comforts, tel. 031-950-
216, fax 031-951-529, www.villaserbelloni.com).

The last two places are inland.

**Hotel Giardinetto**, at the top of town near the TI, 100 steps
above the waterfront, offers 14 squeaky-clean and quiet rooms.
The rooms are stark but the breezy, peaceful garden is a joy
(S-L55,000, D-L80,000, Db-L100,000, Tb-L135,000, breakfast-
L12,000, no CC but personal checks and traveler's checks OK,
Via Roncati 12, tel. 031-950-168, Eugene and Laura Ticozzi SE).

**Albergo Europa**, run with low energy, is in a concrete
annex behind a restaurant, away from the waterfront charm
but offering affordable comfort (10 rooms, Db-L130,000,
CC:VMA, balconies lack views but are quiet, a block from TI
at Via Roma 21, tel. & fax 031-950-471, e-mail: albeuropa
@tiscalinet.it, family Marchesi).

**Eating:** For a good backstreet L30,000 dinner, consider
**Trattoria S. Giacomo** (daily 12:00–14:30, 19:00–21:30, closed
Tue Sept–June, CC:VM, Salita Serbelloni 45, tel. 031-950-329).
For pizza and pasta, try **La Grotta** (daily 12:00–14:30, 19:00–
01:00, closed Mon Oct–June, Salita Cernaia 14, tel. 031-951-152).
Or get picnic supplies at **Gastronomica Mini Market** (at Via
Centrale and Via Monastero, uphill from Hotel Florence).
You'll find picnic benches at spots along the waterfront in
town, lining the promenade south of town, and at the dramatic
Punto Spartivento park north of town.

## Sleeping in Menaggio

**La Primula Youth Hostel** is a rare hostel. Family run for 18 years by Ty and Paola, it caters to a quiet, savor-the-lakes crowd. Located 300 meters south of the Menaggio dock, it has a view terrace; games galore; a members' kitchen; a washing machine; bike, canoe, and kayak rentals (L20,000 a day, L35,000 for non-hostelers); plus easy parking and Internet access. (Closed 10:00–17:00 and Nov–mid-March, L21,000 per night in a 4- to 6-bed room with sheets and breakfast, L23,000 per bed with private plumbing, hearty dinners with a local flair are only L17,000; reserve dinner by 18:00—because of ferry schedules, only possible for people sleeping in Menaggio.) Ty and Paola's newsletter advertises their interesting classes and excursions. The bike ride described under "Sights—Menaggio," above, is a favorite with hostelers. Show this book for a free half-hour Internet connection. (Ostello La Primula, Via IV Novembre 86, 22017 Menaggio, tel. & fax 0344-32356, fax 034-131-677, www.menaggiohostel .com, e-mail: menaggiohostel@mclink.it).

Ty and Paola also offer eight double rooms at **La Marianna**, their B&B in Cadenabbia, two kilometers south of Menaggio (Db with view-L100,000, attached restaurant with lakeside terrace, tel. 0344-30615).

Buses run between Milan's Malpensa airport and Menaggio (2/day year-round, 2 hrs, L25,000 one-way). Last year's departures: direct from Menaggio to Malpensa at 6:30; Malpensa to Menaggio at 12:00.

**Other hostels on Lago di Como:** The Villa Olmo hostel is at the south end of the lake in Como (tel. 031-573-800), and another hostel is in the north at Domaso (tel. 0344-7449).

# Transportation Connections—Varenna

From any destination covered in this book you'll get to Lake Como via Milan. The quickest Milan connection to any point midlake (Bellagio, Menaggio, or Varenna) is via the train to Varenna. If leaving Varenna by train, note that the Varenna station doesn't sell tickets. Purchase a ticket either at the Albergo Beretta bar or the travel agency I Viaggi del Tivano next door. Stamp your ticket in the machine at the station before boarding.

**Milan to Varenna:** Catch a train at Milano Centrale (last year's schedule: 8:15, 9:15, 12:15, 14:16, 16:15, 18:00, 19:10, and 20:15, 60 min, L8,100). In Milan, the large overhead train schedules list Sondrio and Tirano rather than Varenna, a small stop en route (look at the fine print in the departure schedule posted at the station to make sure Varenna is listed). Some cars on long trains don't even get a platform. Ask for help so you don't miss the stop. You may have to open the door yourself.

**Varenna to Milan:** Trains leave Varenna for Milano

Centrale at 6:19, 7:27, 8:25, 10:27, 12:25, 14:25, 16:25, 18:26, and 20:27. (Confirm these times.) Varenna makes a comfy last stop before catching the shuttle from Milan's station to the airport.

**Varenna to St. Moritz in Switzerland:** From Varenna you have fantastic access to the Bernina Express and scenic train to St. Moritz. First take the train to Tirano and then transfer to St. Moritz (3/day, allow 6 hrs with transfer).

# THE DOLOMITES

Italy's dramatic limestone rooftop, the Dolomites, offers some of the best mountain thrills in Europe. Bolzano is the gateway to the Dolomites, and Castelrotto is a good home base for your exploration of Alpe di Siusi, Europe's largest alpine meadow.

The sunny Dolomites are well developed, and the region's famous valleys and towns suffer from *après-ski* fever. The cost for the comfort of reliably good weather is a drained-reservoir feeling. Lovers of the Alps may miss the lushness that comes with the unpredictable weather farther north. But the bold limestone pillars, flecked with snow over green meadows under a blue sky, offer a worthwhile mountain experience.

A hard-fought history has left the region bicultural, with an emphasis on the German. Locals speak German first, and some wish they were still part of Austria. In the Middle Ages, as part of the Holy Roman Empire, the region faced north. Later they were firmly in the Austrian Hapsburg realm. By losing World War I, Austria's South Tirol became Italy's Alto Adige. Mussolini did what he could to Italianize the region, including giving each town an Italian name. But even in the last decade, secessionist groups have agitated violently for more autonomy.

The government has wooed locals with economic breaks that make it one of Italy's richest areas (as local prices attest), and today all signs and literature in the province of Alto Adige/Süd Tirol are in both languages. Many include a third language, Ladin, the ancient Latin-type language still spoken in a few traditional areas. (I have listed both the Italian and German so the confusion caused by this guidebook will match that caused by your travels.)

In spite of all the glamorous ski resorts and busy construc-tion cranes, the local color survives in a warm, blue-aproned,

ruddy-faced, long-white-bearded way. There's yogurt and yodel-
ing for breakfast. Culturally as much as geographically, the area
reminds me of Austria. The Austrian Tirol is named for a village
that is now part of Italy.

## Planning Your Time

Train travelers should side trip in from Bolzano (90 min north
of Verona). To get a feel for the Alpine culture, spend a night in
Castelrotto. With two nights in Castelrotto, you can actually get
out and hike. Tenderfeet ride the bus, catch a chairlift, and stroll.
For mountain thrills, do a six-hour hike. And for a thrill that won't
soon fade away, spend a night in a mountain hut. This means two
nights in Castelrotto straddling a night in a hut.

Car hikers with a day can drive the three-hour loop from
Bolzano or Castelrotto (Val Gardena–Sella Pass–Val di Fassa)
and ride one of the lifts to the top for a ridge walk. Connecting
Bolzano and Venice by the Great Dolomite Road takes two
hours longer than the autostrada but is far more scenic (below).

Hiking season is mid-June through mid-October. The region
is packed, booming, and blooming from mid-July through mid-
September. Spring is dead, with no lifts running, huts closed, and
the most exciting trails still under snow. Ski season is busiest of all.

## Helpful Hints

**Sleeping:** Most towns offer hotels, which charge about L35,000
per person, and private homes, which offer beds for as low as
L25,000 but are often a long walk from the town centers. Beds
nearly always come with a hearty breakfast. Those traveling in
peak season or staying for only one night pay more. Local TIs
can always find budget travelers a bed in a private home (*Zimmer*).
Drivers on a tight budget should pick remote *Zimmers*. Most
mountain huts offer reasonable doubles, cheap dorm (*lager*)
beds, and inexpensive meals. Call any hut to secure a spot before
hiking there (most huts open mid-June–Sept only).

**Eating:** In local restaurants there is no cover charge, and
tipping is not expected. A *Jausenstation* is a place that serves
cheap, hearty, and traditional mountain-style food to hikers.

## BOLZANO (BOZEN)

*Willkommen* to the Italian Tirol! If it weren't so sunny, you could
be in Innsbruck. This enjoyable old town of 100,000 is the most
convenient gateway to the Dolomites, especially if you're relying
on public transportation. It's just the place to gather Dolomite
information and take a Tirolean stroll.

Bolzano is easy. Everything mentioned in Bolzano is a
10-minute walk from Piazza Walther. Leaving the train station,
veer left up the tree-lined Viale Stazione (Bahnhofsallee) and

## Dolomites

walk past the bus station (on your left) two blocks to Piazza Walther, where you'll find the city TI on your right (Mon–Fri 9:00–12:00, 14:00–17:30, Sat 9:00–12:00, closed Sun, tel. 0471-993-808). The excellent Dolomites information center is a block past the big church down Via Posta/Postgasse (Mon–Fri 9:00–12:00, 15:00–17:00, Parrocchia 11, tel. 0471-993-809).

The medieval heart of town is just beyond Piazza Walther. Choose your favorite Italian and bunny hop down the arcaded Via dei Portici to Piazza Erbe, with its ancient and still-thriving open-air produce market.

Archeologists enjoy Bolzano's excellent South Tirol Museum of Archeology, featuring the original Ice Man. "Oetzi the Ice Man" is a 5,000-year-old body found frozen in a glacier by some German tourists a few years ago. With the help of informative displays and a great audioguide, you'll learn about life in this prehistoric period way before ATM machines. And, yes, you actually get to see Oetzi himself lying peacefully inside a specially built freezer (L10,000, L5,000 for students and those over 60 with a passport, audioguide-L3,000, Tue–Sun 10:00–18:00, Thu until 20:00, last entry 60 minutes before closing, closed Mon, Museum-strasse 43, near the river, tel. 0471-982-098).

**Mediocre Side Trip:** Many are tempted to wimp out on the Dolomites and see them from a distance by making the quick trip into the hills above Bolzano (cable car from near Bolzano station to touristy village of Oberbozen, where you'll take a long, pastoral walk to the Pemmern chairlift; ride to Schwarzseespitze and walk 45 more minutes to the Rittner Horn). You'll be atop a 7,000-foot peak with distant but often hazy Dolomite views. It's not worth the trouble.

## Sleeping in Bolzano
**(L2,000 = about $1, country code: 39, zip code: 39100)**
Sleep Code: **S** = Single, **D** = Double/Twin, **T** = Triple, **Q** = Quad, **b** = bathroom, **t** = toilet only, **s** = shower only, **CC** = Credit Card (Visa, MasterCard, Amex), **SE** = Speaks English, **NSE** = No English.

**Gasthof Weisses Kreuz** is your best value, but it's usually booked up (10 rooms, S-L52,000, D-L88,000, Db-L104,000, Tb-L132,000, includes breakfast, 1 block off Piazza Walther in the old town at Kornplatz 3, tel. 0471-977-552, fax 0471-972-273, NSE).

The modern, clean, church-run **Kolpinghaus Bozen** has plenty of rooms with twin beds and all the comforts. It makes one feel thankful (Sb-L85,000, Db-L130,000, Tb-L195,000, includes breakfast, confusing elevator, in the center, 2 blocks beyond Dolomites information center at Spitalgasse 3, tel. 0471-308-400, fax 0471-973-917, e-mail: kolping@tin.it, SE). Its institutional cafeteria is open to all (L15,000 dinners, Mon–Fri 18:30–19:30).

## Eating in Bolzano
**Hopfen and Co.** offers delicious meals (Mon–Sat 9:30–01:00, closed Sun, Piazza Erbe 17, tel. 0471-300-788). **Enoteca Bacaro** is an intriguing spot for a glass of wine and a snack amid locals (located on alley off Via Argentieri 17).

Assemble a scrumptious picnic at the **Piazza Erbe** market; dine in a superb setting in Piazza Walther or in the park along the Talvera River.

## Transportation Connections—Bolzano
**By train to: Milan** (2/day, 4 hrs), **Verona** (hrly, 90 min), **Trento** (hrly, 40 min), **Merano** (hrly, 40 min), **Venice** and **Florence** (via Verona, 3–4 hrs), **Innsbruck** (hrly, 2.5 hrs). Train info: tel. 147-888-088.

**By bus to:** Castelrotto (hrly, 40 min).

## CASTELROTTO (KASTELRUTH)
Castelrotto (population 6,000, altitude 1,060 m), the ideal home base for exploring the Alpe di Siusi, has more village character than

any town I know of in the region. Friday morning is the farmers' market (June–Oct), and a crafts market fills the town square most Thursday mornings. It's touristy but not a full-blown resort—it's full of real people. Pop into the church to hear the choir practice or be on the town square at 15:00 as the bells peal and the moms bring home their kindergartners. On Sundays, townspeople and farmers gather at the church to share a meal and visit.

The TI is on the main square (Mon–Sat 8:30–12:30, 13:30–18:00, Sun 9:00–12:00, tel. 0471-706-333). A cash machine is across the street from the TI (look for Meine Bank sign and go inside). Take a short walk uphill to a pretty viewpoint (facing TI, take road under arch to the right then follow signs to Kalvarien-berg/Calvario; you'll pass the stations of the cross).

## Sleeping in Castelrotto
**(L2,000 = about $1, country code: 39, zip code: 39040)**
**Albergo Torre** (in German, **Gasthof Zum Turm**) is comfortable, clean, and traditional, with great beds and modern bathrooms (prices vary with season, Db-L116,000–190,000, Tb-L200,000–250,000, includes breakfast, L5,000 extra for 1-night stays, CC:VM, behind TI at Kofelgasse 8, tel. 0471-706-349, fax 0471-707-268, e-mail: turm@cenida.it, Gabi and Günther SE). If you're driving, go right through the traffic-free town center (very likely with a police escort). Under the bell tower, go through the white arch to the right of the TI and park (free for guests) in the lot opposite the front door.

**Gasthof zum Wolf** (in Italian, **Al Lupo**) is newly remodeled Tirolean and has all the comforts (Sb-L80,000–115,000, Db-L160,000–220,000, prices vary with season and view, includes breakfast, CNN in rooms, a block below main square at Wolken-steinstrasse 5, tel. 0471-706-332, fax 0471-707-030, www .hotelwolf.it, e-mail: info@hotelwolf.it, Arno SE).

**Hotel Cavallino D'Oro** (in German, **Goldenes Rossl**), on the main square, has plenty of Tirolean character and is run by friendly and helpful Stefan. Every room is different, and locals frequent the bar. If you love antiques by candlelight (or have only credit cards), this 600-year-old hotel is the best in town (Sb-L102,000–135,000, Db-L160,000–190,000 depending on season, discount for 3-night stay, CC:VMA, no elevator, Krausplatz 1, tel. 0471-706-337, fax 0471-707-172, www.cavallino.it, e-mail: cavallino@cavallino.it, SE). Stefan converted his 500-year-old wine cellar into a spa and sauna, complete with heated tile seats and tropical plants.

**Haus Harderer**, below Pensione Castelrotto, rents two rooms (Ss-L46,000, Ds-L92,000, includes breakfast, minimum 2 nights in summer, Plattenstrasse 20, tel. 0471-706-702, run by Inge—SE, plus Oswald, Heinz, Ida, and Mimme the cat). For longer stays, consider their apartment (L160,000/day, no breakfast, 4–6 beds).

**Tirler Hof**, the storybook Jaider family farm, has 35 cows, one friendly *hund*, four Old World–comfy guest rooms, and a great mountain view (D-L80,000, includes breakfast, practical only for drivers, it's the first farm outside of town on the right on road to St. Michael, Paniderstrasse 44, tel. 0471-706-017, e-mail: jaider.klaus@rolmail.net, NSE). The ground-floor double has a private bath. The top-floor rooms share a bathroom and a great balcony. Take a stroll before breakfast.

## Transportation Connections—Castelrotto
Catch buses to get into the heart of the Alpe di Siusi.

**By bus to: Saltria** (4–15/day, toll-free info tel. 800-846-047 or tel. 0471-706-633); **Val di Fassa, Vigo di Fassa,** and **Canazei** (late June–mid Sept only, 4/day, 2 hrs); and **Val Gardena, Ortisei/St. Ulrich,** and **St. Cristina** (summer only, 4/day, 1 hr).

**Summer Shuttle Buses:** From June through mid-October, "Buxi" shuttle buses go about twice hourly from Castelrotto through the Alpe di Siusi to Saltria (8:00–17:00, discounted return tickets). Off-season there's one "SAD" 9:10 bus from Castelrotto to Saltria and a 15:50 bus coming back. Guests at some Castelrotto hotels ride free on Buxi buses—ask.

# ALPE DI SIUSI (SEISER ALM)
Europe's largest high Alpine meadow, Alpe di Siusi, separates two of the most famous Dolomite ski-resort valleys. Measuring five kilometers by 12 kilometers and soaring from 1,800 to 2,000 meters high, Alpe di Suisi is dotted by farm huts and wildflowers, surrounded by dramatic (if distant) Dolomite peaks and cliffs, and much appreciated by hordes of walkers.

The Sasso Lungo (Langkofel) mountains at the head of the meadow provide a storybook Dolomite backdrop, while the spooky Schlern peak stands boldly staring into the haze of the peninsula. The Schlern, looking like a devilish *Winged Victory*, gave ancient peoples enough willies to spawn legends of supernatural forces. The Schlern witch, today's tourist brochure mascot, was the cause of many a broom-riding medieval townswoman's fiery death.

The Alpe di Siusi is my recommended one-stop look at the Dolomites because of Castelrotto's charm as a home base, its easy accessibility to those with and without cars, its variety of walks and hikes, and its quintessentially Dolomite mountain views.

A natural preserve, Alpe di Siusi is closed to cars past Compatsch. The Buxi park bus shuttles hikers to and from key points along the tiny road all the way to Saltria at the foot of the postcard-dramatic Sasso peaks (Sasso Lungo, 3,180 m). Meadow walks, for flower lovers and strollers, are pretty—or maybe pretty boring. Chairlifts are springboards for more dramatic and demanding hikes.

# Alpe di Siusi

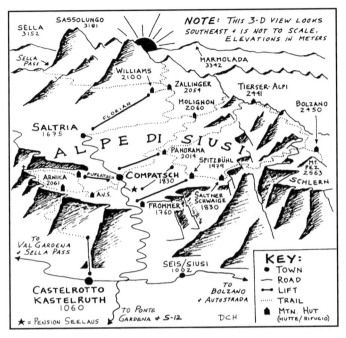

NOTE: THIS 3-D VIEW LOOKS SOUTHEAST & IS NOT TO SCALE. ELEVATIONS IN METERS

SELLA 3152
SASSOLUNGO 3181
SELLA PASS
WILLIAMS 2100
MARMOLADA 3342
ZALLINGER 2054
TIERSER-ALPI 2441
MOLIGNON 2060
BOLZANO 2450
FLORIAN
SALTRIA 1675
ALPE DI SIUSI
PANORAMA 2014
SPITZBÜHL 1939
MT. PEZ. 2563
ARNIKA 2061
PUFLATSCH
COMPATSCH 1830
SCHLERN
A.V.S.
SALTNER SCHWAIGE 1830
FROMMER 1760
TO VAL GARDENA & SELLA PASS
SEIS/SIUSI 1002
TO BOLZANO & AUTOSTRADA
CASTELROTTO KASTELRUTH 1060
TO PONTE GARDENA & S-12
DCH

KEY:
● TOWN
— ROAD
←● LIFT
..... TRAIL
▲ MTN. HUT (HUTTE/RIFUGIO)

★ = PENSION SEELAUS

Trails are well marked, and the brightly painted numbers are keyed into local maps. The Kompass Bolzano map #54 covers everything in this chapter (scale 1:50,000, L8,000). The Wanderkarte map of Alpe di Siusi (produced by Tabacco) offers more detail and focuses on just Alpe di Siusi (scale 1:25,000, L5,000).

**Compatsch**, a kilometer in and as far as you're allowed to drive, is the tourist village (1,870 m) and has a TI (Mon–Sat 9:00–17:00, Sun 9:00–12:00, free WCs behind TI, tel. 0471-727-904). There's also a grocery store (open mid-June–mid-Oct), mountain bike rentals (L10,000/1 hr, L25,000/4 hrs), an ATM, parking (L6,000/day), hotels, restaurants, shops, and so on. Trocker rents horses and provides guides (L25,000/1 hr, L45,000/2 hrs, L62,000/3 hrs, April–Oct, near Compatsch TI, tel. 0471-727-807, NSE).

**Sleeping near the Park Entrance: Pension Seelaus**, a 10-minute walk downhill from Compatsch, is a cozy, friendly, family-run place with a Germanic feel and down comforters (Sb-L79,000–103,000, Db-L148,000–196,000, prices vary with season, includes buffet breakfast and hearty dinner, Via Compatsch 8, tel. 0471-727-954, fax 0471-727-835, www.hotelseelaus.it, e-mail: info@hotelseelaus.it, Roberto SE).

## Hikes in the Alpe di Siusi

Easy meadow walks abound, giving tenderfeet classic Dolomite views from baby-stroller trails. Experienced hikers should consider the tougher and more exciting treks. Before attempting a hike, call or stop by the local TI to confirm your understanding of the time and skills required. Many lifts operate mid-June through mid-October and during the winter ski season. From Compatsch, the Panorama and Puflatsch lifts run further into the off-season.

**Three Easy Walks from Compatsch:** Take a lift to Puflatsch for the two-hour loop north to Arnikahütte and back (elevation gain about 200 m).

**Or:** Ride the lift to Panorama, then hike 90 minutes to Molignonhütte (2,050 m) and back down to Compatsch; or continue 2.5 hours (fairly level) to Zallingerhütte (2,050 m) and another 90 minutes to Saltria and the Buxi bus stop.

**Or:** Bus to Saltria and hike the 2.5-hour loop to Zallinger-hütte (2,050 m, 200 m altitude gain).

**Summit Hike of Schlern (Sciliar):** For a challenging, 19-kilometer (12 miles), seven-hour hike with a possible overnight in a traditional mountain refuge, consider hiking to the summit of Schlern and spending a night in Rifugio Bolzano (Schlernhaus). Start at the Spitzbühl lift and Albergo Frommer (1,725 m, free car park, first bus stop in park). The Spitzbühl chairlift drops you at Spitzbühl (1,935 m). Trail #5 takes you through a high meadow, down to the Saltner Schwaige dairy farm (1,830 m), across a stream, and steeply up the Schlern mountain. You'll meet trail #1 and walk across the rocky tabletop plateau of Schlern to the mountain hotel, Rifugio Bolzano/Schlernhaus, three hours into your hike (2,450 m, D-L60,000, dorm beds-L18,000, tel. 0471-612-024, call for reservation). From this dramatic setting, you get a great view of the Rosengarten range. Hike 20 more minutes up the nearby peak (Mount Pez, 2,560 m) for a 360-degree Alpine panorama. From the Schlernhaus you can hike back the way you came or walk farther along the Schlern (12 km, 2 hrs, past the Rifugio Alpe di Tires, tel. 0471-727-958, D or dorm beds, 2,440 m) and descend back into the Alpe di Siusi and the road where the Buxi bus will return you to your starting point or hotel.

**Loop around Sasso Lungo:** Another dramatic but easy hike is the six-hour walk around Sasso Lungo (Langkofel). You can ride the bus to Saltria (end of the line), take the chairlift to Williamshütte, walk past the Zallingerhütte (overnight possible, tel. 0471-727-947), and circle the Sasso group.

## More Sights in the Dolomites

▲▲**Great Dolomite Road**—This is the definitive Dolomite drive: Belluno/Cortina/Pordoi Pass/Sella Pass/Val di Fassa/Bolzano. Connecting Venice with Bolzano this way (the

Belluno–Venice autostrada is slick) takes two hours longer than the Bolzano–Verona–Venice autostrada. No public transit does this trip. In spring and early summer, passes labeled "closed" are often bare, dry, and, as far as local drivers are concerned, wide open.

▲▲**Abbreviated Dolomite Loop Drive**—See the biggies in half the kilometers (allow 3 hours, Bolzano/Castelrotto/Val Gardena/Sella Pass/Val di Fassa/Bolzano). Val Gardena (Grodner Tal) is famous for its skiing and hiking resorts, traditional Ladin culture, and wood-carvers (the wood carver ANRI is from the Val Gardena town of St. Cristina). It's a bit overrated, but even if its culture has been suffocated by the big bucks of hedonistic European fun seekers, it remains a good jumping-off point for trips into the mountains. Within an hour you'll reach Sella Pass (2,240 m). After a series of tight hairpin turns a mile or so over the pass, you'll see some benches and cars. Pull over and watch the rock climbers. Val di Fassa is Alberto Tomba country. The town of Canazei, at the head of the valley and the end of the bus line, has the most ambience and altitude (4,600 feet). From there a lift takes you to Col dei Rossi Belvedere, where you can hike the Bindelweg trail past the Rifugio Belvedere along an easy but breathtaking ridge to the Rifugio Viel del Pan. This three-hour round-trip hike has views of the highest mountain in the Dolomites—the Marmolada—and the Dolo-mighty Sella range.

▲▲**Reifenstein Castle**—For one of Europe's most intimate looks at medieval castle life, let the friendly lady of Reifenstein (Frau Blanc) show you around her wonderfully preserved castle. She leads tours on the hour, in Italian and German, squeezing in whatever English she can (L6,000, open Easter–Oct, tours on Mon at 14:00 and 15:00, Tue–Thu and Sat–Sun at 9:30, 10:30, 14:00, and 15:00, closed Fri, picnic spot at drawbridge, tel. 0472-647-196).

Just before the Austrian border, leave the autostrada at Vipiteno (Sterzing); follow signs toward Bolzano and then over the freeway to the base of the castle's rock. It's the castle on the west. While this is easy by car, it's probably not worth the trouble by train (from Bolzano, 6/day, 70 min).

▲**Glurns**—Drivers connecting the Dolomites and Lake Como by the high road via Meran and Bormio should spend the night in the amazing little town of Glurns (45 minutes west of touristy Meran between Schluderns and Taufers). Glurns still lives within its square wall on the Adige River, with a church bell tower that has a thing about ringing and real farms, rather than boutiques, filling the town courtyards. There are several small hotels in the town, but I'd stay in a private home (Family Hofer, 6 rooms, Db-L80,000 with breakfast, less for 2 nights, 100 meters from town square, near church, just outside wall on river, tel. 0473-831-597).

# NAPLES, AMALFI COAST, AND POMPEII

If you like Italy as far south as Rome, go farther south. It gets better. If Italy is getting on your nerves, think twice about going farther. Italy intensifies as you plunge deeper. Naples is a barrel of cultural monkeys and Italy in the extreme—its best (birthplace of pizza and Sophia Loren) and its worst (home of the Camorra, Naples' "family" of organized crime). Serene Sorrento, without a hint of big-city Naples and just an hour to the south, makes a great home base. It's the gateway to the much-loved Amalfi Coast. From the jet-setting island of Capri to the stunning scenery of the Amalfi Coast, from ancient Pompeii to even more ancient Paestum, this is Italy's coast with the most.

## Planning Your Time

On a quick trip, give the area three days. With Sorrento as your sunny springboard, spend a day in Naples, a day on the Amalfi Coast, and a day split between Pompeii and the town of Sorrento. While Paestum, the crater of Vesuvius, Herculaneum, and the island of Capri are decent options, these are worthwhile only if you give the area more time. Consider a night train in or out of the area.

For a blitz tour you could have breakfast on the early Rome–Naples express (7:10–9:00), do Naples and Pompeii in a day, and be back in Rome in time for Letterman. That's exhausting but more memorable than a fourth day in Rome. Remember that in the afternoon, Naples' street life slows, and many sights close as the temperature soars. The city comes back to life in the early evening.

For a small-town vacation from your vacation, spend a few more days on the Amalfi Coast, sleeping in Positano, Atrani, or Marina del Cantone.

For most, driving south of Rome is not only stressful—it's impractical. Take advantage of the wonderful public transportation: the slick two-hour Rome–Naples express trains; the handy Circumvesuviana lacing together Naples, Pompeii, and Sorrento; and the regular bus service from Sorrento into the Amalfi region (where parking and car access are severely limited).

## NAPLES (NAPOLI)

Italy's third-largest city (with more than 2 million people) has almost no open spaces or parks, which makes its position as Europe's most densely populated city plenty evident. Watching the police try to enforce traffic sanity is almost comical in Italy's grittiest, most polluted, and most crime-ridden city. But Naples surprises the observant traveler with its good humor, decency, and impressive knack for living, eating, and raising children in the streets. Overcome your fear of being run down or ripped off long enough to talk with people—enjoy a few smiles and jokes with the man running the neighborhood tripe shop or the woman taking her day-care class on a walk through the traffic.

Twenty-five hundred years ago, Neapolis ("new city") was a thriving Greek commercial center. It remains southern Italy's leading city, offering a fascinating collection of museums, churches, and eclectic architecture. The pulse of Italy throbs in Naples. This tangled mess, the closest thing to "reality travel" you'll find in Western Europe, still somehow manages to breathe, laugh, and sing—with a captivating Italian accent.

## Planning Your Time

For a quick visit, start with the museum, do the Slice-of-Neapolitan-Life Walk (see "Sights," below), and celebrate your survival with pizza. Of course, Naples is huge. But with limited time, if you stick to the described route and grab a cab when you're lost or tired, it's fun. Treat yourself well in Naples; the city is cheap by Italian standards.

## Orientation

**Tourist Information:** The TI is in the central train station (Mon–Sat 9:00–18:00, until 20:00 in summer, Sun 9:00–13:00; until 15:00 in summer; with your back to the tracks, TI is in the lobby to your left; then, within the lobby, TI is to your right, tel. 081-268-779). Pick up a map, and even though the odds are against you, ask for the *Qui Napoli* booklet—when they say they're "finished," ask for an old one (but chances are they're out of those, too). If you do manage to snare a *Qui Napoli* booklet, cherish it as you would an autographed first edition of a rare book.

**Arrival in Naples:** There are several Naples stations. You want Naples Centrale (facing Piazza Garibaldi), which has a TI,

## Bay of Naples

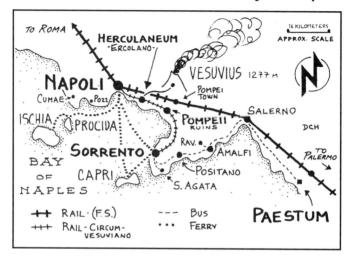

baggage check, and the Circumvesuviana stop for commuter trains to Sorrento and Pompeii. Since Centrale is a dead-end station, through trains often stop at Piazza Garibaldi (actually a subway station just downstairs from Centrale), Campi Flegrei, or Napoli Mergellina across town. The stations of Campi Flegrei and Mergellina (which also has a TI) are connected to Centrale by a direct subway route; a railpass or train ticket to Napoli Centrale covers the ride (subway trains depart about every 10 minutes, less often on Sun). While on the train to Naples, ask the conductor which Naples stations your train stops at. Some trains stop at several, others just at Centrale, and others don't stop at Centrale. Get off at Mergellina or Campi Flegrei only if your train doesn't stop at Centrale or Garibaldi.

## Helpful Hints

**Traffic:** In Naples red lights are discretionary, and pedestrians need to be wary, particularly of the Vespa motorcycles.

**Theft Alert:** Lately Naples, under a new activist mayor, has been occupied by an army of police and feels much safer. Still, err on the side of caution. Don't venture into neighborhoods that make you uncomfortable. Walk with confidence, as if you know where you're going and what you're doing. Assume able-bodied beggars are thieves. Tighten your money belt and keep it completely hidden. Stick to busy streets and beware of gangs of hoodlums. A third of the city is unemployed, and past local governments set an example the Mafia would be proud of. Assume con artists

## Naples Transportation

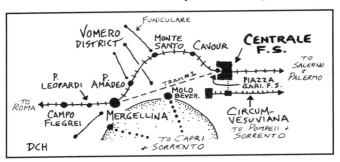

are more clever than you. Any jostle or commotion is probably a thief team smoke screen. Any bags are probably safest checked at the central train station (L5,000, *deposito bagagli* near track #24).

## Getting around Naples

Naples' subway, the Servizio Metropolitano, runs from the Centrale station through the center of town (direction: "Pozzuoli"), stopping at Piazza Cavour (Archaeological Museum), Piazza Dante, and Montesanto (top of Spanish Quarter and Spaccanapoli). Tickets, which cost L1,500, are good for 90 minutes. All-day tickets cost L4,500. If you can afford a taxi, don't mess with the buses. A short taxi ride costs L6,000 to L10,000 (insist on the meter, supplement charged on Sun).

## Sights—Naples

▲▲▲**Museo Archeologico**—For lovers of antiquity, this museum alone makes Naples a worthwhile stop; it offers the only possible peek into the artistic jewelry boxes of Pompeii and Herculaneum. The actual sights are impressive but barren; the best art ended up here in the museum.

**Orientation**: Buy your ticket (L12,000). The bookshop rents audioguides (L7,000 for 3 hrs) and sells a worthwhile green guidebook, titled *National Archeological Museum of Naples* (L15,000).

At the desk next to the ticket booth, you can sign up for a free 20-minute tour of the Secret Room (containing R-rated art from Pompeii and Herculaneum; children under 14 need parental permission). You'll be given a time for your tour; meet at the Secret Room (*Gabinetto Segreto*) on the mezzanine near the *Battle of Alexander* mosaic. These short tours, generally offered at the top and bottom of every hour, are usually given in Italian, but English tours are possible—ask.

Now, face the grand staircase. For the Farnese Collection of marble statues, turn right just before the staircase (and walk way

# Naples

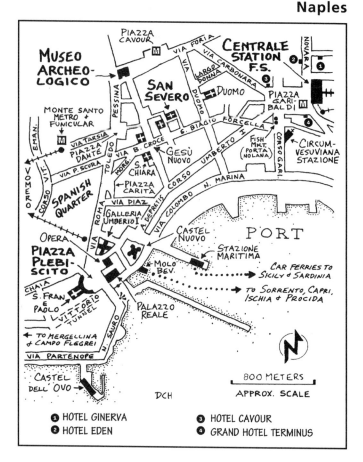

- ❶ HOTEL GINERVA
- ❷ HOTEL EDEN
- ❸ HOTEL CAVOUR
- ❹ GRAND HOTEL TERMINUS

back). The small mezzanine level (up the stairs and on your left) contains the Pompeii mosaics and Secret Room. The huge first floor (which we would call the top floor) contains bronze statues from Herculaneum, frescoes from Pompeii, and vases from Paestum. The WCs are on the ground floor, behind the grand staircase.

**Statues, Frescoes, and Artifacts (top floor):** Climb the stairs to the top floor. Before you enter the great hall, look right to locate the entrance to the bronze statues of Herculaneum. This large collection—including about a dozen bronze statues, plus busts and marble statues—came from Villa Papiri (Papyrus) in Herculaneum. Look into the lifelike blue eyes of the two intense *ateleta* (atheletes); they are bent on doing their best.

Step inside the great hall. With your back to the entrance, the door to the Pompeii frescoes is on your left (in the middle of the hall); it leads to an art gallery lined with paintings, artifacts, and an interesting model of the town of Pompeii (called *plastico di Pompeii*; near the glass objects). Still in the great hall, on your right, the door in the middle of the hall leads to a model of Paestum and ancient vases discovered on site. (Paestum, a temple complex south of Naples, was part of a once-thriving region known as Greater Greece; for more info, see Paestum listing, below.) If you contrast all of this ancient art with the darkness of medieval Europe, it becomes clear that classical art greatly inspired and enlightened the Renaissance greats.

**Mosaics (mezzanine):** On the mezzanine floor below (under the Paestum art section), you'll find a small, exquisite collection of Pompeian mosaics and the Secret Room. A highlight of the mosaics is the grand *Battle of Alexander* (a first-century B.C. copy of a fourth-century B.C. Greek original). Nearby is a delightful, two-foot-high bronze statue of a *Dancing Faun* (a copy is at Pompeii, where it was found). The **Secret Room**, to the left of the *Battle of Alexander* mosaic, contains lascivious works of art discovered at Pompeii and Herculaneum. This small assortment of frescoes, pottery, and statues—which once decorated bedrooms, brothels, and even shops—can be toured only with a guide (see "Orientation," above).

When this earthy art was unearthed in the mid-18th century, people were upset to find their view of the Romans as wise administrators and law makers upended (so to speak). You'll see a lot of phalluses, some hermaphrodites, and acts of intercourse, but much of it seems tame by today's standards. For many years—due to politics and prudishness—this collection was locked up. Judge for yourself whether it's artistic, obscene, or historically educational. If nothing else, the most famous statue—of Pan with a goat—is memorable.

**Farnese Collection (ground floor):** This floor has enough Greek, Roman, and Etruscan art to put any museum on the map, but its highlight is the Farnese Collection—a giant hall of huge, bright, and wonderfully restored statues excavated from Rome's Baths of Caracalla. You can almost hear the Toro Farnese snorting. This largest intact statue from antiquity (a third-century copy of a Hellenistic original) was carved out of one piece of marble and restored by Michelangelo and others. Read the worthwhile descriptions on the walls

**Hours, Cost, Information:** L12,000, Wednesday through Monday 9:00 to 20:00, in summer open until 23:00 on Saturday, closed Tuesday. Tours in English are offered weekdays at 11:30 and 15:30 (except on Tue when museum is closed) and on Saturday and Sunday at 10:00, 12:00, and 15:00 (L6,000, 1.5 hrs, depart

## Naples Walk

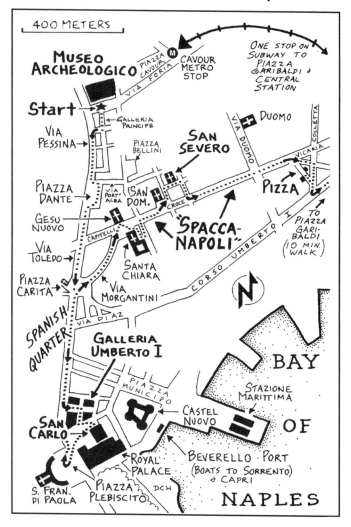

from entry, confirm tour times by calling 081-440-166). Audio-guides cost L7,000 (at bookshop, rentable for 3 hrs). Museum assistants are stationed in various rooms on Saturday and Sunday, available to answer questions. Photos are allowed without a flash.

**Getting to the Museum:** From the Centrale train station, follow signs to Metropolitano (downstairs, buy tickets from

window on right, ask which track—"*Binario?*" to Piazza Cavour—
it's usually track 4, go through a "solo metropolitano" turnstile
and ride the subway one stop). As you leave the metro, take the
exit to the right. Walk through the park. At the end of cluttered
Piazza Cavour, you'll see several pink buildings ahead. The
museum is the pink building on the right side of the street.

▲▲▲**The Slice-of-Neapolitan-Life Walk**—Walk from the
museum through the heart of town and back to the station (allow
at least 2 hours plus lunch and sightseeing stops). Sights are listed
in the order you'll see them on this walk.

Naples, a living medieval city, is its own best sight. Couples
artfully make love on Vespas surrounded by more fights and smiles
per cobble here than anywhere else in Italy. Rather than seeing
Naples as a list of sights, see the one great museum and then
capture its essence by taking this walk through the core of the city.
Should you become overwhelmed or lost, step into a store and ask
for help: "*Dov'è il stazione centrale?*" (DOH-vay eel staht-zee-OH-
nay chen-TRAH-lay) or point in this book to the next sight.

**Via Toledo and the Spanish Quarter (city walk, first
half):** Leaving the Archaeological Museum at the top of Piazza
Cavour (Metro: Piazza Cavour), cross the street and walk through
the ornate *galleria* (the grand, arched gallery) on your way to
Via Pessina. The first part of this walk is a straight 1.5-kilometer
ramble down this boulevard to Galleria Umberto I near the Royal
Palace. Coffee will be waiting.

Busy Via Pessina leads downhill to Piazza Dante. After two
blocks, a tiny pedestrian street (Via Micco Spadaro) to your left
dead-ends at the **Academy of Fine Arts** (Belle Arti). Sneak a peek
inside. Isn't that Michelangelo's *David*?! (The bar/pizzeria in front
serves a decent quick lunch with pleasant outdoor seating.)

At Piazza Dante, notice poor old Dante in the center looking
out over the divine comedy with a hopeless gesture. (Unknow-
ingly, he points the way to Pizzeria Port'Abla, a recommended
restaurant; see "Eating," below.) Past the square, Via Pessina
becomes Via Toledo, Naples' principal shopping street. At Piazza
Sette Septembre, continue straight on Via Toledo (even though
the arterial jogs left). About five blocks below Piazza Dante, at Via
Maddaloni, you cross the long straight street called **Spaccanapoli**
(literally, "split Naples"). Look left and right. Since ancient times,
this thin street (which changes names several times) has bisected
the city. (We'll be coming back to this point later. If you want
to abbreviate this walk, turn left here and skip down to the
Spaccanapoli section.)

Via Toledo runs through Piazza Carita (also known by its
new name, Piazza Salvo D'Acquisto), with fascist architecture
(from 1938, sternly straight lines, no curves) overlooking the
square. Wander down Via Toledo a few blocks past more fascist

architecture—the two banks on the left. Try robbing the second one (Banco di Napoli, Via Toledo 178).

Up the hill to your right is the **Spanish Quarter**, Naples at its rawest, poorest, and most historic. Thrill seekers (or someone in need of a $20 prostitute) will take a stroll up one of these streets and loop back to Via Toledo.

The only thing predictable about this Neapolitan tide pool is the ancient grid plan of its streets, the friendliness of its shop-keepers, and the boldness of its mopeds. Concerned locals will tug on their lower eyelid, warning you to be wary. Pop into a grocery shop and ask the man to make you his best ham and mozzarella sandwich. Trust him on the price—it should be around L5,000.

Continue down Via Toledo to Piazza Plebiscito. From here you'll see the church of San Francesco di Paola with its Pantheon-inspired dome and broad, arcing colonnades. Opposite is the **Royal Palace**, which has housed Spanish, French, and even Italian royalty. The lavish interior is open for tours (L8,000, Thu–Tue 9:00–20:00, Sat until 23:00, closed Wed, shorter hours off-season; a TI is inside the Royal Palace). Next door, peek inside the neo-classical Teatro San Carlo, Italy's second-most-respected opera house (after Milan's La Scala). The huge castle on the harbor front just beyond the palace houses government bureaucrats and is closed to tourists.

Under the Victorian iron and glass of the 100-year-old **Galleria Umberto I**, enjoy a coffee break or sample a unique Neapolitan pastry called *sfogliatella* (crispy scallop shell–shaped pastry filled with sweet ricotta cheese). Go through the tall yellow arch at the end of Via Toledo or across from the opera house. Gawk up.

**Spaccanapoli back to the station (city walk, second half):** To continue your walk, double back up Via Toledo past Piazza Carita to Via Maddaloni. (Consider going via the backstreets.) You're back at the straight-as-a-Roman-arrow Spaccanapoli. Formerly the main thoroughfare of the Greek city of Neapolis, it starts up the hill near the Montesanto funicular.

Turn right off Via Toledo and walk down Via Maddaloni to two bulky old churches on Piazza Gesu Nuovo. Check out the austere, fortresslike church of **Gesu Nuovo** with its peaceful but brilliant Baroque interior. Across the street, the simpler Gothic church of **Santa Chiara** offers a stark contrast (free, Mon–Sat 8:30–13:00, 15:30–18:30, Sun 8:30–13:00). Its bright-tiled cloisters are a peaceful refuge (L6,000, Mon–Sat 9:30–13:00, 14:30–17:30, Sun 9:30–13:00, to reach to cloisters, exit church to the right, walk alongside church to separate entrance at the back).

The rest of this walk is basically a straight line (all of which locals call Spaccanapoli). Continue down traffic-free Via B. Croce to the next square, Piazza S. Domenico Maggiore. To reach **Cappella Sansevero**, detour along the right side of the castlelike San Domenico Maggiore church (and take the first right after that), following yellow signs to Cappella Sansevero (L8,000, Mon and Wed–Sat 10:00–20:00, Sun 10:00–13:30, closed Tue, Via de Sanctis 19). This small chapel is a Baroque explosion mourning the body of Christ, who lies on a soft pillow under an incredibly realistic veil. It's all carved out of marble and is like no statue I've seen (by Giuseppe "howdeedoodat" Sammartino, 1750). Lovely statues, carved from a single piece of marble, adorn the altar. Despair struggles with a marble rope net (on the right, opposite Chastity). No photos are allowed in the chapel (postcards available in gift shop). For the ghoul in all of us, walk down the stairway to the right for a creepy look at two 200-year-old studies in varicose veins. Was one decapitated? Was one pregnant?

Back on Via B. Croce, turn left and continue the Spaccanapoli cultural scavenger hunt. As Via B. Croce becomes Via S. Biagio dei Librai, notice the gold and silver shops and the Ospedale delle Bambole (doll hospital) at #81.

Cross busy Via Duomo. The street and side-street scenes along Via Vicaria intensify. Paint a picture with these thoughts: Naples has the most intact street plan of any ancient Roman city. Imagine life here as in a Roman city (retain these images as you visit Pompeii), with streetside shop fronts that close up after dark to form private homes. Today it's just one more page in a 2,000-year-old story of city activity: all kinds of meetings, beatings, and cheatings; kisses, near misses, and little-boy pisses.

You name it, it occurs right on the streets today, as it has since Roman times. People ooze from crusty corners. Black-and-white death announcements add to the clutter on the walls. Widows sell cigarettes from buckets. For a peek behind the scenes in the shade of wet laundry, venture down a few side streets. Buy two carrots as a gift for the woman on the fifth floor if she'll lower her bucket to pick them up. The neighborhood action seems best around 18:00.

At the tiny fenced-in triangular park, veer right onto Via Forcella. Turning right on busy Via Pietro Colletta, walk 50 meters and step into the North Pole. Reward yourself for surviving this safari with a stop at the Polo Nord Gelateria (Via Pietro Colletta 41, sample their Kiss flavor before ordering). Via Pietro Colletta leads past Napoli's two most competitive **pizzerias** (see "Eating," below) to Corso Umberto.

Turn left on the grand-boulevardian Corso Umberto. From here to the station, it's a 10-minute walk (if you're tired, catch a bus—they all go to the station). To finish the walk, continue on Corso Umberto past a gauntlet of purse/CD/sunglasses salesmen to the vast, ugly Piazza Garibaldi. On the far side is the Centrale station.

**Markets**—Naples' **fish market** is fun for photos, with sawed-off swordfish, wriggly eels in pans, and mussels taking a shower. It's at Piazza Nolana, a few blocks southwest of the train station (at the piazza, follow your nose and go through the old gate; market spills down small street, Vico Sopramuro). A bigger, **general market** starts at the far corner of Piazza Capuana (several blocks northwest of the train station), filling the street Via Sant' Antonio Abate with a mix of clothes, olives, bags of gnocchi, hanging hams, shoes, produce, umbrellas, and shoppers on foot or on Vespas. These colorful markets are both open daily from early in the morning until about 16:00 Monday to Saturday, 13:00 on Sunday.

## Sleeping in Naples
**(L2,000 = about $1, country code: 39)**
Sleep Code: **S** = Single, **D** = Double/Twin, **T** = Triple, **Q** = Quad, **b** = bathroom, **t** = toilet only, **s** = shower only, **CC** = Credit Card (**V**isa, **M**asterCard, **A**mex), **SE** = Speaks English, **NSE** = No English.

    With Sorrento just an hour away, I can't imagine why you'd sleep in Naples. But if needed, here are four safe, clean places (200 meters from the station) plus a hostel. The area is ugly but reasonably safe. Still, be careful after dark.

    **Laundry:** Bolle Blu is four blocks from Piazza Garibaldi (daily 8:30–20:00, L12,000, takes 60 min, head straight out of station to street at far right end of square, Corso Novara 62, intersection with Ferrara, cellular 0338-894-2714).

    **Hotel Ginevra** is quiet, bright, and cheery, with comfortable beds, floral wallpaper, and a L10,000-per-load washing machine. It's run by a friendly family: Bruno and son Lello speak English, Anna speaks Italian (16 rooms, S-L45,000, D-L70,000, Db-L90,000, T-L100,000, Tb-L125,000, Q-L125,000, Qb-L150,000, special 10 percent discount with this book and cash, prices promised through 2001, breakfast in room-L7,500, phones, TV, CC:VMA, turn right out of the station and walk one block up Corso Novara, turn right on Via Genova to #116, second floor, tel. & fax 081-283-210 or 081-554-1757, www.mds.it/ginevra, e-mail: hginevra@tin.it). They also offer private tours of the Amalfi Coast.

    **Hotel Eden**, which is not as cozy, is a big old establishment run with panache by English-speaking Nicola and his brother Vincenzo. Its 45 rooms are clean and come with good beds, brown and gray tones, a phone, TV, and private bath. Front rooms get traffic noise; request a room in the back. To make a statement, ask for a nonsmoking room (Sb-L42,000, Db-L72,000, Tb-L90,000, Qb-L108,000, these prices—which have already been discounted 20 percent for my readers—are good through 2001 with this book and cash, no CC, no breakfast, elevator, turn right out of the station and walk one block up Corso Novara, Corso Novara 9, tel. 081-285-344, fax 081-285-690). Reserve by phone and reconfirm the day before you arrive.

**Hotel Cavour**, a three-star hotel on Piazza Garibaldi, has some Old World architectural charm but many of its 94 rooms are plain, with simple furnishings and tiled floors. The more elegant suites come with parquet floors (Sb-L180,000, Db-L250,000, Db suites-L330,000, Tb-L330,000, prices drop off-season, air-con-L35,000/day but included with suite, parking-L25,000, CC:VM, elevator, some nonsmoking rooms, Piazza Garibaldi 32, with your back to the station, it's on the far right side of the square, tel. 081-283-122, fax 081-287-488, www.cavour .com, e-mail: info@cavour.com, SE).

**Grand Hotel Terminus**, a four-star place across the street from the station, has 168 rooms with all the comforts (Db-L340,000 or so, includes breakfast, air-con, CC:VMA; nonsmoking rooms on second floor, some rooms on fourth to sixth floors have Vesuvius views; elevator, fridges, gym, roof garden, bar, restaurants, hotel is to your immediate left as you leave station, Piazza Garibaldi 91, tel. 081-779-3111, fax 081-206-689, www.starhotels.it, SE).

**Ostello Mergellina** is well run and cheap (L24,000 beds in 6-bed rooms, L30,000 beds in shared doubles, hostel members pay L5,000 less, includes sheets and breakfast, closed 9:00–15:00 and at 24:00, inexpensive meals, Salita della Grotta a Piedigrotta 23, Metro: Mergellina, tel. 081-761-2346).

## Eating in Naples

Drop by one of the two most traditional pizzerias. Naples, baking just the right combination of fresh dough, mozzarella, and tomatoes in traditional wood-burning ovens, is the birthplace of pizza. **Antica Pizzeria da Michele**, a few blocks from the train station, is for purists (Mon–Sat 11:00–23:00, closed Sun, cheap, filled with locals, 50 meters off Corso Umberto on Via Cesare Sersale, look for the vertical red "Antica Pizzeria" sign, tel. 081-553-9204). It serves two kinds: *margherita* (tomato sauce and mozzarella) or *marinara* (tomato sauce, oregano, and garlic, no cheese). A pizza with beer costs L8,000. Some locals prefer **Pizzeria Trianon** across the street. Da Michele's arch rival offers more choices, higher prices, air-conditioning, and a cozier atmosphere (daily 10:00–15:30, 18:30–23:00, Via Pietro Colletta 42, tel. 081-553-9426).

For legendary pizza near the museum, try **Antica Port'Alba Pizzeria** (Thu–Tue 9:00–16:00, 20:00–24:00, closed Wed, several blocks south of museum, just off Piazza Dante, sculpture of Dante points the way, go through old gate, interesting street is lined with book stalls, Via Port'Alba 18, tel. 081-459-713).

## Circumvesuviana Stops
## Between Naples and Sorrento

I list these so you can look at the scenery rather than your watch.

| | |
|---|---|
| Napoli | V. Viuli |
| Gianturco | Trecase |
| S. Giovanni | Torre Annunziata |
| Barra | Pompei Scavi (yes) |
| S. Maria d. Pozzo | Moregine |
| S. Giorgio | Ponte Persica |
| Cavalli di Bronzo | Pioppaino |
| Bellavista | V. Nocera |
| V. Liberta | C. Mare Stabia |
| Ercolano Scavi (yes) | C. Mare Terme |
| Ercolano | Pozzano |
| Miglio D'Oro | Scraio |
| Torre del Greco | Vico Equense |
| V.S. Antonio | Seiano |
| V. del Monte | Meta |
| V. Monaci | Piano di Sorrento |
| Villa della Ginestra | S. Agnello |
| Leopardi | Sorrento (yes) |

## Transportation Connections—Naples

**By boat to: Sorrento** (7/day, 60 min, L12,000), **Capri** (6 hydrofoils/day, 45 min, L16,000).

**By train to: Rome** (hrly, 2–3 hrs), **Brindisi** (2/day, 7 hrs, overnight possible; from Brindisi, ferries sail to Greece), **Milan** (7/day, 7–9 hrs, overnight possible, more with a change in Rome), **Venice** (4/day, 8–10 hrs), **Nice** (4/day, 13 hrs), **Paris** (3/day, 18 hrs). Naples train information: tel. 1478-88088.

**The Circumvesuviana:** Naples, Herculaneum, Pompeii, and Sorrento are all on the handy commuter train, the Ferrovia Circumvesuviana. At Naples' Central Station, signs direct you downstairs. In the long corridor in the basement, the ticket windows—marked Circumvesuviana—are on your left. Nearby, the schedules are posted on the wall. When you buy your ticket, ask which track your train will depart from (*"Che binario?"*—kay bee-NAH-ree-oh). Don't go through the turnstiles opposite the ticket windows. Instead, continue down the corridor and jog right when it does, down another long corridor that has turnstiles at the end (insert your ticket). The platforms are just beyond. The Circumvesuviana also has its own terminal one stop or a 10-minute walk beyond the Central Station. Take your pick.

Two trains per hour marked "Sorrento" get you to Herculaneum (Ercolano) in 15 minutes, Pompeii in 40 minutes, and Sorrento, the end of the line, in 70 minutes (L4,900 one-way, no train passes, not all of the trains go as far as Sorrento—look at the schedule carefully or confirm with a local before boarding to make sure the train is going where you want to). When returning to Naples Centrale station on the Circumvesuviana, get off at the second-to-the-last station, the Collegamento FS or Garibaldi stop (Centrale station is just up the escalator).

## SORRENTO

Wedged on a ledge under the mountains and over the Mediterranean, spritzed by lemon and olive groves, Sorrento is an attractive resort of 20,000 residents and—in the summer—as many tourists. It's as well located for regional sightseeing as it is a fine place to stay and stroll. The Sorrentines have gone out of their way to create a completely safe and relaxed place for tourists to come and spend money. Everyone seems to speak fluent English and work for the Chamber of Commerce. This gateway to the Amalfi Coast has an unspoiled old quarter, a lively main shopping street, and a spectacular cliffside setting. Skip the port and its poor excuse for a beach unless you're taking a ferry.

### Orientation

Sorrento is long and narrow. The main drag, Corso Italia (50 meters in front of the Circumvesuviana train station), runs parallel to the sea from the station through the town center and out to the cape, where it's renamed Via Capo. Everything mentioned (except the hotels on Via Capo) is within a five-minute walk of the station. Many places in Sorrento close in January and February.

**Tourist Information:** At the TI, or Soggiorno e Turismo, get a free *Surrentum* magazine, which has a great map and schedules of boats, buses, and events (Mon–Sat 8:45–19:15, closed Sun, shorter hours off-season, tel. 081-807-4033). To reach the TI from the station, go left on Corso Italia and walk five minutes to Piazza Tasso. Turn right at the end of the square down Via L. de Maio through Piazza Sant Antonino to the Foreigners' Club mansion at #35. You'll pass fake "tourist offices" (travel agencies selling bus and boat tours).

**Helpful Hints:** The Foreigners' Club provides reasonably priced snacks and drinks, relaxation, and views, and a handy place for visitors to meet locals (behind the TI, public WC). It's lively with concerts or dancing every summer evening (starting at 21:00, tel. 081-877-3263). If you need immediate tanning, you can rent a chair on the pier by the port, though the best swimming is at Punta del Capo (see below).

## Getting around Sorrento

Orange city buses run from the station to Punta del Capo and down to the port (L1,700 tickets within the center, sold at *tabacchi* shops). Sorrento Rent a Car also rents mopeds and Vespas (L56,000/3 hrs; open 8:00–13:00, 16:00–21:00, Corso Italia 210, tel. 081-878-1386). In summer, forget renting a car unless you enjoy traffic jams.

## Sights—Sorrento

▲**Strolling**—Take time to explore the surprisingly pleasant old city between Corso Italia and the sea. Views from the public park next to Imperial Hotel Tramontano are worth the detour. Duck into the Church of England. The evening *passeggiata* (along Corso Italia and Via San Cesareo) peaks around 22:00. Check out the old-boys' club playing cards, oblivious to the tourism, under their portico at Via San Cesareo and Via Tasso. This town is filled with Brit-friendly pubs (the Merry Monk is a fun Irish pub). And you haven't heard "Mustang Sally" until you've heard it in Italian.

**Lemon Grove Garden (L'Agruminato)**—This small park in town consists of an inviting lemon and orange grove, lined with paths. It's dotted in the center with benches and a little stand that sometimes offers free tastes of *limoncello*, a drink made of lemons, sugar, and pure alcohol (May–Aug 10:00–20:00, Sept–April 10:00–16:00). You can enter the garden on Corso Italia (across from Panetteria da Franco—Corso Italia 165, see door flanked by tiles, marked "*L'Agruminato, il giardino della città*") or at Via Rota (next to Hotel La Meridiana Sorrento).

▲**Punta del Capo**—For clean water and a pebbly peninsula-tip beach, walk 40 minutes to Punta del Capo (or take the 10-minute bus ride from Piazza Tasso, 2/hrly, L1,700). It's a rocky but accessible, traffic-free swimming area with a stunning view of Sorrento and Naples. The ruined Roman Villa di Pollio marks this discovered but beautiful cape. Leave the road at the American Bar, turn right, and amble down the covered walkway to the beach. For the best swimming, walk over wooden bridge and head to the far left end of the beach (caution: immodest bathers).

## Sleeping in Sorrento

**(L2,000 = about $1, country code: 39, zip code: 80067)**

Unlike many resorts, Sorrento offers the whole range of rooms. Hotels often charge the same for a room whether it has a view, balcony, or neither. At hotels that offer sea views, ask for a room "*Con balcone, con vista sul mare*"—with a balcony with a sea view). "*Tranquillo*" is taken as a request for a room off the street. Hotels listed here are either near the station and city center or along the way to Punta del Capo, a 20-minute walk (or short bus ride) from the station. While many hotels close for the winter, you should

## Sorrento

HYDROFOILS ↑  ↑ BOATS
TO NAPLES & CAPRI   TO NAPLES & CAPRI

MARINA PICCOLA

SAN FRANCESCO

MUSEO CORREALE

STAIRS DOWN TO MARINA

VIA S.F.

VIA CALIFANO

PARCO CORREALE

VIA ROTA

VIA CORREALE

PIAZZA A. LAURO

ORANGE LOCAL BUSES

PARK

VIA CAPASSO

VIA NIZZA

POST

VIA S. MARIA GRAZIE

VIA S. CESAREO

CORSO   ITALIA

CORSO ITALIA

PIAZZA TASSO

VIA FUORIMURA

VIA DEGLI ARANCI

TO NAPLES

TO VIA CAPO HOTELS,
PUNTA DEL CAPO,
CAMPING &
S. AGATA

STAZIONE
CIRCUMVESUVIANA RAILWAY
AND
SITA (BLUE) BUSES

300 METERS

DCH

❶ HOTEL LORELEY & AMBASCIATORI
❷ LA MERIDIANA & PENSIONE MARA
❸ HOTELS DESIREE & TONNARELLA
❹ HOTEL NICE
❺ HOTEL CITY & STANDA MARKET
❻ HOTEL DEL CORSO
❼ SANT ANTONINO
❽ PIZZERIA GIARDINIELLO
❾ HOTEL MIGNON MEUBLE
❿ ZI'ANTONIO REST.

have no trouble finding a room any time outside of August, when the place is jammed and many hotel prices go way up. Spring for a hotel with air-conditioning if you wilt in the heat. Note: The spindly, more exotic, and more tranquil Amalfi Coast town of Positano (below) is also a good place to spend the night.

**Laundromat**: A handy coin-op Laundromat is at Corso Italia 30; turn right down the alley for the side entrance (1 load-L15,000, 2 loads-L25,000).

### Sleeping East of the Center

A block in front of the station, turn right onto Corso Italia and then left down Via Capasso. At the Loreley and Ambasciatori, the private "beach" is actually a sun deck built out over the water.

**Hotel Loreley** is a rambling, spacious, colorful old Sorrentine villa, ideal for those wishing to sit on the bluff and stare at the sea. Of its 27 rooms, 19 are quiet and have sea-view balconies (some balconies are miniscule). Streetside rooms are noisier and lack views. A L5,000 elevator takes you to the hotel's private beach (Db-L150,000; from July 15–Sept 15 half-pension at L110,000 per person is required but the dinner's good; CC:VM, some air-con rooms, unpredictable management cannot guarantee view rooms, easy street parking—L500/hr, follow Via Capasso to the water and turn right to Via Califano 2, tel. 081-807-3187, fax 081-532-9001, SE). **Grand Hotel Ambasciatori**, next door, is a four-star hotel with all the amenities, a pool, and free elevator to the beach (Db-L290,000–460,000 depending on season, includes buffet breakfast, CC:VM, air-con, some balconies, parking, Via A. Califano 18, tel. 081-878-2025, fax 081-8071021, www.manniellohotels.it).

**Hotel La Meridiana Sorrento**, a new three-star place, has everything but character—45 air-conditioned modern rooms and business-class public spaces. Some rooms have front or side sea views (Db-L230,000, Tb-L300,000, half-pension at L150,000 per person required Aug–Sept 15, prices soft when slow, CC:VMA, big rooftop terrace with grand views, next door to public garden with lemon grove, Via Rota 1, tel. 081-807-3535, fax 081-807-3484, www.wel.it).

**Pensione Mara** is a dirty T-shirt kind of place, with 13 simple rooms in a dull building with a good location (S-L50,000, D-L85,000, Db-L100,000, T-L135,000, Tb-L140,000, cheap quads and family room, prices promised through 2001, from Via Capasso turn right at Hotel La Meridiana to Via Rota 5, tel. & fax 081-878-3665, friendly Adelle speaks a little English).

## Sleeping in the Town Center

**Hotel City** is small and bright but on a busy street—there are single-pane windows and double-pain Vespas and cotlike beds. The manager, Gianni, tries to give peace-loving Americans the quiet back rooms (Italians actually prefer the noisy rooms overlooking the action in the street). He runs a newsstand and travel agency in his lobby (Sb-L80,000, Db-L100,000, breakfast-L5,000, cheaper and with breakfast in winter, CC:VMA, 5 percent discount with cash, handy near Piazza Tasso at Corso Italia 221, tel. & fax 081-877-2210).

**Hotel Nice** is a decent value near the station on the noisy main drag. Ask for a room off the street (Sb-L90,000, Db-L120,000, Tb-L170,000, Qb-L200,000, prices increase about L10,000 July–Aug, CC:VMA, includes breakfast, air-con, TV, Corso Italia 257, tel. 081-878-1650, fax 081-878-3086, e-mail: albergo.nice@katamail.com).

**Hotel Mignon Meuble**, with 11 big, clean, and pleasant rooms, is Old World simple on a quiet street off Corso Italia. A five-minute walk from the station, this is the best hotel value

in the town center (Db-L120,000, includes breakfast in the
room, some balconies, no views, CC:VMA, owned by Hotel
Loreley, Via Sersale 9, from station, turn left on Via del Corso,
tel. 081-807-3824, NSE).

**Hotel Del Corso**, a just-renovated Old World hotel, is clean
and comfortable with 20 spacious rooms and urban noise. Family
run, it's well maintained with pride (Db-L160,000, Tb-L240,000,
includes breakfast, half-pension never required, air-con-L20,000/
day—required as package deal in summer and worth it, CC:VMA,
TV, rooftop sun terrace, in town center near Piazza Tasso, Corso
Italia 134, tel. & fax 081-807-3157, tel. 081-807-1016, www
.hoteldelcorso.com, e-mail: info@hoteldelcorso.com). Helpful
Luca speaks English.

**Ostello di Sorrento La Caffetteria**, a tiny hostel run by a
bar five blocks from the train station, offers the cheapest beds
in town (50 beds in triples and quads—L30,000 with bath, L25,000
without, Db-L100,000, includes breakfast, Via degli Aranci 160,
tel. & fax 081-877-1371, SE).

### Sleeping with a View on Via Capo

These hotels are outside of town near the cape (straight out Corso
Italia, which turns into Via Capo; from the city center, it's a 20-
minute walk, a L20,000 taxi ride, or a cheap SITA bus ride). The
bus situation is goofy: There are two competing companies—blue
SITA and orange Circumvesuviana. Tickets for both are sold at
tobacco shops, not on the bus. Orange is more frequent (3/hrly).
From the hotels, it's a 30-minute walk (no bus) to the beach at
Punta del Capo. If you're in Sorrento to stay put and luxuriate,
these accommodations are best (although I'd rather luxuriate on
the Amalfi Coast).

**Pension La Tonnarella** is a Sorrentine villa with several
terraces, stylish tiles, sea views, a dreamy chandeliered dining
room, and uninterested owners (around Db-L230,000 with view
and breakfast, obligatory L140,000 per person half-pension with
dinner in Aug, CC:VMA, air-con, many rooms with great view
balconies, small beach with free elevator access, Via Capo 31,
tel. 081-878-1153, fax 081-878-2169, e-mail: pippo@syrene.it).

**Hotel Désirée**, run by friendly Corinna, is a simpler affair
with humbler views but no traffic noise, all the comforts, and
no half-pension requirements (maximum prices: Sb-L100,000,
small Db-L130,000, Db-L150,000, Tb-L180,000, Qb-L210,000,
includes breakfast, laundry-L15,000, shares La Tonnarella's drive-
way and beach, at Via Capo 31, tel. & fax 081-878-1563). Corinna
is hugely helpful with tips on exploring the penninsula.

**Hotel Minerva** is like a sun worshippers' temple. Catch the
elevator at Via Capo 32. Getting off at the fifth floor, you'll step
into a spectacular terrace with outrageous Mediterranean views

and a small, cliff-hanging swimming pool complementing 48 large, tiled *limoncello* rooms (most have sea-view balconies—request higher rooms for less street noise and more view). Peasants sneak in a picnic dinner and enjoy just hanging out here. Prices increase in September (Db-L240,000/L290,000 in Sept, Tb-L270,000/ L320,000 in Sept, Qb-L300,000/L320,000 in Sept, these discounted prices promised with this book through 2001 only if claimed at time of reservation, includes buffet breakfast and air-con, no summer half-pension requirement, closed Nov–March, CC:VMA, Via Capo 30, tel. 081-878-1011, fax 081-878-1949, www.acampora.it, e-mail: minerva@acampora.it, SE).

**La Minervetta Pension** rents 12 fine rooms built into the cliff below its restaurant and far below the noisy street. Each room comes with perfect quiet and an awesome Mediterranean view (Db-L190,000, includes breakfast, half-pension—at L130,000 per person—is required in Aug, bunky family rooms, parking, 10-minute walk from old center at Via Capo 25, tel. 081-877-3033, fax 081-807-3069, Salvatore SE).

The humble **Pension Elios**, run by Luigi, Maria, and daughter Gianna, offers 14 simple but spacious rooms, most with balconies and views, and a panoramic sun terrace (D-L90,000, Db-L100,000, includes breakfast, family rooms, cheaper off-season, free parking, Via Capo 33, tel. 081-878-1812).

# Eating in Sorrento

## Eating Downtown

**L'Antica Trattoria**, your best Sorrento splurge, serves huge portions of wonderful local cuisine (minimum order of L60,000 per person) in classy candlelit ambience full of dressy waiters and enthusiastic eaters (daily 12:00–15:00, 19:00–24:00, closed Mon off-season, air-con, nonsmoking sections, reservations smart for eves, CC:VM, Via P.R. Giulani 33, tel. 081-807-1082). A few doors downhill, **Davide Gelato** has many repeat customers—so many flavors, so little time (Via P.R. Giuliani 39, off Corso Italia).

**Ristorante Pizzeria Zi 'Ntonio**, just as fancy as L'Antica Trattoria but about half the price, is popular for its local cuisine and its specialty—homemade pasta. Italians like its woody, hanging hams and happy tiled ambience (Wed–Mon 12:00–16:00, 18:30–01:30, closed Tue, air-con, antipasti buffet, CC:VM, Via Luigi de Maio 11, tel. 081-878-1623).

**Pizzeria Giardiniello** is a family show offering good food, good prices, smiles, and a peaceful, tropical garden setting (daily 12:00–24:00, Via Accademia 7, tel. 081-878-4616).

**Sant Antonino's** offers friendly service, red-checkered tablecloths, an outdoor patio, decent prices, and edible food (closed Mon off-season, CC:VM, just off Piazza Sant Antonino on Santa Maria delle Grazie 6, tel. 081-877-1200). Nearby, the smaller and livelier **Pizzeria Da Gigino** is better (first road to the right of Sant Antonino as you face it, daily 12:00–15:00, 18:30–24:00, closed Tue off-season, CC:VM, tel. 081-878-1927).

**Panetteria da Franco**, a fun local hangout with good olive bread, cheap pizzas, and wooden-bench seating, is handy if you're staying east of the center (daily 7:30–02:00, just before turnoff to recommended hotels at Corso Italia 265, across from entrance to public lemon grove).

If you fancy a picnic dinner on your balcony, on the hotel terrace, or in the public garden, you'll find many markets and take-out pizzerias in the old town. The **Standa supermarket** at Corso Italia 223 has it all (Mon–Wed and Fri–Sat 8:30–12:55, 17:00–20:55, Thu 8:30–12:55 only, closed Sun, CC:VM).

### Cliffside Dinners with Sea Views

For a decent dinner on either side of town near recommended hotels, these two places come with great view terraces. **La Minervetta**, a 10-minute walk west of town across the street from the recommended Hotel Minerva, is ideal for tired tourists in need of a low-stress, reasonably priced, quality meal and a soothing view (closed Nov–March, Via Capo 25, tel. 081-807-3069). **Hotel Loreley's restaurant** serves reasonably priced, so-so meals with a spectacular sea view (if it's busy, nonguests may be turned away, 10-minute walk east of town center, see hotel listings).

## Transportation Connections—Sorrento

**By boat to: Capri** (about hrly, 40 min, L9,000; quicker and pricier by hydrofoil and jet boat: 20 min, L13,000), **Positano** (2/day in summer, weekends only in late spring and early fall, 75 min, L10,000). Sorrento's busy port also launches ferries to **Naples** (7/day, 60 min, L12,000) and **Ischia** (schedules available at TI, walk or shuttle-bus to port from Piazza Tasso). Several lines compete, using boats and hydrofoils.

Buy only one-way tickets (there's no round-trip discount) for schedule flexibility, so you can take any company's boat back. Prices are the same. Check times for the last return crossing upon arrival. The first boats leaving Sorrento can be jammed (either arrive early to buy your ticket, or leave closer to 10:00).

**To the Amalfi Coast by bus:** Blue SITA buses depart from Sorrento's train station nearly hourly (in peak season, 20/day) and stop at all Amalfi Coast towns (Positano in 45 min, L2,300; Amalfi in another 45 min, L4,600), ending up in Salerno at the far end of the coast in just under three hours. Buses start running as early as 6:30 and run as late as 21:45. Buy tickets at the tobacco shop nearest any bus stop before boarding. (There's a *tabacchi* at street level at the Sorrento station.) Leaving Sorrento, arrive early to grab a

seat on the right for the best views. There are often two or three
buses leaving at the same time. You have to transfer in Amalfi to
get to Salerno.

**Amalfi Coast tours by taxi:** Fun-loving Carmine Monetti
and his son Raffaele offer five- to seven-hour air-conditioned
trips from Sorrento along the coast visiting Positano, Amalfi, and
Ravello (L200,000 for up to 4 people April–Oct, L200,000 Nov–
March, Carmine's cellular 033-8946-2860, Raffaele's cellular
033-5602-9158, tel. & fax 081-878-4795, taxi #17). Carmine
speaks very little English but is the jolliest Italian man you'll ever
meet. You'll smile less but learn more if you go with Raffaele,
whose English is better.

**To Pompeii, Herculaneum, and Naples by Circumvesu-
viana train:** This handy commuter train runs about every 40 minutes between Naples and Sorrento. From Sorrento it's 30 minutes
to Pompeii, 45 minutes to Herculaneum, and 70 minutes to
Naples (L4,900 one-way). See "Transportation Connections—
Naples," above, for tips on arriving there smartly.

## Sorrento Peninsula

The **bus ride from Sorrento to Sant Agata** is a beautiful
cliff-hanger punctuated by lemon groves, olive orchards, and
wildflowers. Catch the sunset here for the single best view
over both sides of the peninsula. From the end of the line,
Sant Agata, walk toward Sant Agata's church. Follow signs
to the monastery, Il Deserto. Go through the gate and climb
into and on top of the monastery for the views surveying both
the Golfo di Napoli and Golfo di Salerno (look for the Colle
di Fontanelle vista).

The village of **Sant Agata** is nothing special, but you'll find
it refreshingly unspoiled. It's a decent place for dinner or a granita
*caffè con panna* at the old wooden bar about 100 meters from the
bus stop (departures—2/hrly, 20-minute ride—on blue SITA
buses from the Sorrento station; buy 2 one-way L2,000 tickets
in the Sorrento station café).

Sant Agata is the gateway to the scenic but ignored **Sorrento
Peninsula**, which stretches 20 kilometers from Sorrento to the
Campanella point. From here the bus continues to Marina del
Cantone and Termini. From Termini a seven-kilometer walk
takes you to the point under a ruined Norman Tower where you
can almost reach out and touch Capri (bring food and water, buy
a detailed map, get local directions, not good for swimming).

**Marina del Cantone**, a tiny fishing village near Nerano
on a Sorrento Peninsula dead end, is the place to establish a
sleepy, fun-in-the-sun residency (5 buses/day from Sorrento
to Nerano, 60 min, L3,200; less frequent buses continue to
Marina del Cantone, or walk 20 minutes downhill from Nerano).

There are some good hikes from here: Punto Penna is a four- to five-hour loop with great views. A more strenuous hike leads along the coast, past the stunning Gulf of Salerno view at Torca, where buses go back to Sant Agata. Along the trail, don't miss the cliff-hugging fishing village of Crapolla. Bring water and a good map.

**Sleeping in Marina del Cantone:** Sleep at the friendly **Pensione La Certosa**, which offers a beachfront restaurant, organizes boat excursions, and can direct you to a number of peaceful little beaches (16 rooms, Db-L120,000 outside of summer, L160,000 in July, includes breakfast, half-pension required in Aug for L120,000 per person, CC:VM, 80068 Massa Lubrense, tel. 081-808-1209, fax 081-808-1245, www.hotelcertosa.com, run by Alfonso, SE). A fine pizzeria is next door. For cheaper beds, try the bungalows at **Camping Nettuno**, which also runs a diving center (Db-L85,000–110,000, Qb-L125,000–180,000 depending on season, includes kitchen, Via A. Vespucci 39, tel. 081-808-1051, www.villaggionettuno.it).

# THE AMALFI COAST—BY BUS

This trip from Sorrento to Salerno along the Amalfi Coast is a ▲▲▲ sight and one of the world's great bus rides. It will leave your mouth open and your film exposed. You'll gain respect for the Italian engineers who built the road—and even more respect for the bus drivers who drive it. As you hyperventilate, notice that the Mediterranean, a sheer 500-foot drop below, really twinkles.

Cantilevered garages, hotels, and villas cling to the vertical terrain, and beautiful sandy coves tease from far below and out of reach. Gasp from the right side of the bus as you go out and from the left on the way back. Those on the wrong side really miss out. Traffic is so heavy that in the summer, local cars are allowed to drive only every other day—even-numbered license plates one day, odd the next. (Buses and tourists foolish enough to drive are exempt from this system.)

Amalfi Coast towns are pretty but generally touristy, congested, overpriced, and a long hike above tiny beaches. The real thrill is the scenic drive. Catch a blue SITA bus from the Sorrento train station (see "Transportation Connections—Sorrento," above).

If you're thinking of taking a round-trip bus ride along the Amalfi Coast to Salerno and back, consider these two options instead. Get off at a prettier town (such as Cetera) near Salerno and return from there by bus rather than go into the big plain town of Salerno. Or take the bus to Salerno, then catch the ferry back to Amalfi, Positano, or Sorrento; Salerno's ferry dock is conveniently located at the bus stop (see Transportation Connections—Salerno, at the end of this chapter).

## Amalfi Coast

# POSITANO

Specializing in scenery and sand, Positano hangs halfway between Sorrento and Amalfi on the most spectacular stretch of the coast. The village, a three-star sight from a distance, is a pleasant gathering of cafés and women's expensive clothing stores, with a good but pebbly beach. Squished into a ravine, the center of town has no main square, unless you count the beach. There's little to do here but enjoy the beach and views and window-shop. Consider seeing Positano as a day trip from Sorrento; take the bus out and the afternoon ferry home. If you stay the night, save the day for the beach and the cooler morning and evening for hiking up and down this hilly town. The town has a local flavor at night, when the grown-ups stroll and the kids play soccer on the church porch.

**Tourist Information:** The TI is a half block from the beach, in a small building at the bottom of the church steps (daily 8:30–1:50, 16:00–19:30, shorter hours off-season and closed Sun, tel. 089-875-067).

**Arrival in Positano:** The town has only two scheduled bus stops: Chiesa (nearer Sorrento) and Sponda (nearer Amalfi town). To minimize your descent, take the Sponda stop (the second Positano stop if you're coming from Sorrento). It's a 15-minute stroll/shop/munch from here to the beach (and TI).

If you're catching the bus back to Sorrento, remember it may leave from Sponda five minutes before the printed departure; there is no place for the bus to wait, so in case the driver is early, you should be, too. If the walk up is too tough, take the little orange bus (marked Interno Positano) which does a loop from he center of Positano (at Via Columbo and Via del Mulini, across from Bar Mulino Verde) up to the main highway and the SITA bus stops (L1,500, 2/hrly, buy tickets for orange bus on board;

buy tickets for SITA from Bar Mulino Verde or Positour Agency—
both are on Via Columbo).

## Sights—Positano
**Beach**—Positano's wide beach, colorful with beach umbrellas, is
mostly public (free), but also has a private section (L18,000 per person, includes use of sun beds and umbrellas, open April–Oct). At the
harbor, the nearest WC is behind the waterfront Bucca di Bacco bar.
**Boat Trips**—At the right side of the beach (as you face the sea),
you'll see a series of booths selling boat tickets. Boats to Fornillo
make three-minute, L1,500 journeys to Fornillo Beach—a
quieter beach nearby (or an easy 10-minute walk, take trail near
ticket booths).

You could catch a boat to Amalfi (9/day, 30 min), Capri
(7/day, 1 hr), Sorrento (4/day in afternoon, 25 min), or Naples
(1/day, 50 min on hydrofoil); fewer boats run off-season. Or
consider renting a rowboat or taking various boat tours of a
nearby cave (La Grotta dello Smeraldo—Emerald Cave), fishing
village (Nerano), and small islands.

## Sleeping in Positano
**(L2,000 = about $1, country code: 39, zip code: 84017)**
These hotels (but not the hostel) are all on Via Colombo, which
leads from the Sponda SITA bus stop down into the village.
You'll encounter the hotels in this order: Marincanto (on sea
side of road), California (inland), La Tavolozza (seaside), Savoia
(inland), and Bougainville (inland). Neither laundry in town offers
self-service or guarantees same-day service (Lavanderia Elisa, at
Via Columbo 175, is near recommended hotels).

**Albergo California** has great views, spacious rooms, and a
grand terrace draped with vines (Db-L200,000–250,000 depending
on season and amenities, viewless Db-L180,000, includes breakfast, some air-con rooms, free parking, can arrange tours, Via
Colombo 141, tel. 089-875-382, fax 089-812-154, www.hpe.it/
california/, e-mail: albergo.california@hpe.it, Maria SE).

**Residence La Tavolozza** is an attractive eight-room hotel
warmly run by Celeste (cheh-LES-tay). Flawlessly restored, each
room comes with a view, a balcony, fine tile, and silence (Db-
L140,000, breakfast extra, also has small apartment and royal
family apartment, Via Colombo 10, tel. & fax 089-875-040).

**Hotel Bougainville** is spotless, with eager-to-please owners
and 14 comfortable rooms (Db-L130,000 with view balcony,
L110,000 without view, breakfast included with this book,
CC:VMA, some traffic noise and fumes, Via Colombo 25,
tel. 089-875-047, fax 089-811-150, e-mail: bougan@positano
.argosid.it, Carlo, Luisa, and son Christian SE).

**Hotel Marincanto**, with three stars and 25 large, classy, floor-tiled rooms—many with terraces—is worth the splurge (Db-L245,000, L200,000 off-season, Db suite-L300,000, L250,000 off-season, closed Nov–March, CC:VM, elevator, phones, mini-bar, air-con planned for 2001, private stairway to beach, large sun deck below hotel, parking-L30,000/day, Via Colombo 36, tel. 089-875-130, fax 089-875-595, www.webspace.it/marincanto, SE).

**Hotel Savoia**, a three-star hotel run by a friendly staff, has 39 modern, air-conditioned rooms, priced according to the size of room and terrace. A lesser value than the similarly priced Marincanto, this is a fine backup (Db-L250,000 Aug–mid-Sept, otherwise L210,000, deluxe Db-L290,000/L250,000, big Db suite-L340,000/L280,000, includes breakfast, CC:VM, some sea views, TV, phone, mini-bar, elevator, Via Colombo 73, tel. 089-875-003, fax 089-811-844, www.starnet.it/savoia, SE).

**Brikitte Hostel** offers your best cheap dorm-bed option in this otherwise ritzy town (ask bus driver to let you off at Bar Internazionale, Via G. Marconi 358, tel. 089-875-857, www.brikitte.com).

## Eating in Positano

The pizzerias on the beach are overpriced, but pleasant and convenient. At the waterfront **La Tre Sorrelle**, try the zucchini blossoms stuffed with ham and mozzarella (daily 12:00–16:00, 19:00–24:00, CC:VM). The very Italian **Da Vincenzo** is excellent (Wed–Mon 13:00–15:00, 19:00–24:00, Tue 19:00–24:00, above Positano on ridge opposite recommended hotels, a 10- to 15-minute walk from hotels, climb the stairs behind TI or take the road, Viale Pasitea 172, tel. 089-875-128). The family-run **Da Costantino**, so high on the hill that the restaurant sends a van to pick you up and take you home, offers reasonably priced, simple, filling meals (closed Wed, Via Montepertuso 127, ask your hotel to call for the van, tel. 089-875-738).

If a picnic dinner on your balcony or the beach sounds good, Emilia at **Enogastromia Delikatessen** can supply the ingredients (daily in summer 7:00–14:00, 16:00–22:00, in winter closes at 20:00 and on Sun, near recommended hotels, Via del Mulini 5). **Vini e Panini**, another small grocery, is a block from the beach and TI (Mon–Sat 8:00–14:00, 16:30–21:30, Sun 8:00–14:00, just off church steps).

## AMALFI

The waterfront of this most famous of the Amalfi Coast villages is dominated by a bus station, a parking lot, and two gas stations. The main street through the village—hard for pedestrians to avoid—is packed with cars and bully mopeds. Neighboring Atrani, a 15-minute walk away, and Minori, a bit farther on, are more pleasant.

## Sleeping in Amalfi, Atrani, and Agerola

If you're marooned in Amalfi, stay at the **Hotel Amalfi** (40 rooms, Db-L120,000–200,000, includes breakfast, obligatory half-pension in Aug costs L140,000 per person, CC:VMA, no sea views, on a garden, 50 meters from cathedral, Via dei Pastai 3, 84011 Amalfi, tel. 089-872-440, fax 089-872-250, www.starnet.it/hamalfi).

**In Atrani:** Hike 15 minutes (or ride the bus) to the tiny beach town of Atrani and stay in **A'Scalinatella.** This informal hostel—with dorm beds, private rooms, family apartments, and a washer (L10,000/load)—is ideal for a small-town Amalfi hideaway, without the glitz and hill climbing of Positano. The English-speaking owner, Filippo, is friendly and helpful (17 beds, L25,000–40,000 per bed in D or T, D-L70,000–90,000, Db-L90,000–120,000, near main square, 84010 Atrani, tel. 089-871-492).

**In Agerola:** A tiny **youth hostel** is in Agerola on Piazza G. Avitabile (L17,000 per bed, Internet access, catch bus from Amalfi, tel. 081-802-5048).

## CAPRI

Made famous as the vacation hideaway of Roman emperors Augustus and Tiberius, these days Capri is a world-class tourist trap packed with gawky tourists in search of the rich and famous and finding only their prices. The six-by-three-kilometer "Island of Dreams" is a zoo in July and August. Other times of year it provides a relaxing and scenic break from the cultural gauntlet of Italy. While Capri has some Roman ruins and an interesting 14th-century Carthusian monastery, its chief attraction is its famous Blue Grotto, and its best activity is a scenic hike.

**Tourist Information:** The TI at the ferry dock offers a room-finding service (Mon–Sat 8:30–20:30, Sun 9:00–15:00; Nov–March Mon–Sat 9:00–13:00, 15:30–18:45, closed Sun, tel. 081-837-0634). The Kara Mara baggage storage service is nearby. As you exit the pier, the ticket windows (for your return trip) are to your right and the funicular is across the street to your left.

**Getting around Capri:** From the ferry dock at Marina Grande, a funicular lifts you 500 feet to the town of Capri (L1,800, 5 min, 4/hrly). From Capri, cliff-hanging buses run to Anacapri (L1,800, 4/hrly). If you plan to go to Anacapri, it's easiest to buy a round-trip funicular-bus ticket for L7,200 at the base of the funicular in Marina Grande (near the ferry dock). You don't save any money, but you avoid the hassle of buying tickets at each stop.

## Sights—Capri

**Capri Town**—This is a cute but touristy shopping town. The TI is in a closet on the main square (to the left as you exit funicular, same hours as ferry dock TI—listed above, tel. 081-837-0686, WC down stairs behind TI). For a view restaurant with good seafood,

try **Da Gemma** (open
daily, closed in Oct, Via
Madre Serafina 6, from
town square go up stairs
near church and follow
the sign, tel. 081-837-
0461). Overall, Capri
Town is most useful as a
place to catch the bus to
Anacapri (from funicular

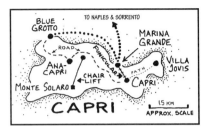

exit, walk straight on shop-lined street; about 100 meters ahead
on your right is the bus station).
**Anacapri**—This is also a cute but more bearable town (TI tel.
081-837-1524). Oddly, there are no ocean views from the town,
but there are hikes worth taking and one sight worth seeing. **St.
Michael's Church** has a remarkable tile floor showing paradise
on earth (L2,000, daily 9:30–18:30, until 17:00 off-season). **La
Rondinella** is a fine seafood restaurant sans view (Fri–Wed 12:00–
15:00, 19:00–24:00, closed Thu, Via Giuseppe Orlandi 245,
8-minute walk from bus stop, follow shop-lined street, left at
Piazza A. Diaz, jog left at Ristorante Eden Paradiso, look for
restaurant on left, tel. 081-837-1583).

　　**Sleeping in Anacapri: Villa Eva**, a 10-minute walk from
town on the Blue Grotto road, is a friendly, family-run place with
a lush setting and a swimming pool (20 rooms, Db-L130,000–
150,000 depending on season, Via la Fabbrica 8, tel. 081-837-
1549, fax 081-837-2040, www.caprionline.com/villaeva). The
cheap **Alla Bussola di Hermes** is ideal for students and backpackers (dorm bed-L35,000, D-L90,000, in center of Anacapri,
Via Traversa la Vigna 14, tel. 081-838-2010, e-mail: bus
.hermes@libero.it, run by lovely Rita).
**Hike down Monte Solaro**—From Anacapri, ride the L9,500
chairlift to the 1,900-foot summit of Monte Solaro for a commanding view of the Bay of Naples and a pleasant downhill hike
through lush vegetation and ever-changing views, past the 14th-
century Chapel of Santa Maria Cetrella, and back into Anacapri.
**Blue Grotto**—To most, a visit to the Blue Grotto is an overrated
and overpriced "must." The boat from Marina Grande costs
L9,000, the Grotto entrance plus the guided rowboat ride is
L16,500 (total L25,500). You can lop off L9,000 if you catch
the bus to Anacapri and hike briskly for one hour to the Grotto
(instead of taking the boat from Marina Grande to the Grotto).
Hikers can dive in for free. And so can anyone after 17:00,
when the boats stop running. Touristy as this is, the Grotto,
with its eerily beautiful blue sunlight reflecting through the
water, is impressive (daily 9:00 until an hour before sunset,
except in stormy weather).

**Villa Jovis**—Emperor Tiberius' now-ruined villa is a scenic one-hour hike from Capri Town. Supposedly Tiberius ruled Rome from here for a decade in about A.D. 30 (L4,000, daily 9:00 until an hour before sunset).

## Transportation Connections—Capri

**By boat to: Sorrento** (nearly hrly, L9,000 for 40-minute ride, L13,000 for 20-minute jet-boat ride), **Naples** (6 hydrofoils/day, 45 min, L18,000). For an untouristy alternative to Capri, consider the nearby island of **Ischia** (easy boat connections from Naples and Sorrento).

## POMPEII, HERCULANEUM, AND VESUVIUS

▲▲▲**Pompeii**—Stopped in its tracks by the eruption of Mount Vesuvius in A.D. 79, Pompeii offers the best look anywhere at what life in Rome must have been like 2,000 years ago. An entire city of well-preserved ruins is yours to explore. Once a thriving commercial port of 20,000, Pompeii grew from Greek and Etruscan roots to become an important Roman city. Then, Pompeii was buried under 30 feet of hot mud and volcanic ash. For archaeologists this was a shake-'n'-bake windfall, teaching them almost all they know about daily Roman life. It was rediscovered in the 1600s, and the first excavations began in 1748.

**Cost, Hours, Information:** L16,000, L26,000 combo ticket includes Herculaneum and three lesser sites—valid three days, March through September daily 8:30 to 19:30, October through February 8:30–17:00. The ticket office closes 1.5 hours before closing time. A good map is included with admission (for more information, check www.pompeiisites.org). A free baggage check is near the ticket window.

Stop by the bookshop. A guidebook is essential. (Books are also on sale in Sorrento.) The small Pompeii and Herculaneum "past and present" book has a helpful text and allows you to recreate the ruins with plastic overlays—with the "present" actually being 1964 (available for L18,000 in bookstore unless they're "finished"; if you buy from a street vendor, pay no more than L18,000). Audioguides may be available—ask. Live guides cluster near the ticket booth. If you gather about 10 people, the price is reasonable if you split the cost 10 ways (L16,000 apiece, total cost about L160,000, 2 hrs). For a local guide, consider Gaetano Manfredi (tel. 081-863-9816, cellular 033-033-7567).

**Background:** Remember that Pompeii was a booming trading city. Most streets would have been lined with stalls and jammed with customers from sunup to sundown. Chariots vied with shoppers for street space, and many streets were off-limits to chariots during shopping hours (you'll still see street signs with pictures of men carrying vases—this meant pedestrians only).

# Pompeii

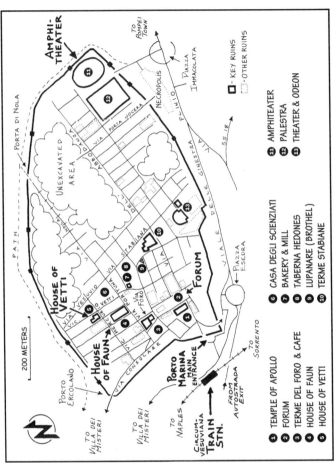

Fountains overflowed into the streets, flushing the gutters into the sea (thereby cleaning the streets). The stones you see at intersections allowed pedestrians to cross the constantly gushing streets. A single stone designated a one-way street (just enough room for one chariot), and two stones meant a two-way chariot street. There were no posh neighborhoods. Rich and poor mixed it up, as elegant homes existed side by side with simple homes throughout Pompeii. With most buildings covered by a brilliant white ground-marble stucco, Pompeii in A.D. 79 was a fine town. Remember, Pompeii's best art is in the Naples museum, described above.

**Tour of Pompeii:** Allow at least three hours to tour the site. Consider the following route, starting at the Porta Marina (town gate) after the ticket booth. Before Vesuvius blew, the sea came right here to Pompeii's door. There would have been large public baths below. As you approach the Porta Marina, notice the two openings—big for chariots, small for pedestrians.

From the Porta Marina, Via Marina leads to the **Temple of Apollo** (*Tempio di Apollo*), surrounded by 48 columns. As you face the altar, the Forum is just to your right (beyond the wall).

The **Forum** (*Foro*), Pompeii's commercial, religious, and political center, is the most ruined part of Pompeii. It's grand nonetheless, with several temples and the "basilica" (Pompeii's largest building, used for legal and commercial business).

Walk along the fenced, roofed area that runs alongside the Forum. Behind the iron fence are piles of pottery, and, at the end, some eerie casts of volcano victims. Continue straight. After you leave the Forum through the gate, take an immediate right, then a left. You're on Via del Foro, passing a convenient 21st-century cafeteria (decent value, gelato, overpriced cards and books, WCs with great rooftop views).

Head down Via del Foro—and enter the impressive baths, **Terme del Foro** (on the left, past the cafeteria). Here, three rooms offered clients a hot bath (*caldarium*), a warm bath (*tepidarium*), and a cold-plunge bath (*frigidarium*).

When you exit the baths, you'll see—across the street—an ancient fast-food stand (notice the holes in the counters for pots). To your left a few doors down is the Casa de Poeta Tragico, with its famous "Beware of Dog" mosaic in the entryway. To your right—roughly two blocks down the street—is the House of Faun (Casa del Fauno, Danzante). A faun is still dancing, just inside the door (original in Naples' Archaeological Museum).

One of Pompeii's largest homes, the **House of Faun** provided Naples' Archaeological Museum with many of its top treasures, including the famous mosaic of the Battle of Alexander. Wander through the many courtyards. The exit is at the rear. Turn right when you exit and look for the exposed 2,000-year-old lead pipes in the wire cage (ahead and down on the ground to your right). Take your first left on Vicolo dei Vetti. Enter Pompeii's best-preserved home, the House of Vetti (Casa dei Vetti).

The **House of Vetti**, which has retained its mosaics and frescoes, was the home of two wealthy merchant brothers who were into erotic wallpaper (cover your eyes as you enter). An immediate right upon entering (open your eyes now) takes you into the slave's sleeping quarters and through to the kitchen and the little hanky pantry off the kitchen filled with erotic art. Enjoy the beautifully preserved rooms as you walk counterclockwise around the central courtyard.

Leaving the House of Vetti, go left past the pipes again. Then turn right onto Vicolo dei Vetti and peek into the Casa degli Scienziati (#43, view mosaic chapel in back). Then turn left onto the Via della Fortuna. From there a quick right on Vicolo Storto leads down a curving street to the bakery and mill (*forno e mulini*). The ovens look like a modern-day pizza oven. Take the first left after the bakery onto Via degli Augustali/Lupanare and check out the mosaics on the left at the Taberna Hedones (must be the tavern of hedonism). Then turn right and follow the signs to the **brothel** (*lupanare*) at #18. Wander into the brothel, a simple place with stone beds, stone pillows, and art to get you in the mood.

If you're tired after the brothel, you've seen the essentials and can head on out. Otherwise, Pompeii's last great sight—the amphitheater—is a worthwhile 10-minute stroll away. Exiting the brothel, turn right onto the same street you entered from and then turn left on Via della Abbondanza, which leads to the well-preserved Stabian baths (Terme Stabiane—about 25 meters down on the left and worth the detour). At the end of Via della Abbondanza, turn right at the "*uscita/per l'anfiteatro*" sign and walk down the pine tree–lined lane to the huge, partially rebuilt **amphitheater** (*anfiteatro*). This is the oldest (80 B.C.) and best-preserved Roman amphitheater in Italy. From the top, look into the giant rectangular **palestra**, where athletes used to train. Vesuvius looms over the theater as it did 2,000 years ago. Retrace your steps all the way down the Via della Abbondanza to the entrance of Pompeii.

**Getting to Pompeii:** Pompeii is halfway between Naples and Sorrento, about a half hour from either by direct Circumvesuviana train (runs at least hourly). Get off at the "Pompei Scavi, Villa dei Misteri" stop. Check your bag at the train station (at the bar) for L1,500, or, better yet, near the Pompeii ticket desk for free. From the station, turn right and walk down the road about a block to the entrance (first left turn). The TI is farther down the street, but not a necessary stop for your visit.

▲▲**Herculaneum (Ercolano)**—Smaller, less ruined, and less crowded than its famous big sister, Herculaneum offers a closer peek into ancient Roman life but with none of the grandeur of Pompeii. (There's barely a colonnade.) Extremely low-tech, you'll find no information or books at the site (guidebooks are on sale in nearby gift shops). Caked and baked by the same A.D. 79 eruption, Herculaneum is a small community of intact buildings with plenty of surviving detail (L16,000, L26,000 combo ticket includes Pompeii and 3 lesser sites—valid 3 days, March–Sept daily 8:30–19:30, Oct–Feb 8:30–17:00, ticket office closes 1.5 hr earlier, free baggage check, 15 min from Naples and 45 min from Sorrento on the same Circumvesuviana train that goes to Pompeii, leave station and turn right, following yellow signs, 8 blocks straight downhill from Ercolano station to end of road, tel. 081-739-0963).

▲**Vesuvius**—The 4,000-foot summit of Vesuvius, mainland
Europe's only active volcano (sleeping restlessly since 1944), is
accessible year-round by car, taxi (L60,000 round-trip), or by the
blue Transporti Vesuviani bus (often 5/day but irregular, roughly
hrly departures 9:00–14:00 from Herculaneum station; 60 min up
with stop at bar, 40 min down). The bus trip, with a two-hour
wait on the mountain, costs about L15,000 (including the L3,000
admission). From the bus and car park, it's a steep and often cold
and windy 30-minute hike to the top for a sweeping view of the
Bay of Naples. Up here it's desolate and lunarlike. The rocks are
hot. Walk the entire crater lip for the most interesting views; the
far end overlooks Pompeii. Be still and alone to hear the wind and
tumbling rocks in the crater. Any steam? Closed when erupting.

## PAESTUM

Paestum is one of the best collections of Greek temples anywhere—and certainly the most accessible to Western Europe.
Serenely situated, it's surrounded by fields and wildflowers and
has only a modest commercial strip.

This town was founded as Poseidonia by Greeks in the sixth
century B.C. and became a key stop on an important trade route.
In the fifth century B.C., Poseidonia was conquered by a barbarous
tribe from the inland, the Lacuns, who changed its name to
Paistom and tried to adopt the cultured ways of the Greeks. The
Romans, who took over in third century B.C., gave Paestum the
name it bears today. The final conquerors of Paestum, malaria-
carrying mosquitoes, kept the site wonderfully deserted for nearly
a thousand years. Rediscovered in the 18th century, Paestum today
offers the only well-preserved Greek ruins north of Sicily.

**Note:** The Temple of Neptune may be covered with scaffolding through early 2001—maybe longer (confirm with TI: daily in
summer 8:00–19:00, off-season daily 9:00–16:30, hours may vary,
tel. 0828-811-016, e-mail: aastp@oneonline.it).

**Arrival at Paestum:** Buses from Salerno (see "Transportation
Connections," below) stop near a corner of the ruins (at a little
bar/café). Arriving by train, exit the station and walk through the
old city gate; the ruins are an eight-minute walk straight ahead. Stop
by the TI (next to museum) to pick up a free map of the site. If you
ask politely, you can store luggage at the TI, site, or museum.

**Cost, Hours, Information:** L8,000-museum, L8,000-site,
L12,000 combo ticket. Both the museum and site open daily at
9:00 (with the exception of the first and third Mon of month,
when museum is closed). Year-round, the museum closes at 19:00
(last ticket sold at 18:30). The site closes one hour before sunset
(as late as 19:30 June–Aug, as early as 15:45 in Dec, last ticket sold
an hour before closing). Several mediocre guidebooks are offered
at the museum's bookshop, including a past-and-present guide.

# Paestum

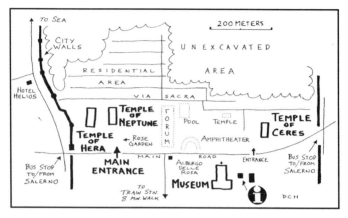

The book with the jumbled title, *Archaeologic Site Temples Museum Paestum*, is the most informative (L15,000). The site and museum have separate entrances. The museum, just outside the ruins, is in a cluster with the TI and a small, early Paleochristian basilica.

**Tour of Paestum:** Allow two hours, including the museum. Start with either the museum or site, depending on your interest and the heat of the day.

**The Museum:** This offers you the rare opportunity of seeing artifacts—dating from prehistoric to Greek to Roman times— at the site where they were discovered. These beautifully crafted works help bring Paestum to life.

The large ground floor (the most impressive part) contains Greek artifacts. Upstairs you'll find the Prehistory exhibits (in a walkway hugging the walls of the building, with displays of pottery, blades, and arrowheads, and nothing in English) as well as the Roman Room (near the elevator; contains statues, busts, and inscriptions dating from the time of the Roman occupation). No matter where you start, you'll feel like you've come in on the middle of something, but about half of the work is described in English, and the art speaks for itself.

The large carvings overhead—wrapping around the first room you see as you enter the museum—once adorned a sanctuary of Hera outside the city. Some of the carvings show scenes from the life of Hercules. In the various rooms of the ground floor, you'll see startlingly well-preserved Greek vases, crumbling armor, and paintings. The highlight of the museum is a rare example of Greek painting, known as the Diver's Tomb (480 B.C.). These slabs—showing a diver and four scenes of banqueting—originally were the sides of a tomb. The simple painting of a diver arcing down into a pool was the top of the tomb (painting faced inward). Though the deceased might have been a diver, it's thought the art more likely represents our dive from life to death. It's rare to see a real Greek statue (most are Roman copies), even rarer to see a Greek painting. The many other painted slabs in the museum date from a later time under Lucan rule. The barbarous people who conquered the Greeks tried to appropriate their art and style, but lacked the Greeks' distinct, delicate touch. Regardless, the paintings, as well as the crisply drawn pictures on dozens of vases, are instructive and enjoyable—consider these as ancient snapshots.

**The Site:** The key ruins are the impossible-to-miss Temples of Neptune, Hera, and Ceres, but the scattered village ruins are also interesting. Lonely Ceres, in an evocative setting, is about a 10-minute walk from Neptune and Hera, which stand together. The entry to the site may return to its original place in front of Neptune (once the scaffolding is off) or it may be still be in front of Ceres.

The misnamed Temple of Neptune is a textbook example of the Doric style. Constructed in 450 B.C. and actually dedicated to Hera, the Temple of Neptune is simply overwhelming. Better preserved than the Parthenon in Athens, this huge structure is a tribute to Greek engineering and aesthetics. Take a seat in the temple (if allowed after scaffolding is removed) and contemplate the word "renaissance"—the rebirth of this grand Greek style of architecture. Notice how the columns angle out and the base bows up (scan the short ends of the temple). This was a trick ancient architects used to create the illusion of a perfectly straight building. All important Greek buildings were built using this technique. Now imagine it richly and colorfully decorated with marble and statues.

Adjacent to the Temple of Neptune is the almost-delicate Temple of Hera, dedicated to the Goddess Hera in 550 B.C.

**Sleeping near Paestum:** Paestum at night, with views of the floodlit ruins, is magic. **Hotel delle Rose**, which has 12 small, fine rooms and a respectable restaurant, is near the site entry, on the street bordering the ruins (Db-L100,000, includes breakfast, CC:VM, tel. 0828-811-070, www.hoteldellerose.com, NSE). The **Seliano Estate for Agritourism** offers spacious, spotless rooms on a farm complete with horses, buffalo, a pool, and great cooking (Db-L100,000 with breakfast, L110,000 in July–Aug, run by an English-speaking baroness, near beach, 1.5 kilometers from ruins, tel. 0828-724-544, fax 0828-723-634).

**Hotel Helios**, a last resort, is a three-star hotel with one-star rooms. After you're wowed by a classy lobby with stained glass and marble as well as the inviting swimming pool, the basic, less-than-clean rooms are a disappointment (Db-L150,000 with breakfast and dinner, Via Principe di Piedmonte 1, tel. 0828-811-451, fax 0828-721-047). Ask to visit the owner's mozzarella farm, located nearby.

## Transportation Connections—
## Salerno and Paestum

Salerno, the big city just north of Paestum, is your transfer point. From Naples or Sorrento, you'll change buses or trains in Salerno for Paestum. Salerno's TI has bus, ferry, and train schedules (Mon–Sat 9:00–14:00, 15:00–20:00, closed Sun, shorter hours off-season, on Piazza Veneto, just outside train station, tel. 089-231-432, toll-free 800-213-289, www.crmpa.it/ept/).

**Salerno to Paestum by bus:** Four companies (CSTP, SCAT, Giuliano, and Lettieri) offer a Salerno–Paestum bus service, all conveniently leaving from the same stop at Piazza Concordia on the waterfront (2–3/hrly, 70 min, schedules extremely sparse on Sun). Buy the L5,500 ticket on the bus, except on CSTP buses (CSTP prefers you buy a ticket at their office next to TI at Piazza Veneto/train station, but driver will grumpily sell you a ticket on bus if necessary). No clear schedule is posted at the Salerno stop. Simply ask a local or a bus rep at the stop for the next bus to Paestum; otherwise, get a schedule at the TI (more impartial, since they don't represent a particular company and their schedule shows all companies and times). Note that orange city buses use the same stop; ignore these.

When leaving Paestum, catch a northbound bus from either of the intersections that flank the ruins (see map on page 300). Flag down any bus, ask "*Salerno?*" and buy the ticket onboard (except for CSTP buses—try to get ticket at bar closest to stop).

**Salerno to Paestum by train:** The train from Salerno to Paestum (3–4/day, 40 min, direction: Paola or Sapri) runs far less frequently than the buses, though it's a quicker ride, immune from traffic jams; check schedules at Salerno's TI or train station (luggage storage-L5,000/12 hrs). The Paestum train station is a 10-minute walk from the ruins (from station, go through old city wall, ruins are straight ahead). If you plan to leave Paestum by train, buy your train ticket at the bar/café near the TI (the station is unstaffed, train schedules at TI). Leaving Paestum, trains bound for Salerno (direction: Battaglia) usually continue to Naples.

**Naples to Salerno by train:** Hourly, 1.5 hour trip (some trains stop at Pompeii).

**Sorrento to Salerno by bus:** The scenic three-hour Amalfi Coast drive (blue SITA bus, 12/day, 3 hrs, easy transfer in Amalfi) drops you in Salerno, on the waterfront at Piazza Concordia, at the same place the buses from Paestum depart. The train station and TI are two blocks inland.

If you plan to take a bus from Salerno to Sorrento (or points in between), buy your bus ticket at Salerno's Bar Ciofi (CHOH-fee), across the square from Piazza Concordia (see map on next page). Ticket vendors change periodically; if Bar Ciofi no longer sells tickets, ask anyone or a clerk at a *tabacchi* shop, "Who sells

## Salerno Connections

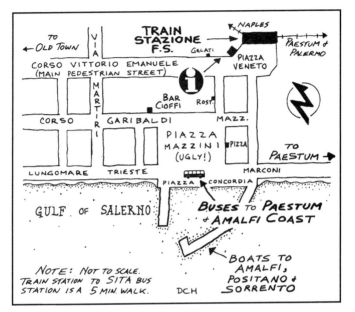

bus tickets to ____?" by saying *"Chi vendi i biglietti dell'autobus per ___?* (kee VEHN-dee ee beel-YET-tee del-OW-toh-boos pehr).

**Salerno by ferry to Amalfi towns:** If you take the bus to Salerno, consider returning by boat. Catch the ferry from Salerno's Piazza Concordia (where the SITA bus drops you off) to **Amalfi** (12/day, 35 min), **Positano** (11/day, 70 min), or **Sorrento** (3/day, 2 hrs, TravelMar, Piazza Concordia, tel. 089-873-190 or 089-872-950).

**Sorrento to Salerno by train:** Ride the Circumvesuviana to Naples Centrale station (hrly, 70 min) and catch the Salerno train (hrly, 1 hr).

**Drivers:** While the Amalfi Coast is a thrill to drive off-season, summer traffic is miserable. From Sorrento, Paestum is three hours via the coast and a much smoother two hours by autostrada. Driving toward Naples, catch the autostrada (direction: "Salerno"), skirt Salerno (direction: "Reggio"), exit at Eboli, drive straight through the modern town of Paestum, and you'll hit the ruins about when you're worried you missed a turnoff. Along the way you'll see many signs for *"mozzarella di bufala,"* the cheese made from the milk of water buffalo that graze here. Try it here—it can't be any fresher.

# APPENDIX

## Let's Talk Telephones

To make any international call, first dial the international access code (of the country you're calling from) and then the country code (of the country you're calling). Next dial the area code (if the country has area codes) and the local number. Many countries in Europe still use area codes. Italy, along with France, Spain, Portugal, Norway, and Denmark, doesn't. For specifics on Italy, see "Telephones" in the Introduction.

If you want to make an international call to a European country that uses area codes, this is the procedure you follow:

Dial the international access code, the country code, the area code (drop the initial zero), and then the local number. For example, to call one of my recommended Munich hotels (tel. 089/264-349) from Italy, dial 00 (Italy's international access code), 49 (Germany's country code), 89 (Munich's area code without its initial zero), then 264-349.

To call long distance within a country that uses area codes, dial the area code (including its zero), then the local number.

### International Access Codes

When dialing direct, first dial the international access code of the country you're calling from. For the U.S. and Canada, it's 011. Virtually all European countries use "00" as their international access code; the only exceptions are Finland (990), Estonia (800), and Lithuania (810).

### Country Codes

After you've dialed the international access code, dial the code of the country you're calling.

| | | |
|---|---|---|
| Austria—43 | Finland—358 | Norway—47 |
| Belgium—32 | France—33 | Portugal—351 |
| Britain—44 | Germany—49 | Spain—34 |
| Canada—1 | Greece—30 | Sweden—46 |
| Czech Rep.—420 | Ireland—353 | Switzerland—41 |
| Denmark—45 | Italy—39 | United States—1 |
| Estonia—372 | Netherlands—31 | |

### Useful Italian Phone Numbers

Emergency (English-speaking police help): 113 or 112
Ambulance: 118
Road Service: 116
Directory Assistance (for L1,000, an Italian-speaking robot gives the number twice, very clearly): 12
Telephone help (in English; free directory assistance): 170 or 176

# Climate Chart
First line, average daily low; second line, average daily high; third line, days of no rain.

| | J | F | M | A | M | J | J | A | S | O | N | D |
|---|---|---|---|---|---|---|---|---|---|---|---|---|
| **Rome** | | | | | | | | | | | | |
| | 40° | 42° | 45° | 50° | 56° | 63° | 67° | 67° | 62° | 55° | 49° | 44° |
| | 52° | 55° | 59° | 66° | 74° | 82° | 87° | 86° | 79° | 71° | 61° | 55° |
| | 13 | 19 | 23 | 24 | 26 | 26 | 30 | 29 | 25 | 23 | 19 | 21 |
| **Milan** | | | | | | | | | | | | |
| | 32° | 35° | 43° | 49° | 57° | 63° | 67° | 66° | 61° | 52° | 43° | 35° |
| | 40° | 46° | 56° | 65° | 74° | 80° | 84° | 82° | 75° | 63° | 51° | 43° |
| | 25 | 21 | 24 | 22 | 23 | 21 | 25 | 24 | 25 | 23 | 20 | 24 |

# Numbers and Stumblers
- Europeans write a few of their numbers differently than we do: 1 = 𝘭 , 4 = 𝟰 , 7= 𝟳. Learn the difference or miss your train.
- In Europe, dates appear as day/month/year, so Christmas is 25-12-01.
- Commas are decimal points and decimals commas. A dollar and a half is 1,50, and there are 5.280 feet in a mile.
- When pointing, use your whole hand, palm downward.
- When counting with fingers, start with your thumb. If you hold up your first finger to request one item, you'll probably get two.
- What we Americans call the second floor of a building is the first floor in Europe.
- Europeans keep the left "lane" open for passing on escalators and moving sidewalks. Keep to the right.

# Metric Conversions (approximate)
1 inch = 25 millimeters       32 degrees F = 0 degrees C
1 foot = 0.3 meter        82 degrees F = about 28 degrees C
1 yard = 0.9 meter        1 ounce = 28 grams
1 mile = 1.6 kilometers       1 kilogram = 2.2 pounds
1 centimeter = 0.4 inch       1 quart = 0.95 liter
1 meter = 39.4 inches       1 square yard = 0.8 square meter
1 kilometer = .62 mile       1 acre = 0.4 hectare

# Public Holidays and Festivals
Italy has more than its fair share of holidays. Each town has a local festival honoring its patron saint. Italy (including most major sights) closes down on these national holidays: January 1, January 6 (Epiphany), Easter Sunday and Monday, April 25 (Liberation Day), May 1 (Labor Day), May 20 (Ascension Day), August 15 (Assumption of Mary), November 1 (All Saints' Day), December 8 (Immaculate Conception of Mary), and December 25 and 26.

## Events in Italy

| | |
|---|---|
| **January** | Epiphany Fair—Jan. 6 (religious festival), Rome |
| **February** | Carnevale—mid-Feb (Mardi Gras), Venice |
| **March** | Rome Marathon—late March, Rome |
| **April** | Vinitaly—early April (wine festival), Verona |
| | Holy Week and Good Friday (processions), All Italy |
| | Scoppio del Carro (fireworks) on Easter, Florence |
| **May** | Florence May Music Festival—early May–mid-June, Florence |
| **June** | Battle of the Bridge—first Sun (medieval festival), Pisa |
| | Regatta of the Great Maritime Republics— first week of June (rowing competition, parade), Amalfi in 2001 (Pisa in 2002) |
| | Venice Biennale—odd years only, mid-June–early Nov (art show), Venice |
| | Calcio Fiorentino—late June (costumed soccer game, fireworks), Florence |
| **July** | Feast of the Redeemer—third Sun (parade, fireworks), Venice |
| | Festa de'Noantri—mid- to late July (neighborhood fair), Rome |
| | Il Palio—July 2 (horse race), Siena |
| | Verona Arena Outdoor Opera, Verona |
| **August** | Venice International Film Festival—late Aug, Venice |
| | Il Palio—Aug 16 (horse race), Siena |
| | Siena Music Week—late Aug, Siena |
| **September** | Historical Regatta—first Sun (boat parade), Venice |
| | Chestnut Festivals (festival, chestnut roasts) Most towns, mainly north of Rome |
| | Festival of San Genarro—Sept 19 (religious festival), Naples |
| **December** | Christmas Market, Rome, Piazza Navona |

For more information on Italian festivals, check visit www.hostetler.net, www.italiantourism.com, www.carnivalofvenice .com, www.festivals.com, and www.whatsgoingon.com.

# Italian Survival Phrases

For 192 more pages of survival phrases for your next trip to Italy,
check out *Rick Steves' Italian Phrase Book and Dictionary*.

| Hello (good day). | **Buon giorno.** | bwohn **jor**-noh |
| Do you speak English? | **Parla inglese?** | **par**-lah een-**glay**-zay |
| Yes. / No. | **Sì. / No.** | see / noh |
| I'm sorry. | **Mi dispiace.** | mee dee-spee**ah**-chay |
| Please. | **Per favore.** | pehr fah-**voh**-ray |
| Thank you. | **Grazie.** | **graht**-seeay |
| Goodbye! | **Arrivederci!** | ah-ree-vay-**dehr**-chee |
| Where is...? | **Dov'è...?** | doh-**veh** |
| ...a hotel | **...un hotel** | oon oh-**tehl** |
| ...a youth hostel | **...un ostello della gioventù** | oon oh-**stehl**-loh day-lah joh-vehn-**too** |
| ...a restaurant | **...un ristorante** | oon ree-stoh-**rahn**-tay |
| ...a supermarket | **...un supermercado** | oon soo-pehr-mehr-**kah**-doh |
| ...the train station | **...la stazione** | lah staht-seeoh-nay |
| ...tourist information | **...informazioni per turisti** | een-for-maht-seeoh-nee pehr too-**ree**-stee |
| ...the toilet | **...la toilette** | lah twah-**leht**-tay |
| men | **uomini, signori** | woh-mee-nee, seen-**yoh**-ree |
| women | **donne, signore** | don-nay, seen-**yoh**-ray |
| How much is it? | **Quanto costa?** | **kwahn**-toh **kos**-tah |
| Cheap(er). | **(Più) economico.** | (pew) ay-koh-**noh**-mee-koh |
| Is it included? | **È incluso?** | eh een-**kloo**-zoh |
| I would like... | **Vorrei....** | vor-**rehee** |
| ...a ticket. | **...un biglietto.** | oon beel-**yay**-toh |
| ...a room. | **...una camera.** | oo-nah **kah**-may-rah |
| ...the bill. | **...il conto.** | eel **kohn**-toh |
| one | **uno** | **oo**-noh |
| two | **due** | **doo**-ay |
| three | **tre** | tray |
| four | **quattro** | **kwah**-troh |
| five | **cinque** | **cheeng**-kway |
| six | **sei** | sehee |
| seven | **sette** | **seht**-tay |
| eight | **otto** | **ot**-toh |
| nine | **nove** | **nov**-ay |
| ten | **dieci** | **deeay**-chee |
| hundred | **cento** | **chehn**-toh |
| thousand | **mille** | **mee**-lay |
| At what time? | **A che ora?** | ah kay **oh**-rah |
| now / soon / later | **adesso / presto / tardi** | ah-**dehs**-soh / **prehs**-toh / **tar**-dee |
| today / tomorrow | **oggi / domani** | **oh**-jee / doh-**mah**-nee |

# Faxing Your Hotel Reservation

Faxing is more accurate and cheaper than telephoning. Use this
handy form for your fax (or find it online at www.ricksteves.com
/reservation). Photocopy and fax away.

## One-Page Fax

To: _____ @ _____
               *hotel*                              *fax*

From: _____ @ _____
               *name*                              *fax*

Today's date: ____ /_____ /____
              *day*   *month*   *year*

Dear Hotel _____ ,

Please make this reservation for me:

Name: _____

Total # of people: _____   # of rooms: _____   # of nights: _____

Arriving: ____ /_____ /____   My time of arrival (24-hr clock): _____
          *day*   *month*   *year*   (I will telephone if I will be late)

Departing: ____ /_____ /____
           *day*   *month*   *year*

Room(s):  Single___  Double___  Twin___  Triple___  Quad___

With:  Toilet___  Shower___  Bath___  Sink only___

Special needs:  View___  Quiet___  Cheap___  Ground Floor___

Credit card:  Visa___  MasterCard___  American Express___

Card #: _____

Expiration date:_____

Name on card: _____

You may charge me for the first night as a deposit. Please fax, e-mail, or
mail me confirmation of my reservation, along with the type of room reserved, the price, and whether the price includes breakfast. Thank you.

_____
*Signature*

_____
*Name*

_____
*Address*

_____
*City*                      *State*          *Zip Code*     *Country*

_____
*E-mail Address*

# Road Scholar Feedback for ITALY 2001

*We're all in the same travelers' school of hard knocks. Your feedback helps us improve this guidebook for future travelers. Please fill this out (or use the on-line version at www.ricksteves.com/feedback), attach more info or any tips/favorite discoveries if you like, and send it to us. As thanks for your help, we'll send you our quarterly travel newsletter free for one year. Thanks!* **Rick**

**Of the recommended accommodations/restaurants used, which was:**

Best _____

      Why? _____

Worst _____

      Why? _____

**Of the sights/experiences/destinations recommended by this book, which was:**

Most overrated _____

      Why? _____

Most underrated _____

      Why? _____

**Best ways to improve this book:**

_____

_____

**I'd like a free newsletter subscription:**

_____ Yes     _____ No     _____ Already on list

_____
Name

_____
Address

_____
City, State, Zip

_____
E-mail Address

***Please send to: ETBD, Box 2009, Edmonds, WA 98020***

# INDEX

**AVALON**
**TRAVEL**
p u b l i s h i n g

# BECAUSE TRAVEL MATTERS.

**AVALON TRAVEL PUBLISHING** knows that travel is more than coming and going—travel is taking part in new experiences, new ideas, and a new outlook. Our goal is to bring you complete and up-to-date information to help you make informed travel decisions.

**AVALON TRAVEL GUIDES** feature a combination of practicality and spirit, offering a unique traveler-to-traveler perspective perfect for an afternoon hike, around-the-world journey, or anything in between.

## WWW.TRAVELMATTERS.COM

Avalon Travel Publishing guides are available at your favorite book or travel store.

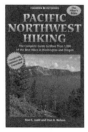

# www.travelmatters.com

**User-friendly, informative, and fun:**
## Because travel *matters.*

Visit our newly launched web site and explore the variety of titles and travel information available online, featuring an interactive *Road Trip USA* exhibit.

## also check out:

### www.ricksteves.com

The Rick Steves web site is bursting with information to boost your travel I.Q. and liven up your European adventure.

### www.foghorn.com

Visit the Foghorn Outdoors web site for more information on the premier source of U.S. outdoor recreation guides.

### www.moon.com

The Moon Handbooks web site offers interesting information and practical advice that ensure an extraordinary travel experience.

# FREE-SPIRITED TOURS FROM

*Rick Steves*

*Great Guides*

*Big Buses*

*Small Groups*

*No Grumps*

**Best of Europe** ■ **Best of Europe II** ■ **Eastern Europe** ■ **Turkey** ■ **Italy** ■ **Britain**
**Spain/Portugal** ■ **Ireland** ■ **Eastern France** ■ **Western France** ■ **Village France**
**Scandinavia** ■ **Germany/Austria/Switzerland** ■ **London** ■ **Paris** ■ **Rome**

Looking for a one, two, or three-week tour that's run in the Rick Steves style?
Check out Rick Steves' educational, experiential tours of Europe. Rather than
seeing Europe as a spectator from a bus window, you'll be encouraged to dive into
daily life. You'll have opportunities to meet the locals, see how local transportation
and services work, and get comfortable wandering off on your own. By the end of the
tour, you'll have the knowledge and confidence it takes to travel through Europe
independently—which is what many of our tour members do before they return home.

Rick Steves' tours include much more in the "sticker price" than mainstream
tours. Here's what you'll get with a Europe or regional Rick Steves tour...

**Group size:** Your tour group will be no larger than 26. **Guides:** You'll have two guides
traveling and dining with you on your fully guided Rick Steves tour. **Bus:** You'll travel
in a full-size 48-to-52-seat bus, with plenty of empty seats for you to spread out and
read, snooze, enjoy the passing scenery, get away from your spouse, or whatever.
**Sightseeing:** Your tour price includes all group sightseeing. There are no hidden
extra charges. **Hotels:** You'll stay in small, characteristic, locally-run hotels in the
center of each city, within walking distance of the sights you came to see. **Price and
insurance:** Your tour price is guaranteed for 2001. Single travelers do not pay an
extra supplement (we have them room with other singles). ETBD includes prorated
tour cancellation/ interruption protection coverage at no extra cost. **Tips and
kickbacks:** All guide and driver tips are included in your tour price. Because your
driver and guides are paid salaries by ETBD, they can focus on giving you the best
European travel experience possible.

**Interested?** Call (425) 771-8303 or visit www.ricksteves.com for a free copy of
Rick Steves' 2001 Tours booklet!

## Rick Steves' Europe Through the Back Door

130 Fourth Avenue North, PO Box 2009, Edmonds, WA 98020 USA
Phone: (425) 771-8303 ■ Fax: (425) 771-0833 ■ www.ricksteves.com

# FREE TRAVEL GOODIES FROM

*Rick Steves*

## EUROPEAN TRAVEL NEWSLETTER

My *Europe Through the Back Door* travel company will help you travel better *because* you're on a budget—not in spite of it. To see how, ask for my 64-page *travel newsletter* packed full of savvy travel tips, readers' discoveries, and your best bets for railpasses, guidebooks, videos, travel accessories and free-spirited tours.

## 2001 GUIDE TO EUROPEAN RAILPASSES

With hundreds of railpasses to choose from in 2001, finding the right pass for your trip has never been more confusing. To cut through the complexity, ask for my 64-page *2001 Guide to European Railpasses.* Once you've narrowed down your choices, we give you unbeatable prices, including important extras with every Eurailpass, *free:* my hour-long "How to get the most out of your railpass" video; your choice of one of my 16 country guidebooks and phrasebooks; and written advice on your one-page trip itinerary.

## RICK STEVES' 2001 TOURS

We offer 16 different one, two, and three-week tours (160 departures in 2001) for those who want to experience Europe in Rick Steves' Back Door style, but without the transportation and hotel hassles. If a tour with a small group, modest family-run hotels, lots of exercise, great guides, and no tips or hidden charges sounds like your idea of fun, ask for my 48-page 2001 Tours booklet.

## YEAR-ROUND GUIDEBOOK UPDATES

Even though the information in my guidebooks is the freshest around, things do change in Europe between book printings. I've set aside a special section at my website (www.ricksteves.com/update) listing *up-to-the-minute changes* for every Rick Steves guidebook.

> *Call, fax, or visit www.ricksteves.com to get your...*

- ☑ **FREE EUROPEAN TRAVEL NEWSLETTER**
- ☑ **FREE 2001 GUIDE TO EUROPEAN RAILPASSES**
- ☑ **FREE RICK STEVES' 2001 TOURS BOOKLET**

## Rick Steves' Europe Through the Back Door

130 Fourth Avenue North, PO Box 2009, Edmonds, WA 98020 USA
Phone: (425) 771-8303 ■ Fax: (425) 771-0833 ■ www.ricksteves.com

# Rick Steves' Phrase Books

Unlike other phrase books and dictionaries on the market, my well-tested phrases and key words cover every situation a traveler is likely to encounter. With these books you'll laugh with your cabby, disarm street thieves with insults, and charm new European friends.

*Each book in the series is 4" x 6", with maps.*

**RICK STEVES' FRENCH PHRASE BOOK & DICTIONARY**
U.S. $6.95/Canada $10.95

**RICK STEVES' GERMAN PHRASE BOOK & DICTIONARY**
U.S. $6.95/Canada $10.95

**RICK STEVES' ITALIAN PHRASE BOOK & DICTIONARY**
U.S. $6.95/Canada $10.95

**RICK STEVES' SPANISH & PORTUGUESE PHRASE BOOK & DICTIONARY**
U.S. $8.95/Canada $13.95

**RICK STEVES' FRENCH, ITALIAN & GERMAN PHRASE BOOK & DICTIONARY**
U.S. $8.95/Canada $13.95